Aircraft Performance Theory
for Pilots

P. J. Swatton

b

Blackwell
Science

© 2000 by
Blackwell Science Ltd
Editorial Offices:
Osney Mead, Oxford OX2 0EL
25 John Street, London WC1N 2BL
23 Ainslie Place, Edinburgh EH3 6AJ
350 Main Street, Malden
    MA 02148 5018, USA
54 University Street, Carlton
    Victoria 3053, Australia
10, rue Casimir Delavigne
    75006 Paris, France

Other Editorial Offices:

Blackwell Wissenschafts-Verlag GmbH
Kurfürstendamm 57
10707 Berlin, Germany

Blackwell Science KK
MG Kodenmacho Building
7–10 Kodenmacho Nihombashi
Chuo-ku, Tokyo 104, Japan

First published 2000

Set in 10/12pt Times
by DP Photosetting, Aylesbury, Bucks
Printed and bound in Great Britain by
The Alden Press, Oxford and Northampton

The Blackwell Science logo is a trade mark of
Blackwell Science Ltd, registered at the United
Kingdom Trade Marks Registry

DISTRIBUTORS

Marston Book Services Ltd
PO Box 269
Abingdon
Oxon OX14 4YN
(*Orders:* Tel: 01235 465500
           Fax: 01235 465555)

USA
Blackwell Science, Inc.
Commerce Place
350 Main Street
Malden, MA 02148 5018
(*Orders:* Tel: 800 759 6102
                781 388 8250
           Fax: 781 388 8255)

Canada
Login Brothers Book Company
324 Saulteaux Crescent
Winnipeg, Manitoba R3J 3T2
(*Orders:* Tel: 204 837-2987
           Fax: 204 837-3116)

Australia
Blackwell Science Pty Ltd
54 University Street
Carlton, Victoria 3053
(*Orders:* Tel: 03 9347 0300
           Fax: 03 9347 5001)

A catalogue record for this title
is available from the British Library

ISBN 0-632-05569-3

Library of Congress
Cataloging-in-Publication Data
is available

For further information on
Blackwell Science, visit our website:
www.blackwell-science.com

Contents

List of Abbreviations

A&AEE	The Aeroplane and Armament Experimental Establishment
ACS	Air Conditioning System
ACN	Aircraft Classification Number
AFM	Aeroplane Flight Manual
AGL	above ground level
AIC	Aeronautical Information Circular
AIP	Aeronautical Information Package
AMSL	above mean sea level
ANO	Air Navigation Order
AN(G)R	Air Navigation (General) Regulations
APS	Aircraft Prepared for Service
ARB	Air Registration Board
	Airworthiness Requirements Board
ASD	Accelerate/Stop Distance
ASDA	Accelerate/Stop Distance Available
ASDR	Accelerate/Stop Distance Required
ATC	Air Traffic Control
AUW	All-Up Weight
BCAR	British Civil Airworthiness Requirements
BE	Brake Energy
BRP	Brake Release Point
C of A	Certificate of Airworthiness
C of P	Centre of Pressure
CAA	Civil Aviation Authority
CAP	Civil Aviation Publication
CAS	Calibrated Airspeed
CBR	Californian Bearing Ratio
CDA	Mean coefficient of drag in the air
CDG	Mean coefficient of drag on the ground
CG	Centre of Gravity
CP	Critical Point
DOE	Department of the Environment (now the Department of Environment, Trade and Regions, DETR)
EAS	Equivalent Airspeed
EGT	Exhaust Gas Temperature
EMD	Emergency Distance

EMDA	Emergency Distance Available
EMDR	Emergency Distance Required
EPR	Engine Pressure Ratio
EROPS	Extended Range Twin Operations
ESWL	Equivalent Single-Wheel Load
ETOPS	Extended Range Twin Operations
FAA	Federal Aviation Administration
FAR	Federal Aviation Regulations
FUSS	Flaps-Up Safety Speed
GFF	Gross Fuel Flow
GFP	Gross Flight Path
G/S	Ground Speed
hPa	Hectopascal
HPC	Horizontal Plane Clearway
IAS	Indicated Airspeed
IAT	Indicated Air Temperature
ICAO	International Civil Aviation Organization
ILS	Instrument Landing System
ISA	International Standard Atmosphere
JAA	Joint Aviation Authority
JAR	Joint Aviation Requirements
JBI	James Brake Index
kg	kilograms
km	kilometres
kts	nautical miles per hour (knots)
LCN	Load Classification Number
LCG	Load Classification Group
LDA	Landing Distance Available
LDR	Landing Distance Required
MAT	Mass-altitude-temperature
M_{CRT}	Critical Mach number
M_{MO}	Maximum Operating Mach number
MPa	Megapascal
MSL	Mean Sea Level
MTWA	Maximum Total Weight Authorized
MZFW	Maximum Zero Fuel Weight
NFP	Net Flight Path
nm	nautical mile
NOTAM	Notice to Airmen
OAT	Outside Air Temperature
OD	Ordnance Datum
ODM	Operating Data Manual
OFZ	Obstacle-Free Zone
PCN	Pavement Classification Number
PFSR	Power Failure Speed Ratio
PNR	Point of No Return
psi	pounds per square inch

QFE	The altimeter sub-scale setting which causes the altimeter to read zero elevation on the ground
QNE	The indicated height on the altimeter at the aerodrome datum point with the altimeter sub-scale set at 1013.2 mbar
QNH	The altimeter sub-scale setting which causes the altimeter to read the elevation above mean sea level, when on the ground
RCR	Runway Condition Reading
RCPC	Runway Continued-Plane Clearway
RESA	Runway End Safety Area
RNP	Required Navigation Performance
RTOG	Regulated Take-Off Graph
RZ	Reference Zero
SAR	Specific Air Range
SFC	Specific Fuel Consumption
SIWL	Single Isolated Wheel Loading
SWL	Single Wheel Loading
TAS	True Airspeed
TAT	Total Air Temperature
TOCS	Take-Off Climb Surface
TOD	Take-Off Distance, Top of Descent
TODA	Take-Off Distance Available
TODR	Take-Off Distance Required
TGT	Turbine Gas Temperature
TOR	Take-Off Run
TORA	Take-Off Run Available
TORR	Take-Off Run Required
TOW	Take-Off Weight
V_1	Decision speed
V_2	Take-off safety speed
V_{2min}	Minimum take-off safety speed
V_3	All-engines-operating steady initial climb speed
V_4	All-engines-operating steady take-off climb speed
V_A	Design maneouvring speed
V_{AT}	Target threshold speed
V_{AT_0}	The target threshold speed with all power units operating
V_{AT_1}	The target threshold speed with one power unit inoperative
V_{EF}	The assumed speed at the time of engine failure
V_{FE}	The maximum speed at which the flaps may be lowered
V_{FTO}	The final take-off climbing speed with one engine inoperative
V_{GO}	The lowest decision speed from which a continued take-off is possible within TODA
V_{IMD}	Velocity of Minimum Drag
V_{IMP}	Velocity of Minimum Power
V_{LE}	The maximum speed with undercarriage (landing gear) extended
V_{LO}	Maximum speed at which the undercarriage (landing gear) may be lowered
V_{LOF}	Lift-off speed

V_{MBE} Maximum brake-energy speed
V_{MC} Minimum control speed with the critical power unit inoperative
V_{MCA} Minimum control speed in the air, take-off climb
V_{MCG} The minimum control speed on or near the ground
V_{MCL} The minimum control speed on the approach to land
V_{MO} The maximum operating speed
V_{MS} The minimum stalling speed
V_{MS_0} Minimum stalling speed with the flaps in the landing setting
V_{MS_1} The minimum stalling speed for the case under consideration
V_{MU} The minimum unstick speed
V_{NE} Never exceed speed
V_P Hydroplaning (aquaplaning) speed
V_R Rotation speed
V_{RA} Turbulence speed or rough-air speed
V_{REF} Reference landing speed
V_S Stalling speed
V_{SR} Reference stalling speed
V_{SR_0} Reference stalling speed in the landing configuration
V_{SR_1} Reference stalling speed in the specified configuration
$V_{S_{1g}}$ Stalling speed at 1g
V_{S_0} The stalling speed with the flaps at the landing setting
V_{S_1} The stalling speed for the configuration under consideration
V_{STOP} The highest decision speed from which an aeroplane can stop within ASDA
V_{SW} The speed at which the onset of natural or artificial stall warning occurs
V_T Threshold speed
$V_{T_{max}}$ The maximum threshold speed
$V_{T_{min}}$ The minimum threshold speed
V_{US} The unstick speed
V_X The speed for the best gradient of climb
V_Y The speed for the best rate of climb
WAT   Weight–altitude–temperature
WC   Wind component
WED   Water equivalent depth
ZFW   Zero fuel weight

Weight and Mass

Most of us know what we mean when we use the term weight and become confused when the term mass is used in its place. In all of its documents the JAA insist on using the term mass whereas the majority of aviation documents produced by the manufacturers use the term weight. The following are the definitions of each of the terms and should help clarify the situation:

Mass   The quantity of matter in a body as measured by its inertia is referred to as its mass. It determines the force exerted on that body by gravity, which is inversely proportional to the mass. Gravity varies from place to place and also decreases with increased altitude above mean sea level

Weight   The force exerted on a body by gravity is known as its weight and is dependent on the mass of the body and the strength of the gravitational force for its value. Weight = mass in kg × gravity in Newtons. Thus the weight of a body varies with its position and elevation above mean sea level but the mass does not change for the same body

The change of weight of an object due to its changed location is extremely small, even at 50 000 ft above mean sea level, however, it is technically incorrect and the term mass should be used. For the sake of simplicity I have retained the colloquial term weight throughout this book, which should be replaced when dealing with the JAA documents by the term mass. *IEM OPS 1.605.*

Preface

The minimum levels of performance which must be attained by every type of public transport aeroplane licensed to carry passengers for hire to, in or from any point in Europe are laid down in **Joint Aviation Requirements (JARs)**. Together with a number of other documents, these Requirements form a set of safety rules designed to ensure that every aeroplane embarking on a public transport flight shall be despatched at a weight which, in the known and forecast conditions, will afford an adequate level of safety throughout its flight and subsequent landing. If the take-off weight has been correctly calculated, and if the prevailing conditions do not differ significantly from those used in making the calculations, then any pilot observing them is unlikely to have to make critical performance decisions while in flight, at times and in situations when the flight-deck crew are likely to be under special pressure.

The growth of the aviation industry has been so rapid and so nationally fragmented that, at the same time as improvements in aircraft performance have compelled JARs themselves to grow in complexity, so also have the regulations of a number of other bodies, national and international, which regulate many aspects of flight traversing national borders, become more numerous and more detailed. An already complex legal situation has become much worse. Today it is difficult, even for an experienced aviator, to understand all the regulations for aircraft performance – let alone to apply them correctly to any given situation.

An examination in Aeroplane Performance is set by the Flight Crew Licensing Department of the Joint Aviation Authority (JAA). To validate a licence a candidate must attain a mark of at least 75% in the examination.

Since the documentation is now so complex that even basic technical terms are often misused and basic principles misunderstood, it is not too much to say that some of those who succeed in passing this examination will do so without really understanding the full meaning of the calculations they have made. The aim of this book is to simplify the daily routine of the initiate and to provide a trustworthy work of reference for all aircrew, flight planners, operations controllers and airport operators. It is collated and presented in such a manner that it will not only help in passing the examination but will also enable experienced personnel to gain a deeper understanding of the subject of Aeroplane Performance and related subjects.

The Handbook of Aeroplane Performance Theory

Part 1 – General Theory   This part is devoted to those aspects of aeroplane performance which are common to all classes of public transport aeroplane. It includes: types of surfaces and their dimensions, types of contaminant and its effect on performance, speed and distance definitions and general principles of flight.

Part 2 – Class 'A' Theory   This part is confined to those requirements which specifically relate to aeroplanes in Class 'A'.

Part 3 – Class 'B' Theory   This is similar to Part 2 and has been confined to those requirements of small aeroplanes in Class 'B'.

Part 4 – Class 'C' Theory   The theoretical performance requirements of large piston-engined aeroplanes are covered by this part.

The author would like to stress that, although *Aircraft Performance Theory* is directed towards explaining Aeroplane Performance theory, the explanations, advice and interpretation given are his alone, and are not necessarily shared by the JAA or by any other Government body. It does not seek to replace any of the works mentioned in the bibliography, but is to be used in conjunction with them. References used in the text compilation were those current in January 2000.

Every effort has been made to ensure that the information contained in *Aircraft Performance Theory* was up-to-date at the time of publication; but readers are reminded that every document listed in the bibliography on which this book is based is subject to amendment, and is in any case completely reviewed about every five years. It is true that major changes of policy are not implemented without adequate warning and publicity; but minor alterations could escape notice and every reader is advised to pay careful attention to the amendment lists and information circulars periodically issued by the CAA and JAA. No responsibility is accepted for any errors or discrepancies.

P.J.S.

Acknowledgements

My grateful thanks go to David Webb who willingly gave of his expertise and spent many hours converting most of my hand drawn diagrams electronically to disc.

I am also grateful to the Civil Aviation Authority, the Joint Aviation Authority, The Boeing Commercial Airplane Group and British Aerospace PLC for their permission to utilize information from their various publications in the text of this book.

Introduction

The development of aircraft as a means of passenger transport early in the 20th century caused Governments to become concerned that no regulations existed to protect the public with regard to their activities. An International Conference was therefore held in Paris in 1910 whose objective was to produce regulations governing aerial navigation which would ensure the safety of persons *on the ground*. (It was possibly felt that the safety of persons *in the air* was not at the time a subject on which useful regulations could be considered at all.)

The Paris Conference failed, since it proved impossible for agreement to be reached between the various national bodies already in existence. The British Government, however, was determined to protect its own public and produced an Aerial Navigation Act in 1911. Though originally introduced to ensure the safety of persons on the ground, it was later expanded to include the safety of passengers as another of its aims. Further attempts to reach international agreement were frustrated by the outbreak of World War I.

That war saw great advances in aircraft design – especially in the size, speed and range of the machines themselves and in the efficiency and reliability of their engines. After the war, a further attempt was therefore made to reach international agreement on safety regulations, and an International Committee for Aerial Navigation met at Vienna in 1919 to decide on a code of requirements that transport aircraft would have to satisfy if they were to obtain a passenger-carrying licence. It was envisaged, in particular, that it would be essential to specify a set of minimum standards in climb performance.

Once again, international agreement proved impossible of attainment and eventually the British again took the lead with a purely national approach. In 1926 they promulgated the first British Government requirements for public transport aircraft in the form of *The Airworthiness Handbook for Civil Aircraft* published by the Air Ministry. The minimum climb performance was defined simply as the altitude to which an aircraft could climb within three minutes of take-off. Aircraft were classified according to their individual stalling speeds, although this was recognized even at the time as being unsatisfactory, and investigations were soon put in hand to find a more rational approach.

In 1933, the Secretary of State for Air set up a Departmental Committee to examine the whole problem of controlling civil aviation, and it was ultimately decided that the best method of approach would be to leave the problems of regulation in the first place in the hands of aircraft constructors, the operators and their insurers. Public interest in so important a matter was retained, however, in the form of a second Air Navigation Act which came into force in 1936. Under this Act, the Secretary of State was empowered to delegate certain of his functions to an appropriately-constituted Board which was to become known as the **Air Registration Board (ARB)**. The Board began work as a limited company in 1937; but with the outbreak of the Second World War civil air transport virtually ceased to operate, and the activities of the ARB were suspended almost 'for the duration'.

World War II saw even greater advances in aviation than had its predecessor, and development in aircraft design and manufacturing techniques produced aircraft with such greatly improved performance that the existing Regulations could no longer achieve their main aim – that of ensuring the maximum level of safety for the public. The prime cause of this deficiency was the increase in the number of possible changes in aircraft configuration during flight, none of which had been envisaged when the 1926 Requirements were formulated.

The outcome was the formation in 1947 of the **International Civil Aviation Organization (ICAO)** – a permanent institution for which the groundwork had been laid at a Convention held in Chicago in 1944. This Convention also produced a report which became the basis for many national conferences on airworthiness requirements. In the same year, 1944, the revived ARB in the United Kingdom began the task of developing the British requirements, which eventually became a *Code of Airworthiness Standards* by means of which the Air Navigation Act (1936) and its consequent **Air Navigation (General) Regulations** could be met.

At almost the same time, in 1945, the Civil Aviation Authority (CAA) in the United States – its name has now been changed to the **Federal Aviation Authority** or **FAA** – produced a comprehensive schedule of flight performance standards which represented operational practice in the USA. It was drawn up in such a way that most current aircraft were able to achieve the standards set.

When this document was offered to ICAO for adoption, however, it was felt that the American requirements did not provide a uniform level of safety for all aircraft operating in all conditions. More specific requirements were formulated by ICAO, and eventually achieved a wide measure of international acceptance.

The United States and the Soviet Union, however, decided not to adopt the ICAO requirements and continued to use their own codes. These codes, though similar, were not as specific as that of the ICAO, which formed the basis of all the airworthiness requirements on which were based the national codes for every other member of ICAO.

During the course of all these negotiations, it became increasingly apparent that the lack of sufficient statistical evidence was making it difficult to rationalize airworthiness requirements. In 1946, therefore, the **Aeroplane and Armament Experimental Establishment (A&AEE)** at Boscombe Down in England began a series of tests designed to determine the effects of engine failure on the take-off performance of aircraft. A Fortress III and a Dakota III were the aircraft types chosen to represent four-engined and twin-engined aircraft, respectively, and the first steps in modern aircraft testing techniques may be said to have been taken.

In the next year (1947), a paper was published by the A&AEE entitled *The Derivation of Airworthiness Climb Standards*. Basing themselves on the information contained in this document, the ARB published a draft issue of **British Civil Airworthiness Requirements (BCARs)** in 1948. These Requirements related to the standards of climb by which aircraft were in future to be classified according to the degree of safety achieved. With aviation a continuously developing science, partial revisions of these Requirements have been made about every five years since 1948. The importance of keeping abreast of these revisions has been stressed in the Preface.

ICAO, meanwhile, was not being idle in gathering information enabling them to produce a set of Aircraft Performance Requirements which could be presented to the international community; and it was as an outcome of this joint research that the first attempt to rationalize aircraft performance requirements based on sound statistical evidence was presented in the *Final Report of the Standing Committee on Performance* in 1953 (DOC 740 Air/Ops/612).

A body of European national representatives accepted the **Federal Aviation Requirements (FARs)** as the basis for the standards to be met by all aircraft certificated after July 1979. These are called the **Joint Aviation Requirements (JARs)**. The mandatory minimum standard performance requirements for the certification of all turbine powered passenger carrying aeroplanes over 5 700 kg are contained in JAR 25, whereas those for smaller turbine-engined aeroplanes and for large piston-engined aeroplanes are contained in JAR 23. The operating regulations for **all** public transport aeroplanes are contained in JAR-OPS which become mandatory from 1 April 1999.

THE AEROPLANE PERFORMANCE EXAMINATION

In the past the subject of Aeroplane Performance referred to scheduled or planned performance but as from 1 July 1999 the examination in this subject will include some topics which were originally contained in the 'Flight Planning' or 'Principles of Flight' examinations. This examination is an optional alternative to the CAA FCL examination in Group "A" scheduled performance until 1 July 2000 when it becomes compulsory for all ATPL examination candidates. To encompass the new syllabus it has been necessary to expand this manual to include these topics.

In the past, the examination concentrated on scheduled performance regulations and requirements. In future a considerable proportion of the subject will be devoted to performance theory, it is therefore necessary to discuss the principles of flight in some detail in this book.

The aeroplane performance examination will be one hour long and consist of between 40 and 50 questions, which will be based upon the JAR-FCL syllabus 032 01 01 00 to 032 03 07 02. The main reference documents for the Performance examination questions are:

(1) JAR-OPS.
(2) JAR-1 Definitions and Abbreviations.
(3) JAR-23 Normal and Commuter Aeroplanes.
(4) JAR-25 Large Aeroplanes.
(5) Civil Aviation Aeronautical Information Circulars.

PART 1
GENERAL THEORY

CHAPTER 1

Regulations and Requirements

Performance regulations and requirements are a set of flight safety rules established to ensure that any aeroplane engaged on a public transport flight is despatched at a weight which, with the known and forecast conditions, will attain the level of safety deemed necessary. If the weight is correctly calculated and the prevailing conditions do not differ significantly from those used for the calculations, the pilot is held to be *unlikely* to have to make critical performance decisions in flight, at times when he is likely to be under pressure.

The foundation of all performance requirements is a scale of probabilities which is based upon the statistics and analysis of past aircraft accidents and incidents. Flying is now ten times safer than it was in 1955 and the probability of a catastrophic accident on a public transport flight now is not significantly greater than the risk of being killed in a private motor car. This probability is about one in one million per hour of flight. Table 1.1 shows the scale of probabilities used for determining performance requirements by the CAA, and adopted by the JAA as the basis for the Table published in JAR 25 Section 2 Page 2-F-5 and shown here as Table 1.2. It gives brief descriptions and examples for each major group.

The primary objective of *scheduled* or planned performance is the determination of the maximum TOW that will ensure the successful attainment of the predetermined safety level in *all* phases of the flight. The CAA was entrusted with the responsibility of ensuring that *all* British registered public transport aeroplanes attain an adequate minimum safety standard irrespective of the size of the aeroplane, its number of engines or the phase of flight. The 'Remote' probability of 10^{-6} was selected as the target for all public transport aircraft scheduled performance and has now been adopted by the JAA as that for all European registered public transport aeroplanes.

To discharge its commission the CAA introduced three measures:

(1)   All public transport aeroplanes were divided into groups in which each type has approximately the same performance capabilities;
(2)   Legislation was devised for each phase of flight, for both high and low performance aeroplanes, that would produce approximately the same level of safety for all groups of aeroplanes; and
(3)   The performance level to be used for all performance calculations was specified, together with the way in which that level has to be determined.

Table 1.1 Scale of probabilities (*BCAR Section D*).

Category	Probability	Examples
Minor Likely to occur during the life of each aircraft.	Frequent	Probable Heavy landing.
	10^{-3}	
Minor Unlikely to occur often during the life of each aircraft.	Reasonably probable	Probable Engine failure.
	10^{-5}	
Major Unlikely to occur to each aeroplane during its life, but may occur several times during the life of a number of aircraft of the type.	Remote	Improbable Low speed over-run. Falling below the take-off net flight path. Minor damage. Possible passenger injuries.
	10^{-7}	
Hazardous Possible, but unlikely to occur in the total life of a number of aircraft of the same type.	Extremely Remote	Improbable High speed over-run. Ditching. Extensive damage. Possible loss of life. Hitting obstacle in the take-off net flight path. Double engine failure on a twin.
	10^{-9}	
Catastrophic	Extremely Remote	Improbable Aeroplane destroyed. Multiple deaths.

Similar measures were introduced by the JAA in 1998 dividing all public transport aeroplanes into Classes and using JAR-OPS as the legislative document.

1.1 THE PERFORMANCE CLASS SYSTEM

For the purposes of scheduled performance regulations and requirements all public transport passenger carrying aeroplanes are divided into five Classes:

Class 'A' Aeroplanes   This Class has the most stringent requirements of all classes and is used for all multi-engined turbo-propeller aeroplanes having ten or more passenger seats *or* a maximum take-off mass exceeding 5700 kg *and* all multi-engined turbo-jet aeroplanes. Those aircraft in this Class may sustain an engine failure at any time between commencement of the take-off run and the end of the

Table 1.2 Scale of probabilities (*JAR 25 Section 3 Page 3-F-13*).

Classification of failure conditions	JAR-25 probability	Effect on aircraft and occupants
Minor	Frequent	Probable Normal.
———————————— 10^{-3} ————————————		
Minor	Reasonably probable	Probable Operating Limitations. Emergency Procedures.
———————————— 10^{-5} ————————————		
Major	Remote	Improbable Significant reduction in safety margins. Difficult for crew to cope.
———————————— 10^{-7} ————————————		
Hazardous	Extremely remote	Improbable Large reductions in safety margins. Crew extended because of workload. Serious or fatal injuries to a small number of passengers.
———————————— 10^{-9} ————————————		
Catastrophic	Extremely remote	Extremely improbable Aeroplane destroyed. Multiple deaths.

landing run, and a forced landing should not be necessary. Furthermore, they are able to operate on contaminated runways and with certain configuration deviations without endangering the safety of the aeroplane. These requirements ensure compliance with the standards promulgated in *Paragraph 2.2 of Part III of ICAO Annex 8* for transport aeroplanes and are those of JAR 25. The performance data are published in the Flight Manual. Examples in this group are: DC10, L1011, B707, B727, B737, B747, B757, B767, HS125, and BAC1-11. *JAR-OPS1.470(a).*

Class 'B' Aeroplanes This Class includes all propeller driven aeroplanes having nine or less passenger seats and a maximum TOW of 5700 kg or less. Any twin-engined aeroplanes in this Class which cannot attain the minimum climb standards specified in Appendix 1 to JAR-OPS 1.525(b) (see Part 3) shall be treated as a single-engined aeroplane. Performance accountability for engine failure on a multi-engined aircraft need not be considered below a height of 300 ft (*IEM OPS 1.535 Paragraph 1*). Single-engined aeroplanes are prohibited from operating at night or in IMC (except under Special VFR) and are restricted to routes or areas in which surfaces are available to permit a safe forced landing to be executed. *JAR-OPS 1.470(b) and 525(a).*

Class 'C' Aeroplanes   This Class includes all piston-engined aeroplanes with ten or more passenger seats or a maximum TOW exceeding 5700 kg Aircraft included in this Class are able to operate on contaminated surfaces and are able to suffer an engine failure in any phase of flight without endangering the aeroplane. *JAR-OPS 1.470(c).*

Unclassified   Aeroplanes which have specialized design features that affect the performance in such a manner that it is impossible to fully comply with the requirements of the appropriate Class of aeroplanes are considered to be 'Unclassified.' (e.g. Seaplanes, Supersonic aeroplanes). Specialized performance requirements applied to these aircraft ensure an equivalent level of safety is attained as though the aeroplane had been included in the relevant Class. *JAR-OPS 1.470(d).*

No Group   Multi-engined turbo-propeller aeroplanes having ten or more passenger seats *and* a maximum TOW of 5700 kg or less unable to attain the performance requirements of Class 'A' may continue to operate until 1 April 2000 provided the minimum performance requirements of Class 'B' can be achieved. *JAR-OPS 1.470(e) and (f).*

> The manner in which a particular aircraft type is to be flown, the purpose for which it may be used and the absolute maximum TOW are specified in the Flight and Operating Data Manuals. These are issued as part of the Certificate of Airworthiness.

1.2 PERFORMANCE LEGISLATION

The minimum performance standards deemed acceptable by the JAA for each class of aeroplanes and for each phase of flight are published in the appropriate airworthiness requirements manual.

Because of the wide disparity of the safety standards between performance classes it was necessary to introduce two complemetary measures which when imposed together produce a uniform safety standard for all public transport aeroplanes, irrespective of the performance class. They were:

(1)   Operating Regulations which were introduced on 1 April 1998 in JAR-OPS.
(2)   Airworthness Requirements which are the minimum acceptable performance levels in all phases of flight are detailed in JAR 25 and 23.

1.2.1 Operational regulations

The operational regulations regarding the weight and performance of aeroplanes used for public transport are legally permitted by ANO Article 30 and 'prescribed' in AN(G)Rs which are legally enforceable by virtue of Statutory Instrument No. 1989/669. These will be superseded by those in JAR-OPS when an appropriate statute is approved by Parliament. For each performance class contained in this document there is a set of despatch rules which are aimed at producing a maximum

TOW using the forecast conditions for take-off, route, destination aerodrome and alternate aerodrome. To obtain an approximately uniform level of safety for all public transport flights these have the *least stringent operational regulations* for the performance group which has the *most stringent airworthiness requirements* and vice-versa.

The application of these rules ensures that the aircraft performance characteristics as scheduled in the Flight Manual are properly matched to the route and climatic conditions. A summary of the regulations and requirements that apply to each performance Class is given in Table 1.3.

Table 1.3 Applicability of JARs (All references in this table are to JAR paragraphs).

Performance class	A	A	B	C
JAR document	25	OPS1	OPS1	OPS1
Take-off				
(a) WAT limit	117	490(a)	530(a)	565(a)
(b) Field length	109	490(b)	530(b)	565(b)
(c) Flight path	115	–	–	–
One engine inoperative	111/121	495	535	570
En-route				
All engines operating	–	–	–	575
Inoperative power units				
(a) One engine	123(b)	500	540	580
(b) Two engines	123(c)	505	–	585
Landing				
(a) WAT limit	121	510(a)	545	590
(b) Field length (dry)	125	515	550	595
(c) Field length (wet)	–	520	555	600
(d) Climb all engines	119	–	525(b)	–

1.2.2 Airworthiness requirements

The law governing the operation of public transport aeroplanes in the UK is contained in the **Air Navigation Order (ANO)** and requires all aeroplanes to be registered (Article 3) and to have a valid Certificate of Airworthiness (Article 7). All public transport aircraft on the UK register are certificated according to the appropriate airworthiness code of a particular performance class.

For over 30 years the Air Registration Board (ARB) were responsible under powers delegated to them by the relevant Ministries for matters relating to aircraft performance. They published the minimum performance requirements which stated the specific detailed technical and handling standards to which an aircraft on the British register must conform. These are the **British Civil Airworthiness Requirements (BCARs)**. Since the reorganization of civil aviation administration in 1979, the JAA Airworthiness Division has taken over the responsibility for formulating, updating and amending JARs which replaced BCARs. The initials ARB now stand for 'Airworthiness Requirements Board' which is comparable to the Council of the former ARB, and is similarly constituted. It is this ARB which acts in an advisory capacity to the CAA.

JAR-OPS, JAR 25 and JAR 23 are the current regulatory documents for the operation of public transport aeroplanes and are discussed in detail in this book. They are mandatory for all passenger carrying aeroplanes requiring registration in the UK or any other European country.

1.3. AEROPLANE PERFORMANCE LEVELS

Measured Performance   The performance actually achieved in both high and low performance conditions is measured by the manufacturers. After sufficient measurements have been recorded, the makers produce a set of *measured* performance figures. These are the average performance figures of an aircraft or group of aircraft, being tested by the required method under specified conditions. However, they are unrealistic because they are measurements of a brand new aeroplane being flown by a highly skilled test pilot. So they have to be adjusted by the *engine fleet mean performance* or the *minimum acceptance power or thrust* to obtain the aircraft's *gross* or average performance.

Gross Performance   All aeroplanes of the same type perform slightly differently, even when flown by the same pilot in exactly the same conditions and in accordance with the techniques prescribed in the Flight Manual. Gross performance therefore represents the average performance that a fleet of aircraft can be expected to achieve if they are satisfactorily maintained. There is at least a 50% probability of 'gross' performance level being exceeded by the actual performance of any aircraft of the specified type, measured at any time. In other words it is the level of performance that an average pilot flying an average aeroplane could be reasonably expected to attain.

Net Performance   To account for further variations in performance caused by manoeuvring, piloting technique and temporary below average aircraft performance the gross performance values are further diminished for each phase of flight, as specified by the JAA. This is the safety factorization. The resulting net performance figures are those used in the Flight Manual and Operating Data Manual. Where the gross performance is the average in a normal distribution, the net performance correponds to approximately five standard deviations. It is based on an incident probability rate of one in one million flights, making it a *remote* probability, that the aircraft will not achieve the specified performance level.

CHAPTER 2
Performance Planning

The prime objective of the JAA in formulating Joint Aviation Requirements is safety. These regulations ensure that the aircraft is constructed and operated in the safest manner possible and that all aircraft operators are legally obliged to fly within the limitations imposed by these rules and regulations.

To operate within these boundaries the aircraft must be able to manoeuvre safely, even after the critical engine fails at the most crucial point in flight. Thus space is of paramount importance. The space required to manoeuvre must *never* exceed the space available. Sound performance planning ensures that this goal is achieved.

Time and fuel used in manoeuvring are relatively unimportant; but operators must be concerned that maximum profitability is achieved. Thus the maximum take-off weight permissible must be calculated, to ensure that the maximum traffic load is carried. Because weight is variable and controllable, the operator is seeking the optimum weight within the constraints imposed.

2.1 ESSENTIAL DATA

To enable the calculations and computations to be made, and to comply with JAR-OPS, information is required from two sources:

(a) Aerodrome   The various distances, runway slopes, obstructions and elevation can be extracted from the UK *Aeronautical Information Package,* and for overseas aerodromes from the ICAO Aeronautical Chart catalogue.

(b) Meteorological   The temperature used at aerodrome level may be measured or forecast. However, the altitude used in all performance computations is the airfield pressure altitude which is the reading of an altimeter at aerodrome level with 1013.2 hPa set on the sub-scale. This altitude often is not available and the QFE or QNH has to be used to convert the airfield elevation to a pressure altitude. To do this Fig. 2.1 should be used for the conversion using QFE or Fig. 2.2 if QNH is to be used. Figure 2.2 can also be used to convert obstacle elevations to become pressure altitudes.

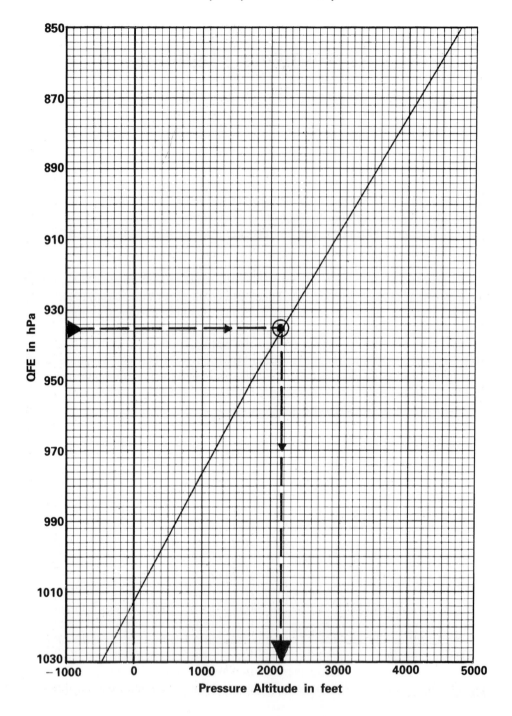

Fig. 2.1   Conversion from QFE to standard pressure altitude.

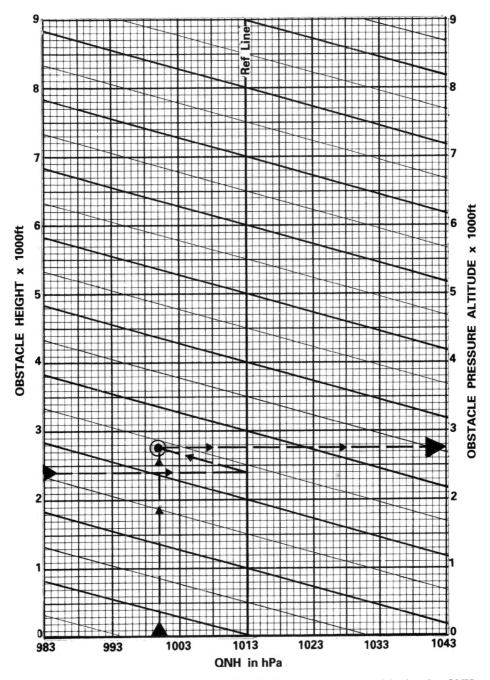

Fig. 2.2 The conversion of aerodrome or obstacle elevation to pressure altitude using QNH.

2.2 THE INTERNATIONAL STANDARD ATMOSPHERE

The basis for all performance calculations is the **International Standard Atmosphere (ISA)** which is defined as a perfect dry gas, having a mean sea level temperature of +15°C, which decreases at a rate of 1.98°C for every 1000 feet increase of altitude up to an altitude of 36 090 ft where the temperature is assumed to remain constant at –56.5°C. The mean sea level (MSL) pressure is assumed to be 1013.2 hPa. (29.92 in. Hg). These characteristics are shown in Table 2.1.

Table 2.1 International standard atmosphere (dry air).

Pressure	Temperature		Density	Height		Thickness of 1 hPa layer	
hPa	°C	°F	gm^{-3}	m	ft	m	ft
1013.2	15.0	59.0	1225	0	0	8.3	27
1000	14.3	57.7	1212	111	364	8.4	28
950	11.5	52.7	1163	540	1773	8.8	29
900	8.6	47.4	1113	988	3243	9.2	30
850	5.5	41.9	1063	1457	4781	9.6	31
800	2.3	36.2	1012	1949	6394	10.1	33
750	–1.0	30.1	960	2466	8091	10.6	35
700	–4.6	23.8	908	3012	9882	11.2	37
650	–8.3	17.0	855	3591	11780	11.9	39
600	–12.3	9.8	802	4206	13801	12.7	42
550	–16.6	2.1	747	4865	15962	13.7	45
500	–21.2	–6.2	692	5574	18289	14.7	48
450	–26.2	–15.2	635	6344	20812	16.1	53
400	–31.7	–25.1	577	7185	23574	17.7	58
350	–37.7	–36.0	518	8117	26631	19.7	65
300	–44.5	–48.2	457	9164	30065	22.3	75
250	–52.3	–62.2	395	10363	33999	25.8	85
200	–56.5	–69.7	322	11784	38662	31.7	104
150	–56.5	–69.7	241	13608	44647	42.3	139
100	–56.5	–69.7	161	16180	53083	63.4	208

ISA Deviation It is necessary to present performance data at temperatures other than the ISA temperature for all flights levels within the performance spectrum envelope. If this were to be attempted for the actual or forecast temperatures, it would usually be impractible and in some instances impossible.

To overcome the presentation difficulty and still retain the coverage or range required, it is necessary to use ISA deviation. This is simply the algebraic difference between the actual (or forecast) temperature and the ISA temperature for the flight level under consideration. It is calculated by subtracting the ISA temperature from the actual or forecast temperature for that particular altitude. This is shown at Fig. 2.3.

Table 2.2 ISA height in feet above the standard pressure level.*

Pressure (hPa)	0	2	4	6	8
1030	−456	−509	−563	−616	−670
1020	−185	−240	−294	−348	−402
1010	+88	+33	−22	−76	−131
1000	+363	+308	+253	+198	+143
990	640	584	529	473	418
980	919	863	807	751	695
970	1200	1143	1087	1031	975
960	1484	1427	1370	1313	1256
950	1770	1713	1655	1598	1541
940	2059	2001	1943	1885	1828
930	2351	2293	2235	2176	2117
920	2645	2587	2528	2469	2410
910	2941	2882	2823	2763	2704
900	3240	3180	3120	3060	3001
890	3542	3482	3421	3361	3300
880	3846	3785	3724	3663	3603
870	4153	4091	4029	3968	3907
860	4463	4401	4339	4277	4215
850	4777	4714	4651	4588	4526
840	5093	5029	4966	4903	4840
830	5412	5348	5284	5220	5157
820	5735	5670	5606	5541	5476
810	6061	5996	5930	5865	5800
800	6390	6324	6258	6192	6127
790	6722	6656	6589	6523	6456

* Enter with QFE to read aerodrome pressure altitude. Enter with QNH to read the correction to apply to aerodrome/obstacle elevation to obtain pressure altitude.

ISA Deviation = Ambient Temperature − Standard Temperature

Usually 5°C bands of temperature deviation are used for data presentation in Flight Manuals to reduce the size of the document or to prevent any graphs becoming overcrowded and unreadable. The temperatures measured on an actual ascent would reveal that, when converted to ISA deviations, they all fall into a narrow band spread of deviations.

JSA Deviation As an alternative to ISA deviation some aircraft manuals use Jet Standard Deviation (JSA) which assumes the temperature lapse rate to be 2°C/1000 ft and that the atmosphere has no tropopause, the temperature is, therefore, assumed to continue decreasing at this rate beyond 36 090 ft.

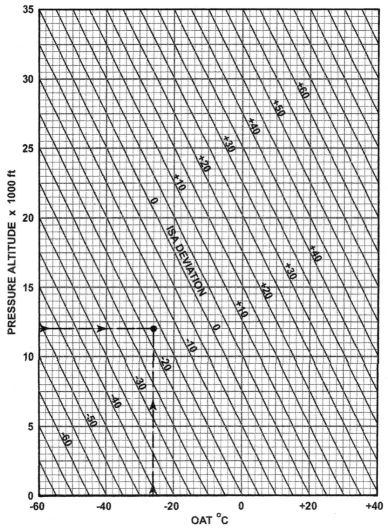

Fig. 2.3 ISA conversion graph.

Height and altitude   Three parameters are used in aviation for vertical referencing of position. They are the airfield surface, mean sea level (MSL) and the standard pressure level of 1013.2 hPa. It would be convenient if the performance data could be related to aerodrome elevation because this is published in the *Aeronautical Information Package* and is fixed.

However, it is impractical because of the vast range that would have to be covered. Mean sea level and pressure altitude are the only permissible references for assessing altitude for the purposes of aircraft performance calculations, provided that the one selected by the manufacturers for the Flight Manual is used consistently throughout. Alternatively, any combination of them may be used in a conservative manner.

Using MSL avoids the problem of the range of heights and would be ideal from a safety viewpoint; but again this would be too variable because of the temperature and pressure range. The only practical datum to which aircraft performance can be related is the standard pressure level of 1013.2 hPa. In the case of jet aircraft performance the CAA recommends the use of this datum.

Pressure altitude   In Aeroplane Flight Manuals (AFMs) the word *altitude* refers strictly to *pressure altitude* which can be defined as the vertical distance from the 1013.2 hPa pressure level. Thus, aerodrome and obstacle elevations must be converted to pressure altitude before they can be used in the performance graphs. Figure 2.1 or 2.2 may be used for these purposes or, with the aircraft on the ground, the altimeter sub-scale may be set to 1013.2 hPa and the altimeter reading used for the take-off performance calculations. Many large aerodromes provide the aerodrome pressure altitude as part of their hourly weather reports.

Density altitude   The performance data for piston-engined aeroplanes is calculated using density altitude, which is the pressure altitude corrected for non-standard temperature (see Fig. 2.4). It is the altitude in the standard atmosphere at which the prevailing density occurs and can be calculated by dividing the ambient density by the actual density lapse rate or by using the formula:

Density Altitude = Pressure Altitude + (118.8 × Temperature Deviation)

Temperature Considerations   The temperature of the air quoted for the aerodrome surface is measured by a thermometer hung in a louvred screen 4 ft above the ground, which shields it from the direct rays of the sun. Thus it is not a true measurement of the temperature at the runway threshold, which *is* exposed to the sun and also re-radiates heat. The difference between these two temperatures is not significant in temperate and cold climates, but in tropical and sub-tropical climates it can make a considerable difference to the take-off and landing performance of an aircraft. In these circumstances, the performance calculations are too optimistic because the reported temperature is too low. *Aircrew are therefore advised that when operating in hot climates in daylight hours it is prudent to increase the reported surface temperature by 2°C before using it in any performance computations.*

2.3 THE PRACTICAL APPLICATION OF PERFORMANCE STANDARDS

When considering any aspect of scheduled performance it must be remembered that the measured performance figures were those taken when a brand new aircraft was being flown extremely accurately by a trained expert test pilot. Such measurements are therefore unrealistic and simply the starting point from which the authorities derive the gross and net performance standards.

Gross performance is the average level achieved by an average pilot in an average aircraft.

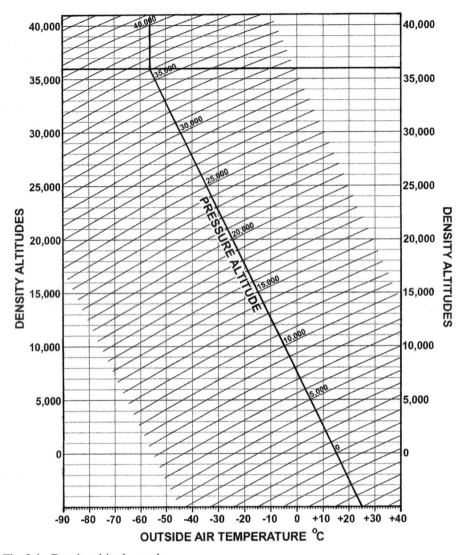

Fig. 2.4 Density altitude graph.

This standard is that which it could be reasonably expected for most aeroplanes of the type to accomplish. Thus gross height is the true height and gross distance the true distance that the pilot could rationally expect his aeroplane to attain. *Gross height is, therefore, the uncorrected pressure altimeter indication for the height being considered.*

The net performance level is that which the authorities have determined should be used to ensure that the aeroplane will achieve the set level of safety probability.

Thus net heights, distances and gradients are those parameters which are used for comparison with the actual heights of obstacles or with runway distances to guarantee the mandatory safety level.

This level of performance equates to that which would be achieved by the average pilot flying the worst fleet aeroplane in the worst conditions. It is therefore a performance level that all fleet aeroplanes must be capable of obtaining and a level that most will exceed. This then is the foundation of aeroplane scheduled performance.

CHAPTER 3

Flight Manuals

The Flight Manual is a legal document and forms an integral part of the Certificate of Airworthiness. (ANO Art. 7 & 8.) It contains all the information essential, from the Scheduled Performance viewpoint, to the safe operation of the aircraft. Absolute limiting values quoted in the Manual are therefore legally enforceable, and can only be exceeded for a particular flight if specific permission is obtained from the CAA or JAA before the flight begins. If any particular limitation is exceeded, the aircraft's Scheduled Performance guarantee is automatically invalidated.

Performance data are presented by the manufacturers in a simple, clear and unambiguous layout in the Flight Manual to enable the aircraft operator to make the best use of the aeroplane with the maximum degree of safety. Thus the most suitable layout compatible with the aircraft type is selected, within the constraints of the regulations imposed by the CAA or the JAA. The conditions observed in the construction of all graphical data and the range of data which must be included is specified in both AN(G)R and JAR-OPS. The *minimum* amount of information provided in any particular aircraft Flight Manual must be sufficient to enable it to be operated in at least one region of the world in which the prevailing meteorological conditions would only infrequently be outside the range provided. Manufacturers usually determine and schedule sufficient data to enable the aircraft to be safely operated anywhere in the world. On the rare occasions when the prevailing meteorological conditions fall outside the range covered by the Flight Manual, any information required *must not be extrapolated from the graphs, unless specifically permitted.* The manufacturer is also compelled to include data in the Flight Manual which allow for the effect of any equipment or configuration peculiar to that specific aeroplane type which, if used, would have a significant effect on its performance. Examples are anti-icing systems, water-methanol injection, etc.

3.1 VALIDITY OF INFORMATION

All Flight Manuals include a statement regarding the validity of the performance information they contain. The data scheduled cannot be considered valid unless this statement includes the following mandatory clauses:

(1) The performance class in which the aeroplane is classified.
(2) Extrapolation of performance data is only valid if specifically permitted and within the limitations stated.

(3) Performance data for any temperature beyond the maximum of the range scheduled are not valid.

(4) The appropriate WAT-limited weight for take-off or landing is the maximum for that phase of flight. If it is exceeded, the related performance data are automatically invalidated.

(5) The maximum altitude at which an attempt to relight or restart an inoperative power unit may be made is clearly stated.

(6) A representative TAS is given that is to be used in calculating any route limitation and is termed the 'Over-Water Speed'.
   (a) For normal operations in the event of two power units becoming inoperative.
   (b) For ferrying flights in the event of a serviceable power unit becoming inoperative.

(7) Equipment limitations. The aeroplane manufacturers are legally required to include in the aircraft Flight Manual the following details of equipment or configuration that will affect the scheduled performance:
   (a) A list defining the certificated flap setting for the aeroplane type and the way in which performance data are used if flap is selected.
   (b) The effect on performance data of operating specific equipment.
   (c) The effect on performance data of the unserviceability of specific equipments.

Some of these legal requirements may be contained in a Configuration Deviation List (CDL). From this list it will be seen that reverse thrust and anti-skid are the only two factors considered to have a significant effect on take-off and landing performance. A statement is included for every piece of equipment listed in the CDL to enable planning calculations to be made in the event of unserviceability. It details, in particular, any factorization or correction that must be used if such is the case.

3.2 SPECIFIC CONDITIONS AND ASSOCIATED RANGES

3.2.1 Aerodrome altitude

Although the requirements only specify that aerodrome altitudes must be scheduled in Flight Manuals from 1000 ft below MSL to 2000 ft above MSL, it is usual for manufacturers to present a range from 1000 ft below to 10 000 ft above MSL. The aerodrome altitude is normally presented as a pressure altitude which, if not readily available, will require the airfield elevation to be converted by one of the following methods:

(1) With the aircraft on the ground, set the altimeter sub-scale to 1013.2 hPa and read off the pressure altitude.

(2) Enter the altitude conversion graph at Fig. 2.1 or Table 2.2 with QFE and extract the pressure altitude.

(3) If only QNH is known, pressure altitude may be calculated from Table 2.2 or

by the following formula or by entering Fig. 2.2 with the QNH and extracting the pressure altitude:

$$\text{Pressure Altitude} = \text{Airfield Elevation} + [30 \times (1013 - \text{QNH})]$$

3.2.2 Cruising altitude

The data range required for the en-route phase of flight is from MSL to the maximum altitude at which the aeroplane is able to operate having regard to its own AUW and to the ambient temperature.

3.2.3 Temperature

The range of temperatures required for all performance data is from ISA+15°C to ISA–15°C. However, most manufacturers provide data up to a maximum temperature of ISA+30°C.

3.2.4 Wind

Aircraft manufacturers are only obliged to provide take-off and landing performance data for a range of wind speeds from 15 kts head component to 5 kts tail component. If these limitations were observed, they would unnecessarily penalize the operator; so most Flight Manuals are produced with a wind component range from 40 kts head to 10 kts tail.

Before these wind components are used in take-off and landing calculations AN(G)Rs, JAR-OPS and JAR 25.105(d)(1) require that all headwinds be reduced by 50% and all tailwinds be increased by 50%. This factorization, made for the purposes of safety, may already be incorporated in the scheduled data of the wind grids in the various graphs by changing the slope of the grid-lines or by varying the scale of the grid so that the forecast wind can be used directly on the wind grid without alteration. *The effect of this safety factorization is diminished if the wind is at 90° to the runway.*

If the wind is gusting over a range of speeds, the component which must be used in all performance planning calculations is the most unfavourable one. Crosswind effect is not usually scheduled. If, however, the JAA decides that within the maximum crosswind limitation the effect is significant above a certain speed, the performance data must take this into account. A statement of this fact will be included in the Flight Manual of any aircraft so affected. Wind at an airfield is measured at a height of 10 m above the surface level.

3.2.5 Runway slope

Runway slope for the purposes of take-off and landing performance is assumed to be uniform over the entire runway length. The range of slopes included in the Flight Manual is from +2% to –2% and the effective runway gradient is to be used for take-off computations. *JAR 25.105(d)(2).*

If slope varies along the runway length then the average slope is the one which is promulgated. This slope should be used for all field lengths used in take-off performance planning calculations. For Class 'A' aeroplane *scheduled landing* performance computations, the average slope *must* be used if it exceeds 2% and *may* be used if so desired for lower values. A prudent operator would always use the runway slope in these calculations. However, for in-flight landing performance calculations, when approaching or arriving overhead the landing aerodrome, then the slope for the landing runway should be used irrespective of its value. *JAR-OPS1.515*. The runway slope formula is:

$$\text{Slope} = \frac{\text{Change of height in feet}}{\text{Runway length in feet}} \times 100$$

CHAPTER 4

Altimeter Corrections

As explained in Chapter 1, Scheduled Performance is directed towards achieving the highest possible degree of flight safety in the circumstances that prevail. When meteorological conditions make it necessary to fly the aircraft solely by reference to instruments, the only means of establishing the aircraft's vertical distance above any particular datum is a pressure altimeter. The construction of this instrument is such that it will only indicate the true height above MSL if the actual conditions of temperature, pressure and lapse rate are precisely the same as the International Standard Atmosphere (ISA) values for these factors. Rarely do these circumstances occur, and an error is introduced to the indications given which can be directly attributed to the deviation from the ISA conditions. The magnitude of any such error, in particular barometric and temperature, is related to the size of the deviation. Although they can be calculated, neither can be compensated for in the instrument. Other errors inherent in the construction of the instrument and the nature of its operation can be calibrated, listed on a correction card and due allowance made for them.

Because Scheduled Performance calculations are concerned with ensuring that the aircraft obtains adequate vertical clearance of all obstacles encountered during any particular flight, it is important that the two errors which cannot be calibrated and are caused by non-standard atmospheric conditions be properly understood to ensure that adequate allowance is made for them. Obstacle heights are TRUE heights above MSL. To enable accurate clearance height over the obstacle to be calculated, it is essential that the aircraft's indicated altitude be corrected for all errors to obtain TRUE altitude.

This is particularly important for the period of flight during the initial climb directly after take-off, when for Class 'A' aeroplanes the minimum net obstacle clearance legally required is only 35 ft in straight flight or 50 ft during a turn; and during the landing phase when the obstacle clearance limit (OCL) may be as low as 200 ft above the surface level.

4.1 BAROMETRIC ERROR

Barometric error is caused when the MSL pressure differs from the ISA value of 1013.25 hPa. It can be compensated by offsetting the datum from which the altimeter measures the aircraft height to the value of the actual MSL pressure. This is done by means of a setting knob which is directly linked to a sub-scale. It enables the measuring datum to be set to any desired value.

This error is of particular significance in mountainous areas if an aircraft is flying at the safety altitude, or is compelled to descend to safety altitude when the local MSL pressure is unknown and the sub-scale has to be set to the forecast value. If the MSL pressure is unknown at take-off the sub-scale can be adjusted so that the instrument indicates the aerodrome elevation plus the height of the altimeter above the aerodrome surface. This method ensures that the indicated altitude is only subject to temperature error plus the calibrated instrument error for this phase of flight.

Figure 4.1 illustrates the effect on instrument indications if the altimeter sub-scale is *not reset* during the flight to the local MSL pressure. An aircraft flying from an area of HIGH pressure to one of LOW pressure will, if the altimeter sub-scale is not reset, cause the altimeter to *over-read* by an amount approximately equal to (30 × pressure difference in hPa) in feet.

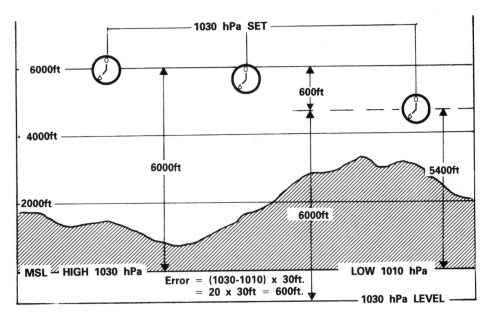

Fig. 4.1   Barometric error.

4.2 TEMPERATURE ERROR

Because of the close relationship between temperature and pressure, any deviation between the surface temperature and the ISA assumed value of +15°C is compensated when the sub-scale is set to the local MSL pressure value. However, this correction cannot compensate for the different lapse rate of temperature that will be experienced if the actual temperature differs from ISA. The error so caused in the altimeter indications is referred to as **temperature error**. Cold air is denser than warm air and therefore has a greater lapse rate. This causes the pressure at any given level above the surface to be lower than it would be at the same level in warm air. Figure 4.2 shows an example.

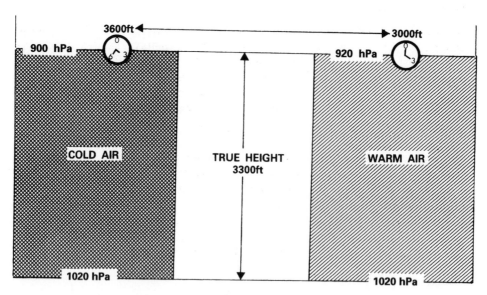

Fig. 4.2 Temperature error.

Because the lapse rate of temperature in cold air is greater, the altimeter over-reads, falsely indicating the aircraft to be higher than it really is. When the actual temperature is below that of ISA, the error is particularly dangerous if no allowance is made for it when estimating obstacle clearance, because the actual vertical separation will be less than that indicated.

An investigation made in 1979 confirmed that an allowance of 4 ft per 1000 ft of indicated altitude must be made for every 1°C difference of the actual temperature from the ISA temperature at that altitude. If the static air temperature is lower than the ISA temperature, the correction must be subtracted from the indicated altitude to obtain the true altitude above the datum set on the sub-scale. It is estimated that the error involved if temperature error is uncorrected can be up to 9.44% of the indicated altitude in temperate climates, but in extreme temperature conditions it can be as much as 25%. The corrected indicated altitude is within 1.5% of the true altitude under normal temperature conditions and within 3% under extreme temperature conditions. The formula to be used for temperature error correction is therefore:

(1)   Altitude Correction $= 4 \times$ ISA Deviation $\times \dfrac{\text{Indicated Altitude}}{1000}$

(2)   Temperature *below* ISA then:
       True Altitude = (Indicated Altitude − Correction)
       or Indicated Altitude = (True Altitude + Correction)

(3)   Temperature *above* ISA then:
       True Altitude = (Indicated Altitude + Correction)
       Indicated Altitude = (True Altitude − Correction)

Take-off and landing

Scheduled Performance calculations are completed before flight to determine the manner in which the aircraft should be operated to comply with the regulations. All obstacle and Gross Flight Path heights are TRUE heights. To enable the pilot to conform with the performance plan during the take-off climb, the gross height of flap retraction and the gross height at the end of the net flight path must be converted to indicated altitudes. Similarly, the obstacle clearance limiting altitude on the final approach is a true height which must be converted to an indicated altitude.

A graph which covers the complete range of ISA deviations may be used for these calculations which must be made accurately. Because of the wide range of aerodrome elevations the graph is based on the aerodrome surface level, i.e. with the altimeter sub-scale set to QFE. If it is normal for the pilot to have QNH set on the altimeter sub-scale for take-off and landing, it is necessary to add the aerodrome elevation to the corrected altitude to obtain indicated altitude.

The procedure for take-off and landing computations using Fig. 4.3 is therefore as follows:

(1) Enter the graph with the gross height at the carpet of the graph.
(2) Extract the corrected altitude.
(3) Apply the calibration correction from the altimeter correction card.
(4) Add aerodrome elevation.

The result is the indicated altitude required with the altimeter sub-scale set to QNH. If no QNH is available, the sub-scale should be set for take-off so that the altimeter reads the aerodrome elevation. For landing the best available forecast value should be used.

4.2.2 En-route

The minimum obstacle clearance permissible en-route is 2000 ft or safety altitude, dependent on the Performance Class. If the performance planning has been accurately completed, there should be no difficulty in maintaining this minimum separation. However, should it become necessary to make an emergency descent, it is important that the pilot have a fairly accurate indication of the aircraft's true altitude. The altimeter sub-scale must be set to the most recent actual or forecast QNH for the area of the descent. With this setting the instrument will then indicate the uncorrected altitude above MSL.

A similar graph to that on Fig. 4.4 can be used to convert indicated altitude to true altitude for the en-route case. Because the accuracy does not have to be so precise and the results have to be based on the MSL datum, the graph can include a much wider altitude range. Since the requirement is usually to convert indicated altitude to true altitude, the procedure to adopt is as follows:

(1) Apply the calibration correction to the indicated altitude.
(2) Enter the right or left hand vertical axis of Fig. 4.4 with the corrected altitude.
(3) Extract true altitude.

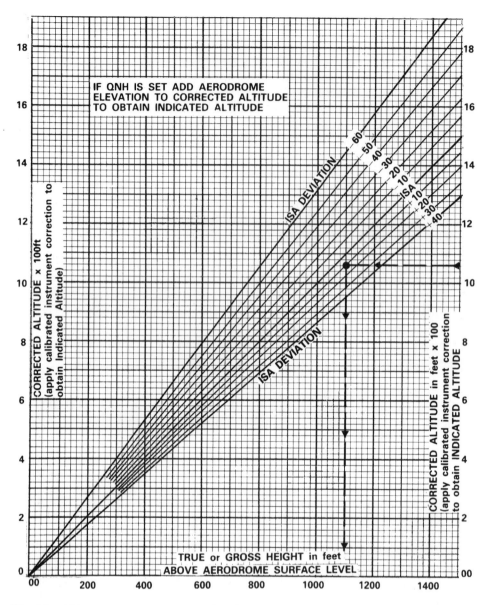

Fig. 4.3 Altimeter temperature correction (for take-off and landing with QFE set on subscale).

If it is required to convert obstacle height or safety height to an indicated altitude, the reverse of this procedure should be used. It is, therefore, only necessary to apply the calibrated instrument correction to the corrected altitude to obtain the indicated altitude.

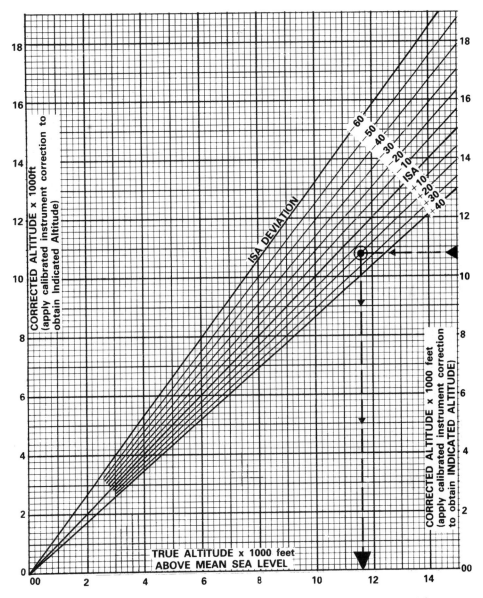

Fig. 4.4 Altimeter temperature correction (en-route with QNH set on sub-scale).

Test Paper 1

Q1. The scheduled performance target probability factor is:
    (a) Extremely remote – 10^{-8}.
    (b) Remote – 10^{-6}.
    (c) Reasonably probable – 10^{-4}.
    (d) Frequent – 10^{-2}.

Q2. Gross performance is:
    (a) Measured performance diminished by five standard deviations.
    (b) Net performance adjusted by safety factorization.
    (c) Measured performance adjusted so that all aeroplanes of the type have a 50% chance of exceeding it.
    (d) Measured performance diminished to allow for manoeuvring, piloting technique and temporary below average performance.

Q3. Pressure altitude is:
    (a) The altimeter indication when 1013.2 hPa is set on the sub-scale.
    (b) The altimeter indication when QNH is set on the sub-scale.
    (c) The altimeter indication when QFE is set on the sub-scale.
    (d) The altitude above mean sea level.

Q4. During daylight hours in hot climates, the allowance to the reported temperature that prudent aircrew should make in their scheduled performance calculations is:
    (a) $-2°$C.
    (b) $+1°$C.
    (c) $+2°$C.
    (d) $+4°$C.

Q5. The minimum range of runway slopes required to be included in the Flight Manual is:
    (a) $+1\%$ to -2%.
    (b) $+2\%$ to -1%.
    (c) $+2\%$ to -1%.
    (d) $+2\%$ to -2%.

Q6. Barometric error is caused when:
    (a) The surface pressure is not standard.
    (b) Mean sea level pressure differs from 1013.2 hPa.
    (c) The pressure lapse rate is not 30 ft per hPa.
    (d) The sub-scale is not set to 1013.2 hPa.

Q7. If the static air temperature is $-15°C$ and the indicated altitude is 10 000 ft then the true altitude is:
    (a) 10 400 ft.
    (b) 10 600 ft.
    (c) 9400 ft.
    (d) 9600 ft.

Q8. If aerodrome elevation is 1000 ft, the ambient temperature is $+30°C$ and QNH is set on the altimeter sub-scale the altimeter indication will be:
    (a) 932 ft.
    (b) 880 ft.
    (c) 1068 ft.
    (d) 1120 ft.

Q9. The operational regulations regarding scheduled performance are contained in the following document:
    (a) Joint Airworthiness Requirements-Operations (JAR-OPS).
    (b) Joint Airworthiness Requirements (JAR 23).
    (c) Joint Airworthiness Requirements (JAR 25).
    (d) Federal Aviation Requirements (FAR 25).

Q10. The minimum acceptable performance requirements for a Class 'A' aeroplane are contained in the following document:
    (a) JAR-OPS1.
    (b) JAR 23.
    (c) JAR 25.
    (d) FAR 25.

Q11. En-route in the Northern Hemisphere an aeroplane flying with QNH set on the sub-scale of the altimeter, is experiencing $15°$ port drift. The altimeter, if the sub-scale is not reset, will:
    (a) Read the correct height above MSL.
    (b) Over-read.
    (c) Under-read.
    (d) Not be affected.

Q12. The factorization of the reported along track wind component required by JAR-OPS1 when making performance calculations is:
    (a) 50% of any headwind and any tailwind.
    (b) 50% of any headwind and 150% of any tailwind.
    (c) 150% of any headwind and 50% of any tailwind.
    (d) 100% of any headwind and 150% of any tailwind.

Q13. Given: pressure altitude = 31 000 ft; ambient temperature = $-30°C$. The ISA
temperature deviation is:
      (a) $+17°C$.
      (b) $-17°C$.
      (c) $+32°C$.
      (d) $-32°C$.

Q14. Given: pressure altitude = 40 000 ft; JSA deviation = $+10°C$. The ambient
temperature is:
      (a) $-75.5°C$.
      (b) $-66.5°C$.
      (c) $-55.5°C$.
      (d) $-46.5°C$.

CHAPTER 5

Field-Lengths Available

The *International Standards and Recommended Practices Annex 14* written and published by ICAO is a guide for airfield operating authorities to use as a basis for the construction, layout and modernization of aerodromes. In the UK this has been incorporated by the CAA in CAP 168. The standards recommended to the operating authority are primarily concerned with the safety of flying operations, but all are genuinely aimed at not being unnecessarily restrictive or limiting to the aircraft operator.

The type of aircraft that may operate at an aerodrome is determined by the size of the airfield, the runway lengths and surface strengths. At least one runway, together with its stopway and/or clearway, should be long enough to meet the requirements of all anticipated traffic in still air, making due operational allowances. *CAP 168 Chapter 3 Paragraph 1*.

Field lengths determined by these standards affect the performance calculations made for commercial aeroplanes operating at the aerodrome, and are criteria that have fixed quantities. They are the 'available' distances which are promulgated by the operating authority and which must *never* be exceeded in performance computations.

Aerodrome reference codes.   Specific minimum measurements for aerodromes are decided by the CAA and allocated according to the 'Aerodrome Reference Code' which is determined by a combination of the Reference Field Length and the aeroplane wing span or outer main wheel span. Details of this coding are given in *CAP 168 Chapter 3 Table 3.1* and Table 5.1 here is an abbreviated version.

5.1 THE RUNWAY STRIP

CAP 168 Chapter 3. ICAO Annex 14 Paragraph 3.3 To protect aircraft from unnecessary damage in case of unintentional or accidental deviation from the runway track on the ground or in the air, the runway is included in an area referred to as the **runway strip.** This is an area of defined dimensions in which strict limitations are imposed regarding obstacles, grading, slope and strength. Operational parameters used to formulate these limitations include take-off ground swing,

31

Table 5.1 Aerodrome reference codes.

Code no.	Reference field length	Wing span	Wheel span
1	Less than 800 m	Less than 15 m	Less than 4.5 m
2	800 m–1199 m	15 m–23.9 m	4.5 m–5.9 m
3	1200 m–1799 m	24 m–35.9 m	6 m–8.9 m
4	1800 m and over	36 m–59.9 m	9 m–13.9 m

aborted take-off overrun and the low overshoot procedure. The area is free of all obstacles, is graded and is capable of supporting the weight of the intended user aircraft. Unless every obstacle liable to endanger the aircraft on the ground or in the air is removed from this envelope, the declared distances will have to be restricted. Figure 5.1 shows the runway strip envelope and Fig. 5.2 shows the strip envelope for an instrument runway strip for Code 3 and 4 aerodromes. *CAP 168 Chapter 3 Paragraph 4.3.3(a).*

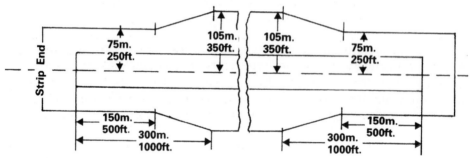

Fig. 5.1 Runway strip envelope (Codes 3 & 4). *CAP 168 Fig. 3.3.*

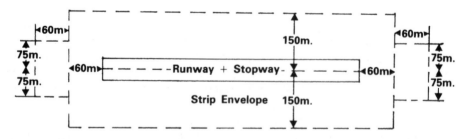

Fig. 5.2 Instrument runway strip (Codes 3 & 4). *CAP 168 Paragraph 4.3.3(a).*

The runway strip is flush with the runway and stopway and is constructed so as to avoid sudden horizontal changes in bearing strength. It is capable of bearing the aircraft it is intended to serve at maximum weight, without suffering significant damage.

These characteristics extend up to 60 m (200 ft) beyond and 23 m (75 ft) from the edge of the runway on both sides. Beyond 45 m (150 ft) from the centre line the bearing strength gradually reduces in order to assist the arrest of the aeroplane, beyond the envelope, but remain negotiable by Fire and Rescue vehicles.

The runway ends are gradually sloped to ensure that the runway does not become a buried vertical obstruction to aircraft wheels moving over soft ground. Other runway design features that should not present a hazard are drainage channels and catchpits.

5.2 FIELD-LENGTHS

For the purposes of aircraft performance it is only necessary to examine in detail the runway, its approach and extended centre-line areas.

Next to flight safety, profitability is the major interest of both the aircraft and the airfield operators. Increased profit for the aircraft operator is achieved by increased traffic loads which are limited by the maximum TOWs. Greater airfield utilization is necessary for the airfield operator to spread overhead costs and increase profits. Thus it is in the interests of both operators of aeroplanes and aerodromes to increase the ground run available for take-off. For the aircraft operator this will raise the limiting TOW imposed by the field lengths, and the airport authority may find that the aerodrome becomes usable by a wider range of aircraft.

During take-off an engine failure would reduce an aircraft's acceleration and ability to climb. It is this factor that imposes the TOW limitation with respect to the available field-lengths. When an engine failure is experienced, the pilot either abandons take-off or continues to become airborne and climb away. If the take-off is to be abandoned, sufficient ground run and prepared surface must be available to bring the aircraft safely to a halt. If the take-off is continued, the aircraft must be able to clear all obstacles by a safe margin with the reduced power available.

For each aircraft and TOW there is one speed, under certain conditions a range of speeds, at which both the conditions for abandoning and continuing take-off can be met. This is the speed at which the pilot must decide which course of action to follow and is referred to as **decision speed** commonly called V_1.

If the speed at the time of engine failure is below decision speed, the take-off *must* be abandoned because the distance required to accelerate to take-off speed would be considerably increased. Should the engine fail at a speed above decision speed, the take-off *must* be continued because there would be insufficient ground distance available to stop the aircraft safely, and because it will have already attained a high enough speed for a safe climb-away.

The total distance available is, therefore, an important factor in determining to what speed the aeroplane can safely accelerate and then be able either to safely stop or to continue the take-off. Many other factors have also to be considered when calculating decision speed; these are discussed fully in the appropriate chapter of this book.

An airfield which has only the runway available for the ground run may unnecessarily restrict the aircraft's TOW if the topographical and physical features of the runway area are suitable for an extension to be constructed or cleared. Increased distance can be made available by the airport authorities in a number of ways depending on the physical and economic constraints imposed.

If there are no obstacles in the take-off climb flight path a short ground run can be enhanced by a simple runway extension. Generally the airfields of today already have a runway of the maximum possible length; further extension is very expensive and therefore may not be a viable proposition. Construction of a take-off extension will reduce the capital outlay, however it will not enhance the landing distance available. The provision of a stopway and/or clearway could provide a cheap and effective alternative which may overcome these difficulties.

5.2.1 Take-off run available

Take-off run available (TORA) is defined as the distance between the point on the surface of the aerodrome at which the aeroplane can commence its take-off run to the nearest point, in the direction of take-off, at which the surface of the aerodrome is incapable of bearing the weight of the aeroplane, under normal operating conditions.

AN(G)R 1985 Paragraph 5(3) and JAR-OPS 1.480 Paragraph a(9) define it as the length of runway which is declared available by the appropriate Authority and suitable for the ground run of an aeroplane taking off. That is the gross weight of the aeroplane, which includes everything and everyone carried in it or on it at the commencement of the take-off run. CAP 168 Chapter 3 Paragraph 13.1(a) states that in most cases it will correpond to the length of the runway pavement. ICAO Annex 6 page 44 states that it is the length of runway declared available and suitable for the take-off ground run.

Length   Usually TORA corresponds to the physical length of the runway; but in some circumstances the proximity of roads, variations in the pavement strength or some other obstruction of a permanent nature may compel the airfield operating authority to declare a portion of the runway unavailable for take-off. The declared TORA, in such cases, is then less than the actual tarmac or paved length. This may also be the case for aerodromes at which it is necessary to use part of the declared runway for an aeroplane to line-up on the runway.

Runway alignment reduction   The reduction necessary to the declared distances available to allow for line up before take-off only applies to large aeroplanes. The amount of reduction to be made is stated in the Flight Manual by the manufacturers. Due account must be made for this loss before commencing any calculations. *JAR-OPS 1.490(b)(6)*. A full description is provided at the end of this chapter.

Starter extension   Where, because of the requirements of the anticipated traffic, it is desirable to increase the TORA but physical conditions do not permit a full extension of the runway, a starter extension may be used. This type of extension has the same strength as the runway, a maximum length of 150 m (500 ft) and a minimum width of two thirds of the normal requirement. *CAP 168 Chapter 3 Paragraph 3.2.2.*

Temporarily reduced TORA length Work in progress, surface damage or some other temporary obstruction can cause a temporary reduction in the declared TORA by the airfield operating authority. The amount by which the threshold is displaced will vary with the individual circumstances of each situation giving regard to the nature, type and level of traffic, the size and location of the obstacle and the limiting cloudbase and visibility in which the runway will be used.

It is the responsibility of the airfield operating authority to measure and promulgate the revised declared distances and the height of the restricting obstruction above the aerodrome surface level. The details are then notified to aircraft operators by NOTAM. *CAP 168 Chapter 3 Appendix 3B.*

Slope For the purposes of performance calculations, the take-off surface is regarded as a plane of infinite extent and of uniform slope in the direction of take-off. It must be free of irregularities which may cause undesirable bouncing, pitching or vibration which could adversely affect braking efficiency. The overall longitudinal slope of the runway is significant to aircraft operators. It is determined and declared by the airfield authority and is the tangent of the angle of climb or descent of the surface to the horizontal plane, expressed as percentage. It is calculated by dividing the difference in elevation between the end points of TORA by its length. In the UK this is not permitted to exceed 1% for Codes 3 and 4 or 2% for Codes 1 and 2. *CAP 168 Chapter 3 Paragraph 3.3.1.*

Where the slope of any individual portion is significantly different to the overall slope it, also, is declared. Runways having non-uniform slopes, therefore, have the mean slope and the significant slope changes declared. The effect that slope has on performance calculations is discussed in Chapter 17.

Width Any part of the runway which is included in the declared TORA has to be suitable for the ground run of aeroplanes throughout its full width, and have a uniform load bearing strength throughout its length and width appropriate to the aircraft it is intended to serve. The minimum width varies with the Aerodrome Reference Code and is specified in CAP 168 Chapter 3 Paragraph 3.2 and Table 3.2. For the purposes of this book only runways of a minimum width of 45 m and suitable for aeroplanes classified as 'A' or 'B' have been considered. Runway strength is dealt with in detail in Chapters 8 and 9.

Promulgation The airfield operating authority is obliged to declare all the details described above, and is also required to include the magnetic bearing, displaced threshold position and surface type. All declared details are published in the *United Kingdom Aeronautical Information Package (AIP)* for British airfields. Foreign airfield runway details are contained in the equivalent publication for that country.

5.2.2 Obstacles

All fixed, permanent or temporary, and mobile objects, or parts thereof, that are located on an aircraft movement surface area, or extend above a defined surface level intended to protect aircraft in flight, are defined as obstacles.

The authorities usually consider all roads (except aerodrome service roads when vehicular traffic is under the direct control of the aerodrome authorities and co-ordinated with ATC) and highways to be obstacles extending 4.8 m (16 ft) above the crown of the road. Furthermore railways, regardless of the amount of traffic, are considered to be obstacles extending 5.4 m (18 ft) above the top of the rails.

Frangibility   The ability of an object to retain its structural integrity and stiffness up to a desired maximum load is the measure of its *frangibility*. If on impact from a greater load the object distorts, yields or breaks into pieces in such a manner that the remaining configuration presents the minimum hazard to aircraft, it is considered to be frangible.

Lights which have to be positioned on the extended runway centre-line are of lightweight construction on frangible mountings. They have the minimum height consistent with their operational efficiency, and should not exceed 0.9 m (3 ft) above ground level or the clearway plane (described later in this chapter). As such they do not limit the length of the declared distances.

Some navigational aids cannot operate efficiently if sited away from the runway or approach area. It is, therefore, permissible to site equipment essential to approach, landing or overshoot in the area of the runway as low as possible on frangible mountings.

Objects offering resistance to impact likely to aggravate the consequences of a ground swing are sited as far from the runway as possible and outside of the runway strip but may impose a limitation on the distance declared.

Runway length enhancement   The most economical method of increasing the usable length of the ground run, while remaining within the legal requirements of the CAA, is to make the maximum use of the surrounding topography by constructing a stopway beyond the end of the runway on which an aircraft can safely come to rest after abandoning take-off. The construction costs are minimal.

Long runways can be further enhanced by ensuring the predicted flight path is cleared of all obstacles to form a clearway for aircraft that become airborne after engine failure. This will effectively increase the length of the ground run available that may be utilized in the continued take-off case. In certain circumstances the take-off distance required limits the maximum TOW in which case having a clearway is then a distinct advantage.

5.2.3 Stopway

JAR 1 page 12. CAP 168 Chapter 3 Paragraph 8. To meet the take-off field length requirements of some aircraft, a long runway is necessary. An economical substitute for part of the ground run available is the stopway. If it is necessary to provide similar field lengths in both directions for the same runway, a stopway must be provided at both ends of the runway. Thus the overall runway strip is longer than would have been necessary if the runway had been extended. The decision to extend the runway or provide stopways will be dictated by the relative costs, and by the physical characteristics of the terrain along the extended runway centre-line.

A stopway is an area of ground, beyond the end of TORA in the direction of take-off, which is prepared entirely free of obstructions and designated by the CAA as a suitable area on which aircraft of the type for which the airfield is intended can be safely stopped in the event of an abandoned take-off. *CAP 168 Chapter 3 paragraph 8.1.1.*

Its width is no less than that of the runway with which it is associated. Its length is determined by the first upstanding obstacle of a non-frangible nature which would cause structural damage to the aircraft in the event of an abandoned take-off, or by a deterioration in the surface load bearing strength or braking characteristics or by a ditch or depression. Slopes and changes of slope on the stopway are generally within the requirements of the runway. The rate of change of slope will not exceed 0.3% per 30 m. *CAP 168 Chapter 3 Paragraph 8.4.1.*

Because it is regarded as being for infrequent use, a stopway does not necessarily have to be of the same strength or wearing quality as the runway with which it is associated, although it must be capable of supporting the weight of the type of aircraft it is intended to serve without inducing structural damage to the aircraft. The wheels of a moving aircraft must not sink more than a few inches and therefore it is essential that all sub-surface obstructions are at least 0.3 m (12 in.) below the surface and constructed with shallow sloping sides. However, the stopway is constructed in such a manner that the passage of Rescue and Fire-fighting vehicles is unimpeded. Furthermore, it does not have to be maintained to the same standard as the runway and may not be swept as frequently or cleared of snow.

Stopways having similar appearance to the runway, because of the surface treatment of the stopway, are differentiated by a distinctive marking method at the end of the runway. If the stopway characteristics are substantially different from those of a smooth hard-surfaced runway then correction factors included in the take-off data will enable account to be taken for the differences in all seasonal conditions. *JAR 25.109(d).*

In some areas it is possible that ground which is suitable for use as stopway during a dry season is not suitable during a wet season. Should any doubt exist as to whether or not a stopway is usable, it *must* be assumed that it is not. In most cases the wet season problems are resolved by adequate land drainage. If the stopway is grass surfaced and associated with a hard surfaced runway most operators of large public transport aeroplanes will refrain from accounting it in any take-off calculations. They prefer the reduced TOW so caused, than to take the risk involved if an aeroplane abandoned a take-off.

5.2.4 Accelerate/Stop Distance Available

The Accelerate/Stop Distance Available (ASDA), which used to be known as the Emergency Distance Available, is defined as the distance from the point on the surface of the aerodrome at which an aeroplane commences its take-off run to the nearest point, in the direction of take-off, at which the aeroplane cannot roll over the surface of the aerodrome and be brought to rest in an emergency without risk of accident. *AN(G)R 5(3); JAR-OPS 1.480(a)(1); ICAO Annex to Part 1 Attachment C.*

It is therefore the total distance available for an aircraft to accelerate to decision speed, abandon take-off and then brake to a halt which is the length of TORA plus the length of the stopway, if such a stopway is declared available by the appropriate authority and is capable of bearing the aeroplane weight in the prevailing operating conditions. (TORA + stopway) = ASDA is shown in Fig. 5.3. *JAR-OPS 1.480(a)(1); ICAO Annex to Part 1 Attachment C.*

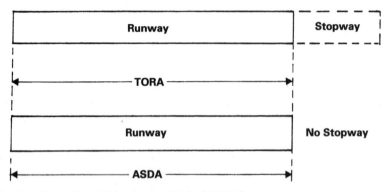

Fig. 5.3   Accelerate/Stop Distance Available (ASDA).

If there is no stopway available then the Accelerate/Stop Distance Available (Emergency Distance Available) = Take-Off Run Available. In 'shorthand', ASDA (EMDA) = TORA

5.2.5 Clearway

A clearway is an area which may be provided beyond the end of TORA, in the direction of take-off which is free of obstacles that could cause a hazard to aeroplanes in flight. *CAP 168 Chapter 3 Paragraph 9. JAR 1 page 2; ICAO Annex 14 Paragraph 3.5.*

It is an area over which an aeroplane taking off from the associated TORA can make a safe initial climb and is, therefore, an alternative means of increasing the usable length of runway in some circumstances. When TORA is less than 900 m it is not usual to provide a clearway. Because it is associated with the part of take-off after the aircraft becomes airborne, it may extend over land or water and does not require any bearing strength. It is the responsibility of the airport operating authority to ensure that if any clearway extends beyond the airfield boundary it is kept free of obstacles, or infringement. Table 5.2 gives clearway widths for UK aerodromes.

Types of clearway   To take into account the effect of down sloping ground in the clearway, the CAA have introduced three main types of clearway which are fully described in CAP 168 Chapter 3 Paragraph 9.4. They are the **normal**, the **horizontal-plane** and the **runway-continued-plane** clearways, each of which is limited in a different manner. This differentiation is for the purpose of the Airport Licensing

Table 5.2 Clearway widths for UK aerodromes.

Airfield code	Starting semi-width	Finishing semi-width
3 & 4	75 m	90 m
2	40 m	75 m
1	30 m	75 m
ICAO	75 m	75 m

Authority to determine the length of clearway to be declared. Aircrew and operations staff need only concern themselves with the distance actually declared, for the purposes of performance calculations.

Width   The width of the clearway at the end of TORA is not less than the width of the runway strip for the visual runway with which it is associated and expands linearly to its maximum width either side of the extended centre-line by the end of TODA for airfields in the UK. Its shape is therefore that of a truncated triangle. Airfields outside of the UK, which adhere to ICAO Annex 14, Paragraph 3.5.3 have rectangular clearways that extend 75 m (250 ft) either side of the extended runway centre-line.

Length The length of the clearway is determined by the position of the first non-frangible obstacle, or frangible obstacle exceeding 0.9 m, above the local ground level or a surface irregularity that could cause structural damage to the aircraft in its initial climb after take-off.

If the length is not limited in this manner then the maximum length that is permitted to be used for the purposes of performance calculations is restricted to one half of the length of the associated TORA. *AN(G)R 5(3); CAP 168 Chapter 9 Paragraph 9.3.1; ICAO Annex 14 Paragraph 5.*

Although it is permissible to declare a maximum clearway length equal to 50% of TORA, the airworthiness requirements imposed on the aircraft performance effectively restrict the amount of usable clearway for these purposes to 20% of TORA.

Slope   The surface beneath a clearway does not require special preparation. Minor irregularities, including isolated depressions such as ditches, are permitted. However, the slope changes and transition area conform to those of the associated runway out to the width of that runway either side of the extended centre-line. Over the remainder of the clearway no part of the ground may project above a slope measured at the start of clearway of 1.25% (1:80) for runways of Code 3 or 4 aerodromes. If this plane is infringed by any part of the terrain, it is considered to be the limiting obstacle for the purposes of calculating clearway length. *CAP 168 Chapter 3 Paragraph 9.*

5.2.6 Take-off Distance Available (TODA)

JAR-OPS 1.480(a)(7); CAP 168 Chapter 3 Paragraph 13.

Take-off Distance Available is the distance from the start of TORA to the nearest obstacle in the direction of take-off projecting above the surface of the aerodrome and capable of affecting the safety of the aeroplane when in flight, up to a maximum distance of 150% TORA (Fig. 5.4). *AN(G)R 5(3); CAP 168 Paragraph 9.5; ICAO Annex 14 Paragraph 6.*

Length   The length of TODA can, therefore, be either the total of TORA plus clearway (not exceeding 150% of TORA) or just equal to TORA if no clearway exists.

Slope   Where no clearway is available, the slope of TORA and TODA are the same. However, when a clearway is declared, the slope is calculated by dividing the difference in elevation between the start of TORA and the end of clearway by the length of TODA. If the slope of the clearway is significantly different to that of the runway then the operating authority will promulgate the elevations required to facilitate the calculation of the correct slope.

Obstacles   By definition, no obstacles capable of hazarding the aircraft in the airborne phase of take-off may exist in the declared clearway. Beyond the end of TODA the CAA imposes a **Take-off Climb Surface (TOCS)** with a slope of 2% to establish which obstacles penetrate the climb surface and have to be considered in Net Flight Path (NFP) calculations.

5.2.7 Balanced Field Lengths

ICAO Annex 14 Attachment A Paragraph 2.5; CAP 168 Chapter 3 Appendix 3c Paragraph 2.1.3. The original concept of a **Balanced Field Length** was a runway that had no declared stopway or clearway. It was the equality of the runway with ASDA (EMDA) and TODA that caused the term to be introduced. For aircraft such as the DC6 it was normal practice to use 'Balanced Field Lengths' to calculate the maximum permissible TOW. The requirements of stopway and clearway were later changed so that credit could be taken in the TOW calculations for cleared areas beyond the runway which would benefit the operator. Because of the background of the term, some early Operating Data Manuals (ODMs) contained simplified graphs to resolve TOW with a balanced field.

Currently the term 'Balanced Field Length' refers to a runway where ASDA(EMDA) = TODA. It is the equality of the stopway and clearway which is now referred to as 'balanced,' and the runway length is no longer a limiting consideration, except when there is no clearway or stopway (see Fig. 5.5).

5.2.8 Unbalanced Field Lengths

Where the stopway does *not* equal the clearway, the field lengths are considered unbalanced because ASDA (EMDA) does not equal TODA. By full utilization of

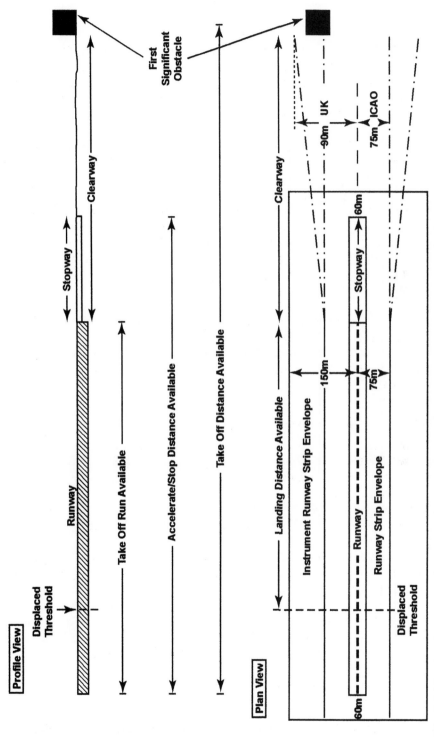

Fig. 5.4 Declared aerodrome distances (*CAP 168 Chapter 3 Figure 3.10*).

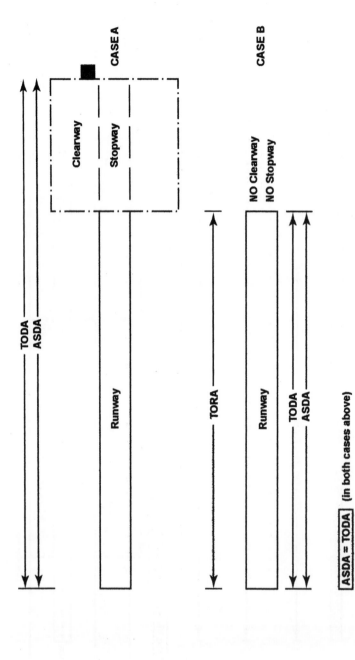

Fig. 5.5 Balanced field lengths.

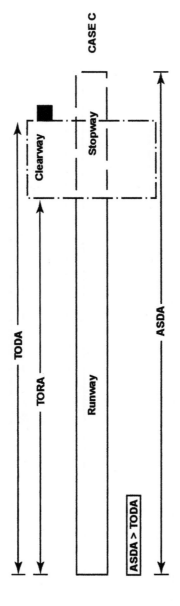

Fig. 5.6a Unbalanced field length.

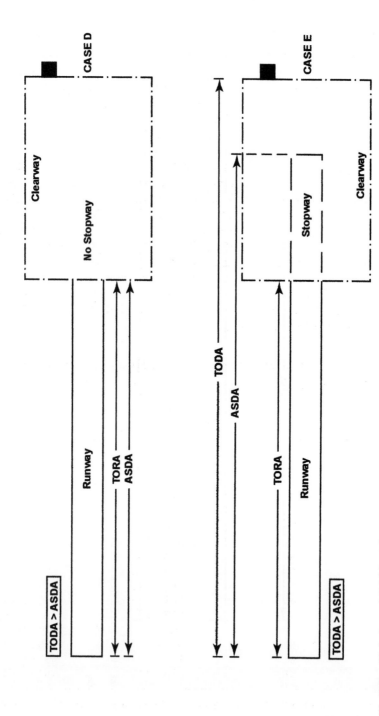

Fig. 5.6b　Unbalanced field lengths.

the varying amounts of stopway and clearway, the highest possible TOW for the field lengths under consideration will be obtained (see Fig. 5.6).

5.2.9 Runway alignment reduction

JAR-OPS 1.490(c)(6) requires that the published available distances be reduced by the amount taken by an aeroplane to line up with the runway. This correction is to be made before computation of the take-off performance. The amount of reduction is dependent on the runway turn geometry and the aircraft type.

The adjustment to TODA is based on the distance from the commencement to the position of the main wheels after line up correction A. This is because the take-off distance required is measured from the start of the take-off run to the point at which the aeroplane attains screen height with the undercarriage extended. The TORA is reduced by the same amount because the take-off run required is the distance from the start of the take-off run to the point where the main wheels leave the ground. However, the adjustment to ASDA is based on the nose-wheel position after line-up correction B. This is because, in the event of an abandoned take-off, the nose-wheel must come to rest before the end of the stopway. See Fig. 5.7.

Manufacturers publish the distances taken to line-up for 180° and 90° turns on to the centre-line. In assessing the distance corrections a minimum edge safety distance (m) is used which is specified in ICAO Annex 14. For the example aeroplanes quoted in Table 5.3, the Boeing 737-400, this is 3.04 m and the 747 and the 777-200 is 4.57 m. See Figs 5.7–5.10 and Table 5.3.

Table 5.3 Example runway alignment reductions; 90° taxiway entry* (courtesy of the Boeing Company).

Aircraft type	Max. eff. steering angle (°)	Min. line up distance correction TODA ft (m)	ASDA ft (m)
737-200	75	30.4 (9.3)	67.7 (20.6)
737-300	75	31.4 (9.6)	72.2 (22.0)
737-400	75	33.0 (10.1)	79.8 (24.3)
737-500	75	30.2 (9.2)	66.5 (20.3)
737-600	75	31.5 (9.6)	68.6 (20.9)
737-700	75	32.6 (9.9)	73.9 (22.5)
737-800	75	35.3 (10.8)	86.7 (26.4)
747 ALL	63	78.4 (23.9)	162.4 (49.5)
747-SP	63	69.9 (21.3)	137.2 (41.8)
757-200	60	63.6 (19.4)	123.6 (37.7)
757-300	60	71.3 (21.7)	144.6 (44.1)
767-200	61	68.7 (20.9)	133.3 (40.6)
767-300	61	74.3 (22.6)	149.0 (45.4)
767-400	61	80.4 (24.5)	166.1 (50.6)
777-200	64	77.5 (23.6)	162.3 (49.5)
777-300	64	86.0 (26.2)	188.4 (57.4)

* Includes the minimum edge safety distances required by ICAO Annex 14 of 10 ft (3.04 m) for 727/737 and 15 ft for all other types.

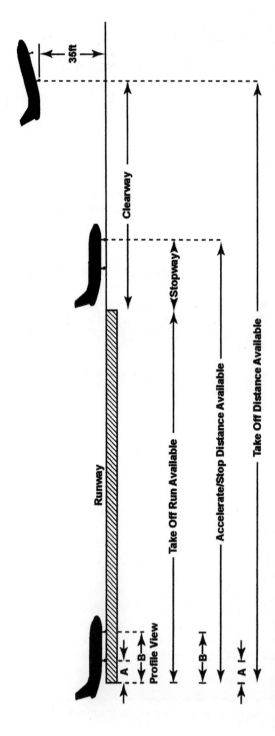

Fig. 5.7 Take-off distance adjustments.

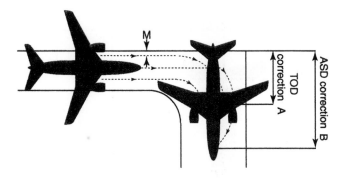

Fig. 5.8   90° turn on to centre-line.

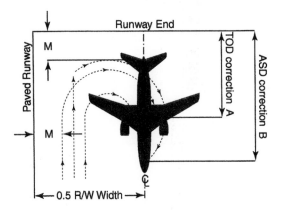

Fig. 5.9   180° turn on to centre-line.

5.2.10 The calculation of runway slope

Runway slope is defined as the average inclination of the runway surface to the horizontal expressed as a percentage. It is, therefore, the change of elevation in feet per hundred feet measured along the surface. If the TORA is quoted in metres it must first be converted to a distance in feet by multiplying the length by 3.28 before using the following formula to determine the runway slope. If the TORA in opposite directions on the same runway are of different lengths then one has a displaced threshold and this displacement is being utilized as stopway for the opposing runway (Fig. 5.11). The TORA to be used in the formula must always be the shorter of the two TORAs. Note the runway slope is determined from the shorter TORA length and no other distance is involved. The formula is:

$$\frac{\text{Difference in threshold elevations}}{(\text{Take-off run available} \times 3.28)} \times 100 = \%$$

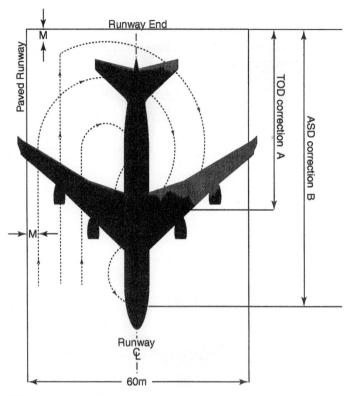

Fig. 5.10   180° turn on to a 60 m runway.

Example 1   Given: R/W 27, Threshold elevation 3290 ft; TORA 1000 m; EMDA
1100 m; TODA 1200 m. R/W 09, Threshold elevation 3350 ft; TORA 900 m; EMDA
1000 m; TODA 1100 m. Calculate the runway slope for runway 09.

$$\frac{(3350 - 3290)}{900 \times 3.28} \times 100 = 2.03\% \ \text{downhill.}$$

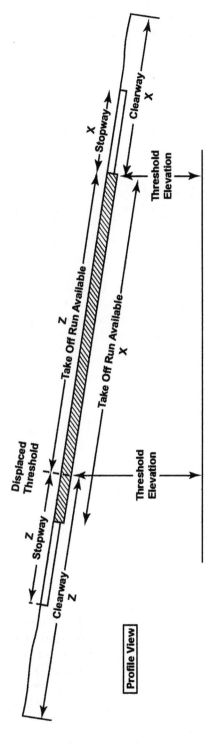

Fig. 5.11 Runway with a displaced threshold.

CHAPTER 6

The Take-off Climb Area

To ensure a full and complete knowledge of scheduled performance, all the related factors must be examined in detail. One of them which is often overlooked is that of the obstacles that require consideration during the take-off climb. Although these obstacles are usually listed for each runway, it is to the aircrew's benefit to know the method that was used to decide which obstacles to include and which not.

Airfield operators are required by the CAA to establish a take-off climb area for each runway direction intended to be used for the take-off of aircraft. The dimensions of the area are specified and form a **Take-Off Climb Surface (TOCS)** for the runway. Any immovable objects that project through this surface are notified to the CAA by a survey party. The obstacle is then plotted on a chart which relates the horizontal distance and height of the top of the obstacle to the take-off runway.

6.1 CLIMB SURFACE DIMENSIONS

CAP 168 Chapter 4 Paragraph 2. The dimensions prescribed for the TOCS area for aerodromes in each of the codes are listed in Table 6.1 and are depicted in Fig. 6.1a,b. A description of each measurement follows.

Table 6.1 Take-off climb surfaces (copyright CAA). *CAP 168 Table 4.1.*

Code number	3 or 4	2	1
Length of inner edge	180 m	80 m‡	60 m‡
Distance of inner edge from end of take-off run*	60 m	60 m	30 m
Divergence each side	12.5%	10%	10%
Final width	1200 m	580 m	380 m
	1800 m†		
Length	15000 m	2500 m	1600 m
Slope	2%	4%	5%
	(1:50)	(1:25)	(1:20)

* Where clearway is provided the inner edge is at the end of the clearway.
† When the intended track includes changes of heading greater than 15° the final width of the take-off climb surface for runways code 3 or 4 is 1800 m.
‡ Where clearway is provided the length of the inner edge should be 150 m.

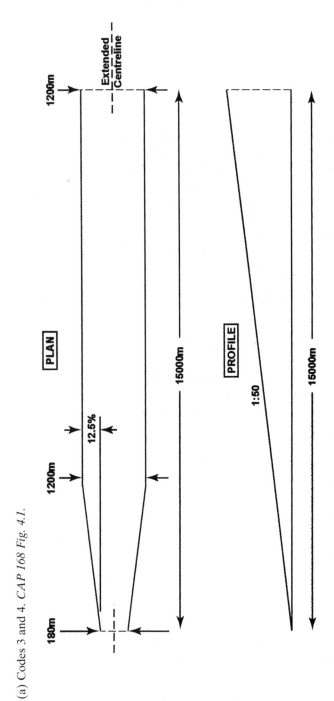

(a) Codes 3 and 4. *CAP 168 Fig. 4.1.*

Fig. 6.1a Take-off climb surface (copyright CAA).

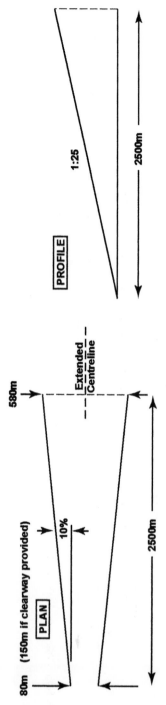

(b) Code 2. *CAP 168 Fig. 4.2.*

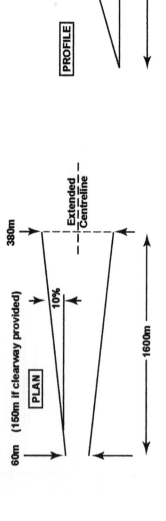

(c) Code 1. *CAP 169 Fig. 4.3.*

Fig. 6.1b   Take-off climb surface (copyright CAA).

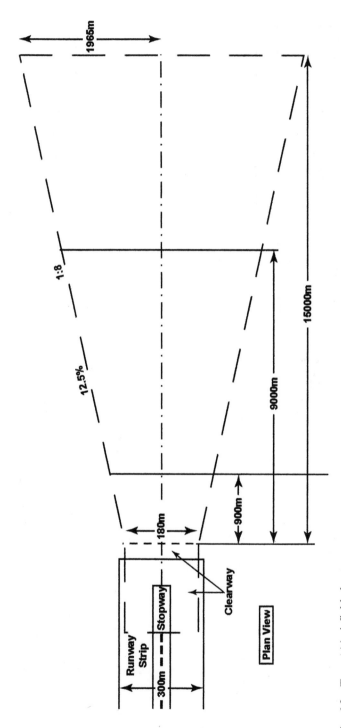

Fig. 6.2 Type 'A' airfield chart.

6.1.1 Inner edge

An imaginary line perpendicular to the runway centre-line at the end of the clearway; or, if no clearway exists, a minimum distance of 60 m (200 ft) from the end of the runway in the direction of take-off for Codes 2, 3 and 4 or 30 m for Code 1. The inner edge is 180 m long for Codes 3 and 4, 80 m for Code 2 and 60 m for Code 1.

6.1.2 Funnel

The funnel commences at the ends of the inner edge and diverges at the prescribed rate until it reaches the maximum length, except for Codes 3 and 4 which reach their maximum width at a distance of 4080 m measured along the extended centre-line from the inner edge.

6.1.3 Final width (straight climb Codes 3 and 4 only)

The final width of the take-off climb surface area extends 600 m (1970 ft) either side of the extended centre-line until a total distance of 15 000 m (49 213 ft) from the inner edge is reached.

6.1.4 Final width (change of heading Codes 3 & 4 only)

If the intended track includes a change of heading greater than 15°, the final width is 900 m (2950 ft) either side of the extended centre-line until a total distance of 15 000 m (49 213 ft) from the inner edge is reached.

6.1.5 Slope

For main take-off runways the slope of the surface is 2% for Codes 3 and 4, 4% for Code 2 and 5% for Code 1 from the inner edge. The height of the end of the take-off surface area in all cases is approximately 1000 ft above the surface level at the end of the clearway, or runway if no clearway exists.

A climb surface that involves a turn is considered to be a complex surface such that the normal at any point is a horizontal line at the same height above the end of the runway, or clearway, as would have been achieved if the flight path had been straight for the same distance flown.

Where the runway width is substantially greater than the minimum, the length of the inner edge of the TOCS is extended so that it is not less than the appropriate strip width. The initial part of the surface is formed by the sides drawn from the strip edges parallel to the extended centre-line until they intersect the diverging sides of the normal TOCS.

6.2 TYPE 'A' AIRFIELD CHARTS

Although airfield operators declare an obstacle limitation surface, this is not the criterion used to establish the location and height of obstacles for the aircraft operator. Before an aerodrome operating authority is granted a licence, details of all obstacles have to be surveyed, measured and plotted on a type 'A' chart. This chart has a horizontal scale of 1:10 000 and a vertical scale of 1:1 000 as illustrated in Fig. 6.2.

If the chart dimensions exceed 1 m, the scale may be altered to 1:20 000 horizontally and 1:2 000 vertically so that the resulting chart is of a reasonable size. The elevations or heights of all the obstacles included in the survey area and penetrating the survey surface are numbered and plotted above the Ordnance Datum, which is the elevation at the end of TODA. This was the datum to which all obstacles were related until 1992. Since that date obstacle distances are related to the brakes release point (BRP) and obstacle heights to MSL which means they are now quoted as elevations.

6.2.1 Obstacle shadows

CAP 168 Chapter 4 Paragraph 10. The principle of shielding is employed when a substantial object or natural terrain already penetrates an obstacle limitation surface. When it is considered that such an obstacle is permanent, objects of equal or lesser height around it may at the CAA's discretion be permitted to penetrate the surface.

Obstructions are considered to cast an horizontal shadow forward at the elevation of the top of the obstacle away from the runway and also a backward shadow 10% downward towards the runway. All shadows cast by obstacles are considered to be cast from the full width of the obstacle decreasing with sides parallel to the relevant protecting surface until they converge or intersect the TOCS. Thus the plan view takes the form of a triangle or truncated triangle.

Any obstacle that falls within the forward shadow and lies beneath a negative slope of 10% is not considered to be significant, and does NOT have to be shown on the type 'A' chart or declared by the aerodrome operating authority.

Aircraft operators are advised that they are legally responsible for avoiding all obstacles in their aeroplane obstacle domain even those not declared or plotted on the type 'A' chart as being significant.

The area covered and the profile formed by the existing requirements are used as the basis for plotting all take-off-climb obstacle charts in the UK. These are the airfield type 'A' charts, one of which is published for each take-off runway. All are reviewed annually and completely re-surveyed every three years, or every six years if the area has no tree growth *and* is unlikely to be developed.

Obstacle information is extracted from these charts for promulgation. If the aerodrome has not been recently re-surveyed then the obstacles details quoted use the physical position and elevation of the end of TODA as the reference point. If, however, the aerodrome has recently been surveyed then the data used are the BRP and MSL. Care is required if the AIP is used to determine these details because it currently contains a mixture of the two methods.

CHAPTER 7

The Aerodrome Landing Surface Area

The phase of flight termed the 'landing' in fact refers to the complete approach from 1500 ft above the landing surface level to the termination of the landing roll. It is therefore necessary to study both the airfield and the surrounding area.

7.1 THE AERODROME

7.1.1 Runway End Safety Area (RESA)

A runway end safety area is provided on almost all runways. Its minimum dimensions are 90 m long and twice the width of the runway with which it is associated. Its purpose is to minimize the risks that arise when an aeroplane over-runs or undershoots a runway. It is symmetrically disposed about the extended centre-line and has a bearing strength great enough not to endanger the aircraft or hinder movement of rescue and fire-fighting vehicles. The area must be clear of non-frangible obstacles and free of abrupt gradient changes. If land is not available for the purpose of providing a RESA, all declared distances are reduced to accommodate such an area. *CAP 168 Chapter 3 Paragraph 5.*

7.1.2 Landing Distance Available (LDA)

The use to which a runway is put determines the criteria applied in measuring the distances declared. LDA means the distance from the point on the surface of an aerodrome above which the aeroplane can commence its landing, having regard to the obstructions in its approach path, to the nearest point in the direction of landing at which the surface is incapable of bearing the weight of the aeroplane under normal operating conditions or at which there is an obstacle capable of affecting the safety of the aeroplane. It usually extends from the end of the touchdown threshold, along the full length of the runway. *AN(G)R 5(3).*

The length of the LDA declared is determined by whether a paved stopway is available if the threshold is displaced, because of obstacles in the approach area, and by whether the runway is for visual or instrument approaches. The effect these factors have on the declared LDA is shown in Fig. 7.1.

The basic reference code for runway lengths, including stopway and/or clearway when provided, is Code 3 or 4 which have a length greater than 1200 m. *CAP 168 Chapter 3 Paragraph 2.3 and ICAO Annex 14 Table 1.1.*

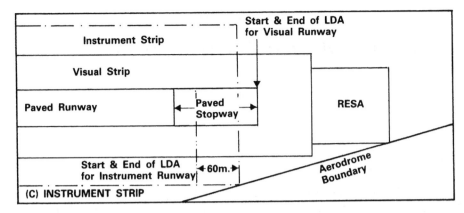

Fig. 7.1 Factors affecting the declared LDA. Instrument runway Codes 3 and 4. *CAP 168 Fig. 3.12.*

7.1.3 Runway threshold

The threshold is the start of that part of a runway which is declared as available for landing. It is normally located at the beginning of a runway if the strip width, length and RESA dimensions are met. If any of these requirements are lacking, or if an obstacle extends above the approach surface, it may be necessary to offset the threshold from the runway end. The amount of displacement will vary with the circumstances, regard being given to:

(1) Nature, type and the level of traffic;
(2) Whether it is a visual or instrument runway with a precision or non-precision approach;
(3) The position of any obstacle that affects the RESA or infringes the approach surface;
(4) Any obstacle that affects the obstacle clearance height;
(5) The glidepath angle and calculated obstacle clearance height;
(6) The limiting visibility and cloudbase for that runway.

7.1.4 The approach surface

The approach surface is an inclined plane or combination of planes preceding the threshold of each runway intended for landing, in which all permanent obstacles are clearly marked and mobile obstacles controlled. The dimensions of the approach surface vary with the code of the runway and on whether or not it is a precision instrument runway, a non-precision runway or a visual runway.

The plan view of the approach surface area is funnel-shaped. A horizontal inner edge at right-angles to the runway centre-line is located at 60 m before the touchdown threshold, a width of 300 m and at the same elevation. From this edge the sides diverge at 15% until the outer edge is reached. The first section has a length of 3000 m and a slope of 2% and the second section a length of 3600 m and slope of 2.5%. This is followed by a horizontal section 8400 m long which has an outer edge width of 4800 m (see Fig. 7.2).

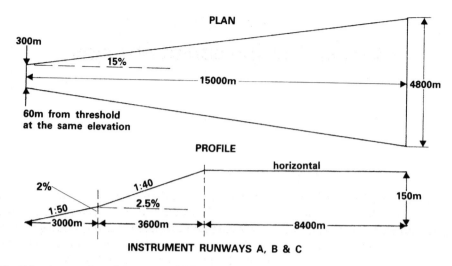

Fig. 7.2   Approach surface areas. *CAP 168 Fig. 4.5.*

CHAPTER 8
Aerodrome Pavement Strength

The operation of aircraft from any type of airfield surface can never be safely undertaken without knowing full details of the aircraft load characteristics and the surface strength. Forty years ago it was common practice for aerodrome operators to classify surfaces in broadly-defined categories. Since then aircraft weights and tyre pressures have increased, and wheel arrangements changed, so much that the original categories have become meaningless.

Although a simple system of load comparison between the aircraft and surface is necessary, it has to be accurate and easy to apply. Many tests were carried out using steel plates and known weights to compile surface failure/load tables. From these tests various systems have been developed to meet the requirements of modern aircraft.

In general, an aerodrome pavement should be strong enough for an aircraft to operate without risk of damage to either pavement or aircraft under normal circumstances. The system of load bearing comparison developed in the UK was accepted by ICAO, and is now one of the methods in use throughout the world. Originally the system was known as **Load Classification Numbers (LCN)** from which developed the **Load Classification Group (LCG)** system.

Pavement types   Two main pavement types exist: 'rigid,' when the bearing strength is derived from a concrete slab; and 'flexible', when the strength is obtained from a series of layers of compacted substance usually finished with a surfacing of bituminous material. The strength of the surface is a measure of its load-bearing capability. Flexibility or relative stiffness of the surface is related to the strength of the ground beneath the pavement and the thickness of the pavement. Rigid pavements have a measure of relative stiffness which is quoted in 'l' inches and flexible pavements in 'h' inches.

Stress effects   The stress effect an aircraft has on a pavement varies with AUW, tyre pressure, number and spacing of wheels, type of pavement and the actual or equivalent thickness of that pavement. Aircraft with multi-wheel arrangements are better able to spread their load and are often less limited by thin flexible pavements than by thick ones, which may suffer a multi-loaded fracture area between the wheels at the base of the pavement (see Fig. 8.1).

Airfield surface weight limitations   All airfield surfaces, including hard standings, parking areas, hangar floors, taxiways and runways, whether constructed of tarmac

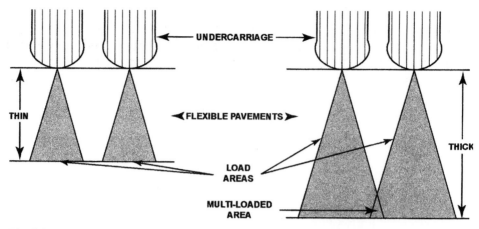

Fig. 8.1 The effect of a multi-wheeled undercarriage.

or concrete, are classified according to their strength. Each area is given the load classification number (LCN) or single wheel loading (SWL) of its weakest point. The LCN or SWL of the aircraft must not exceed the figures laid down by the airport authority at any point which the aircraft is likely to traverse before getting airborne.

Runway surfaces The surface of runways should be without irregularities that would cause loss of braking action, affect the aircraft steering or otherwise adversely affect the take-off or landing of an aircraft. The coefficient of friction in both wet and dry conditions must reach a satisfactory standard. If abnormal quantities of water are present on the runway the pilot must be notified of its depth and of its likely effect on braking action.

The surface areas beyond the end of the runway must be the same width as the runway and have a bearing strength not less than 30% that of the associated runway. The area up to 60 m (200 ft) beyond the runway or stopway end, and 23 m (75 ft) from each side of the runway and stopway, must be capable of bearing the maximum weight of all aircraft that it is intended to serve without causing significant damage to the aircraft. Beyond these limits the remainder of the runway strip is graded but not prepared to the same standard. The bearing strength does not decrease until a distance of 45 m (150 ft) from the runway centre-line, and then at a gradual rate to assist the arrest of the aeroplane.

Runway extensions must always remain negotiable by Fire and Rescue vehicles.

8.1 THE LOAD CLASSIFICATION NUMBER SYSTEM

The original system was based on aircraft with single wheel units having a minimum tyre contact area of 200 sq. in. With the introduction of heavier aircraft with multiple wheel arrangements and high tyre pressures, the system became unusable because the tyre contact area was considerably reduced.

To overcome this difficulty for each arrangement of closely grouped wheels, an **Equivalent Single Wheel Loading (ESWL)** was calculated; which, at the tyre pressure of the assembly, enabled it to be compared with a single wheel unit. Thus a direct relationship exists between LCN and ESWL. A selected list of loads is shown in Table 8.1.

Table 8.1 Conversion of ESWL to LCN.

Wheel load (lb)	Tyre pressure (contact area) (sq. in.)	LCN
100 000	120	100
90 000	115	90
80 000	110	80
70 000	105	70
60 000	100	60
50 000	95	50
40 000	90	40
30 000	85	30
20 000	80	20
10 000	75	10

By comparing the known characteristics of an aircraft and the airfield surface it is possible to determine whether an airfield is suitable for a particular type of aircraft by the use of the LCN.

The aircraft LCN should not exceed the airfield LCN if the number of aircraft movements is to be unrestricted, without additional maintenance work to the airfield being required.

8.1.1 Airfield LCN overload

Airfield operators are permitted to accept aircraft with an LCN up to 10% higher than the pavement LCN without restricting the number of movements. Continuous operation at this overload is liable to reduce the interval between pavement major maintenance work.

Although it is permissible to exceed the airfield LCN still further, this will increase the maintenance requirements of the surface and is directly related to the degree of overload and the number of movements, because there may well be failure of the pavement which could cause damage to the aircraft. The aerodrome operators, if they are willing to accept the damage that may be caused to the surface, will inform the aircraft's captain of the surface state and degree of risk involved. It is then the captain's decision whether or not to use the surface.

Table 8.2 summarizes the excess loading and pavement life. *An aircraft movement is defined as one landing, one take-off or one passage over a section of pavement.* Some surfaces, particularly of the flexible type, are unsuitable for high tyre

Table 8.2 Conditions for exceeding surface LCN.

Amount A/C LCN exceeds A/F LCN	No. of A/C moves during pavement life	Conditions imposed
10%–25%	3000	Nil
25%–50%	300	Nil
50%–100%	Extremely limited	Experienced Civil Engineer examine pavement history. Give likely damage and permission.
Over 100%	Emergency only	Serious damage to aircraft and surface.

pressures and may fail even if the aircraft LCN is lower than the pavement LCN. Maximum permissible tyre pressures are shown on the LCN plans of aerodrome pavements tested by DOE engineers.

8.2 LOAD CLASSIFICATION GROUPS

Although the LCN system is accurate; an aerodrome plan could contain many surfaces of varying LCN strength, and the ICAO decided that it was unnecessarily complicated. The DOE therefore evolved a system of simple pavement classification groups based on the original LCN calculations. This system, Load Classification Groups (LCGs), takes local variation of LCN into account and divides the whole LCN spectrum into seven groups, as depicted in Table 8.3.

Table 8.3 LCG and LCN equivalence.

LCG	Aircraft type	LCN
I	Heavy aircraft	101+
II		76–100
III		51–75
IV		31–50
V		16–30
VI		11–15
VII	Light aircraft	1–10

8.2.1 Surface deterioration

The deterioration suffered by any particular surface can be due to any one cause, or to a combination of causes. They include the repetitive loading by different wheel arrangements having a cumulative effect. Other factors affecting the life of the surface are climate, sub-surface type and moisture content, type of surface and amount of maintenance work carried out.

8.2.2 Airfield LCG overload

A safe loading below the maximum permissible load of any airfield surface is guaranteed by the safety factor incorporated in the LCG system. Prior permission from the airfield operating authority must be obtained if it is required to exceed the pavement LCG.

To avoid undue damage being caused to the pavement, only infrequent movements of aircraft exceeding the airfield LCG by one group are permitted. An aircraft exceeding the LCG of the airfield surface by two or more categories may only use the airfield in an emergency.

8.3 OTHER CLASSIFICATION SYSTEMS

Outside the UK there are four main types of airfield surface classification systems which are described below.

(a) Acceptable aircraft   A particular aircraft type, e.g. Britannia or DC6, is quoted as the limiting size of aircraft which can safely use the surface. This does not give an exact measurement of the maximum permissible surface load because it takes no account of wheel configuration or tyre pressures.

(b) Acceptable AUW   The maximum AUW which can traverse the surface is stated as a weight, or a weight qualified by the type of wheel arrangement. By comparing the aircraft LCN with that of a limiting aircraft for the airfield having a similar weight and wheel arrangement, a rough guide to the suitability of the airfield can be obtained.

(c) Equivalent Single Wheel Load (ESWL) or Single Isolated Wheel Load (SIWL)   The load of several wheels of a multi-wheeled unit is represented by the load which a single wheel at the same tyre pressure would impose on the runway surface.

(d) New pavement strength reporting method   A relatively new pavement strength reporting system was introduced in 1984 and is fully described in Chapter 9.

Figure 8.2 enables LCN to be converted to LCG and ESWL.

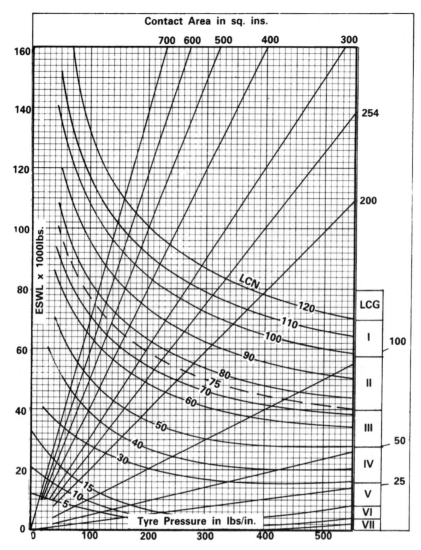

Fig. 8.2   Relationship of LCN to LCG and ESWL.

CHAPTER 9

The ACN/PCN Reporting System

All Member States of ICAO are required by ICAO Standard Practices Annex 14 to promulgate their aerodrome pavement strengths in their individual AIPs. Of the pavement strength classification systems currently in use, only four were acceptable to ICAO for the purposes of complying with this requirement. They were: **the maximum gross aeroplane mass allowable**, **the maximum undercarriage leg load allowable**, **the load classification number (LCN) system** and **the load classification group (LCG) system**. Freedom of selection between these four acceptable choices resulted in a variety of different systems being used by Member States, and even between aerodromes of the same State. This situation complicated performance planning.

To resolve this problem and to maximize the pavement surface life, it was decided by ICAO that a new method of reporting pavement strength should be adopted to replace the other existing acceptable methods. The new method is detailed in Amendment 35 to Annex 14 ICAO Standard Practices. The aim is to introduce uniformity and standardization of pavement strength reporting and at the same time be easily used for all aircraft types.

The criteria developed from the load classification (LCN) or load classification group (LCG) will continue to be used for the design and evaluation of pavements. However, the original pavement strength classification has been converted to units of the new reporting method by the aerodrome operating authority and promulgated by the appropriate national civil aviation authority.

9.1 THE ACN/PCN REPORTING SYSTEM

Only the method of reporting pavement strength has been altered by the introduction of the ACN/PCN system. The base datum used for this reporting method is common to both pavement and aeroplane, so as to facilitate easy comparison. All civilian and many military aeroplane types have been classified to this datum and a comprehensive list was published in the amendment.

There are two basic procedures contained in Amendment 35. The first procedure is designed for use with pavements intended for aeroplanes having a maximum total weight authorized (MTWA) of 5700 kg (12 500 lb) or less. The second procedure is used for reporting the strength of all other pavements and is that which has been adopted by the CAA for implementation in the UK.

Pavement strengths reported in other Member States using the first procedure

65

will contain a simple statement in words of the maximum allowable aircraft weight and the maximum allowable tyre pressure. No aeroplane having a weight and/or tyre pressure that exceeds the limiting pavement strength values so stated is permitted to use the pavement. An example of a report using the first procedure would appear in the AIP as 500 kg/0.45 MPa (note: 1 Megapascal (MPa) = 145 psi).

The second procedure is used for reporting the strength of those pavements intended for use by heavy aircraft. It was adopted by the CAA for use by civilian aerodromes and aeroplanes from 26 November 1981. This reporting method is referred to as the **Aircraft Classification Number – Pavement Classification Number (ACN/PCN)** system.

9.1.2 The Pavement Strength Report

Using this system the pavement strength report is divided into five parts, each of which is coded and promulgated in the AIP in a prescribed order to ensure that the decode is unambiguous. The five parts of the report are:

(a) Pavement Classification Number (PCN)   This is a number given to the pavement strength which expresses the relative effect of an aircraft on the pavement for a specified sub-grade strength, and represents the bearing strength of the pavement for an UNRESTRICTED number of movements.

Classification numbers commence at zero and are on a continuous scale with no upper limit. A pavement load rating of one PCN is that strength which would be just sufficient to support a single wheel of mass 500 kg at a tyre pressure of 1.25 MPa (181.5 psi). Sample coded report: PCN 60.

(b) Pavement type   The reporting procedure for pavement type is divided into 'rigid' and 'flexible' – the same as that used for the evaluation of aircraft classification numbers. The type reported depends on its relative stiffness. If the surface bearing strength is derived from a composite material or from layers of a compacted substance, the pavement type could fall in either category. If it is derived from a concrete slab, it is normally designated 'rigid'. The code used for the report is 'R' for rigid and 'F' for flexible.

(c) Sub-grade strength category   The strength of the pavement sub-grade is measured and classified in one of four groups for the appropriate pavement type and is classified either high, medium, low or ultra-low and are coded for the report as: 'A' – High, 'B' – Medium, 'C' – Low or 'D' – Ultra-Low.

(d) Tyre pressure category   Tyre pressures are arbitrarily divided into four groups and coded:

'W' – High tyre pressure with no upper limit.
'X' – Medium, maximum tyre pressure 1.5 MPa (217.5 psi).
'Y' – Low, maximum tyre pressure 1.0 MPa (145 psi).
'Z' – Very Low, maximum tyre pressure 0.5 MPa (72.5 psi).

Thus the maximum tyre pressure that a pavement can withstand is reported by the appropriate group code.

(e) Evaluation method   Only two methods may be used to determine pavement qualities. They are code 'T' or 'U'. If a full technical evaluation of the pavement has been carried out, it is reported 'T'. If the evaluation is based on the experience gathered from user aircraft, it is reported as 'U'. This information is useful to manufacturers and operators should it become necessary to study the aerodrome pavement in detail.

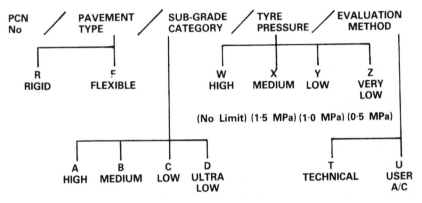

Fig. 9.1   ACN/PCN pavement strength reporting method.

The introduction of the ACN/PCN reporting method has given the aerodrome operating authority greater freedom in deciding the maximum permissible aircraft weight than was possible before. In the past an aerodrome operating authority had to restrict the aircraft maximum weight to that which was determined by the LCG assessment method. Now, if the aerodrome operating authority so desires and considers it safe, it can permit the unrestricted movement of larger aircraft types by utilizing the 'U' symbol and reporting the limiting PCN equal to the upper ACN of the required aircraft type. Of course this may subsequently result in the PCN being lowered if the pavement performance does not meet with expectations and begins to deteriorate.

An example of pavement strength reported in the recommended manner is PCN 60/F/B/X/T which, when decoded, becomes:

- Pavement Classification Number 60
- Flexible Pavement
- Medium Strength Sub-Grade
- Medium Tyre Pressure limited to 1.5 MPa (217.5 psi).
- Pavement characteristics were all evaluated technically.

An **Aircraft Classification Number (ACN)** is a number which expresses the relative effect of an aircraft mass on a pavement of a specified sub-grade strength. A single wheel supporting a mass of 500 kg at a tyre pressure of 1.25 MPa (181.25 psi) is considered to have a load rating of 1 ACN. To enable a simple comparison to be made between aircraft mass and pavement strength ICAO have prepared a table of ACNs which include the majority of civilian aircraft types currently in use having an MTWA exceeding 5700 kg (12 500 lb). MTWA is the maximum total weight authorized. Normally this is the maximum take-off weight plus taxi fuel, i.e. maximum ramp weight.

The table was constructed to the same base datum as PCN and produced by means of a computer programme designed for the purpose. In future, aircraft manufacturers will have to calculate ACN information for new aircraft types and publish it in the appropriate Flight Manuals. A sample of the table produced by ICAO is reproduced as Table 9.1.

Use of the table is relatively simple. Enter the line appropriate to the aircraft type and travel horizontally to intercept the 'Pavement Type' block, at the relevant sub-grade strength category. Extract the upper and lower ACNs and interpolate for the actual ramp weight for the departure or actual landing weight for arrival. The method of exact interpolation for weight is shown in the following paragraphs.

Unless prior permission has been obtained from the aerodrome operating authority the ACN and the tyre pressure for the actual weight must *not* exceed the maximum PCN and tyre pressure published in the AIP. Details of overload operating conditions are given later in this chapter.

The Aircraft Classification Numbers table only quotes the numbers for each pavement type, and the sub-grade strength for two aircraft weights – the maximum weight and the empty weight. To find the ACN for any weight between these two it is necessary to complete the following calculation:

$$ACN_{act} = ACN_{max} - \frac{(Max\ Wt - Act\ Wt)(ACN_{max} - ACN_{empty})}{(Max\ Wt - Empty\ Wt)}.$$

For example a Boeing 737-100 using a rigid pavement with a medium strength sub-grade at an actual weight of 35,000 Kgs. will be seen from Table 9.1 to have an ACN_{max} of 26 and an ACN_{empty} of 13 at a tyre pressure of 1.02 MPa. Therefore:

$$ACN_{act} = 26 - \frac{(45722 - 35000) \times (26 - 13)}{(45722 - 25942)}$$

$$= 26 - \frac{(10722) \times 13}{(19780)}$$

$$= 26 - (0.542 \times 13)$$

$$= 26 - 7.05$$

$$= 18.95$$

This type of calculation will no doubt be avoided in the future by aircraft operators producing graphs similar to those shown in Fig. 9.2.

A feature of the new reporting system is that guidance is given on the criteria to

Table 9.1 Example aircraft classification numbers.

Aircraft type	Maximum take-off mass / Operating mass empty kg	Load on one main gear leg	Tyre pressure MPa	psi	kg/cm²	ACNs relative to subgrade category							
						On rigid pavements				On flexible pavements			
						High K=150	Med K=80	Low K=40	Ultra low K=20	High CBR=15%	Med CBR=10%	Low CBR=6%	Ultra low CBR=3%
A300 B2	142 000	46.5	1.23	179	12.58	37	44	52	60	40	45	55	70
	85 690					19	22	26	30	21	23	26	35
B707-320B	148 778	46.0	1.24	180	12.65	39	46	55	63	42	47	57	73
	64 764					14	15	18	20	15	16	17	23
B727-200 (Standard)	78 471	46.4	1.15	167	11.74	46	48	51	53	41	43	49	54
	44 293					23	25	26	27	21	22	24	28
B737-100	45 722	46.3	1.02	148	10.40	24	26	28	29	22	23	26	30
	25 942					12	13	14	15	12	12	13	15
B747-100	334 751	23.125	1.55	225	15.81	44	51	60	69	46	50	60	81
	162 703					18	20	23	26	19	20	22	28
Concorde	185 066	48.0	1.26	183	12.86	61	71	82	91	65	72	81	98
	78 698					21	22	25	29	21	22	26	37
DC8-63	162 386	47.6	1.34	195	13.70	50	60	69	78	52	59	71	87
	72 002					17	19	23	26	18	19	22	29
DC9-41	52 163	46.65	1.10	160	11.24	32	34	35	37	28	30	33	37
	27 821					15	16	17	18	13	14	15	18

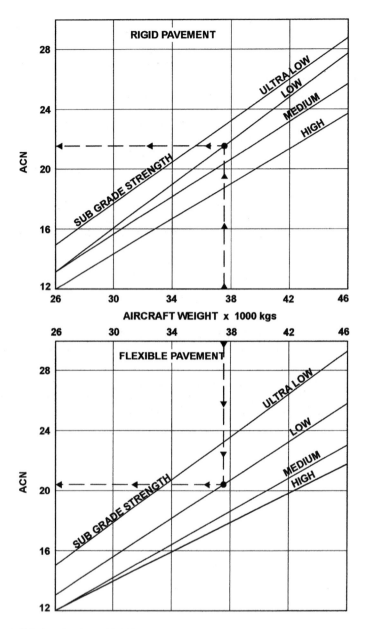

Fig. 9.2   ACNs for Boeing 737-100.

be used by aerodrome authorities for regulating overload operations. The design life of a pavement is such as to ensure that it can sustain a defined load for a specified number of movements, and that, save in the case of a massive overload, the pavement will not suddenly or catastrophically fail. Continuous operations with loads below the limiting PCN value will extend the design life of the pavement, but those operations with loads greater than the published PCN value will shorten the life.

Table 9.2 Conditions for exceeding PCN.

% ACN exceeds PCN	Conditions to be satisfied before movement can be considered acceptable
10%	(a) Pavement older than 12 months. (b) No visible signs of pavement distress. (c) Overload operations do not exceed 5% of the total annual movements. (d) Overload operations are spread over the year.
10%–25%	(e) (a) to (d) inclusive, plus regular inspections by a competent person. (f) Immediate curtailment of overload operations when signs of pavement distress become visible. (g) Overload operations not resumed until pavement strengthening work is complete. (h) Special circumstances only. (j) Scrutiny of pavement records by a pavement engineer.
25%–50%	(k) Thorough inspection by pavement engineer before and after movement.
Over 50%	(l) EMERGENCY MOVEMENT ONLY.

Aerodrome operating authorities may occasionally permit operations when the ACN exceeds the PCN but this will slightly shorten the pavement life expectancy and accelerate the surface deterioration for such movements.

Test Paper 2

Q1. The semi-width of the stopway is:
  (a) 60 m.
  (b) 75 m.
  (c) 90 m.
  (d) The same as the associated runway.

Q2. A balanced field is said to exist when:
  (a) TORA = EMDA.
  (b) TORA = TODA.
  (c) TODA = EMDA.
  (d) There is no stopway.

Q3. The maximum length of clearway is:
  (a) 50% TODA.
  (b) 50% EMDA.
  (c) 150% EMDA.
  (d) 50% TORA.

Q4. Any frangible obstacle in the take-off path:
  (a) Will limit stopway length.
  (b) Present a minimum hazard to an aircraft on impact.
  (c) Must be sited away from the runway strip.
  (d) Will aggravate the ground swing on impact.

Q5. Clearway length is limited by:
  (a) The first upstanding obstacle liable to damage the aircraft in the event of an abandoned take-off after engine failure.
  (b) A ditch or depression.
  (c) A deterioration of load bearing strength.
  (d) The first upstanding obstacle liable to damage the aeroplane in the event of a continued take-off after engine failure.

Q6. The distance BD in the diagram below is:
(a) The stopway.
(b) The clearway.
(c) EMDA.
(d) TODA.

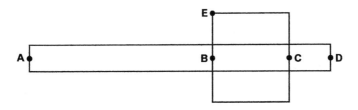

Q7. At Code 3 & 4 airfields the semi-width BE in the above diagram is:
(a) 60 m.
(b) 75 m.
(c) 90 m.
(d) 40 m.

Q8. The maximum length of stopway is not limited by:
(a) The first upstanding non-frangible obstacle.
(b) A deterioration of the load bearing strength.
(c) 50% of the runway length.
(d) A ditch or depression.

Q9. For scheduled performance calculations the forecast or actual wind is always factored by:
(a) 50% for a tailwind and 150% for a headwind.
(b) 150% for a tailwind and 100% for a headwind.
(c) 150% for a tailwind and 50% for a headwind.
(d) 50% for a tailwind and 50% for a headwind.

Q10. A remote probability is 10^{-6} and is described as a:
(a) Minor effect.
(b) Major effect.
(c) Hazardous effect.
(d) Catastrophic effect.

Q11. At FL320 the ambient temperature is –34°C. The temperature deviation is:
(a) +15°C.
(b) –15°C.
(c) +30°C.
(d) –30°C.

Q12. Given: R/W 27 touchdown elevation 277 ft, TORA 2000 m, EMDA 2100 m, TODA 2300 m; R/W 09 touchdown elevation 167 ft, TORA 2200 m, EMDA 2300 m, TODA 2400 m. The runway slope for R/W 09 is:
  (a) 1.52% up.
  (b) 1.52% down.
  (c) 1.68% up.
  (d) 1.68% down.

Q13. The altimeter sub-scale of an aircraft is set to 1013.2 hPa and is not reset during flight. If the aircraft flies from an area of high pressure to an area of low pressure the altimeter reading will:
  (a) over-read.
  (b) under-read.
  (c) remain the same.
  (d) decrease.

Q14. The normal horizontal scale for a type 'A' chart is:
  (a) 1:5000.
  (b) 1:10 000.
  (c) 1:20 000.
  (d) 1:25 000.

CHAPTER 10

Contaminated Surfaces

The effect that contaminated surfaces have on the performance of an aircraft is different for each type because of weight, speed, tyre and undercarriage variations. If an aircraft is permitted to operate on contaminated surfaces, the Flight Manual will contain a statement to this effect giving any limitations and special handling techniques that may be necessary to ensure compliance with the appropriate regulations.

10.1 RUNWAY CONDITION DEFINITIONS

The definitions used to describe the state of a runway surface are:

(a) Contaminated runway   A runway is considered to be contaminated when more than 25% of the runway surface area (whether in isolated areas or not), within the required length and width being used, is covered by one of the following:

(i)   Surface water more than 3 mm (0.125 in.) deep, or loose snow or by slush equivalent to more than 3 mm (0.125 in.) of water;
(ii) Snow which has been compressed into a solid mass which resists further compression and will hold together or break into lumps if picked up (compacted snow) or
(iii) Ice, including wet ice, causing low braking action.

JAR-OPS 1.480(a)(2); AMJ 25x1591 Paragraph 2.

(b) Damp runway   A runway is considered damp when the surface is not dry, but when the moisture on it does not give it a shiny appearance.
JAR-OPS 1.480(a)(3).

(c) Wet runway   A runway is considered as wet when it is well soaked but without significant areas of standing water. A runway is well soaked when there is sufficient moisture on the runway surface to cause it to appear reflective.
AMJ 25x1591 Paragraph 2.2; JAR-OPS 1.480(a)(10).

(d) Dry runway A dry runway is one which is neither wet nor contaminated, and includes those paved runways which have been specially prepared with grooved or porous pavement and maintained to retain 'effectively dry' braking action even when moisture is present. *JAR-OPS 1.480(a)(4).*

Most aerodrome authorities take action to minimize the effect of ice, snow and rain but it is still necessary to measure the braking action on the surface. The most reliable and uniform method of providing this type of information is to measure the amount of friction on the surface. Not only the runways require testing, other surfaces such as holding bays, taxiways and aprons should be checked for satisfactory braking.

Various methods may be used to measure surface friction, which is considered to be the maximum value of friction afforded when a wheel is braked but is still rolling. The most suitable method of assessment is generally determined by operational considerations. The method used to measure surface friction and then to report it is of uniform type to enable pilots to correctly interpret the meaning of the value stated. The equipment used for this purpose provides continuous measurement of the maximum friction along the entire runway.

10.1 Braking coefficient of friction

Operationally, a pilot needs to know how his aeroplane will perform on a contaminated surface compared with how it would perform on a dry hard surface. Braking action information may be passed by R/T in descriptive terms or as a coefficient of friction, which is the tangential force applied by a surface, expressed as a proportion of the normal dry surface force upon a loaded, smooth-tyred aeroplane. The relationship between the braking coefficient of friction and the aircraft's groundspeed for a reference *wet* hard surface is derived in accordance with AMJ25X1591 Paragraph 3.2.3 a or b. The wheel is considered to be travelling parallel to the surface at a speed of slip which is close to the groundspeed.

10.1.2 Contaminated surface measurements

Before the airport operating authority declares a surface fit for use by aircraft, the depth of contaminant and the braking action have to be measured. The depth of snow or slush on the runway is measured with a standard depth gauge every 300 metres along the runway between 5 and 10 metres either side of the centre-line and clear of any ruts. The average reading of depth for each third of the runway is then promulgated. The depth of ice covering runways is not measured.

A continuous runway friction measuring trailer (Mu-meter) and a brake testing decelerometer (Tapley meter) carried in a light van or truck are used to measure the effect of ice, snow, slush and water on braking action.

10.2 BRAKING ACTION ASSESSMENT METHODS

Assessment of braking action will be made by one of the following methods:

10.2.1 Continuous recording friction measuring trailer (Mu-meter)

This method employs a runway friction measuring trailer (Mu-meter) towed by a vehicle at 40 mph. The equipment provides a continuous register of the mean coefficient of friction values either on a paper trace or by means of a digital read-out that is used in conjunction with a hand computer. The principle employed in this case is the measurement of the side-force coefficient generated between the surface and a pair of pneumatic tyres set at a fixed toe-out angle. This device should normally indicate that a possibility of 'slushplaning' exists by giving a low value coefficient of friction.

10.2.2 Brake testing decelerometer (Tapley meter)

An assessment is made of the coefficient of friction using a brake testing decelerometer carried in a van or light truck. The brakes are applied at 25–30 mph. The van or truck has standardized characteristics and a standard procedure to ensure uniformity in technique. The principle employed is the assessment of the coefficient of friction between skidding pneumatic tyres and selected points on the surface being tested.

This method is limited to use on ice (gritted or ungritted) and dry snow, because it is likely to produce misleadingly high readings in slush, wet snow or water (for example, it will not detect that there is a possibility of 'slushplaning'). Braking action, therefore, will not be assessed in the latter conditions.

Most major airfields use the Mu-meter as the prime method of measurement with the Tapley meter as a back-up. Minor airfields may only use the Tapley meter for measuring braking action. Tests for braking action are made along the full length of the runway and stopway approximately 10 metres either side of the centre-line in two runs. Average readings for each third of the runway length are then promulgated. Decelerometer tests are made every 300 metres along the runway. Mu-meter readings which do not fall below 0.50 for any third of the runway are not normally passed to the pilot unless specifically requested.

10.2.3 Improvement of braking action

To increase the friction value of aircraft maneouvring areas affected by ice or snow, grit may have to be put on the surface if poor braking conditions persist. The specification of grit used is the best compromise between improving friction and causing least damage to aircraft. The risk to aircraft when using reverse thrust (or pitch) is high, and extreme caution is necessary particularly after a sudden thaw which results in grit lying on a bare surface.

10.3 REPORTING BRAKING ACTION TO THE PILOT

When the Mu-meter reading for any one-third of the runway falls below 0.50 but not below 0.40, a single mean value for the whole runway will be passed by R/T to the pilot. This is preceded by the corresponding qualitative term and by a descriptive term of the conditions (e.g. 'Braking action medium 0.46. Heavy rain. Time of measurement 1030').

Should the value for any one-third fall below 0.40 then the values for each third will be given in order starting with the one nearest the threshold, preceded by the qualitative term appropriate to the whole runway and followed by a descriptive term of the conditions (e.g. 'Braking action poor 0.46 0.37 0.39. Standing water. Time of measurement 1530').

10.4 INTERPRETATION OF BRAKING ACTION ASSESSMENTS

On take-off, as on landing, the aerodrome authorities measure the runway surface coefficient of friction and estimate the braking action required. The reported braking action passed to the pilot is that of a vehicle unaffected by any condition other than that of the surface. It is therefore the pilot who must assess the other factors affecting the aircraft, such as crosswind and AUW, to place the appropriate interpretation on the reported conditions. A broad guide (which should nevertheless be used with discretion) is as follows:

Good   Aircraft pilots can expect to take-off and/or land within the scheduled wet distances without undue directional control or braking difficulties caused by the runway conditions. Untreated ice does not come into this category but gritted ice could produce the friction required.

Medium   Aircraft are likely to use all of the wet scheduled distance, including the safety factor part of the distance. Directional control may be impaired. The achievement of satisfactory landing performance depends on the precise execution of the recommended flight technique.

Poor   The pilot must expect the aircraft to run at least the full 'very wet' or aquaplaning distance, where this too is scheduled. There may be a significant deterioration in braking performance and in directional control. It is advisable to ensure that the landing distance specified in the Flight Operations Manual for very wet conditions does *not* exceed the landing distance available.

10.5 INTERNATIONAL MEASUREMENT OF RUNWAY SURFACE CONDITIONS

There are several methods used to measure runway surface conditions throughout the world. These measurements can then be reported to the pilot using any one of a number of different ways. Consequently it can be difficult to correctly interpret the meaning of the report. Figure 10.1 is of an advisory nature only and facilitates the conversion of the reported condition to a term with which the pilot is more familiar. *Caution: although the terminology used in Europe and North America is similar it may be interpreted differently.*

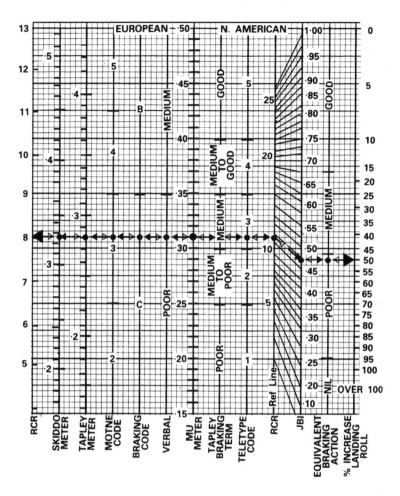

Fig. 10.1   Conversion of measured runway surface conditions.

10.6 SURFACE CONTAMINANTS

10.6.1 Dry snow

Loose hard snow is usually in the form of dry pellets which can be blown, or if compacted by hand, will fall apart again upon release. For this contaminant to be present the temperature must be below −5°C (and not risen since the snow fell). Its specific gravity is up to but not including 0.35. The maximum permissible depth for take-off or landing is 60.00 mm (2.4 in.) on any part of the runway, measured by ruler.

10.6.2 Wet snow

Loose snow taking the form of large flakes which if compacted by hand will stick together to form a snowball (it forms a white covering on all surfaces which when stamped upon does not splash up). The temperature for this type of snow is between −5°C and −1°C, with a specific gravity of 0.35 up to but not including 0.5.

For take-off and landing the maximum permissible depth is 15.0 mm (0.6 in.). A rough guide to this depth is the same as the welt of a shoe.

10.6.3 Compacted snow

Snow which has been compressed into a solid mass and resists further compression is compacted snow. It will hold together or break into lumps if picked up. This type of covering is normally caused by the transit of vehicles over the surface when snow is falling. Its specific gravity is 0.5 and over. *AMJ 25X1591 Paragraph 2.4.*

10.6.4 Slush

A mixture of water and snow which is displaced with a splatter when a heel-and-toe slapping motion is made on the ground. The temperature is at or around 0°C. A maximum depth of 15.0 mm (0.6 in.) is permissible for take-off and landing. Specific gravity is 0.5 up to 0.8.

10.6.5 Water

Visible puddles, usually of rain, standing on the surface causing paved surfaces to glisten when the temperature is above 0°C. On a natural surface it is assumed that more than 3 mm of water exists if under a firm foot pressure the water rises to the surface.

10.6.6 Mixtures

Mixtures of ice, snow and/or standing water may, especially when rain, sleet or snow is falling, produce a substance having an SG above 0.8. This substance is transparent at higher SGs, and is easily distinguished from slush which is cloudy.

10.6.7 Ice

A frozen layer of surface moisture, the thickness of which varies and produces a poor coefficient of friction according to the condition of the surface.

10.7 WATER EQUIVALENT DEPTH (WED)

The limitations and corrections given in most Flight Manuals are calculated for a uniform layer of contaminant at the maximum permissible depth and Specific Gravity quoted in Table 10.1. Flight Manuals that do contain this information express the correction in terms of **Water Equivalent Depth (WED)**; which is the contaminant depth multiplied by its Specific Gravity (see Fig. 10.2). Because WED values are not available to aircrew, operators are advised to quote the limitations and corrections in the Operations Manual in terms of contaminant depth. Estimated data are not acceptable for WEDs exceeding 15 mm.

Table 10.1 Contaminant limitations recommended by the CAA. (*CAA AIC 61/1999 (Pink 195) Paragraph 2.1.*)

Contaminant	SG	Maximum depth (mm)	WED
Very dry snow	<0.35	80	<28
Dry snow	<0.35	60	<21
Wet snow	0.35 to 0.5	15	5.25 to 7.5
Compacted snow	<0.5	15	>7.5
Slush	0.5 to 0.8	15	7.5 to 12
Standing water	1.0	15	15

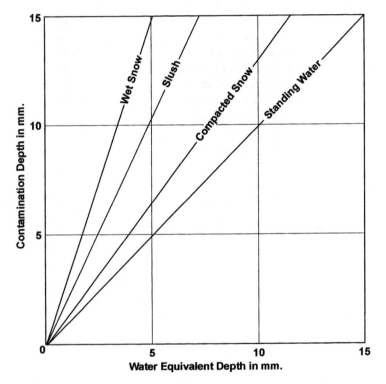

Fig. 10.2 Conversion from WED to contaminant depth.

CHAPTER 11

The Effects of Runway Contamination

All aeroplane operators are required by AN(G)Rs to take into account the condition of the runway surface when calculating the field-length-limited TOW. This regulation refers to operations from runways contaminated with snow, slush or deep water, which should be avoided if possible. Most Flight Manuals contain performance data for these conditions and assume that all engines are operating throughout the take-off. The usual safety margins in the event of an engine failure are not generally available on contaminated runways, but the Flight Manual will contain advice on the procedure to be used.

There is one Civil Aviation Information Circular of particular significance regarding aircraft performance calculations for contaminated runway operations. It is 61/1999 (Pink 195).

It is important to realize that this AIC was current at the time of writing this book but may have been superseded by the time you read this chapter because all AICs are replaced approximately every five years. Every effort must be made to obtain the most up to date version of them. The following is a general description of the contents and should be used only as a guide.

11.1 AIC 61/1999 (PINK 195) 'RISKS AND FACTORS ASSOCIATED WITH OPERATIONS ON RUNWAYS AFFECTED BY SNOW, SLUSH OR WATER'

This circular advises all aeroplane operators to avoid using contaminated runways if at all possible. It describes each type of contaminant and lists the maximum permissible depth beyond which suitable allowances must be made to the aircraft scheduled performance.

It is now mandatory for all new aircraft to have take-off performance scheduled for a dry runway. Manufacturers may, at their discretion, provide additional take-off performance data for use on a wet runway. A wet runway is one that has been wetted by rain or has more than 80% of its total area covered by fully melted ice or snow. The depth of water assumed in aircraft performance figures is 3 mm or less (which is the depth during or just after heavy rain in the UK). It would be unusual for a continuous water depth of 3 mm to persist for more than 15 minutes after the rain has ceased. If the depth of water, slush or wet snow exceeds 3 mm (or 10 mm of dry snow) the depth is considered to be 'significant' and only 25% of the runway surface area needs to be covered for it to be considered wet. *AMJ 25X1591 Paragraph 2.3.* In such conditions the *take-off performance may be adversely affected by additional drag, loss of power, reduced wheel braking performance or directional control difficulties.* There is also the possibility of a system malfunction or of structural damage caused by the spray impingement. If aquaplaning occurs, it could add to directional control and wheel braking problems. *CAA AIC 61/1999 (Pink 195).*

Even if the average depth of contaminant does not exceed 3 mm, isolated areas of standing water, or slush 15 mm or more deep, can cause an ingestion hazard to some aircraft if the puddles occur in the area where the aircraft approaches V_1. Temporary fluctuations of power so caused could impair safety. The most important area when the likely effect of the runway contamination on aircraft performance is being assessed is the upwind half of the runway. If the estimated braking action is poor or if the Mu-meter reading is below 0.40 on this portion of the runway, it is possible that in the event of an abandoned take-off at V_1, the aircraft may not be brought safely to a halt before the end of the stopway is reached. If surface conditions are such, it would be prudent to delay take-off until the depth of contaminant has drained below the significant level of 3 mm. When there is any doubt about the depth of water, slush or snow, or about the area of standing water on the runway DELAY TAKE-OFF.

AIC 61/1999 emphasizes the difficulty in measuring the coefficient of friction on a contaminated runway and the inability to predict the effect it will have on aircraft scheduled performance. It also stresses that in the event of an engine failure during take-off, irrespective of the Performance Class, there may be a time interval during which the aeroplane is unable to continue with the take-off or to stop within the distance available without risk of an accident. The duration of the 'risk period' is impossible to forecast because of the indeterminate nature of acceleration and deceleration on such a surface. The best way to minimize this period is to *keep the TOW as low as possible* by ensuring that unnecessary fuel is not carried.

If the runway surface braking coefficient does not exceed 0.50, the V_1 that must be used is that for a wet runway. The use of this decision speed is intended to cover the effect of icy surfaces or aquaplaning, and ensures that the Accelerate/Stop Distance Required does not exceed the Accelerate/Stop Distance Available. Some manufacturers schedule the effects of aquaplaning separately where more accurate assumptions can be made.

For aeroplanes that have an approved procedure for take-off on runways having a 'significant' depth of contamination the Flight Manual will state the latest point at which a decision to abandon take-off may be made and the earliest point at which a decision to continue the take-off with one engine inoperative may be made.

In such instances the Accelerate/Stop Distance Required will not exceed the Accelerate/Stop Distance Available because the manufacturers have, in their performance calculations, to allow for 150% of the actual contaminant depth. Information is also given of the penalties incurred if less than full reverse thrust is used.

If the braking coefficient of friction is 0.05 or less, the runway is considered to be icy or very slippery. Most Flight Manuals contain advisory information for abandoning take-off on such a surface and refer to V_{STOP}. This is the maximum speed from which the aeroplane can be safely stopped, with all engines operating, on a contaminated runway, by the end of the stopway and is sometimes referred to as 'maximum abandonment' speed. It is based on the use of all available means of retardation, although the data scheduled is that using only 50% of full reverse thrust on all engines.

'Maximum abandonment speed' is *not* V1 because it does not imply an ability that take-off may be safely continued after an engine failure has been suffered. Unlike V1, this speed can be less than VMCG.

11.1.1 General recommendations for take-off. *CAA AIC 61/1999 (Pink 195) Paragraph 3*

The CAA require all airlines to publish an Operations Manual; one section must cover operations from contaminated runways and detail the limitations and corrections necessary to performance calculations. The CAA recommends that the maximum depth of contaminant on any part of the runway should not exceed the following measurements if operations are to continue:

(1) 15 mm of water, slush or wet snow.
(2) 60 mm of dry snow.
(3) 80 mm of very dry snow.

Any limitations or performance corrections given in the aircraft Flight Manual must be strictly obeyed. It is wise to allow an additional margin of distance for the effects that a small temperature change can have on the surface condition. *Allow for a deterioration.*

Some aircraft have performance scheduled for alternative flap settings. If such is the case, the length of the ground run can be reduced by electing to use the maximum flap setting permitted for take-off. The TOW and V speeds which must be used are those applicable to a wet runway – because the abandoned take-off case is less risky so long as the continued take-off remains safe.

Take-off in a crosswind should be avoided if possible, because it will add to the directional control problems that may be experienced. The effects of a crosswind can be minimized by using a runway into wind if the distances are not limiting. Do NOT attempt to take-off in tailwinds or in crosswinds that exceed 10 kts if the runway is contaminated.

On the pre-flight inspection of the aircraft, all devices on the aeroplane which contribute to braking performance such as wheel brakes, reverse pitch or reverse thrust and lift dumpers must be fully serviceable. Ensure that the tyres are not worn, and that those fitted are of the same type as those used in the performance plan calculations. Inspect the aircraft to ensure that it is clear of snow, frost and ice. Even a small amount left uncleared can be critical to aircraft performance. Finally, make certain that maximum take-off power is obtainable – if necessary by carrying out a power check.

If all these checks have proved satisfactory and it is decided to take-off, the following points should be noted. To minimize the adverse effects of a contaminated runway the aeroplane should then be operated in a careful manner.

(1) Taxi slowly avoiding the use of reverse thrust to keep the amount of contaminant adhering to the aeroplane to a minimum.

(2)   Use the normal take-off speeds and technique for maximum take-off power within the limitations (this does not apply to EPR-limited engines). To reduce the possibility of engine malfunction or loss of power due to the ingestion of contaminant, use the ignition override. No optional technique for improving the gradient of climb may be used.

(3)   Use the maximum runway distances available keeping the runway alignment reduction to a minimum. On the take-off roll, if permitted, raise the nose wheel early to reduce the ingestion of slush or water.

(4)   Be aware of the effect that accumulated slush can have on the controls, undercarriage and flaps. After take-off, exercise the undercarriage to dispose of excess moisture that could subsequently freeze.

11.2 THE EFFECT OF HEAVY RAIN

The FAA sponsored a research programme to discover the effect that heavy rain has on aircraft performance. The results showed that:

(1)   The impingement and rapid accumulation of water sufficiently distorts the shape of the upper wing surface, albeit only temporarily, to diminish the total lift developed by up to 30% of its normal value.

(2)   The impact of the rain on the aircraft and its lowered undercarriage increases drag to such an extent that it decreases the aircraft's forward speed.

(3)   When operating in such conditions a jet engine is slow to respond to rapid demands for power.

(4)   The weight of the rain can momentarily adversely affect the aircraft weight.

The total effect of these factors is to produce a much lower level of performance for any aircraft experiencing such weather conditions. The weight increase raises the stalling speed, whilst the reduced lift and increased drag together reduce the forward speed achieved. For an aeroplane in the take-off or landing configuration, this situation is *extremely dangerous* because of the close proximity of the normal operating speed to the stalling speed. There is, therefore, a very high risk of the aircraft stalling when it is close to the ground.

If there is a possibility of encountering *heavy rain* during take-off, it is advisable to *delay* the *departure*. If the danger is during the landing phase, it would be prudent to divert to an alternative aerodrome or to hold off until the rain has cleared the area. It could prevent a disaster.

11.3 TAKE-OFF PERFORMANCE CALCULATIONS

In most Flight Manuals the performance information given for take-off from contaminated runways is based on all engines operating throughout the take-off or abandoned take-off. No account is taken of the possibility of engine failure and no safety margin included in the calculations for such an eventuality. Accordingly *no*

V_1 is possible. However, most aeroplane manufacturers provide advisory information regarding the maximum speed from which an aircraft may be safely brought to rest in the event of an abandoned take-off on an icy or very slippery runway. This speed is referred to as 'maximum abandonment speed'.

11.4 TAKE-OFF RECOMMENDATIONS

The maximum TOW calculated for a contaminated runway must *not* exceed the maximum TOW calculated for a dry runway. If the normal TOW is limited by an obstacle in the Net Flight Path then the obstacle limited TODR for a dry runway should be used as the TODA for the TOW calculations on a contaminated runway.

Take-off calculations for a contaminated runway are made for the all-engines-operating configuration, therefore a V_1 cannot be calculated and is replaced by a 'maximum abandonment' speed on a slippery runway which offers no guarantee of stopping in the available distance in the event of an engine failure. Some older aeroplane Flight Manuals do not contain take-off information for a contaminated runway, the AIC advises that the CAA should be consulted on whether operations can take place or how the data can be obtained.

Usually the factorization equates to $1.15 \times$ TODR for all-engines-operating at the maximum TOW.

11.5 GENERAL RECOMMENDATIONS FOR LANDING
AIC 11/1998 (PINK 164)

It is generally agreed by the various licensing authorities that the point at which the adverse effects of runway contaminants become significant with regard to aircraft performance begin when the depth of water, slush or wet snow reaches 3 mm or when dry snow reaches 10 mm. Although depths of contaminant less than these may not be considered significant, they are unfavourable and cause aircraft performance to deteriorate from that which would normally be expected of it on a dry runway.

Thus with the runway surface contaminated to less than a significant depth, the landing distance required increases to that calculated for a wet surface, which *must not* exceed the landing distance available.

If the aircraft has been certificated by the 'Reference' landing system, the normal calculated landing distance required already relates to a wet runway surface and no correction is necessary. But if the aircraft was certificated for landing according to the 'Arbitrary' system, the calculated landing distance required relates to a dry runway and must be multiplied by 1.15 to obtain the landing distance required on a runway with a wet surface.

When the contaminant depth becomes significant, the adverse effects liable to be experienced on landing are a system malfunction caused by spray ingestion or impingement (which could also cause structural damage to the aircraft), and/or reduced wheel-braking performance. Ultimately it could lead to aquaplaning and the loss of directional control on the ground. Because of the nature of these unfavourable factors, it is usual for aircraft manufacturers to reduce by a considerable amount the maximum crosswind in which an aircraft may be landed when the surface is contaminated. This reduces the possibility of the crosswind component aggravating any tendency to swing on landing.

The general technique for landing on a contaminated surface is to touch down firmly, without bouncing, in the centre of the runway touch-down area. Use aerodynamic braking to slow the aircraft initially; lower the nose wheel promptly; but delay the application of wheel brakes until after the wheels have had a chance to spin up. Use maximum reverse thrust as soon as possible. If the aircraft is fitted with an anti-skid brake system, apply continuous pedal pressure.

Should the aeroplane not be fitted with this system, or if the system is unserviceable, gently apply pressure up to the maximum which will not lock the wheels; then release brake pedal pressure and gradually increase it again. Repeat the procedure so as to avoid bursting the tyres. If possible, the aircraft should be slowed to a crawl before it reaches the last 500 metres of the runway, because this is the touchdown area for the reciprocal runway and is therefore likely to be covered in rubber film, making handling even more difficult.

If there is a crosswind, the crab approach technique is preferred to the wing-down method of approach. Landing under these circumstances is particularly hazardous because the wind will tend to push the aircraft to the downwind side of the runway after touchdown and will also cause it to weathercock into wind. Only the friction of the tyres can prevent this happening – and in these conditions that friction is liable to be very low.

In the absence of a crosswind, it is recommended that full reverse thrust be applied as early as possible during the landing run if the aircraft is pointing down the runway and if its use will not cause rudder blanking. Long-fuselaged aeroplane operators are recommended by the manufacturers to avoid this technique. As always, the best advice is to consult the Flight Manual or aeroplane Operating Notes for the best technique to adopt for any specific type of aircraft.

It is best to avoid landing at all where these conditions exist. If possible divert to a suitable alternate aerodrome and eliminate the risk of accident. But if a landing under such conditions is unavoidable, the controllability and braking action should be reported to Air Traffic Control as soon after landing as possible to enable other landing aircraft to be accurately informed before they are committed to landing.

Most Flight Manuals provide a correction table to enable the operator to convert the calculated landing distance required to the landing distance required on a very slippery surface, or on one which aquaplaning is likely to occur.

11.6 VERY LOW FRICTION SURFACES

Aeroplanes that have data included in the Flight Manual for landing on a very low friction surface account for the landing distance by correcting the 'Arbitrary System' landing distance on a normal surface to that required on a runway having a braking coefficient of friction of 0.05 with all engines operating and all means of retardation used. In addition information is given of the penalties incurred for using less than full reverse thrust, exceeding the target threshold speed and, if approved, landing on a surface having more than a significant amount of contamination.

CHAPTER 12

Hydroplaning (Aquaplaning)

The tyre friction required by an aeroplane to maintain directional control and effective braking is a finite quantity for each aircraft type. The amount of friction actually obtained can be adversely affected by any surface contaminant. Water is particularly dangerous because it can cause an almost total loss of tyre friction. Such a condition is referred to as **hydroplaning** or **aquaplaning.** It is the condition which exists when the tyre footprint, the contact area, is lifted from the surface by fluid pressure until it rides on top of the fluid film. The result is negligible braking and difficulty in maintaining directional control.

The effects of aquaplaning on aircraft handling characteristics are similar to those experienced on an icy or very slippery surface. Some Flight Manuals contain information on handling characteristics and aircraft performance when such surface conditions exist. The guidance given should be used at all times when the contaminant depth is 'significant'. Some degree of hydroplaning is possible at any time when the runway is contaminated by water or some other foreign substance.

Two types of hydroplaning can occur, either individually or together, on wet or icy runways. They are known as **dynamic** and **viscous**, and they differ in their initial cause and total duration.

12.1 DYNAMIC HYDROPLANING

For this phenomenom to occur, two essential conditions must be present. First, the surface must be flooded to a depth which exceeds the total depth of the runway texture plus the tyre tread. This is the **critical depth** and is normally 3 mm.

The second condition is that the aircraft must be travelling at or above the critical speed, which is the tyre speed at which the standing inertia of the water is such that the water is unable to escape from under the tyre. If both conditions are present, dynamic hydroplaning is likely to occur.

It has been determined by research that the size of the tyre footprint directly affects the aircraft's hydroplaning characteristics. If the tyre is correctly inflated, its footprint is unaffected by changes in AUW. But if the tyre is underinflated, the size of the footprint is increased irrespective of the AUW. *An underinflated tyre is more likely to hydroplane than one that is correctly inflated, and it will do so at a lower groundspeed than that at which hydroplaning would normally occur.* It therefore follows that to reduce the risk of hydroplaning it is good airmanship to ensure that the aircraft tyres are in good condition, have adequate tread and are inflated at the correct pressure. If a choice of tyres that can be fitted exists, multi-rib tyres should be selected because they delay the onset of aquaplaning.

The airfield operating authorities, during the construction or repair of runways, can assist the pilot by delaying the onset or even preventing hydroplaning by ensuring the runways are porous or grooved to give better tyre traction and that there is adequate drainage to prevent a build up of moisture. However, strong crosswinds can defeat good drainage on the windward side of the runway. Aircraft manufacturers during aircraft design can also assist by incorporating tandem wheel arrangements because they can travel through greater depths of contaminant with less difficulty than others.

Dynamic hydroplaning, after its onset, will continue whilst the two essential conditions are maintained. If either the groundspeed falls below the critical speed or the water depth reduces below the critical depth, this type of hydroplaning will not persist.

The speed at which braking efficiency begins to deteriorate is indeterminate because it is a gradual process, but the speed at which it becomes total can be determined. Tests carried out with an aircraft fitted with bald tyres on a smooth, wet surface revealed that the speed at which hydroplaning occurred can be calculated from the following formula:

Where V_P is the aquaplaning groundspeed in knots.
(1) For a non-rotating tyre
V_P (spin up) in knots $= 7.1\sqrt{P}$. If P is the tyre pressure in lb/ in.^{2}.
(2) For a rotating tyre (*AMJ 25 x 1591 Paragraph 4.3a.*)
V_P (spin down) in knots $= 9\sqrt{P}$. If P is the tyre pressure in lb/in.^{2} or
V_P (spin down) in knots $= 34\sqrt{P}$. If P is the tyre pressure in kg/cm^2.

On take-off, the tyre commences to roll on a wet surface, and at slower speeds the water present is able to escape to the sides of the tyre until the speed approaches the critical speed. At this point a wedge of water builds up in front of the tyre and lifts it clear of the surface. To avoid hydroplaning during take-off do *not* attempt to roll

Table 12.1 Example of dynamic hydroplaning speeds.

Aircraft type	Tyre pressure		Tyre hydroplaning speed in kts	
	MPa	psi	Non rotating	Rotating
A300 B2	1.23	178.4	103	120
B707-320B	1.24	179.8	103	121
B727-200	1.15	166.8	99	116
B737-100	1.02	147.9	94	109
B747-100	1.55	224.8	115	135
Concorde	1.26	182.8	104	122
DC8-63	1.34	194.4	107	125
DC9-41	1.10	159.5	97	114

unless the water depth is less than critical for the entire length of the take-off run required.

For landing the non-rotating formula should be used to calculate the dynamic hydroplaning speed. If the depth of contaminant exceeds the critical depth, the landing should be delayed until it has drained below the critical depth. The keyword in these circumstances is *caution.*

Remember the old maxim that a good landing is the result of a good approach. Make every attempt to obtain an accurate touchdown speed. Every 1% increase in touchdown speed above that recommended for the aircraft weight increases the landing distance required by 2%.

12.2 VISCOUS HYDROPLANING

The only essential condition for viscous hydroplaning to occur is a smooth surface covered by a thin film of moisture. It happens at much lower groundspeeds than dynamic hydroplaning and is usually of very short duration. On normal landings at the touchdown point the aircraft tyres slip and skid momentarily until they spin up to their rotational speed. Usually the texture of the runway surface is coarse enough to break up the liquid film, but any deposits of rubber or oil prevent this dissipation taking place. The heat generated by the initial slippage of the tyre is enough to cause a thin layer of rubber to melt and adhere to the runway.

Successive landings cause the deposits to form a rubber sheet at the runway ends which reduces braking efficiency by 65% in hot weather and up to 100% if the surface is wet.

12.3 COMBINED HYDROPLANING

The loss of tyre friction on wet or flooded runways is generally the result of the combined effects of dynamic and viscous hydroplaning. If dynamic hydroplaning is predominant the area of the tyre under which the bulk of the water is trapped enlarges as the speed increases. If the contaminant is of less than critical depth, however, and there is no bulk of water present, the major part of the footprint is in contact with a thin film of moisture and viscous hydroplaning is the controlling element.

12.4 REVERTED RUBBER SKIDS

When a tyre is hydroplaning, although the friction available is insufficient to rotate the wheel it does generate sufficient heat, on high pressure tyres, to melt the rubber at the contact point and wear a flat spot on the tyre. The heat also converts water or ice on the runway in the path of the tyre into steam. The tyre therefore rides on a layer of steam. This is particularly dangerous not only because of the ineffectiveness of the brakes but also because of the loss of directional control when the wheels are in a locked condition. Avoidance of *reverted rubber skids,* as they are called, depends on the pilot using the anti-skid systems of the aircraft to their maximum advantage, and calls for the application of skilful take-off and landing technique.

Test Paper 3

Q1. For flying operations to continue, the CAA recommend that the maximum depth of dry snow on any part of the runway does not exceed:
    (a) 15 mm.
    (b) 30 mm.
    (c) 60 mm.
    (d) 80 mm.

Q2. The CAA recommend that the maximum crosswind for take-off on a contaminated surface is:
    (a) 5 kts.
    (b) 10 kts.
    (c) 15 kts.
    (d) 20 kts.

Q3. The critical depth of surface water for dynamic hydroplaning is:
    (a) 3 mm.
    (b) 5 mm.
    (c) 7 mm.
    (d) 9 mm.

Q4. Wet snow is comprised of:
    (a) Loose snow pellets.
    (b) Loose snow in large flakes.
    (c) Snow which has been compressed.
    (d) A mixture of water and snow.

Q5. Water equivalent depth is:
    (a) The measured depth of the contaminant.
    (b) The depth of water in the contaminant.
    (c) The contaminant depth × specific gravity.
    (d) The contaminant depth × 0.5.

Q6. For a contaminant to be considered significant its depth must exceed:
    (a) Water – 3 mm.
    (b) Slush – 6 mm.
    (c) Wet snow – 8 mm.
    (d) Dry snow – 12 mm.

Q7. Maximum abandonment speed is the maximum speed from which the aircraft can:
 (a) Safely abandon take-off in the event of an engine failure.
 (b) Safely continue take-off in the event of an engine failure.
 (c) Safely continue or abandon take-off in the event of an engine failure.
 (d) Safely abandon take-off with all engines operating.

Q8. Heavy rain does not temporarily cause:
 (a) Increased weight.
 (b) Increased stalling speed.
 (c) Reduced forward speed.
 (d) Increased volumetric efficiency.

Q9. A very low friction surface has a braking coefficient of friction of:
 (a) 0.5 or less.
 (b) 0.05 or less.
 (c) 0.005 or less.
 (d) 5.0 or less.

Q10. The amount of runway surface area that must be covered by a significant depth of contaminant for it to be declared wet is:
 (a) 25%.
 (b) 50%.
 (c) 70%.
 (d) 80%.

CHAPTER 13

Level Flight

The four main forces acting on an aeroplane in level, unaccelerated flight are lift, weight, thrust and drag. If the aircraft is to maintain level flight these forces must remain in equilibrium. Lift must be equal and opposite to weight and thrust must balance drag. Each has its own point through which it acts, lift through the centre of pressure (C of P) and weight through the centre of gravity (C of G). Thrust and drag act approximately parallel to the longitudinal axis in opposite directions, through points that vary with the aeroplane design and its attitude; thrust acting forward in the direction of travel. Because the C of P and the C of G are not at the same point the lift and weight forces couple produce a pitching moment which must be counteracted by the thrust/drag couple to maintain level flight and a constant IAS. Ideally the C of G should be forward of the C of P. See Fig. 13.1.

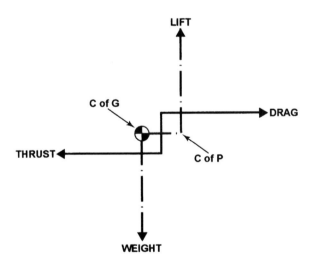

Fig. 13.1 The forces acting in level, unaccelerated flight.

13.1 LIFT

Lift may be defined as that force acting on an aeroplane which is at right angles to the direction of the airflow, through the centre of pressure. It can be calculated for level flight at any specified weight and altitude by the formula:

$$\text{Lift} = C_L \tfrac{1}{2} \emptyset V^2 S,$$

where C_L = the coefficient of lift (a constant mathematical factor); $\emptyset$ = air density; V = free air velocity; S = wing area.

To maintain level, unaccelerated flight the formula must remain in balance for a given wing if the weight and altitude are fixed then the only remaining variables in the formula are the coefficient of lift and the free air velocity.

The coefficient of lift is dependent on the angle of attack for its magnitude. Thus if the speed is increased the angle of attack must be reduced to maintain level flight, otherwise the aeroplane will climb. Similarly if the speed is reduced then the angle of attack must be increased or else the aircraft will descend. For every angle of attack there is a corresponding IAS. Level flight can only be maintained if the formula remains in balance. An alternative to increasing the angle of attack is to lower the flaps, which alters the effective angle of attack, however power may have to be increased to overcome the increased drag. The coefficient of lift does not vary with altitude for the same IAS. See Fig. 13.2.

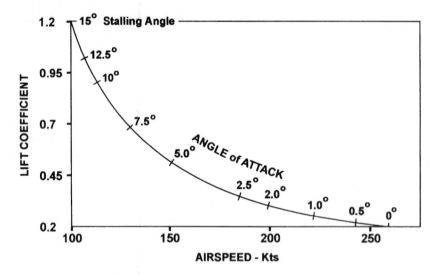

Fig. 13.2   Coefficient of lift vs. IAS.

13.2 THRUST AND POWER

13.2.1 Thrust

The force produced by the engine(s) of an aeroplane in a forward direction is thrust and directly opposes drag. The unit of measurement is the Newton which is calculated by multiplying Mass (kg) by Acceleration (m/s^2). The thrust generated by a jet engine is directly proportional to the engine RPM and inversely proportional to the ambient temperature and altitude. Airspeed does not affect thrust significantly.

The speed attained at the intersection of the thrust available curve and the drag curve is that at which the aeroplane should fly for level, unaccelerated flight. If the thrust available exceeds that required for level flight the aeroplane will accelerate.

13.2.2 Power

The rate of doing work is power, which is the product of thrust and speed and is a measure of the work done by the engine(s). For any specific weight and altitude, graphs may be plotted of the power and thrust, both attained and required, against speed. Examples of such graphs are shown at Fig. 13.3.

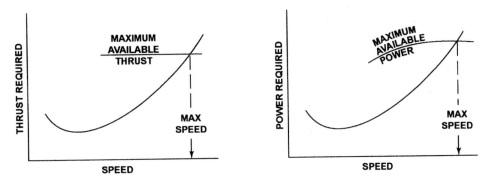

Fig. 13.3 Level flight performance.

From these graphs it is possible to ascertain the power required to attain a particular speed or to determine the speed achieved at a particular power setting. The highest speed the aeroplane can achieve, at the altitude and weight specified for the graph, is determined by the point at which the maximum power available equals the power required. The minimum speed is not usually defined by the power or thrust but by conditions of stability, control or stall. However, flying at any speed below V_{IMD} will require an increase in thrust.

For a constant altitude and angle of attack (ignoring compressibility) an increase in weight will require both the power and the airspeed to be increased.

13.3 DRAG

The force acting in opposition to thrust and parallel to the airflow, in other words the resistance to forward motion, is called drag. It comprises two main components: induced drag and profile drag.

13.3.1 Induced Drag

As an aerofoil moves through the air it creates vortices which oppose forward movement and is referred to as induced drag; the larger the vortices the greater the induced drag. It is, therefore, dependent on the angle of attack for its magnitude. High angles of attack create large vortices, whereas low angles of attack cause small vortices. Thus *induced drag increases with decrease of speed, and reaches its highest value at* V_{S_0} for a constant weight and altitude.

13.3.2 Profile drag

The resistance caused by the aerofoil shape, the boundary layer surface friction and the poor or inadequate streamlining is known as profile drag. It is present at all speeds but has an increasingly detrimental effect on aeroplane performance as the speed increases.

13.3.3 Total drag

The resultant of all the drag caused by an aeroplane's movement through the air is the total drag. It is slightly more than the sum of the induced drag and the profile drag and is illustrated for both piston/propeller-driven and jet-engined aeroplanes in Fig. 13.4. The total drag increases in proportion to the square of the speed, e.g. if the speed is doubled then the drag will be quadrupled. This is known as the 'speed squared law'. Total drag also increases with weight, as does the required airspeed. *The maximum speed is achieved when the maximum thrust is equal to the total drag.*

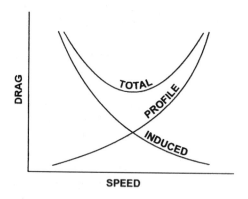

Fig. 13.4   Aircraft drag.

13.3.4 The velocity of minimum drag

The lowest point on the total drag curve is the velocity of minimum drag, V_{IMD}. When plotted on a power curve this point is the tangent to the curve. See Fig. 13.5. The drag vs. speed graph shows that the velocity of the minimum drag for the piston/propeller-driven aeroplane is approximately 1.3Vs whereas for the jet-engined aircraft it is 1.6Vs, in the clean configuration. From this it can be deduced that it is necessary to fly a jet aircraft at a relatively high speed to maintain speed stability but

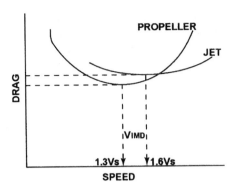 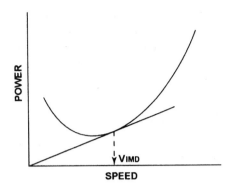

Fig. 13.5 The velocity of minimum drag.

the piston engined aeroplane, to maintain steady flight, can be flown at a relatively low speed. Vs is the stall speed or the minimum steady flight speed at which the aeroplane is controllable. *JAR 1 page 15.*

For jet aeroplanes the minimum drag V$_{IMD}$ speed is always greater than the speed of minimum power V$_{IMP}$.

13.3.5 The lift/drag ratio

For any given weight and altitude, level flight can be maintained at any speed between the maximum and the minimum limits by adjusting the angle of attack to keep the lift formula in balance, so that the lift developed is equal to the weight. However, as the angle of attack increases so also does the drag which, to counteract it, will require a greater amount of thrust. Thus the fuel consumption will increase. This is clearly an inefficient way to maintain level flight. The most efficient manner to operate the aeroplane would be to fly at the angle of attack that creates the most lift and causes the least drag. Therefore, the most efficient angle of attack is that which produces the highest lift/drag ratio. This angle of attack is the same for all weights and altitudes.

There is only one airspeed at the most efficient angle of attack that will keep the lift formula in balance. This, then, is the most economical cruising speed, as an equivalent airspeed it will be the same at all altitudes but it will increase slightly with increased weight.

The lift/drag ratio can be calculated for a range of angles of attack and plotted as in Fig. 13.6. In the example the highest lift/drag ratio of 12:1 occurs at 4°; and the stalling angle, the angle at which the lift developed is insufficient to support the weight, is 15° and has a lift/drag ratio of 4.8:1.

Although lift increases with greater flap angles so also does drag but to a much greater extent, particularly at angles of attack above that which produces the best lift/drag ratio. Thus, lowering flaps almost always worsens the lift/drag ratio and, although it is possible to fly at a lower speed, the power required increases.

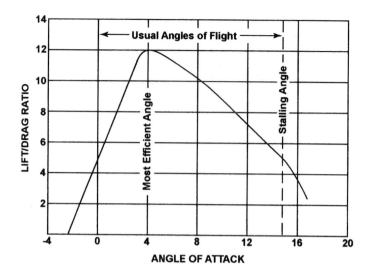

Fig. 13.6 The lift/drag curve.

13.4 WEIGHT

Weight is the force acting on an aeroplane in a vertically downward direction through the C of G . In level flight it is lift which has to oppose weight exactly. If the weight changes the lift must alter to match this change in order to ensure that the lift formula remains in equilibrium. During flight an aeroplane burns fuel, continually reducing its weight.

If the speed remains constant then the excess lift produced over the weight will cause the aeroplane to gradually climb. This is called a cruise climb. However, if level flight is maintained, by reducing the angle of attack, then the aeroplane will gradually increase its forward speed. To maintain level, unaccelerated, flight the thrust must be reduced. V_{IMD} decreases with weight.

In other words, as the weight reduces the excess power available increases and the power required decreases. If the weight were to increase the power available would decrease and the power required would increase. The change to the power curves is similar to that resulting from a change of altitude. See Fig. 13.7.

13.4.1 The effect of altitude

An increase of altitude results in a decreased air density, with the following effects.

(a) Lift At a constant weight the relationship between EAS and the angle of attack is not affected by a change of altitude. However, less lift will be developed due to the reduced density and if level flight is to be maintained then either the angle of attack must be increased or the speed must be increased. At high cruising TAS the loss of lift is increased by the effects of compressibility and would require further compensation.

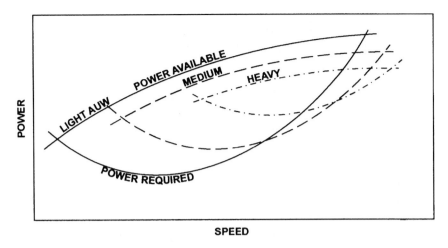

Fig. 13.7   Effect of weight.

(b) Drag   By itself the decreased density at increased altitude would cause the drag generated to decrease. If level unaccelerated flight is to be maintained then the increased angle of attack required by (a) would cause an increase in drag which would cancel the benefits of the decreased density. The overall effect of increased altitude on drag is, therefore, to make little change. However, the TAS will increase.

(c) Power   Irrespective of the type of engine, the power attained decreases with an increase of altitude. Because drag is virtually unchanged at all altitudes then the power required to maintain level flight increases with altitude. Therefore, the power available and power required curves become closer together, resulting in a decrease of the maximum speed possible and an increase of the minimum speed. That is, the range of speeds available in level flight decreases with an increase of altitude. If the curves are plotted against EAS they move up the graph but when plotted against TAS they also move to the right. Both the power required and the TAS increase by the same percentage with increased altitude. Figure 13.8 shows this for a jet aircraft; the same principle applies to a piston-engined aeroplane.

An aeroplane at high altitude in the cruise configuration is in a condition when the forces acting on the aeroplane are in equilibrium. Because of the high TAS at these altitudes, any disturbing force will cause a large deviation from the original state. The dynamic stability is reduced and the damping of any deviation is diminished. The aeroplane is less stable and any control movements to recover to the original attitude and/or altitude must be made slowly and smoothly.

13.4.2 Buffet

This is the rapid small movements of the control surfaces and vibrations of the airframe caused by turbulent airflow. It occurs at very low and very high forward speeds and limits the manoeuvring load factor at high altitude.

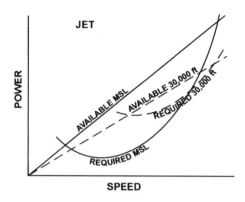

Fig. 13.8   The effect of altitude – jet aircraft.

Low speed buffet.   At high angles of attack, usually approximately 14°, and with low forward speed the airflow becomes turbulent and causes buffet. The IAS at which this occurs is just above the stalling speed, usually approximately 1.2Vs, when the stall warning device should activate.

High speed buffet   At very high Mach numbers the shock wave above the upper surface of the wing causes the airflow to become turbulent towards the trailing edge of the wing which results in rapid, small movements of the controls. This speed is the maximum operating speed Vmo/Mmo. It is possible to exceed this limit inadvertently because of gust upsets, unintentional control movements, passenger movement, or when levelling from a climb or a descent from Mach to airspeed limit altitudes. A maximum speed needle on the ASI shows Vmo up to the altitude at which Vmo = Mmo where the datum becomes Mmo. An aural warning will sound at approximately 10 kts above Vmo or 0.01 above Mmo.

13.4.3 The Buffet Onset Boundary Chart

The amount of stress imposed on an airframe can be determined from the load factor, which is the total lift divided by the total weight. Using a range of load factors and speeds for a specific aeroplane type it is possible to define a 'Manoeuvre Envelope' within which it is safe to operate the aeroplane. From this, for the cruise, can be developed the 'Buffet Onset Boundary' chart which uses the low and high speed buffet speeds as limitations for the envelope. The lower limit is the pre-stall buffet speed which increases with weight. The upper limit is Vmo/Mmo and is constant for all weights. The difference between these limiting speeds decreases with increased altitude and/or weight. This causes the manoeuvrability to become increasingly restricted with altitude which is of great significance in bad weather. The 'manoeuvre' ceiling, for any particular weight, is that altitude at which both the low and the high speed buffet coincide. Inadvertent excursions beyond the buffet envelope boundaries may not result in unsafe operations. *JAR 25.251(e).*

For any given weight, centre of gravity position and airspeed, the maximum operating altitude is that at which a normal positive acceleration increment of 0.3 g is achieved without exceeding the buffet onset boundary. *ACJ 25.1585(c)*. It is, therefore, common practice to draw the 'Buffet Onset Boundary' chart for a range of cruise weights at 1.3 g. See Fig. 13.9.

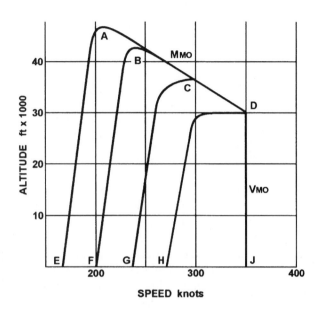

Fig. 13.9   Example 1.3 g Buffet Onset Boundary Chart.

Manoeuvre ceilings:
A – Light weight.
B – Light/medium.
C – Medium weight.
D – Heavy weight.

High speed buffet boundaries:
AD – Mmo.
DJ – Vmo.

Low speed buffet boundaries:
AE – Light weight.
BF – Light/medium.
CG – Medium weight.
DH – Heavy weight.

13.5 ENGINE PERFORMANCE

13.5.1 Definitions

Gross or static thrust   This is the total thrust produced when an engine is stationary and is the product of the mass of air passing through the engine and the jet velocity at the propelling nozzle.

Momentum drag   The drag caused by the momentum of the air passing through the engine relative to the velocity of the aeroplane is known as momentum drag.

Net thrust   The product of the mass of air passing through an engine in flight and the change of velocity given to it is the net thrust.

13.5.2 Thrust rating

The gas loads consequential to the pressure and momentum changes of the gas stream reacting on the engine structure and its rotating parts are the thrust forces in a jet engine. Some of these are forward and exceed those that are rearward. The excess forward force is referred to as the rated thrust of the engine. It is measured by comparing the turbine discharge or the jet pipe pressure to the compressor inlet or intake pressure and is known as the engine pressure ratio (EPR) and is displayed on a gauge in the cockpit. The pilot can set a particular EPR setting by adjusting the thrust levers.

The fuel flow is automatically adjusted to account for changes of altitude, airspeed and ambient temperature and to maintain the EPR set. This retains the thrust at a constant value, thus in a dense atmosphere the fuel flow is reduced. However, this adjustment is limited and if the air density is such that the fuel flow cannot be reduced further then the EPR must be restricted to prevent damage being caused to the engine by exceeding the maximum temperature limitation. This is referred to as the 'flat rating cut-off' and is shown by a line across the EPR graph in the AFM.

13.5.3 Weight

A high weight requires a large amount of lift to be generated by the wings. To increase the lift in the cruise at a constant speed, the angle of attack would have to be increased resulting in increased drag. To overcome this the thrust must be increased with the consequent increase of fuel flow.

13.5.4 RPM

Mass flow is directly affected by the RPM. High RPM increases mass flow which consequently requires an increased fuel flow and increases the thrust output. Most jet aeroplanes cruise at between 85% and 90% of the maximum RPM. If the air density is low, thrust for a given RPM will fall. To restore the lost thrust during take-off it is necessary to inject water or water–methanol into the engine.

During the approach to land it is important to keep the RPM high in case it is necessary to go-around. If this is done the time taken to 'spool up' after the initiation of the go-round procedure is reduced.

13.5.5 Airspeed

The speed of the air at the intake increases with TAS. Because the maximum permissible jet pipe temperature limits the jet pipe speed, the acceleration given to the airflow by the engine is decreased. As speed increases the action of the compressor is added to by ram effect which increases the mass flow. Thus one effect is increasing the thrust whilst the other is decreasing the thrust. Overall they tend to cancel out one another. Thus the thrust of a jet engine is, therefore, not significantly affected by forward speed.

CHAPTER 14

Climbing Flight

Obstacle avoidance is of primary importance to public transport aeroplanes, especially just after take-off. Therefore the angle of climb is a predominant requirement during the take-off climb. Of secondary importance during this phase of flight is the rate of climb, which governs the time taken to reach a given altitude.

14.1 THE FORCES ACTING ON AN AEROPLANE IN A CLIMB

The power required to climb at a given EAS is greater than that required to maintain level flight at the same EAS. This is because the thrust has not only to counteract the effects of drag but also that component of weight which acts in the same direction as drag. The lift requirement in a climb is reduced from that of level flight because it only has to counterbalance the component of weight at right angles to the airflow. See Fig. 14.1.

> Thrust Required = Drag + (Weight × sine angle of climb).
> Lift Required = Weight × cosine angle of climb.

The *gradient* of climb, that is the height gain per unit of horizontal distance, is determined by the amount of *thrust* remaining available after counteracting drag and can be calculated from the forces acting in the climb (see Fig. 14.1). For climb gradients up to 15° it is safe to assume that lift equals weight and that the climb gradient equals the sine of the climb angle. The climb gradient can be calculated:

> Total thrust = Number of engines × Newtons per engine/g m/s/s kg
> Total drag = Lift / L/D ratio kg
> Weight component along climb path = Thrust − Drag kg
>
> Climb Gradient = (Thrust − Drag) kg × 100 / (weight) kg

The *rate* of climb, which is the height gain per unit of time, is determined by the amount of excess *power* available. ROC = Climb Gradient × TAS.

For a jet aeroplane climbing at constant IAS and maximum climb thrust both the climb gradient and the pitch angle will decrease with increasing altitude, which may cause the maximum operating Mach number (Mмo) to be exceeded, but the drag remains constant. In an unaccelerated climb the thrust equals the drag plus the

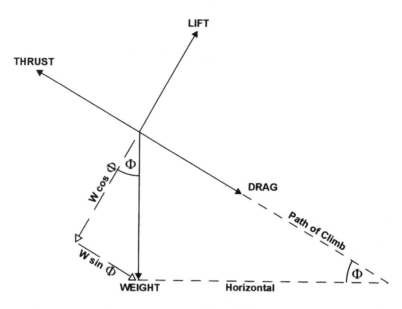

Fig. 14.1   The forces acting on an aeroplane in a climb.

weight component acting along the climb path. With a constant power setting any acceleration during the climb will reduce both the gradient and rate of climb.

14.2 THE MAXIMUM GRADIENT OF CLIMB

To attain the maximum angle of climb the aircraft should be flown at the speed that affords the greatest difference between *thrust available* and the *drag* curves when plotted on a 'Drag vs. Speed' graph. This speed is known as Vx. By transposition of formula the maximum gradient of climb can be found for piston/propeller and jet aeroplanes:

$$\text{Gradient of Climb} = \text{ROC} \div \text{TAS in still air}$$

14.2.1 Piston/propeller aeroplanes.

For piston/propeller-driven aeroplanes, because thrust varies with speed, the best angle of climb is obtained at a speed below the minimum drag speed (VIMD) and below the minimum power speed (VIMP) which is just above unstick speed (VUS). See Fig. 14.2.

14.2.2 Jet aeroplanes

Because thrust does not vary much with speed for a jet-engined aircraft the maximum angle of climb is achieved near the minimum drag speed, when the lift/drag

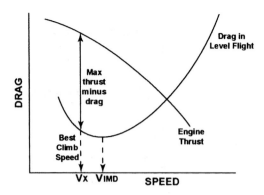

Fig. 14.2 Maximum gradient of climb – piston/propeller aircraft.

ratio is at its highest. See Fig. 14.3 and Fig. 14.6. Climbing at a constant Mach number will cause the coefficient of lift to increase with altitude.

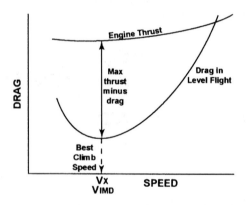

Fig. 14.3 Maximum gradient of climb – jet aircraft.

14.3 THE MAXIMUM RATE OF CLIMB

The speed required to attain the maximum rate of climb is V_Y. The maximum rate of climb is determined by the amount of excess *power* available above that which is required for the climb and can be calculated by the formula:

$$\text{Rate of Climb} = \text{Excess power available/Weight.}$$

14.3.1 Piston/propeller aeroplanes

The climbing speed that gives the best rate of climb for a piston/propeller-driven aircraft is the velocity of minimum power because at this point the difference between the power available and the power required curves is at its maximum. See Fig. 14.4.

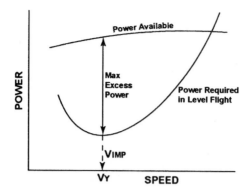

Fig. 14.4   Maximum rate of climb – piston/propeller aircraft.

14.3.2 Jet aircraft

Because both power available and drag increase with speed it is essential to compromise between the two and climb at a speed slightly above V_{IMP} to obtain the maximum rate of climb. See Fig. 14.5.

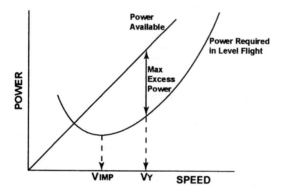

Fig. 14.5   Maximum rate of climb – jet aircraft.

14.4 THE EFFECT OF ALTITUDE ON CLIMB PERFORMANCE

The power attained by both piston/propeller and jet driven aeroplanes decreases with altitude. The power available curves are therefore lowered whilst the power required curves are displaced upwards and to the right. Thus the power required to fly at V_{IMD} is increased and the rate of climb reduces. The range of speeds available between minimum and maximum is also reduced.

14.5 AIRCRAFT CEILING

At the point at which the power available curve only just touches the power required curve a climb is no longer possible. At this altituded, there is only one speed possible in level flight. This is the **absolute ceiling**, which is of little practical use because it is a long slow process to reach it.

For practical purposes an artificial ceiling called the **service ceiling** is introduced which is defined as that altitude at which with all engines operating the maximum rate of climb is 500 fpm (2.5 m/s) for jet aircraft and 100 fpm (0.5 m/s) for piston/propeller-driven aeroplanes. In scheduled performance this is referred to as the 'gross' ceiling. A further artificial ceiling is introduced for safety reasons known as the 'net' ceiling at which a maximum rate of climb of 750 fpm and 150 fpm is achieved respectively.

Similar artificial ceilings exist in scheduled performance for the one-engine-inoperative configuration. The same rates of climb both gross and net must be attained, however, these ceilings are referred to as 'stabilizing altitudes'. For aeroplanes having three or more engines there are also stabilizing altitudes for the two-engine-inoperative configuration.

14.5.1 Climbing speed

The manufacturers of many types of aeroplanes recommend climbing at a constant EAS, or IAS, until a specific pressure altitude is attained and then to continue the climb at a constant Mach number. The pressure altitude at which this change occurs is referred to as the 'speed change point' or 'cross over altitude'. It is that pressure altitude at which both the IAS and the Mach number convert to the same TAS.

The changeover of climbing speeds causes the gradient of climb to alter. In the initial climb, when maintaining a constant IAS, the TAS gradually increases with increasing altitude. Therefore, the distance travelled during a specific time period, irrespective of the wind component, gradually increases so the climb gradient gradually decreases. However, below the tropopause, in the final climb, when a constant Mach number is being maintained the TAS gradually decreases with increasing pressure altitude. This results in a decreasing distance travelled in a specific time interval which causes the climb gradient to gradually increase. *Therefore, at the speed change point the climb gradient changes from one which is decreasing to one that is increasing, with increasing pressure altitude.*

The speed change point pressure altitude is determined by the ambient temperature of the air. Using the standard atmosphere then the examples in Table 14.1 would be correct.

Table 14.1 Example of speed change points.

Pressure altitude (ft)	Initial climb IAS (kts)	Final climb Mach No.	ISA Temp. (°C)	TAS (kts)
24 000	250	0.6	−33	362
22 500	300	0.7	−30	425
21 500	350	0.8	−28	490

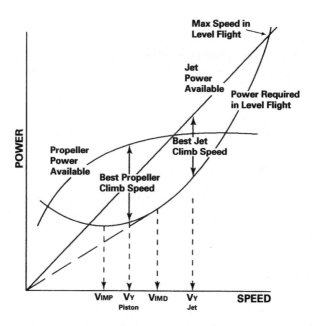

Fig. 14.6 Typical power curves at mean sea level.

If the climb schedule is changed to a higher IAS for a given Mach number the speed crossover point occurs at a lower altitude.

Climbing at a constant Mach number will cause both the TAS and the IAS to decrease in a normal atmosphere. To maintain a specific climb gradient then the angle of attack, C_L, must be increased.

CHAPTER 15
Descending Flight

A steady descent at a constant IAS usually requires no power and is, therefore, a glide descent which has no thrust vector. However, the remaining force vectors, lift, weight and drag, must remain in equilibrium or be balanced. The potential energy derived from the weight of the aeroplane at altitude and descending at an angle enables the weight vector, which acts vertically downward, to be divided into two component vectors. The component vector that acts in the direction of flight parallel to the longitudinal axis directly opposes and balances the drag vector. The component vector of the weight that acts downward at 90° to the longitudinal axis downward opposes and balances the lift vector. See Fig. 15.1.

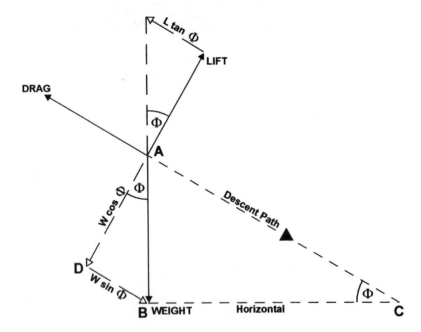

Fig. 15.1 The forces acting on an aeroplane in a glide.

The value of the two vectors can be calculated from the formula:

Forward Vector = Weight × sine descent angle.
Downward Vector = Weight × cosine descent angle.

The three variables in a glide descent, the IAS, the configuration and the glide angle can be manipulated to achieve either of two goals, endurance or range. If it is required to take as long as possible to complete the descent, then the aeroplane must descend at the lowest *rate* of descent which is known as 'gliding for endurance'. Whereas, if the goal is to cover the maximum *distance* during the descent, then it is necessary to maintain as shallow a glide angle as possible and is referred to as 'gliding for range'. The attainment of either goal is dependent on the speed flown during the descent. During a glide at constant Mach number the lift coefficient decreases and the low speed buffet margin will increase, because the IAS increases, but the pitch angle will decrease. It is possible that during this type of descent V_{MO} may be exceeded.

The gliding speed for maximum endurance The speed used during a descent is the rate of movement of the aeroplane along that path and can be divided into two components: horizontal and vertical. The horizontal component is the aeroplane's forward movement through the air and the vertical component is its rate of descent. To produce the maximum endurance the vertical component must be minimized. This means that the descent speed of the aeroplane and the rate of descent must be as low as possible. In Fig. 15.2 V is the descent speed of the aeroplane and the rate of descent is $V \times \sin \Phi$, where Φ is the glide angle.

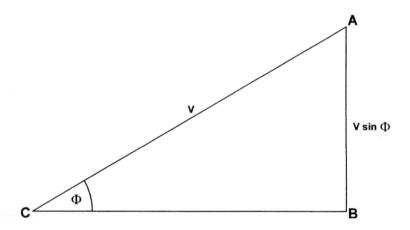

Fig. 15.2 The descent speed components.

The power required is the product of the speed multiplied by the drag. Therefore, the lowest rate of descent is attained at the speed for which the least power is required. For any given weight this speed occurs at the lowest point on the power required curve which may be determined by the point at which a horizontal line is tangential to the curve. This is illustrated in Fig. 15.3. Gliding endurance is directly affected by the weight. The greater the weight, the greater both the rate of descent and the EAS, but the gliding endurance is diminished. The wind component does *not* affect the gliding endurance.

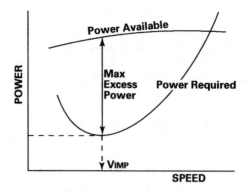

Fig. 15.3 The gliding speed for maximum endurance.

The gliding speed for maximum range   The gliding angle is a gradient of descent, that is a height change per unit of horizontal distance travelled. The gliding angle is minimum when the horizontal distance travelled is maximum. From Fig. 15.1 it will be seen that triangle ABC is similar to triangle BDA.

Cotangent Φ = Distance/Height = (Wcos Φ)/(Wsin Φ) = Lift/Drag or Cl/Cd

Therefore, the greatest distance travelled for the least loss of height, the lowest gliding angle, is when the lift/drag ratio is greatest. In other words, at the speed that causes the least drag. This speed is derived from the power required curve by drawing the tangent to the curve from the datum point of the graph. This is shown in Fig. 15.4, which is a graph of the power required vs. TAS. However, drag is dependent on EAS for its value therefore the descent must be made at a constant EAS to ensure that drag remains as low as possible. This means that the TAS decreases as altitude decreases, therefore, the glide *angle* will *increase* but the *rate* of descent will *decrease.*

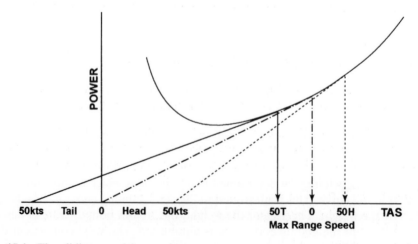

Fig. 15.4 The gliding speed for maximum range.

The effect of wind component   Wind component has the same effect on the glide angle as it has on the climb gradient. A *tailwind* will increase the distance travelled over the ground, thus *decreasing* the descent *gradient*, whilst a *headwind* will *decrease* the distance travelled over the ground thus *increasing* the descent gradient. However, to maintain the best lift/drag ratio it is necessary to adjust the gliding TAS, decreasing it for a tailwind and increasing it for a headwind. This is illustrated in Fig. 15.4.

The effect of weight   The gliding angle is not affected by changes in weight provided that the speed is adjusted to accommodate the weight. The EAS must be increased for a heavier weight or decreased for a lighter weight. Such changes directly affect the time taken to descend and consequently the exposure time to the wind component. Hence, it is more beneficial when gliding for range into wind, for the aeroplane to be heavy, i.e. do not jettison fuel.

An aeroplane in a steady glide at constant EAS will have an increased rate of descent and glide angle, because the TAS and distance travelled is decreased with altitude.

15.1 CLIMB AND DESCENT CALCULATIONS

Distance   The distance travelled in the climb or descent may be calculated using either the gradient or rate of climb (ROC)/rate of descent (ROD).

(1)   Gradient = (Height Difference × 100)/Distance Travelled
(2)   Distance Travelled = (Height Difference × 100)/Gradient. (By transposition)

To allow for the effect of the along track wind component and convert the result into nautical miles (nm.) the formula becomes:

(2)(a)   Ground Distance Travelled
        = (Height Difference/Gradient) × 100/6080 × (Groundspeed/TAS) nm.

However, if the rate of climb (or rate of descent) is known the ground distance travelled, allowing for the along track wind component, may be found by the following formula:

(3)   Ground Distance Travelled
     = Height Difference/[ROD (or ROC)] × (Groundspeed/60) nm.

Gradient   The equality of (2)(a) and (3) above enables the climb (or descent) gradient to be calculated because they both facilitate the determination of ground distance.

(2)(a)   (Height Difference/Gradient) × 100/6080 × (Groundspeed/TAS) nm. =
(3)   Height Difference/[ROD (or ROC)] × (Groundspeed/60) nm.

Then, by cancellation:

$$(1/\text{Gradient}) \times 100/6080 \times 1/\text{TAS} = 1/[\text{ROC (or ROD)}] \times 1/60$$

and, by transposition:

Gradient = [ROC (or ROD)/TAS] × 6000/6080

(4) Gradient = ROC (or ROD)/TAS in still air (approximately) or
(5) Gradient = ROC (or ROD)/Groundspeed (approximately) allowing for the
     along track wind component.

Constant speed descent A constant Mach number descent, in a normal atmosphere, causes the TAS and the IAS to increase. Consequently the groundspeed and
ground distance travelled will gradually increase during the descent causing the
descent angle to decrease progressively throughout the descent. This will increase
the low-speed buffet margin and decrease the high-speed buffet margin. Descending
at a constant IAS, in a normal atmosphere, will cause the TAS to decrease; consequently, the ground distance travelled will decrease which will increase the descent gradient. To maintain a constant descent gradient with a constant IAS the angle
of attack must be increased.

Angle of attack and pitch angle In a glide descent the range is maximized at the
pitch angle that produces the optimum angle of attack, which gives the best lift/drag
ratio. Increasing the pitch angle beyond the optimum will decrease the range
because of the increased drag. Decreasing the pitch angle below the optimum will
increase the forward speed thus decreasing the time taken to descend and therefore
the distance travelled.

The effect of flap The use of flap is restricted to the period of the descent when the
IAS has fallen below the maximum speed for lowering flap. Thus it is limited to the
final approach path. Using flap will increase the lift generated. To maintain the
same glide-path the pitch angle has to be increased and the forward speed
decreased, both are beneficial because together they afford a better view of the
runway at a slower speed.

CHAPTER 16
Maximum Range and Endurance

16.1 CRUISE CONTROL

Before cruise control can be examined in detail it is essential to understand the following definitions

16.1.1 Specific Fuel Consumption (SFC)

The amount of fuel used to generate the thrust output is the Specific Fuel Consumption. It can be calculated by dividing the fuel flow per hour by the thrust.

At a constant Mach number the fuel flow decreases with increased altitude and/or increased ambient temperature. However, at constant thrust and altitude it slightly increases with increased airspeed. But thrust decreases with decreased RPM, increased temperature and increased altitude. Thus the overall effect is that the SFC reduces with decreased ambient temperature and increased RPM (up to the optimum value). Speed in the cruise does not affect SFC significantly.

16.1.2 Specific Air Range

The still-air distance travelled per unit of fuel is the Specific Air Range (SAR). In level, unaccelerated flight it can be calculated by the formula:

$$\text{Specific Air Range} = (\text{TAS/Drag}) \times (1/\text{SFC}).$$

To maximize SAR the aeroplane should be flown to achieve the maximum value of the TAS/Drag ratio. At low altitudes this is achieved at $1.32 V_{IMD}$, but above the altitude at which this equates to M_{CRIT} it will be attained at the manufacturer's specified optimum Mach number. The TAS/Drag ratio improves with altitude to a maximum value which is attained at the pressure altitude where V_{IMD} is equivalent to the manufacturer's specified Mach number.

To further enhance the SAR the induced drag may be reduced by transferring fuel between tanks to position the CG just forward of the aft limit of the CG envelope. This is referred to as flying the 'flat aeroplane'.

16.1.3 Optimum altitude

The altitude at which an aeroplane attains the maximum Specific Air Range is the optimum altitude. Any increase of altitude above the optimum will result in a reduction in SAR, due to compressibility and engine limitations. *As weight decreases the optimimum altitude increases.*

It would be advantageous to fly up to 4000 ft below the optimum altitude only if the headwind is considerably less, or the tailwind considerably greater, than that at the optimum altitude. Although, for a given Mach number, the fuel flow will increase at the lower altitude so also will the TAS, compensating for the fuel flow.

16.1.4 Cruise climb

As a flight progresses fuel is used and the aircraft weight reduces. V_{IMD} is proportional to the square root of the aeroplane weight and therefore reduces as the flight proceeds. To maintain equivalence with the specified Mach number the optimum altitude is increased. This is the cruise climb technique which is executed using a constant Mach number, constant angle of attack and a fixed throttle setting. Below the optimum altitude the Mach number for the Long Range Cruise (LRC) decreases with altitude.

16.1.5 Stepped climb

Because of the gradually increasing altitude, the Cruise Climb technique is not compatible with the requirements of Air Traffic Control en-route. It is, therefore, necessary to fly a profile that approximates to the cruise climb. This is achieved by climbing to the first semi-circular cruising level approximately 1000 ft above the optimum altitude and commencing a level cruise at the optimum Mach number. The cruise continues level until the aeroplane is approximately 3000 ft below the optimum cruise altitude at which point it is climbed 4000 ft to the next semi-circular cruising level. The RPM in the cruise must be reduced to ensure the safe operating limitations of the engines are not exceeded. At high altitude the ability to execute a stepped climb may be limited by the onset of buffet at g-loads greater than one because the maximum altitude is restricted to the 1.3-g altitude. The stepped cruise will achieve a range equal to 95% of that of a cruise climb in the same environmental conditions.

16.2 MAXIMUM RANGE

Flying for range signifies travelling the greatest possible ground distance, using the fuel available. To achieve *maximum* range using a given quantity of fuel, an aeroplane must consume the lowest possible amount of fuel for each nautical mile travelled over the ground. In other words it must attain the lowest possible gross fuel flow:

$$\text{Gross fuel flow (GFF)} = \text{fuel flow/groundspeed.}$$

If work done was the only consideration then maximum range would be obtained by flying at V_{IMD}. Unfortunately such is not the case, because although V_{IMD} is the most efficient *airframe* speed it is not necessarily the most efficient *power unit* speed.

16.2.1 Piston/propeller power units

As speed increases, the thrust developed by a piston/propeller unit combination decreases. Therefore power unit efficiency is greater at low IAS. Maximum *airframe* efficiency is attained at the speed at which the lift/drag ratio is the highest. Thus V_{IMD} will accommodate both the airframe and power unit requirements. For comfort and controllability, however, the aeroplane should be flown at a speed just above V_{IMD}. The manufacturers usually recommend $1.1V_{IMD}$. The highest measure of *aeroplane* efficiency can be attained at only one particular altitude, any deviation from this altitude results in a loss of efficiency.

16.2.2 Jet power units

At a set RPM, the thrust developed by a jet engine is almost constant for all speeds. Fuel consumption is directly proportional to thrust and, therefore, to RPM but is unaffected by speed. Thus greater *engine* efficiency is obtained at high IAS. If this were the only consideration then maximum range would be obtained at an IAS much higher than V_{IMD}. However, speed affects the angle of attack, which in turn affects the lift/drag ratio. Maximum *airframe* efficiency is attained at the highest lift/drag ratio. The ideal aerodynamic cruise speed for a jet aircraft is at the IAS obtained at the tangent to the drag curve. See Fig. 16.1. *This is the maximum IAS for the least amount of drag*, V_I/D_{max}. Thus, the most efficient manner in which to operate a jet aircraft is at the angle of attack and IAS which together produce the best V_I/D ratio. If the cruise is at a constant altitude then both the IAS and the drag will reduce as the flight progresses.

Because maximum range requires the lowest possible gross fuel flow then the aeroplane should be flown at the altitude at which the IAS produces the highest TAS. *At 40 000 ft the TAS produced for a given IAS is almost double that produced at MSL.* An additional benefit of high altitude flight is that, for a given RPM the fuel

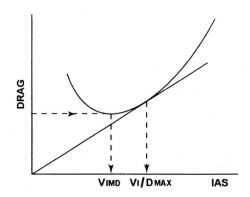

Fig. 16.1 The drag curve.

flow reduces because of the decreased air density. The GFF is, therefore, reduced by both the increased TAS and the decreased fuel flow. *Maximum range for a jet aircraft is, therefore, increased with altitude.*

Specific Air Range = TAS/Fuel Flow.

16.2.3 Weight effect

Irrespective of the type of power unit, if weight is increased then the speed must be increased to develop more lift as a counterbalance. But this increases the drag to a greater extent and causes the lift/drag ratio and the operational efficiency to decrease. *Therefore, decreased weight increases the optimum altitude and the maximum range.*

16.2.4 C of G position

The maximum range of the aeroplane can be improved if the C of G position is maintained at a point just forward of the aft limit of the C of G envelope. This reduces trim drag and can be achieved by transferring fuel between tanks.

16.2.5 Wind effect

Maximum range is dependent on the gross fuel flow, which is a measure of operational efficiency. To increase the range GFF must be reduced. Thus to improve range it is necessary to increase the groundspeed or to reduce the fuel flow or both. The factors affecting fuel flow have already been described and showed that for maximum efficiency the aeroplane should be flown at the optimum altitude. However, this altitude is not necessarily the most efficient *operational* altitude by reason of the ambient temperature or along track wind component.

To obtain the highest possible groundspeed the altitude may have to be reduced to take advantage of the prevailing wind and/or temperature at a lower altitude. More often than not a compromise altitude will have to be flown because the effect that temperature and altitude have on fuel flow and TAS must be considered, as well as the along track wind component effect on groundspeed, at each altitude. To obtain the maximum range the most beneficial balance has to be calculated. If the problem is one of radius of action, instead of range, then any wind component will reduce the distance to the furthermost point from the departure point.

16.3 MAXIMUM ENDURANCE

Flying for endurance denotes remaining airborne for as long as possible, using the fuel available. Therefore, maximum endurance is obtained for a given quantity of fuel at the lowest rate of fuel consumption, i.e. the lowest fuel flow per unit of time.

If the airframe were the only consideration, maximum endurance would be obtained by flying at the condition that requires the minimum amount of work to be done to overcome drag, per unit of time. As the rate of doing work is equal to power, then the best operating condition would be at the speed of minimum power, V$_{IMP}$, which is slightly lower than V$_{IMD}$. However, the airframe is not the only consideration because the efficiency of the power units must also be taken into account.

16.3.1 Piston/propeller power units

The power output of a piston/propeller combination is approximately constant for a given fuel flow:

$$\text{Power required} = \text{drag} \times \text{true airspeed.}$$

However, this power requirement increases with height at a constant IAS because of the increased TAS necessary to overcome a given amount of drag. It is, therefore, necessary to fly at low altitude to minimize TAS and hence reduce the power required. Altitude does not significantly affect fuel flow.

Figure 16.2 shows the piston/propeller power available curve has the greatest reserve of power available over power required to be at V$_{IMP}$ (Position A). At this point the fuel flow is at the minimum possible. The IAS at V$_{IMP}$ is relatively low which makes accurate flying quite difficult. Consequently the manufacturers usually recommend a higher more comfortable speed or even the use of a small amount of flap to increase controllability. This adjustment ensures that any minor disturbance does not cause the IAS to drop to a point on the 'wrong' side of the drag curve.

Maximum endurance is, therefore, dependent on altitude, weight and the fuel available.

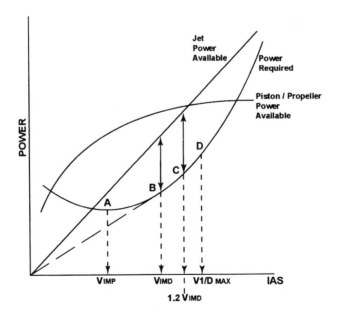

Fig. 16.2 The power curves.

16.3.2 Jet power units

Fuel flow for a turbo-jet engine is approximately proportional to the thrust produced, irrespective of speed or altitude. Since thrust required is equal to drag then the minimum thrust and hence the minimum fuel flow is at the point of minimum drag, VIMD (Position B). Therefore, maximum endurance is attained at VIMD. As drag is constant at all altitudes for a given IAS and thrust decreases with increased altitude as does the fuel flow then the specific fuel consumption is virtually unchanged.

Figure 16.2 shows that the reserve of power available above the power required remains constant for all speeds between VIMD and 1.2VIMD (Position B to C). The manufacturers usually recommend that, for maximum endurance, the speed should be above VIMD to improve the handling qualities, but at high altitude this increase should not be so high as to cause a significant increase in drag. The speed for the maximum endurance is always less than that required to obtain the maximum range.

16.3.3 Summary

The best conditions to attain maximum range or maximum endurance are:

Piston/propeller aircraft
(1) Maximum range – VIMD, at the most efficient altitude for the power units.
(2) Maximum endurance – VIMP, at the lowest practicable altitude. This is approximately equal to the speed to attain the maximum rate of climb.

Jet aircraft
(1) Maximum range – V_I/D_{max}, at the highest practicable altitude.
(2) Maximum endurance – VIMD, at the highest practicable altitude.

Test Paper 4

Q1. Induced drag is caused by:
  (a) The aerofoil movement through the air.
  (b) The aerofoil shape.
  (c) Boundary layer surface friction.
  (d) Inadequate streamlining.

Q2. V$_{IMD}$ is:
  (a) The tangent to the drag curve.
  (b) The lowest point on the power curve.
  (c) The tangent to the power curve.
  (d) 1.6Vs for propeller driven aircraft.

Q3. The angle of attack that produces the best lift/drag ratio is the same for all weights and altitudes. For most aircraft this angle is:
  (a) 2°.
  (b) 4°.
  (c) 6°.
  (d) 8°.

Q4. Increased altitude decreases air density which, if level flight is to be maintained, causes:
  (a) No effect on lift.
  (b) Little overall change to drag.
  (c) The power attained to improve.
  (d) The lift/drag ratio to increase.

Q5. The lift required for climbing flight is:
  (a) Increased above that required in level flight.
  (b) Equal to drag × cosine angle of climb.
  (c) Decreased below that required in level flight.
  (d) Equal to weight.

Q6. The maximum angle of climb for a jet-engined aircraft is attained at:
  (a) V$_{IMP}$.
  (b) 1.2V$_{IMP}$.
  (c) V$_{IMD}$.
  (d) 1.1V$_{IMD}$.

Q7. The maximum rate of climb for a propeller-driven aircraft is attained at:
   (a) V_{IMP}.
   (b) $1.2V_{IMP}$.
   (c) V_{IMD}.
   (d) $1.1V_{IMD}$.

Q8. The service ceiling is defined as the altitude at which the maximum rate of climb is:
   (a) 0 fpm for both jet and propeller driven aircraft.
   (b) 100 fpm for jet aircraft.
   (c) 500 fpm for propeller aircraft.
   (d) 100 fpm for propeller driven aircraft.

Q9. Gross fuel flow is:
   (a) The fuel consumed per hour.
   (b) The fuel consumed per minute.
   (c) The fuel consumed per nm.
   (d) The fuel consumed per leg.

Q10. Maximum range for a jet aircraft is attained at:
   (a) V_{IMD}.
   (b) $1.1V_{IMD}$.
   (c) V_{IMP}.
   (d) V_I/D_{max}.

Q11. The effect of an increase of flap angle has on the lift/drag ratio is:
   (a) None.
   (b) An increase.
   (c) A decrease.
   (d) An increase above 15° of flap.

Q12. The effect an increase of weight has on the power required curve is:
   (a) None.
   (b) Moves up and to the right.
   (c) Moves down and to the left.
   (d) Moves horizontally right.

Q13. The point on the diagram below that determines the maximum range speed for a jet aeroplane is:
   (a) A.
   (b) B.
   (c) C.
   (d) D.

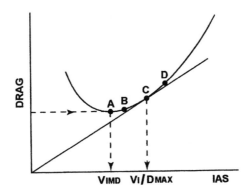

Q14. The force that exactly opposes and balances lift in a climb is:
    (a) Weight × cosine climb angle.
    (b) Weight × sine climb angle.
    (c) Thrust × cosine climb angle.
    (d) Thrust × sine climb angle.

Q15. The effect that an increase of pressure altitude has on the power required curve is:
    (a) None.
    (b) Moves up and to the right.
    (c) Moves down and to the left.
    (d) Moves horizontally right.

CHAPTER 17

The General Effect of the Variables

The take-off and landing performance of an aeroplane is influenced by many different factors. Because several of them can change, the resulting effect on the aeroplane's performance will vary, hence they are referred to as the 'variables'.

The factors considered to be variables are:

(1) Air density.
(2) Wind component.
(3) Aeroplane flap setting.
(4) Aeroplane weight.
(5) Aerodrome runway slope.
(6) Aerodrome runway surface.
(7) Aeroplane air conditioning system.
(8) Centre of Gravity.

17.1 AIR DENSITY

The value of air density is dependent on three contributory influencing factors. They are altitude, air temperature and water vapour content.

At middle latitudes an increase of altitude from mean sea level to 1000 ft above mean sea level on average results in a decrease of 3% in air density. However, in a normal atmosphere that would result in a decrease of temperature of 2°C which would cause an increase of air density of 0.66%. Thus the overall decrease of air density due to the change in altitude is a decrease of 2.34%. This, therefore, shows that *the change of altitude has by far the greater effect on the air density than the change in temperature.* If it didn't density would increase with increase of altitude. A change of water vapour content of the atmosphere can only be brought about by a change of air mass. If the water vapour content increases then the air density decreases.

Hence an increase in air temperature, altitude or water vapour content either individually or together will decrease the air density.

A description and definition of density altitude is given in Chapter 2.

17.1.1 The effect of air density

Engine performance   The amount of thrust produced by an aeroplane engine is directly proportional to the input air density. The greater the density of the air, the greater the thrust produced. Thus the thrust output diminishes as air density decreases and is only partially compensated in a normal atmosphere by the reduced temperature. Thrust gradually decreases up to the tropopause where the compensation ceases, because of the isothermal layer above it. Above this altitude the thrust decreases at a greater rate with increased altitude. Hence it is more beneficial, in terms of thrust, to cruise just below the tropopause. It follows that, if the value of any of the three contributory factors that influence air density, altitude, temperature or water vapour content increases, then the thrust developed by the engine decreases.

A dense atmosphere not only increases the thrust output of the engine, but also the temperature within the engine. There is a maximum limitation to the temperature permitted in the engine, which if exceeded could result in structural damage to the engine. To prevent such an occurrence it is necessary to restrict the thrust output at take-off in conditions of high air density. This limitation is referred to as the 'flat rating cut-off' and is generally achieved by setting the thrust levers to a predetermined lower setting in such atmospheric conditions.

In conditions of low air density (i.e. when the air temperature is high or the aerodrome pressure altitude is high) the thrust output at take-off is low. This will result in a slow acceleration to the required take-off speeds and will increase the length of the ground run and the distance taken to reach screen height. These distances are not permitted to exceed the distances available. If such is the case then the TOW will have to be reduced to comply with this requirement.

After attaining screen height the aeroplane is required to attain at least the minimum gradient of climb deemed by the CAA and the JAA to be acceptable as specified in JARs. In conditions of low air density it may be necessary to reduce the TOW to attain this gradient. This limitation is called the 'weight-altitude-temperature limitation' or the 'WAT limit'. In some countries this is referred to as the 'climb- limited take-off mass (TOM)'. It can therefore be deduced that *a low air temperature and/or altitude increases the climb gradient and the WAT limited TOW and that a high air temperature and/or altitude decreases the climb gradient and the WAT limited TOW.*

Speed   The speeds of an aeroplane to be used for take-off or for landing are specified by the manufacturers in values of calibrated airspeed (CAS) or equivalent airspeed (EAS). No matter which, the values for small aeroplanes, less than 5700 kg maximum authorized weight, are usually only significantly affected by the aeroplane weight and the flap setting made. *The speeds increase with an increase of weight and/or a decrease of flap angle.* They are tabulated by the manufacturers for various weights at the recommended flap settings.

The same is true for large aeroplanes but, in addition, the value of the speeds also varies with density. Increased density increases V_{MCG}, V_{MC} and V_2 but decreases the values of V_1 and V_R. These changes are relatively small, but of greater significance is the effect density has on the conversion of CAS to TAS and consequently on groundspeed. For example using a CAS of 120 kts the conversions are as shown in Table 17.1.

Table 17.1   Conversion of 120 kts CAS to TAS.

Ambient temperature	0°C	+5°C	+15°C
Press. Alt.			
MSL	117 kts	118 kts	120 kts
5000 ft	128 kts	129.5 kts	132 kts
10 000 ft	141 kts	142.5 kts	145 kts

Table 17.1 shows that the density decrease caused by the increased altitude has a much greater effect than the decrease of density due to high air temperature.

Combined effect   The low thrust output caused by the low air density results in a low rate of acceleration during take-off. Therefore, the distance taken from the brakes release point to the point at which lift-off speed is attained is increased. Because of the low air density the lift-off speed produces a higher true airspeed and a higher groundspeed. Consequently the high groundspeed over a long ground run results in a high rotational velocity of the wheels causing high tyre temperatures.

All tyres have a maximum speed limitation which is imposed to prevent the tyre reaching the temperature at which the heat plug will blow out and cause the tyre to deflate. Thus, when the air density is low it may be necessary to restrict the TOW to prevent such an occurrence. This is the 'tyre speed' limit on TOW.

The efficiency of any braking system can only be guaranteed up to the maximum operating temperature which is normally between 450°C and 500°C. In the event of an abandoned take-off, if the temperature of the braking system exceeds this limit it will fail to stop the aeroplane in the distance available. Thus, the maximum operating temperature imposes a restriction on the TOW of the aeroplane to ensure that a rejected take-off is safe. This is the 'brake energy limitation' on TOW and is directly affected by the ambient air density. If the condition of low air density is combined with a runway downslope and a tailwind the rotational velocity of the wheels becomes very high. Should the take-off be abandoned at V1, in such circumstances, then the brake system temperature may exceed the upper limit. If such is the case the TOW must be decreased to ensure compliance.

17.2 WIND COMPONENT

A wind velocity is a wind direction and a wind speed. If the wind velocity is related to a runway direction it may be resolved into the along and across track components. These components can be calculated by the following formulae:

Along track component = windspeed × cosine relative direction
Across track component = windspeed × sine relative direction.

17.2.1 Along track component

The along track component is referred to as a headwind if it is in the opposite direction to that of travel and a tailwind if it is in the same direction as that of travel.

All take-off speeds are determined by the density, the flap setting and the weight of the aeroplane. For any given V_R a headwind will cause the groundspeed to be less than that in still-air. Consequently the ground distance travelled during the take-off from the brakes release point to both the point at which the wheels leave the ground and to the point at which screen height is attained are both reduced. These distances may not exceed those that are available. Therefore, *take-off into wind produces a low groundspeed and enables a higher TOW to be used than would be obtained in still air with the same distances available.* A take-off downwind increases the ground-speed and distance travelled and, therefore, causes the TOW to be reduced below the still air value for the same distance. See Fig. 17.1.

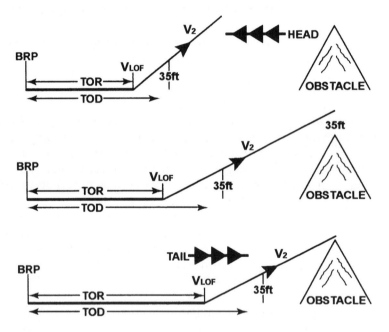

Fig. 17.1   The effect of wind component on climb gradient.

Similarly in the climb, after reaching screen height with one engine inoperative, the aeroplane must continue the climb at the free air safety speed V_2 to flap retraction altitude. The distance travelled to reach this point in a headwind is less than that required in still air. Therefore, the gradient of climb is greater than the still-air equivalent. *The climb gradient is increased by a headwind.* However, the rate of climb (ROC) (i.e. the height gain in a specific time period) is *not* affected by the wind component, as indeed is the WAT-limited TOW, because this is dependent on the minimum gradient requirement which is in still air.

Whilst climbing, the aeroplane is legally required to avoid all obstacles it encounters in the obstacle domain by a minimum vertical interval of 35 ft. Because of the improved gradient of climb in a headwind the obstacle clearance, for any given TOW, is improved. Alternatively, if an increase in TOW is required then the TOW can be increased until the minimum clearance is just attained.

The effect of a headwind on landing is that it shortens both the landing distance from screen height and the landing ground run. It also increases the descent gradient which facilitates a better view of the runway for the pilot at this critical stage of flight.

The effect of a tailwind on the take-off, climb and landing performance is the reverse of that experienced with a headwind. The groundspeed is greater than the TAS, therefore the distance travelled is increased. As a result the gradient of climb or descent is reduced below the still-air value and once again the ROC is unchanged. A tailwind makes it more difficult to attain obstacle clearance in the climb after take-off and may cause the TOW to be reduced if the legal minimum vertical separation from any obstacle in the domain is not obtained.

The wind effective gradient may be calculated by the following formula:

$$\text{Wind effective gradient} = \text{Still-air gradient} \times (\text{TAS/Groundspeed}).$$

17.2.2 The across track component

The across track component of the wind velocity is that which is at 90° to the direction of travel and affects the directional control of the aeroplane. The size of the fin and rudder determines the maximum amount of rudder authority that can be exercised to produce the moments necessary to counteract the crosswind. There-fore, for each aeroplane type, there is a maximum crosswind limitation quoted for a runway with a normal coefficient of friction. If the runway surface has a low coef-ficient of friction, as happens with ice or contamination on the surface, the limiting crosswind speed is considerably reduced below that for a normal surface.

Most aircraft types have a maximum crosswind stipulated for take-off and landing by the manufacturer. If the across track component exceeds this value then the runway cannot be used by that aeroplane for take-off or landing.

17.3 THE AEROPLANE FLAP SETTING

The flaps on an aeroplane enable the pilot to alter the camber of the wing and to change the effective angle of attack of the main plane. This not only alters the lift generated by the wings but also the induced drag. For every aeroplane the manu-facturer recommends a specific flap setting to be used for take-off and another for landing. For a normal take-off the recommended flap setting is usually between 10° and 12° and will produce the greatest amount of lift for the smallest increase of drag. This flap setting is referred to as the 'optimum flap setting' and produces the best lift/drag ratio.

Deploying flap of any angle will increase lift and, therefore, reduce the stalling speed, V_1, V_R and V_{LOF} thus decreasing the ground run of the aeroplane or permitting an increased field-length-limited TOW for the available distance. However, once the aeroplane becomes airborne the induced drag has a major influence on the performance of the aeroplane. It reduces the climb gradient attained as well as the rate of climb and, although the length of the ground run is reduced, the distance taken from V_{LOF} to screen height may well be unchanged at the lower flap settings which means that the take-off distance is unchanged. At much larger flap settings, such as those used for short-field operations, the take-off ground run and the take-off distance are both considerably shorter than those distances for lower flap settings and the WAT limited TOW is also reduced because of the low climb gradient. See Fig. 17.2.

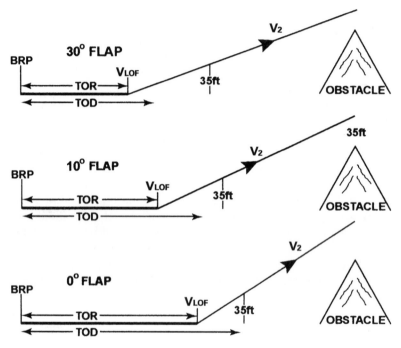

Fig. 17.2   The effect of flap on take-off performance.

A large flap setting, such as 30°, is used for such take-offs and produces a dramatic increase in the lift generated at the expense of a huge increase of drag. This technique does produce a very short take-off ground run, take-off distance and very low associated speeds but the climb performance is very poor. Therefore, obstacle clearance after take-off is more difficult to attain than would be the case normally.

During landing, the use of flaps slows the aeroplane and as a consequence reduces the landing distance from screen height and the length of the landing ground run. The use of large flap angles will shorten these distances considerably and will also give the pilot a much improved visual aspect of the runway.

17.4 AEROPLANE WEIGHT

The weight of an aeroplane at the commencement of the take-off run directly affects the distance travelled from the brakes release point to both the lift-off point and to the screen height. It is that force which acts vertically downward through the centre of gravity of the aeroplane. The opposing balancing force is lift, which has to be generated by the movement of the aircraft through the air. The greater the weight the more lift is required to balance it. Movement of the aeroplane through the air is the result of the forward thrust force produced by the engines overcoming the opposing drag force. If the weight is increased then the engines will have to produce more thrust to increase the forward speed to enable sufficient lift to be generated to counteract the weight.

An increase in weight will cause the stalling speed, V_1, V_R, V_2 and V_{AT} to increase. In any given air density with the maximum permissible engine settings made, the thrust generated is constant so the distances taken to achieve the appropriate speeds are increased if the weight is increased. In such circumstances, on take-off both the ground run and the distance are increased in length, as are the landing distance and the ground run for that phase of flight.

After take-off, despite the increased speeds, the gradient and the rate of climb are both reduced with increased weight, making obstacle clearance more difficult to achieve. This is because the increased weight not only requires a greater lift force to balance it but the drag is also increased by the larger rearward component of the heavier weight. Hence more thrust is required but is not available because the thrust levers are already at the maximum permissible setting. So the overall effect of an increased weight on take-off performance is adverse. The greater the increase of the TOW the worse is the performance.

A decreased TOW has the reverse effect lowering all the speeds, shortening the distance taken, increasing the gradient and the rate of climb. Thus obstacle clearance after take-off is more easily attained.

For landing, an increased landing weight has a similar effect. Because the stalling speed is higher the approach speed must be higher which results in a longer landing distance from screen height and a longer ground run. The combination of the high approach speed and the heavier weight requires a longer ground run to bring the aeroplane to a halt.

17.5 AERODROME RUNWAY SLOPE

A take-off on an upsloping runway will have a reduced rate of acceleration because an element of the thrust available is used to overcome the component of weight that acts in the opposite direction to that of take-off. This results in a longer ground run and take-off distance. A down sloping runway has the reverse effect on take-off decreasing the distances because the weight component is now acting in the direction of take-off and assists the acceleration of the aeroplane. The effect of runway slope during the landing phase is opposite to that of take-off. Upslope shortens the landing distance and the landing ground run, whereas downslope increases both the distances.

17.6 AERODROME RUNWAY SURFACE

All of the graphs published in the aeroplane performance manual are based on a hard, dry, level runway surface having a coefficient of friction greater than 0.4. If the runway surface is other than dry and hard due allowance must be made for it. Full details regarding the effects of different surface types and different contaminants are contained in Chapter 11.

Generally, the surface condition affects the ability of an aeroplane to accelerate or to decelerate. On take-off, spray ingestion and impingement will slow the acceleration of the aeroplane, thus increasing the length of the take-off ground run and the take-off distance. In the event of having to abandon the take-off, the stopping distance will be increased in length by an incalculable amount. This is because the braking effectiveness is dependent on the surface coefficient of friction which is a variable. Therefore, it is not possible to schedule a speed from which the aeroplane can be guaranteed to stop safely within the distance available. However, it is possible to determine an advisory speed from which the aeroplane *should* be able to stop in an emergency within the available distance. This is the 'maximum abandonment speed'.

17.7 AEROPLANE AIR CONDITIONING SYSTEM

The air conditioning system when selected on bleeds air from the engines thus depleting the power produced. The reduced power will cause the length of the take-off run and the take-off distance to increase but will reduce the climb gradient, the rate of climb and the WAT limited TOW.

17.8 CENTRE OF GRAVITY

The CG must remain within safe limits at all times. If it is positioned towards the aft limit of the envelope it will decrease the stalling speed and the trim drag, which decreases the fuel flow and increases the range. If it is towards the forward limit the reverse is true. More details are given in Chapter 20.

CHAPTER 18
Take-off and Climb Speeds

To ensure a thorough understanding of performance it is absolutely essential to be familiar with all of the definitions of the various speeds used in performance and the effect the variables have on these speeds. This chapter and the next include only those speeds directly related to aeroplane performance and contains detailed explanations of them, whereas Chapter 47 of this book contains only definitions of all speeds that may be encountered in aviation.

18.1 GENERAL

All speeds specified by the manufacturers are given in terms of calibrated airspeed (CAS) or equivalent airspeed (EAS). It is, therefore, important to know what speed the pilot should be looking for on the airspeed indicator in each phase of flight and how the value of these speeds will affect other aspects of flight or be affected by the variables.

Airspeed Indicated Reading (ASIR)   The reading on the airspeed indicator without correction is the ASIR. The correction made to allow for inaccuracies in the construction of the instrument, which are permissible within its normal working accuracy, are referred to as instrument error. The ASIR becomes the indicated airspeed (IAS) when corrected for instrument error.

Indicated Airspeed (IAS)   This is the speed of the aeroplane as shown on its pitot/static airspeed indicator calibrated to reflect standard atmosphere adiabatic compressible flow at mean sea level *uncorrected* for airspeed system errors, but corrected for instrument error. *JAR 1 page 8.*

Rectified Airspeed (RAS)   The airspeed value that is obtained when ASIR has been corrected for both instrument and position error. This term is rarely used in civil aviation performance, preference being given to the term calibrated airspeed which has the same value.

Calibrated Airspeed (CAS)   The IAS corrected for position (or system) error is calibrated airspeed which is equal to equivalent airspeed and true airspeed in a standard atmosphere at mean sea level. *JAR 1 page 3.*

Equivalent Airspeed (EAS)   The CAS when corrected for adiabatic compressible flow at a particular altitude becomes equivalent airspeed. Which means that in a standard atmosphere at mean sea level the values of CAS and EAS are the same. *JAR 1 page 6.*

True Airspeed   This is the speed of the aeroplane relative to the undisturbed air. *JAR 1 page 6.*

To summarize, then, if the IAS is corrected for position and instrument error in a standard atmosphere at MSL it is equal to CAS, EAS and TAS. Rarely do the conditions of a standard atmosphere at MSL occur. Either the surface temperature or the altitude or both do not conform to these conditions, in which case the corrections must be applied in sequence.

The corrections required for position and instrument error are normally combined and tabulated on a card. Corrections are shown for the whole range of indicated airspeeds at which it is possible for that aeroplane type to fly from zero to the never-exceed speed (VNE). If there is only one pitot/static system in the aeroplane then the same correction card will apply to all airspeed indicators fed by that system. However, if more than one pitot/static sytem is fitted to the aeroplane then separate correction cards must be provided for each system and used for the appropriate airspeed indicators fed by each of the systems.

Usually the correction card provided is for the flaps up configuration because this is the only configuration that can be used for the whole range of indicated airspeeds possible and it is normally at the maximum certificated weight of the aeroplane. If altitude or weight make a significant difference to the corrections for this configuration then the card will be replaced with a graph from which it is possible to interpolate for intermediate weights and/or altitudes.

For take-off and landing it may be possible to use one of a variety of flap settings. If such is the case, then a series of graphs will be provided in the Aeroplane Flight Manual, a separate graph for each flap setting to enable the pilot to determine the correction to apply to the IAS. The application of this correction, no matter whether from a card or a graph, is a simple addition or subtraction applied to the indicated airspeed.

Compressibility of the air causes a significant error to the reading given by the airspeed indicator with speeds in excess of 300 kts TAS. The value of the correction varies with speed and altitude and may be determined from a graph or by means of a navigation computer. Application of the correction to CAS produces EAS. For take-off and landing the effect of compressible flow is negligible irrespective of the aerodrome elevation. So, for these phases of flight CAS and EAS may be considered to be one and the same. That is why some manufacturers specify the performance speeds in EAS and others in CAS.

Irrespective of which speeds are used for take-off and landing due allowance must be made for density error if TAS is to be computed. Density error is that which is caused by the difference between the ambient density and that which was used to calibrate the instrument. Air density is affected by both air temperature and altitude. It is, therefore, these two factors that must be used to determine the correction to be applied. It may be applied either graphically or by means of the navigation computer to obtain the TAS.

Because the manufacturers specify the speeds for take-off and landing in terms of CAS or EAS the pilot must apply the corrections for instrument and position error in the opposite sense to determine what the target speed should be on the airspeed indicator.

Vs This is the stalling speed and is the greater of:

(1) The minimum CAS obtained when the aeroplane is stalled (or the minimum steady flight speed at which the aeroplane is controllable with the longitudinal control on its stop).
(2) A CAS equal to 94% of the one-g stall speed (Vs_{1g}). *JAR 25.103(b)*.

Vs_{1g} This is the 'One-g Stalling Speed' which is the minimum CAS at which the aeroplane can develop a lift force (normal to the flight path) equal to its weight whilst at an angle of attack not greater than that at which the stall is identified. *JAR 25.103(c)*.

Vs_1 This is the stalling speed with the aeroplane in the configuration under consideration. *JAR 1 page 1–15*.

The aeroplane may be considered stalled when the behaviour of the aeroplane gives to the pilot a clear distinctive indication of an unacceptable nature that the aeroplane is stalled. This indication may be:

(1) A nose-down pitch that cannot be readily arrested and which may be accompanied by a rolling motion which cannot be immediately controlled.
(2) Severe buffeting, of a magnitude and severity that is a strong and effective deterrent to further speed reduction or
(3) In the case of dynamic stalls only, a significant roll into or out of a turn which is not immediately controllable. *JAR 25.201(d)*.

The value of stalling speed is affected by the aeroplane weight, flap setting, air temperature and pressure altitude. The stalling speed is decreased by any one or any combination of the following:

(1) Decreased weight.
(2) Increased flap angle.
(3) Decreased air temperature.
(4) Decreased pressure altitude.
(5) CG towards the aft limit.

18.2 TAKE-OFF SPEEDS

The speeds for take-off are defined in the sequence in which they are encountered during the take-off procedure. They are depicted in Fig. 18.1.

V_{MCG} This is the minimum control speed on the ground and is the CAS, at which, when the critical engine is suddenly made inoperative during the take-off run and

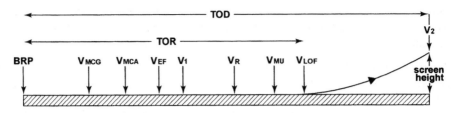

Fig. 18.1 The take-off speeds.

with its propeller, if applicable, in the position it automatically takes, it is possible to maintain control with the use of primary aerodynamic controls alone *(without the use of nosewheel steering)* to enable the take-off to be safely continued using normal piloting skill. The path of the aeroplane from the point of engine failure to the point at which recovery to a direction parallel to the centre-line of the runway is attained may not deviate by more than 30 ft laterally from the centre-line at any point. *JAR25.149(e).*

V_{MC} This is the lowest CAS, at which, when the critical engine is suddenly made inoperative, it is possible to maintain control of the aeroplane with that engine still inoperative, and maintain straight flight with an angle of bank of not more than 5° without a change of heading greater than 20°. It may not exceed 1.2Vs. *JAR 25.149(b) and (d).*

Because V_{MC} and V_{MCG} are both control speeds they are affected only by the air density and no other variable. In conditions of high air density the engine produces a high thrust output so the loss of one engine is a proportionate loss of a high output. This will require a considerable amount of force to counteract any yaw tendencies which can only be achieved at a high CAS. The loss of an engine in low air density, whilst being proportionately the same, can be counteracted at a lower CAS. Thus both control speeds are decreased in conditions of low air density and increased when the air density is high.

V_{EF} This is the CAS at which the critical engine is assumed to fail. It is never less than V_{MCG} and is always less than V_1. *JAR25.107(a)(1).*

V_1 Commonly referred to as 'decision speed', V_1 is never less than V_{EF} plus the speed gained, with the critical engine inoperative, during the time interval between the instant the engine failed and the instant the pilot recognizes and reacts to the failure, as indicated by the pilot's application of the first means of retardation, which should be to close the throttles. *JAR 25.107(a)(2).*

Usually the time interval allowed for recognition and reaction is two seconds. This means that the lowest V_1 is normally two seconds after V_{EF}. The exact value of V_1 is determined by the pressure altitude of the aerodrome, the ambient temperature, the aeroplane weight, the aeroplane flap setting, the runway slope, the wind component and the relative lengths of TORA, ASDA and TODA.

Therefore V_1 can never be less than V_{MCG}, plus the speed increase to the first means of retardation is applied, and must not exceed either V_R or V_{MBE}. It is the maximum speed at which the pilot must take the first action to stop the aeroplane within ASDA and is the minimum speed at which the pilot can continue the take-off and achieve screen height within TODA, following a failure of the critical engine.

If the actual TOW is less than the field-length limited TOW then a range of V_1s is possible. The lowest V_1 is restricted by either TORA or TODA whichever is limiting. This may be referred to as V_{GO}, which is the lowest decision speed from which a continued take-off is possible within TODA. The highest V_1 of the range is called V_{STOP} and is the highest decision speed from which the aeroplane can safely stop within the accelerate/stop distance available (ASDA). *AMJ 25X1591 b. Note.*

Should an engine fail *before* attaining V_1 then the *take-off must be abandoned* because there is insufficient airspeed to successfully complete the take-off. If an engine should fail *after* accomplishing V_1 then the *take-off should normally be continued* because there is insufficient distance remaining to safely stop the aeroplane before reaching the end of the stopway. It is only when an engine fails exactly at V_1 that the pilot must decide on the course of action to be implemented. A sensible pilot will not have waited for the event to occur before making the decision. Before leaving the briefing room a decision should have been made on the procedure to adopt in the event of such an occurrence. This decision will be based on the state of the runway, the state of the stopway, the cloud base, any turbulence and the visibility that obtains at the time of take-off.

Some pilots mistakenly use the term 'balanced V_1' when the TORR is equal in length to TODR. These are not the distances which have to be equal for a balanced situation to exist but those of ASDA and TODA. The use of such a term for which there is no official definition or recognition should be discouraged.

If the V_1 used for take-off is greater than the calculated value then the associated guarantees are invalidated. The option to abandon take-off is no longer available and in the event of an engine failure then the take-off must be continued. A recent accident in the Far East highlighted the point that in the event of an engine failure the take-off should not be abandoned after V_1 has been attained. In this accident the pilot abandoned take-off at V_R and as a consequence destroyed the aeroplane and caused a large number of fatalities.

Note that V_1 only accounts an engine failure on take-off not a structural failure. Two recent accidents of note involved a failure of the engine pylon at the speed of V_R when an engine became detached from the aeroplane. In each case the pilot sensibly abandoned take-off and caused minimal damage to the aircraft.

V_1 is affected by the variables in the following manner:

(1) **Weight.** As weight increases the speed required to develop enough lift to counteract the weight increases thus the speed must be increased to enable the continued take-off to be an option but this is restricted by its ability to stop in the available distance.
(2) **Density.** If the air density decreases as a result of increased pressure altitude and/or ambient temperature then the speed must be increased to develop sufficient lift, again this will be tempered by the stopping distance available.
(3) **Flap setting.** Increasing the flap setting will increase the lift developed and enable V_1 to be reduced for any given set of conditions.
(4) **Runway slope.** Because a component of the aeroplane weight increases the drag force then at maximum take-off power a higher V_1 will have to be

attained with an uphill slope so that sufficient thrust is generated to counteract the drag force and enough lift is developed for the continued take-off case to remain an option. Furthermore, in the abandoned take-off case, in such circumstances the uphill runway slope will assist the aeroplane to stop because of the increased drag force caused by the rearward component of the weight which will enable the higher V_1 to comply with the requirement of being able to stop the aeroplane within the length of the available stopway. A downhill slope requires V_1 to be decreased.

(5) **Wind component.** The effect that wind component has on the value of V_1 is attributable to the abandoned take-off case. A tailwind will increase the distance travelled in stopping the aeroplane. Therefore, V_1 must be at a lower speed than in the still air case because ASDA is a fixed distance. A headwind will assist in stopping the aeroplane in the event of an abandoned take-off, thus V_1 can be a higher value than in still air, if the other conditions remain the same.

V_R This is the speed at which, in both the all engines operating case and the one-engine-inoperative configurations, the pilot should initiate a change to the aeroplane attitude on the ground run, by raising the nose-wheel and rotating the aircraft about its lateral axis. Its exact value varies with TOW, flap setting, pressure altitude and ambient air temperature. It may *not* be less than:

(1) V_1
(2) 105% V_{MC}
(3) The speed required to attain V_2 by screen height
(4) The speed required to ensure that V_{LOF} is 110% V_{MU} with all engines operating and not less than 105% V_{MU} with one-engine-inoperative, except that if lift-off is limited by the geometry of the aeroplane or by elevator power the margins are reduced to 108% with all engines operating and 104% with one-engine-inoperative. *JAR 25.107(e).*

The effects the variables will have on V_R are as follows:

(1) **Weight.** An increase of weight causes the V_R to increase. This is because more lift is required to counteract the heavier weight which must be derived from the forward speed. Thus the speed must be increased to produce the required lift.
(2) **Density.** Decreased density produces decreased lift. Therefore, for any given weight the speed must be increased to produce the required lift with decreased density.
(3) **Flap setting.** An increase of flap angle increases the lift generated, Therefore, for any given weight the rotation speed will decrease with increased flap angle.
(4) **Runway slope.** This has no effect on the value of V_R.
(5) **Wind component.** This has no effect on the value of V_R.

Rotation For all aeroplane types there is a rotation rate which is 'natural'. The rotation rate will vary according to the weight and flap setting. In ambient conditions that produce high aeroplane performance (i.e. low weight, low altitude and low temperature) the rotation rate is increased and in low performance conditions it is reduced. The correct attitude required for the aeroplane to leave the ground is the same for all weights for that type of aeroplane. Although, as with everything in scheduled performance, a safety factor is included in all speeds, distances and heights, if the calculations are to remain valid then *it is essential that rotation is made at the correct speed, at the correct rate to the correct attitude.*

Over rotation   Rotating the aeroplane at a rate faster than that required for the conditions can lead to 'ground stalling' the aeroplane. In other words, attaining a high angle of attack at low speed on the ground which will not generate sufficient lift to enable the aeroplane to leave the ground. A 'snatch' rotation will achieve the same result. Apart from the fact that there is a strong possibility of damaging the rear end of the aeroplane by 'tail dragging' the aeroplane will not leave the ground at the scheduled V_{LOF}, if it leaves the ground at all. Should the take-off be abandoned in these circumstances, which it shouldn't be after V_1 is attained but there is no choice, then there will be insufficient distance remaining to bring the aeroplane safely to a halt before the end of the stopway is reached. However, should the take-off be continued in such circumstances then not only may the aeroplane stagger into the air at a speed perilously close to stalling speed, but also the gradient and rate of climb attained would be dangerously low and any obstacle encountered after take-off may not be cleared by the statutory minimum.

Despite the fact that rotation may be initiated at the correct speed, *over rotation will cause a low climbing speed, a low gradient of climb and a low rate of climb or if the take-off is abandoned increase the stopping distance.*

Under rotation   Even if rotation is made at the correct speed, should the rotation rate be too slow, despite the fact that it may eventually attain the correct attitude, it will nullify the scheduled performance calculations. A longer ground distance will be taken from the brakes release point to V_{LOF} bringing the aeroplane not only nearer to the end of TORA, ASDA and TODA but also closer to any obstacles that have to be avoided after take-off.

Early rotation   Notwithstanding the fact that the aeroplane is rotated at the correct rate to the correct attitude, if it is rotated before the correct speed is reached then it will take a longer ground run to reach V_{LOF}. However, if early rotation is combined with either over or under rotation it will simply aggravate the situation using an even longer ground run.

Late rotation   This has a similar effect to that of early rotation and extends the ground distance taken to reach V_{LOF} with its associated consequences.

V_{MU} This is the CAS at and above which the aeroplane can safely lift off the ground, to continue the take-off and climb to screen height without undue hazard. It is the lowest unstick speed for any set of conditions. *JAR 25.107(d).*

V_{LOF} The CAS at which the aeroplane first becomes airborne for a specified set of conditions. If the aeroplane is rotated at V_R the main wheels should lift-off the ground at V_{LOF} in the ambient conditions. It is sometimes referred to as V_{US} or unstick speed and has a fixed relationship to V_R. Therefore, it varies in value in accordance with the density, weight and flap setting in the same manner as V_R. *JAR 25.107(f)*.

V_{MBE} This is the maximum brake energy speed which is the highest speed from which the aeroplane on the ground can be safely brought to a halt in the prevailing conditions, within the brake energy capabilities of the aeroplane braking system. This limitation is caused by the maximum operating temperature of the brake system, which is usually between 450°C and 500°C. At temperatures above this maximum the efficiency of the system is impaired and in the event of an abandoned take-off will fail to stop the aeroplane in the distance available. For this reason the brake temperature should be checked to be within safe limits before take-off.

Any condition which causes the temperature of the system to increase will exacerbate the situation. Thus the V_{MBE} limit on TOW is likely to be imposed for a take-off in conditions of low air density, downhill runway slope and tailwind component. Low air density will cause the conversion of CAS to TAS to realize a high value and consequently a high groundspeed. Furthermore, because low air density produces a low thrust force forward the ground run necessary to achieve the required CAS for V_R and V_{LOF} is increased in length. Thus, the high groundspeed is present over a long ground run resulting in an increased rotational velocity of the wheels and increased tyre and, if applied, brake system temperatures. Taking off downhill and/or downwind will cause the limiting speed and temperature to be reached that much sooner in the ground run. To prevent the maximum temperature being exceeded in the event of an abandoned take-off the TOW may have to be reduced should the combination of conditions show this to be likely.

V_1 may not exceed V_{MBE}, because V_1 implies that the pilot can elect to abandon the take-off and is guaranteed to be able to safely stop the aeroplane by the end of ASDA. If V_1 exceeds V_{MBE} this guarantee is invalidated. So V_1 must be reduced to comply with the requirement.

The value of V_{MBE} is affected by the weight, pressure altitude, air temperature, runway slope and wind component.

(1) **Weight.** If the weight is increased the value of V_{MBE} decreases and vice-versa. Heavy weights produce high brake temperatures.
(2) **Density.** At low aerodrome pressure altitudes and for low ambient air temperatures the value of V_{MBE} increases. However, in a normal atmosphere a 2000 ft increase of pressure altitude will result in a decrease of air temperature of 4°C. The change of altitude has by far the greater affect on V_{MBE}, decreasing it by approximately six times the increase brought about by the change of temperature.
(3) **Flap setting.** The value of V_{MBE} is not affected by the flap setting.
(4) **Runway slope.** Uphill slope assists in stopping the aeroplane in the event of an abandoned take-off. Therefore, this allows the V_{MBE} to be a higher value than on a level runway and enables take-off to be made at a higher weight. A downhill slope requires the value of V_{MBE} to be reduced to less than the level runway value because the aeroplane is more difficult to stop in the event of an abandoned take-off.

(5) **Wind component.** Similar reasoning may be used for a headwind as that for an uphill slope except when calculating the value of V_{MBE} only 50% of the benefit of any headwind may be used but 150% of any tailwind impairment must be used. This factorization of the wind component is normally already accounted in any graph or table used to calculate the speed.

V_2 Commonly referred to as the free air safety speed, V_2 is the speed to which the aeroplane, with one-engine-inoperative, must naturally accelerate after rotating at V_R and lifting off at V_{LOF} appropriate to the prevailing conditions. In terms of CAS it must enable the aeroplane to attain at least the minimum permissible gradient of climb in the second segment of the take-off net flight path (NFP). It is the lowest speed at which it is deemed safe to climb the aeroplane and may not be less than:

- V_{2min}; and
- V_R plus the speed increment attained before reaching 35 ft. *JAR 25.107(c).*

V_2 is not the most efficient climb speed – it is simply the lowest CAS at which it is safe to climb and that which will attain the gradient requirements of the NFP. The climb speed that will produce the highest climb gradient is V_X and for the greatest rate of climb the speed to use is V_Y.

The value of V_2 is affected by the aeroplane weight, the ambient air density and the flap setting. It has a variable relationship with V_R. The effect of the variables is as follows:

(1) **Weight.** An increase of weight requires an increase in the value of V_2, because a greater forward speed is necessary to generate sufficient lift to counterbalance the increased weight and maintain the minimum climb gradient required. For a reduced weight the reverse is true.
(2) **Density.** The effect an increase of altitude has is to decrease the air density which decreases the thrust produced and the natural acceleration from V_R so that the speed increment is reduced. Hence, V_2 decreases with increased altitude. The theoretical reason for this is the same as that given for V_{MC} and V_{MCG}. A temperature increase without a change of altitude has the same effect but to a lesser extent. Therefore, in a normal atmosphere, the combined effect of an increase of altitude and a decrease of temperature is to reduce the value of V_2 by a relatively small amount.
(3) **Flap setting.** An increased flap setting angle produces an increase in the lift generated and therefore enables the aeroplane to climb at the required gradient at a lower CAS. Lower flap settings at the same weight require a higher CAS to develop sufficient lift to attain the required minimum gradient of climb.
(4) **Runway slope.** The value of V_2 is unaffected by runway slope.
(5) **Wind component.** This does not affect the value of V_2.

V_{2min} Is the lowest speed that V_2 may be in any ambient conditions or any configuration. In terms of CAS V_{2min} may not be less than:

(1)   1.2Vs for:
  (a)   Two- and three-engined turbo-propeller aeroplanes and
  (b)   Turbo-jet aeroplanes without provisions for obtaining a significant reduction in the one-engine-inoperative stalling speed.
(2)   1.15Vs for:
  (a)   Four-engined turbo-propeller aeroplanes and
  (b)   Turbo-jet aeroplanes having provisions for obtaining a signifcant reduction in the one-engine-inoperative stalling speed.
(3)   1.10V$_{MC}$. *JAR 25.107(b).*

V_3 The steady initial climb speed with all engines operating at screen height is called V$_3$. *JAR 1 page 16*. It is the speed to which the aeroplane must naturally accelerate after V$_{LOF}$, if it does *not* suffer an engine failure. Its value is usually V$_2$ + 10 kts and is, therefore, affected by the variables in the same manner as V$_2$.

Two variables not often considered as such are the air conditioning system (ACS) and anti-icing system either of which, when switched on, bleed air from the engines. This reduces the efficiency of the engines and therefore reduces the amount of thrust developed. Their use, therefore, diminishes the performance of the engines and the aeroplane.

Table 18.1 shows the effect that each of the variables has on the take-off speeds. The first column is the datum column with which the following eight columns, in which just the boxed variable has been changed, should be compared to determine the effect on the speeds. In the remaining columns an increasing number of variables have been changed to compare with the second datum.

18.3 TAKE-OFF LENGTHS

Take-off Run (TOR)   The distance from the brakes release point to V$_{LOF}$ is the take-off run. The length of the TOR is increased beyond its still air value on a hard, level surface by:

(1)   Increased weight.
(2)   Uphill runway slope.
(3)   Tailwind component.
(4)   Increased air temperature.
(5)   Increased aerodrome pressure altitude.
(6)   ACS packs on.
(7)   Decreased flap setting.
(8)   Surface contamination.
(9)   Any combination of 1 to 8.

The TOR is decreased by the reverse of the above.

Accelerate/stop Distance   The distance measured from the brakes release point to the point at which the aeroplane is brought to a complete standstill, having suffered an engine failure and having abandoned the take-off. The length of ASD is

Table 18.1 The effect of the variables on take-off speeds.

	Datum									Datum			
Variables													
Tow (1000 kg)	100	120	100	100	100	100	100	100	100	100	100	100	100
Pres Alt.	MSL	MSL	4000 ft	MSL	MSL	MSL	MSL	MSL	MSL	4000 ft	4000 ft	4000 ft	4000 ft
Amb Temp (°C)	+15	+15	+15	+40	+15	+15	+15	+15	+15	+40	+40	+40	+40
Flap (°)	5	5	5	5	15	5	5	5	5	5	15	15	15
R/W Slope (%)	0	0	0	0	0	2D	2U	0	0	0	0	2D	2D
Wind Comp. (kts)	0	0	0	0	0	0	0	15T	40H	0	0	0	15T
Speeds													
V_{MCG} CAS (kts)	113	113	109	112	113	113	113	113	113	104	104	104	104
V_{MC} CAS (kts)	116	116	111	115	116	116	116	116	116	105	105	105	105
V_1 CAS (kts)	133	143	134	134	124	132	135	130	135	132	127	125	121
V_R CAS (kts)	135	145	136	136	126	135	135	135	135	137	127	127	127
V_2 CAS (kts)	145	154	144	144	134	145	145	145	145	143	133	133	133
V_2 TAS (kts)	145	154	155	151	134	145	145	145	145	161	150	150	150

Key: D = Down; U = Up; T = Tailwind; H = Headwind.

increased by the same factors as the TOR except downhill slope increases ASD and uphill slope decreases ASD. Additionally if V_1 is increased the ASD is increased in length.

Take-off Distance   This is the distance from the brakes release point to the point at which screen height is attained. It is affected by the variables in exactly the same manner as the TOR, except, the increases and decreases are proportionately less than those of the TOR for runway slope and for flap setting.

18.4 THE V_1/V_R RATIO

As has been shown, V_1 is decison speed and V_R is rotation speed. The values of both V_1 and V_R are affected by weight, air density, flap setting and the ACS packs. However, V_1 is additionally influenced by the runway slope, the wind component and the relative lengths of the available distances, TORA, ASDA and TODA.
   It is common practice to use the ratio of V_1 to V_R as a means of determining the field-length-limited (FLL) TOW and the associated V speeds. The additional variables that affect V_1 therefore influence the value of the V_1/V_R Ratio. Table 18.2 shows how each of these factors affects the V_1/V_R Ratio. Once again the left column is the datum and should be used for comparison. It will be seen that a headwind increases the V_1/V_R Ratio and a tailwind decreases the ratio. The effect the relative values of TORA, ASDA and TODA have on the ratio is shown by the last three columns. However, as you will have realized the combination of the three relative distances is infinitely variable and only an example can be shown of the likely result. The exact effect can only be determined by using the precise value of each of the distances in any calculation.

18.5 SCREEN HEIGHT

This is the height of an imaginary screen placed at the end of the TODR or at the beginning of the LDR which an aeroplane with the *wings level* and the *undercarriage extended* would just clear.

18.6 CLIMB SPEEDS

Vx   This is the term generally used to describe the CAS at which the highest gradient of climb will be achieved after reaching screen height during the take-off procedure and therefore provides the maximum vertical separation from obstacles during the take-off climb. It is affected by the variables in precisely the same manner as V_R.

Vy   The CAS used to obtain the highest rate of climb is commonly referred to as V_Y. After reaching screen height in the take-off procedure it is the speed that should be used instead of V_3 if the goal is to obtain the greatest rate of climb possible. The variables affect this speed in exactly the same way as they do V_R. *JAR 1 page 16.*

Table 18.2 The effect of the variables on the V$_1$/V$_R$ ratio.

	Datum								
TORA (m)	3000	3000	300	3000	3000	3000	3000	3000	3000
EMDA (m)	3000	3000	3000	3000	3000	3000	3500	3000	3500
TODA (m)	3000	3000	3000	3000	3000	3000	3000	3500	3500
Wind Comp. (kts)	0	20 H	20 T	0	0	0	0	0	0
R/W Slope (%)	0	0	0	2 UP	2 DOWN	0	0	0	0
ACS	OFF	OFF	OFF	OFF	OFF	ON	OFF	OFF	OFF
CEMDA (m)	3000	3320	1910	2840	3060	2950	3500	3000	3500
D'Value (m)	2910	3170	2150	2540	3230	2840	3040	3098	3230
V$_1$/V$_R$ Ratio	0.92	0.932	0.849	0.95	0.891	0.921	0.97	0.899	0.948
TOW (1000 kg)	203	211	176	191	213	201	207	208	213

Variable

Key: H = Headwind; T = Tailwind.

V_4 The steady take-off climb speed with all engines operating which must be attained before reaching minimum flap retraction height is referred to as V_4. It is the minimum speed in this configuration that will ensure the gross flight path attained is no less a gradient than that from which the minimum acceptable net gradients were derived. It is often used as the speed required for noise abatement procedures after take-off. It is never less than $1.2V_{MC}$ or $1.3V_{MS_1}$.

CHAPTER 19

Landing Speeds

The variables affect the landing speeds in a similar manner to the take-off speeds.

V_{LE} This is the maximum speed that the aeroplane may be flown with the undercarriage (landing gear) extended.

V_{LO} This is the maximum speed at which the undercarriage may be lowered.

19.1 CONTROL SPEEDS

V_{MCL} This is the minimum control speed during the approach to land with all engines operating; it is never less than the CAS at which it is possible:

(1) With the critical engine inoperative, and its propeller, if applicable, feathered and the remaining engines producing maximum take-off power or thrust:
   (a) To maintain straight flight using no more than 5° of bank.
   (b) To roll through 20° from straight flight away from the inoperative engine in five seconds.
(2) As for 1(b) but in a 5% gradient of descent in 3.5 seconds.
(3) To recover control without reducing power. *JAR 25.149(f)*.

V_{MCL_1} The minimum control speed during the landing approach with one engine inoperative. The conditions are exactly the same as for V_{MCL}. *JAR 25.149(g)*.

V_{MCL_2} For three-engined and four-engined aeroplanes it is the minimum control speed during the landing approach with two engines inoperative. The conditions are exactly the same as for V_{MCL}. *JAR 25.149(h)*.

The values of the minimum control speeds are only influenced by the density of the air and then to a very minor extent. Generally, most manufacturers specify a single speed for all weights and air densities.

Discontinued approach speed Sometimes referred to as the 'approach climb' speed is the discontinued approach speed in the one-engine-inoperative configuration, with the undercarriage retracted and the remaining live engines set at the available take-off power or thrust at the maximum landing weight. It may never exceed 1.5Vs and will attain a minimum gradient of climb of 2.1% for a twin-engined aeroplane, 2.4% for a three-engined aeroplane or 2.7% for a four-engined aeroplane when the approach is discontinued from decision height. Its value is affected by the ambient air density, increasing slightly with an increase in density. *JAR 25.121(d).*

Landing climb speed This is the climbing speed for an aeroplane in the landing configuration with all engines operating at the thrust or power developed eight seconds after selecting take-off power. It is:

(1) Not less than V_{MCL}.
(2) Not more than the greater of $1.3V_S$ and V_{MCL}.
(3) $1.15V_S$ for four-engined aeroplanes on which the application of power significantly reduces stalling speed or $1.2V_S$ for all other aeroplanes. *JAR 25.119.*

It is the speed to be flown for the initial part of the climb after an abandoned landing attempt and will produce a steady gradient of climb of 3.2% or more. This gradient determines the landing WAT limit which, as for take-off, increases in a dense atmosphere and vice-versa. It is affected by the flap setting which decreases the WAT limited landing weight with increased flap angle. It is affected by the variables in precisely the same way as V_2.

V_{REF} The reference landing speed of an aeroplane is that which it attains in a specified landing configuration at the point where it descends through the landing screen height in the determination of the landing distance for a manual landing. *JAR 1 page 11.* This used to be referred to as V_{AT_0}, with all-engines-operating, and is not permitted to be less than $1.3V_{S_0}$ following a steady gradient of descent of not greater than 5%.

Landing approach speed The speed at which a stabilized approach is maintained in the final approach to a height of 50 ft. It is never less than $1.3V_S$. *JAR 25.125(a)(2).*

V_T This is the threshold speed. It is the speed that the pilot aims to cross the threshold and is an average speed calculated for conditions of light winds and slight turbulence. Its value is determined by the air density, the aeroplane weight and flap setting. The speed is decreased with decreased weight, increased density and increased flap setting either individually or together. *JAR 1 page 15.*

$V_{T_{max}}$ This is the maximum value that the threshold speed may be in any condition or configuration. *JAR 1 page 15.*

Although the following speeds are no longer defined in JARs they are still to be found in some Flight Manuals. V_{REF} is now used in place of them.

V_{AT} This is the target threshold speed and is that which the pilot aims to cross the threshold at screen height when landing. It is an average speed calculated for conditions of light winds and slight turbulence, and is determined by the aeroplane weight and flap setting. It may be used for any configuration of the engines, such as

V_{AT_0} for all-engines-operating, V_{AT_1} for one-engine-inoperative and V_{AT_2} for two-engines-inoperative.

V_{AT_0} The target threshold speed for an all-engines-operating approach which is not less than $1.3V_{S_0}$ following a steady descent to screen height of not greater than 5%.

V_{AT_1} The target threshold speed for a one-engine-inoperative approach and is never less than V_{AT_0}.

CHAPTER 20
Performance Calculations and Limitations

20.1 PERFORMANCE CALCULATIONS

The four phases of any flight are take-off, take-off climb, cruise and landing. For each phase there is a set of operating regulations in JAR-OPS and a set of minimum acceptable performance criteria specified in JAR 25 or JAR 23.

The data provided in the AFM by the manufacturers are based on the assumption that the aeroplane is fully serviceable and is operated in accordance with the recommended techniques and power settings. It is further assumed that it is operating on a hard, dry, level runway with a co-efficient of friction of 0.5 or greater in still-air.

If any of these assumptions are incorrect, due allowance must be made for them in the performance computations. Usually all take-off and landing graphs include grids which apply the effect of runway slope, wind component and the use of the air conditioning system and the anti-ice system. However, separate graphs are normally provided to account any other irregularity such as a very slippery surface, anti-skid system unserviceable, reverse thrust inoperative and high lift devices inoperative. If any of these abnormalities are present at take-off then the ASDR is increased, only the unserviceability of the high lift devices will increase the TODR.

If the pilot uses a rolling technique to line-up and start the take-off whilst applying power, instead of a stationary start and applying full power against the brakes, then all the calculations will be invalidated. This is because some of the available distance is used up during the period that the engines are 'spooling up' to maximum take-off power and the calculations assume full take-off power over the whole distance available.

The take-off stage of flight is defined as that phase which commences at the beginning of the take-off run and ends at a screen height of 35 ft. Factors which affect the safe performance of an aircraft *before* take-off and which therefore need consideration are covered in this chapter. Their very nature means that they are unrelated to one another except for the fact that each can individually constitute a performance limitation.

For take-off, the manufacturers in the data provided assumed that the aeroplane would be lined up and held against the brakes whilst the take-off power setting is selected. If this is not done and a rolling start to take-off is made then any calculation made is invalidated. When the correct technique is used the maximum take-off power for a jet engine or the maximum efficiency of the propellers for propeller-driven aeroplanes is achieved between 40 and 80 kts during the take-off run. The

152

distance taken to accelerate during take-off is directly affected by the flap setting, the angle of attack and the thrust/weight ratio. An increase of flap setting, angle of attack or weight will increase the acceleration distance. During the take-off run it is normal for jet engine thrust to diminish very slightly due to ram effect, which reduces the thrust/weight ratio and also will increase the acceleration distance.

The importance of V_1 has already been stressed in Chapter 18. If V_1 is miscalculated and is lower than the correct value then both ASDR and TODR will be less than their true values. If the miscalculated V_1 is higher the reverse is true.

Should an aerodrome have a stopway and/or a clearway available then this enables the field-length-limited TOW to be higher than it would be without these distances. A stopway permits a longer ASDR and a clearway allows a longer TODR than would be the case for a balanced field. If the field-lengths are unbalanced then using balanced field graphs unnecessarily restrict the TOW to a value lower than that which is legally permitted. The V_1 associated with this weight will also be below the correct value for the unbalanced distances.

If the actual TOW is less than the calculated field-length-limited TOW a range of V_1s is available for use. The minimum is limited by TODA and the maximum by ASDA. Using a V_1 below the optimum will reduce the accelerate/stop distance, whereas using a value higher than the optimum will reduce the take-off distance.

Remember, an *available* distance is that which is published in the Aeronautical Information Publication (AIP) and does not change. A *required* distance is a calculated distance which results from the application of the effects of the variables and the minimum performance requirements. It is therefore a net distance. A distance unqualified by a suffix (e.g. TOR, ASD or TOD) is the actual distance taken by an aeroplane in the specified configuration and operating in the prevailing conditions, and is therefore a gross distance.

20.2 LIMITATIONS

The Certificate of Airworthiness issued for a particular aircraft type states the manner in which the aircraft must be flown and the purpose for which it may be used. The weight limitations stated therein are absolute if the maker's guarantee of performance and handling is to remain valid. Under exceptional circumstances the manufacturers and the JAA together may grant permission to exceed any particular limiting weight – in which case the stated performance will almost certainly not be achieved. All Classes of public transport aeroplanes are subject to the following restrictions.

20.2.1 Structural limitations

The maximum permitted weights for take-off, for landing and for the aeroplane without usable fuel, the zero fuel weight, are all absolute values which are specified in the AFM. If any one of these limitations is ignored it could have disastrous consequences. If it is permissible to exceed the maximum normal TOW, a maximum overload weight will be quoted in the Flight Manual. There is no guaranteed performance for this weight, but if this limitation is exceeded, there is a real danger of structural failure. Only the maximum landing weight may be exceeded without prior permission being obtained, and then only in an emergency.

The effects of overloading include:

(1)   Reduced acceleration and increased take-off speeds.
(2)   Longer take-off run and take-off distance.
(3)   Decreased gradient and rate of climb.
(4)   Increased difficulty in clearing obstacles by the statutory minimum after take-off.
(5)   Imposition of excessive loads on the undercarriage, especially if the runway is rough.
(6)   Reduced ceiling and reduced range.
(7)   Impaired manoeuvrability and controllability.
(8)   Increased stalling speeds.
(9)   Increased landing speeds requiring a longer runway.
(10) Decreased brake effectiveness, particularly on surfaces having a low coefficient of friction.
(11) Reduced structural strength margins.
(12) Inability to climb or maintain height after engine failure on a multi-engined aeroplane.
(13) Possibility of exceeding the brake energy and/or the tyre speed limitation.

20.2.2 The centre of gravity envelope

The centre of gravity (CG) is that point on the longitudinal axis through which all of the aircraft weight acts vertically downward. The centre of gravity must remain within the safe limits defined by the manufacturers. The area between the maximum forward and aft safe limits is referred to as the C of G envelope. The position of the C of G for take-off is fixed by the distribution of the load and the fuel. In flight the location of the C of G can be manipulated by using the fuel in a particular sequence from various tanks or by transferring fuel between tanks.

It is usual to position the C of G toward the aft limit for take-off to assist rotation at V_R. In the cruise the fuel should be managed in such a manner that the C of G is positioned just forward of the aft limit of the envelope. This is often referred to as 'flying the flat aeroplane' because trim drag is minimized. If, in these circumstances, the power setting remains unchanged the TAS will increase and improve the maximum range. However, if the requirement is to increase the endurance the TAS should be kept constant and the power reduced, which will reduce the fuel flow. For landing the C of G should be moved forward. Exceeding the limits of the C of G envelope can have serious consequences.

(1)   Exceeding the forward limit may result in:
    (a)   Difficulty in rotating during take-off.
    (b)   Increased stalling speed.
    (c)   Greater induced drag which increases fuel consumption and reduces range.
    (d)   Insufficient nose-up trim available during approach to land making a stable approach difficult.

(e) Difficulty in flaring and holding the nose-wheel off the ground at touch down.

(f) Increased load on the nose wheel.

(2) Exceeding the aft limit usually results in:

(a) Premature rotation on take-off.

(b) Inadvertent stall in the climb.

(c) Trimming difficulties especially at high power settings.

(d) Longitudinal instability, particularly in turbulence.

(e) Degraded stall qualities.

20.2.3 Crosswind limitation

The displacement of aircraft control surfaces to maintain the runway track during the take-off run produces drag on some aircraft (e.g. Boeing 707) which reduces the acceleration up to V_R. However, it is the size of the fin and rudder and the length of the fuselage that determines how large the counteracting moment generated will be, to oppose the weathercocking tendency of the aeroplane in a crosswind. The maximum value of crosswind that can be adequately counteracted without adversely affecting performance or handling is quoted in the Aeroplane Flight Manual.

It is a legal requirement that an aerodrome in the UK should have sufficient runways (marked as such), to ensure that on not less than 97% of occasions there is at least one direction of take-off and landing available with a crosswind component acceptable for the types of aeroplane likely to use the aerodrome. This usually means that the maximum crosswind experienced at most major aerodromes is 20 kts. If the physical geography does not allow the main runway to be constructed into the prevailing wind, the maximum permissible crosswind for flying operations for the aerodrome may be reduced by the licensing authority. The safety factorization imposed by JAR-OPS on the use of the along track wind component, i.e. 50% of a headwind and 150% of a tailwind, loses its effectiveness with 90° crosswinds.

20.2.4 Brake-energy limitation

The energy absorption capability of the aircraft braking system has a design limitation, usually a maximum operating temperature of between 450°C and 500°C, beyond which it will fail to stop the aircraft in the distance available. The ability of the braking system to stop an aircraft decreases with an increase of altitude, and/or temperature, and/or weight, and with a tailwind and/or downhill slope, so the design limitation is reached sooner. This limitation is normally related to the aircraft's speed and is referred to as V_{MBE}. Decision speed, V_1 must never exceed V_{MBE}. If it does, the AUW must be reduced until $V_1 = V_{MBE}$.

V_{MBE} is a design limitation on the take-off run itself; but if the aircraft has had a period of prolonged taxi-ing and an insufficient time for the brakes to cool before commencing the take-off run, the brake temperatures will already be fairly high. This will reduce their energy absorption capacity, and is a factor which cannot be accurately scheduled.

20.2.5 Tyre speed limitation

With the increased weights and speeds of modern transport aircraft, tyre temperatures can become very high. Most tyres are fitted with fusible plugs which give protection against overpressure due to high wheel temperatures caused by excessive braking. Every type of tyre has a maximum speed specified in the Flight Manual to ensure that at maximum TOW the temperature generated remains within safe limits. Thus V_{LOF} converted to a groundspeed is the critical speed.

A graph is provided in the Flight Manual on which the maximum tyre speed is clearly annotated. The graph combines the entries of aerodrome pressure altitude, air temperature and wind speed to enable the maximum TOW to be calculated. If this weight is lower than is that dictated by any of the other considerations, it becomes the limiting TOW. It follows then that the most adverse conditions for the tyre speed limitation are a high elevation aerodome, a high surface temperature and a tailwind. The tyre limiting speed is sometimes, incorrectly, referred to as V_{TIRE}.

20.2.6 Practical considerations

When the actual TOW is less than the field-length limited TOW a range of V_{1}s is available, the lowest value being limited by TODA or V_{MCG} whichever produces the higher restriction and the highest value by ASDA or V_R whichever causes the lower restriction. The lowest value is normally used by jet aircraft, because of the large excess of power available over power required, the higher value is usually used by turbo-prop aeroplanes that do not have this excess of power.

For an aerodrome with unbalanced field distances the V_1 will be higher than the V_1 for the same aerodrome if the field distances are balanced. Using a V_1 below the balanced distance V_1 ensures that there is ample distance in which to stop the aircraft if the take-off has to be abandoned. However, this distance is reduced if the V_1 used is greater than the balanced field V_1. The actual take-off distance is affected by the acceleration from V_1 with one-engine-inoperative to reach V_R, which is determined by the TOW. This distance will be greater than that for a balanced field if the V_1 used is lower than the balanced field V_1 and less if the V_1 used is greater. The reverse is true for the accelerate/stop distance.

20.2.7 Noise abatement procedures

The procedure to be adopted after take-off to ensure the aircraft noise remains at an acceptable level to those on the ground is determined by the position of the noise sensitive area to the end of TODR. Procedure 'A' is adopted if that area is some distance from the aerodrome and procedure 'B' for those areas close to the aerodrome. Both procedures have three segments.

20.2.7.1 Procedure 'A'

First segment The first segment, from screen height to 1500 feet above the aerodrome surface level, is conducted with all engines operating at take-off power/

thrust, with take-off flap set and at a speed of V_2 + 10 to 20 kts with the under-carriage retracted. The speed and configuration remain the same until 3000 ft is attained.

Second segment However at 1500 ft, where the second segment commences, the power/thrust is reduced to the climb setting and remains so until the aeroplane reaches a height of 3000 ft above the take-off surface level.

Third segment The third segment commences at 3000 ft when the aeroplane is accelerated, still climbing, until the en-route climb speed has been attained. The flaps are retracted on attainment of the appropriate speed for each setting. The climb is continued to the cruising altitude at the en-route climb speed (see Fig. 20.1).

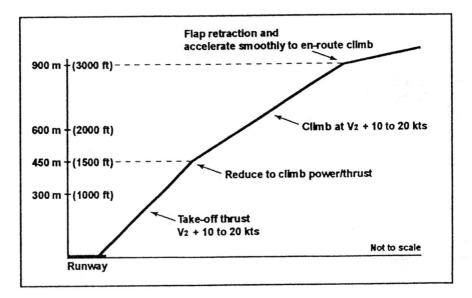

Fig. 20.1 Noise abatement procedure 'A'.

20.2.7.2 Procedure 'B'

First segment The first segment, from screen height to 1000 ft above the aero-drome surface level is conducted with all engines operating at take-off thrust/power and take-off flap set at a speed of V_2 + 10 to 20 kts.

Second segment At 1000 ft the aeroplane is accelerated to the minimum safe manoeuvring speed with zero flap, V_{ZF} and the climb continued to 3000 ft. During this segment of the climb the thrust must be reduced to normal climb thrust for high by-pass ratio engines but for low by-pass ratio engines it must be reduced to less than the normal climb thrust yet not less than that required to maintain the final segment climb gradient of the one-engine-inoperative gross flight path. For aero-planes having a slow rate of flap retraction the thrust should be reduced at an intermediate flap setting. Throughout this segment the aeroplane must continue to accelerate to V_{ZF} + 10 kts.

Third segment   On attaining 3000 ft the aeroplane is once again accelerated to the en-route climb speed and the climb continued to the cruise altitude (see Fig. 20.2).

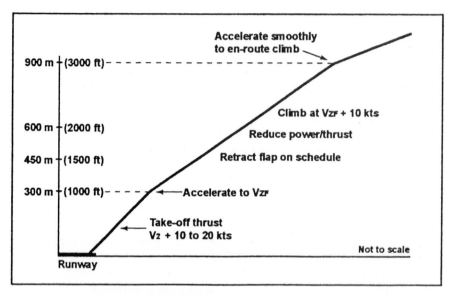

Fig. 20.2   Noise abatement procedure 'B'.

Test Paper 5

Q1. What effect does an increase of flap setting have on the lift/drag ratio?
  (a) None in a low density atmosphere.
  (b) Increase the ratio.
  (c) Decrease the ratio.
  (d) None in a high density atmosphere.

Q2. The maximum safety margin provided by V_{MC} over V_{S_0} is:
  (a) 20%.
  (b) 30%.
  (c) 40%.
  (d) 50%.

Q3. If a V_1 in excess of the calculated value is used for take-off then:
  (a) The V_1/V_R ratio is unaffected.
  (b) The continued take-off option is void.
  (c) The abandoned take-off option is void.
  (d) Both continued and abandoned take-off options are void.

Q4. V_{REF} is defined as:
  (a) The speed attained for a specific configuration on passing through screen height on landing.
  (b) The reference speed used for all manual landing distance calculations
  (c) The speed used to determine the landing distance required.
  (d) The datum speed on the ASI.

Q5. Fill in the words to correctly complete the following sentence. V_1 must never be less than ... and must not exceed ... or ... .
  (a) V_R; V_{MBE}; V_2.
  (b) V_{MCG}, V_R, V_{MBE}.
  (c) V_{MCG}, V_{MBE}, V_2.
  (d) V_R, V_{MC}, V_{MBE}.

Q6. What is the relationship between V_{EF} and V_1?
  (a) V_1 is always 3 kts after V_{EF}.
  (b) V_{EF} is always 3 s before V_1.
  (c) V_1 is approximately 2 s after V_{EF}.
  (d) V_1 is approximately 2 kts after V_{EF}.

Q7. Compared with a level runway a 2% runway upslope will cause the value of V_1 to:
  (a) Remain unchanged.
  (b) Decrease.
  (c) Increase.
  (d) Equal V_R.

Q8. Compared with still-air a tailwind will cause the value of V_1 to:
  (a) Remain unchanged.
  (b) Decrease.
  (c) Increase.
  (d) Equal V_R.

Q9. The effect an increase of TOW will have on the value of V_R is to cause it to:
  (a) Remain unchanged.
  (b) Decrease.
  (c) Increase.
  (d) Equal V_2.

Q10. An increase of aerodrome pressure altitude causes the value of V_{MCG} to:
  (a) Remain unchanged.
  (b) Decrease.
  (c) Increase.
  (d) Equal V_{MC}.

Q11. The safety margin of V_{REF} over V_{S_0} is:
  (a) 20%.
  (b) 30%.
  (c) 40%.
  (d) 50%.

Q12. V_2 is defined as:
  (a) The one-engine-inoperative free air safety speed attained at screen height.
  (b) The all-engines-operating free air safety speed attained at screen height.
  (c) The climb speed necessary to obtain the highest gradient of climb.
  (d) The climb speed necessary to obtain the highest rate of climb.

Q13. Which of the following combinations of the variables will most likely cause the take-off distance to have the greatest increase:
  (a) Headwind; downslope; high surface temperature.
  (b) Headwind; downslope; low surface temperature.
  (c) Tailwind; downslope; high surface temperature.
  (d) Tailwind; upslope; high surface temperature.

Q14. If the take-off flap setting is increased from 0° to 15° the take-off distance will most likely:
   (a) Remain unchanged.
   (b) Decrease.
   (c) Increase.
   (d) Have a longer ground run.

Q15. If the take-off flap setting is decreased from 15° to 0° the value of V$_{LOF}$ will:
   (a) Remain unchanged.
   (b) Decrease.
   (c) Increase.
   (d) Become closer to V$_R$.

Q16. The effect that an increase of aerodrome pressure altitude has on the value of V$_R$ is to cause it to:
   (a) Remain unchanged.
   (b) Decrease.
   (c) Increase.
   (d) Become closer to V$_2$.

Q17. An increase in ambient temperature will ... the gradient of climb and ... the WAT limited TOW. The words to correctly complete the sentence are:
   (a) Increase; increase.
   (b) Increase; decrease.
   (c) Decrease; increase.
   (d) Decrease; decrease.

Q18. The combination of the influencing factors that will most adversely affect the brake-energy limiting speed are:
   (a) High pressure altitude; high air temperature; runway downslope; a headwind.
   (b) High pressure altitude; high air temperature; runway downslope; a tail-wind.
   (c) High pressure altitude; low air temperature; runway downslope; a tail-wind.
   (d) Low pressure altitude; high air temperature; runway downslope; a tail-wind.

Q19. A headwind when compared with still-air will ... the take-off distance, ... the climb gradient and ... the WAT limited TOW. The words to correctly complete the above sentence are:
   (a) Increase; increase; not affect.
   (b) Increase; decrease; increase.
   (c) Decrease; increase; decrease.
   (d) Decrease; increase; not affect.

Q20. Given: Still-air gradient of climb 4%; TAS 100 kts; Groundspeed 120 kts. The wind effective climb gradient is:

   (a) 4.8%.
   (b) 4.17%.
   (c) 4.0%.
   (d) 3.3%.

PART 2

CLASS 'A' AEROPLANES: THEORY

Class 'A' aeroplanes include all multi-engined aeroplanes powered by turbo-propeller engines with a maximum approved passenger seating configuration of more than nine or a maximum take-off weight exceeding 5700 kg and all multi-engined turbo-jet aeroplanes.

The Specimen aeroplane used by JAA FCL for Class 'A' is the Medium Range Jet Transport (MRJT) and calculations for this aeroplane will require the use of CAP 698.

CHAPTER 21

Field-Length Requirements

The performance requirements for all aircraft registered in the UK are prescribed by BCARs and JARs and are based on a flight technique that ensures adequate control of the aircraft at all points during take-off in the event of a power unit failure, cross-winds or a wet runway, or for any reasonable combination of these conditions. In addition, AN(G)Rs and JARs demand that the take-off field-lengths required do *not* exceed the field-lengths available.

The maximum take-off weight that attains all these requirements is referred to as the Field-Length Limited TOW (FLL TOW).

Because safety is the paramount consideration, the most critical power unit is assumed to fail at the most unfavourable point during take-off – that is at the position where the field lengths available are *just* adequate to meet those required to both abandon the take-off and to continue the take-off. The power unit failure is further assumed to result in the complete and immediate loss of propulsive power from the affected power unit, except for that momentarily supplied by the inertia of the moving parts. No further auxiliary power is assumed to be supplied from that particular power unit either.

If such a failure should occur at the point where the field lengths available are just equal to the field lengths required, the pilot has a choice of whether to abandon or continue take-off and *must* decide which course of action to follow. Accordingly this point of distance equality is referred to as the **decision point**. Engine failure *before* this point dictates that the take-off *must be abandoned*; because although there would be sufficient ground run remaining to brake the aircraft safely to a halt, there would be insufficient distance remaining to continue the take-off and accelerate, using the reduced power available, to attain flying safety speed. If such were the case the Take-Off Distance Required (TODR) would exceed Take-Off Distance Available (TODA).

Similarly, if an engine failed *after* the decision point had been passed, the pilot has no choice but to *continue with the take-off* because the Accelerate/Stop Distance Available (ASDA) would not be long enough to bring the aircraft safely to a halt. The **decision point** is, therefore, the most crucial point at which an aircraft can suffer an engine failure during take-off.

21.1 V₁, DECISION SPEED

The most ready and reliable means of identifying decision point is the airspeed indicator. In using this instrument, the speed at the decision point is referred to as **decision speed** (V_1). *AIC 141/1998.*

Although this speed is safe in relation to the field-lengths, other factors cause additional safety limitations to be imposed on it. These are:

(1)   The lowest permitted speed for V_1 is the minimum speed on the ground at which the aircraft can be safely controlled in the event of the critical power unit failing (V_{MCG}).

(2)   The maximum speed limit for V_1 is either V_R, which is the speed at which the pilot initiates a change in the attitude of the aeroplane with the intention of becoming airborne, or V_{MBE} which is the maximum speed on the ground from which the aircraft can be safely brought to a halt within the brake energy capabilities of the aircraft, whichever is the lower.

The most important speed during take-off is therefore V_1, which must be accurately calculated. In certain circumstances it is possible to have a range of V_1 speeds from which to choose the most advantageous in the prevailing conditions, these are described in Chapter 22.

The lower speeds of the range are used if the stopway is less limiting than clearway, i.e. ASDR is less limiting than TODR. The higher speeds are utilized if the reverse is true. Thus, it is advantageous to use the higher speeds when obstacles in the take-off area make it necessary to keep TODR to a minimum.

21.1.1 V₁ 'wet'

The friction characteristics and the braking action of a wet runway are very different to those of a dry one, because the ability of an aircraft to decelerate on a wet surface decreases, and the distance required to brake it to a halt increases. Accordingly, the 'wet' value of V_1 is between 5 and 10 kts less than its value on a dry runway. Only recently has it become mandatory for the manufacturers to schedule wet runway performance figures, in accordance with JAR 25x1591, which take these facts into account. Thus separate values of V_1 are scheduled for 'wet' and 'dry' surface conditions. The actual difference between the 'dry' and 'wet' values is calculated by the manufacturers using the gross all-power-units operating acceleration and is subject to an overriding maximum time difference limitation of four seconds, imposed by the CAA.

Before it became mandatory to produce wet figures, some Regulated Take-Off Graphs (RTOGs) (see Chapter 23) were produced using V_1 dry. *If dry RTOGs are used for a wet runway, the four seconds time difference in V₁ speeds becomes a risk period should a power unit fail.* This is because the pilot, having passed V_1 wet, is committed to take-off but, not having reached V_1 dry, is not certain of being able to reach the required height by the end of TODR. The aircraft will in fact achieve a screen height of between 15 ft and 35 ft at the end of TODR.

Screen height is the height of an imaginary screen located at the end of TODR which an aircraft would *just* clear in an unbanked attitude, with the undercarriage extended.

21.2 JOINT AVIATION REQUIREMENTS – TAKE-OFF

JARs are formulated in such a manner that each of the field-length distances that has to be derived from the Flight Manual graphs is the most limiting of separate requirements. There are three sets of requirements – Take-off Run, Accelerate/Stop Distance and Take-off Distance. Thus, to produce these graphs a comparison of each requirement in a set has already been made by the manufacturers. *JAR 25.105(a),(b) & (c).*

21.2.1 Take-Off Run Required (TORR). *JAR 25.113(b)*

In the event of no clearway being available, the TORR is less limiting than the Accelerate/Stop Distance Required and therefore does not need consideration. If, however, the take-off distance includes a clearway, the **Take-Off Run Required** is the greatest of the following distances and must not exceed TORA. *JAR-OPS 1.490(b)(3):*

TORR – all-power-units-operating The total of the gross distance from the start of the take-off run to the point at which V_{LOF} (the speed at which the main wheels leave the ground if the aircraft is rotated about its lateral axis at V_R), assuming that V_{EF} is consistent with the lowest V_1 at which a continued take-off is possible within TODA, is reached, plus one half of the distance taken from V_{LOF} to the point at which the aircraft reaches a screen height of 35 ft consistent with the air-craft attaining V_4 (the steady initial climb speed with all engines operating), *by* 400 ft above reference zero, is factorized by 1.15 to obtain the all-power-units operating net TORR. This factorization ensures that the gross TORR is within 87% of TORA and is depicted in Fig. 21.1. *JAR 25.113(b)(2) & AMJ 25x1591 paragraph 3.2.1.c.ii.*

TORR – one-power-unit-inoperative (dry runway) The horizontal distance from the commencement of the take-off roll to a point equidistant between V_{LOF} and the point at which a height of 35 ft above the take-off surface is reached on a dry runway, assuming the critical power unit is inoperative at V_{EF}. This requirement is shown in Fig. 21.2. *JAR 25.113(b)(1) & JAR 25.111(a).*

TORR – one-power-unit-inoperative (wet runway) The gross horizontal distance from the commencement of the take-off roll to the point at which V_{LOF} is reached on a reference wet hard surface, assuming the critical power unit becomes inop-erative at V_{EF}, corresponding to V_{GO}, which is the lowest V_1 from which a continued take-off is possible within TODA. This requirement is shown in Fig. 21.3. *AMJ 25x1591 paragraph 3.2.1.c.i.*

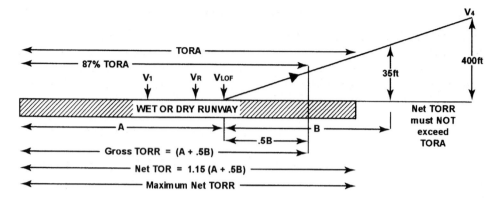

Fig. 21.1 TORR – all-power-units-operating (wet and dry runway). A = Gross Distance to V_{LOF}; B = Gross Distance from V_{LOF} to 35 ft.

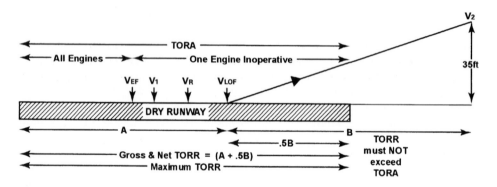

Fig. 21.2 TORR – one-engine-inoperative (dry runway). A = Gross Distance to V_{LOF}; B = Gross Distance from V_{LOF} to 35 ft.

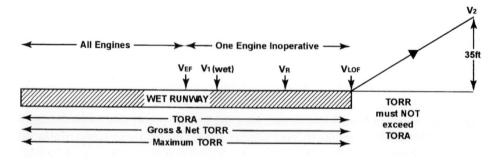

Fig. 21.3 TORR – one-engine-inoperative (wet runway).

21.2.2 Accelerate/Stop Distance Required (ASDR). *JAR 25.109.*

With the implementation of JARs a relatively new term has been introduced to performance to describe the minimum distance which the aircraft requires to come to rest in the case of an abandoned take-off. Originally termed the Emergency Distance Required it is now called the Accelerate/Stop Distance Required (ASDR). Because AN(G)Rs 7(2) and JAR-OPS 1.490(b)(1) stipulate that the distance required must not exceed that which is available then the TOW for this requirement is limited to that which is obtained when ASDR just equals ASDA.

In accordance with JAR 25.109 it is the greatest of the following four total distances:

(a) ASDR – all-engines-operating (dry hard surface) This requirement is the sum of the distances required to accelerate from a standing start with all-engines-operating to $V_1 + 2$ seconds, and to decelerate from this point to a full stop on a dry hard surface with all engines still operating. The two second time delay is that time assumed for the pilot to react and to disengage any automatic take-off thrust control system. This requirement is depicted in Fig. 21.4. *JAR 25.109(a)(2).*

(b) ASDR – all-engines-operating (wet hard surface) As for (a) except that the surface is a reference wet hard surface and the acceleration continues to $V_{STOP} + 2$ seconds. V_{STOP} is the highest V_1 from which the aeroplane can stop within ASDA. See Fig. 21.4. *AMJ 25x1591 Paragraph 3.2.1.a.ii.*

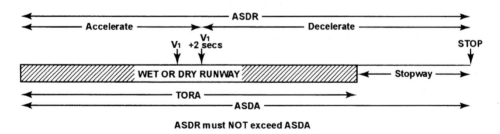

Fig. 21.4 ASDR – all-power-units-operating (wet and dry runways).

(c) ASDR – one-engine-inoperative (dry hard surface) This requirement is the sum of three distances:

(1) The distance necessary to accelerate from a standing start with all-engines-operating to V_{EF}.
(2) The distance covered in a continued acceleration for two seconds past V_1 with one-power-unit-inoperative.
(3) The distance taken to come to a full stop on a dry hard surface with one-power-unit-inoperative. See Fig. 21.5. *JAR 25.109(a)(1).*

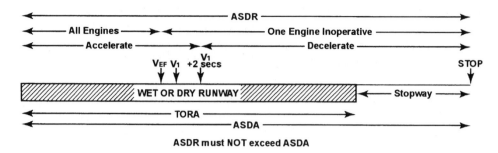

Fig. 21.5 ASDR – one-engine-inoperative (wet and dry runways).

(d) ASDR – one-engine-inoperative (wet hard surface).   The same conditions as (c) above except that the surface is a reference wet hard surface and that V1 is replaced by VSTOP (see (b) above). See Fig. 21.5. *AMJ 25x1591 Paragraph 3.2.1.a.i.*

21.2.2 Take-Off Distance Required (TODR). *JAR 25.113(a).*

Take-Off Distance Required is the total distance it takes for an aircraft to reach screen height, 35 ft above the take-off surface level, from the commencement of the take-off roll. It is stipulated that TODR is to be the greatest of the following four distances and must *not* exceed TODA. *JAR-OPS 1.490(b)(2).*

(a) TODR – all-engines-operating (dry hard surface)   This is 115% of the gross horizontal distance travelled, with all engines operating, to reach a height of 35 ft above the take-off surface level in such a manner that V4 (not less than V2 + 10 kts) is achieved by 400 ft above Reference Zero (an imaginary plane passing through a point 35 ft vertically beneath the aircraft at the end of TODR). See Fig. 21.6. *JAR 25.113(a)(2).*

(b) TODR – all-engines-operating (wet hard surface)   The same conditions as (a) except the surface is a reference wet hard surface. See Fig. 21.6. *AMJ 25x1591 paragraph 3.2.1.b.ii.*

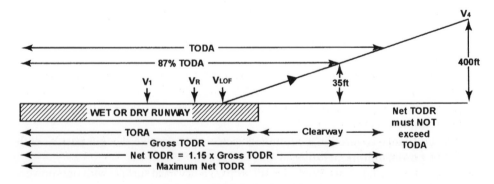

Fig. 21.6 TODR – all-power-units-operating (wet and dry runways).

(b) TODR – one-engine-inoperative (dry runway) The gross horizontal distance from the commencement of the take-off roll to the point at which the aircraft reaches 35 ft above the take-off surface level, assuming the critical power unit fails at V_{EF} on a dry, hard surface. See Fig. 21.7. *JAR 25.113(a)(1)*.

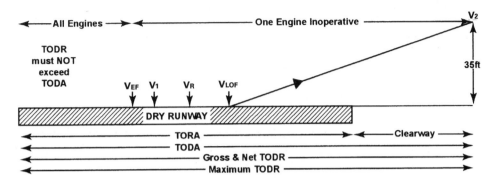

Fig. 21.7 TODR – one-engine-inoperative (dry runway).

(c) TODR – one-engine-inoperative (wet runway) The gross horizontal distance from the commencement of the take-off roll to the point at which the aircraft reaches 15 ft above the take-off surface level, assuming the critical power unit fails at V_{EF}, corresponding to V_{GO}, and a reference wet hard surface, achieved in a manner consistent with obtaining V_2 by 35 ft above the same level. See Fig. 21.8. *AMJ 25x1591 paragraph 3.2.1.b.i.*

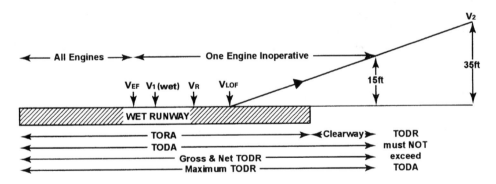

Fig. 21.8 TODR – one-engine-inoperative (wet runway).

The factorization imposed by the airworthiness requirements on the all-engines-operating TORR and TODR ensures that the probability of the net distances required exceeding the distances available is less than 10^{-6}, in the 'remote' range, using a standard deviation of 3%.

Only when an engine failure occurs at the most critical speed will the full distances available be required. The probability of this event occurring is also 'remote' and is held not to necessitate the gross distances required being factorized.

A comparison of the above two requirements is depicted in Fig. 21.9.

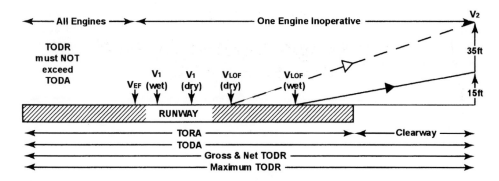

Fig. 21.9 TODR – one-engine-inoperative comparison.

CHAPTER 22
Field-Length Limited Take-off Weight Analysis

The performance requirements prescribed by the CAA achieve the desired safety standards by factorizing every condition that has to be considered, BCARs specify the legal minimum requirements for aircraft registered before July 1979, and JAR 25 for those registered after that date. *All regulations state that the Net Distances Required must never exceed the Actual Distances Available. AN(G)Rs 1981 Paragraph 7(2) and JAR-OPS 1.490(b).*

The factorization imposed by the aviation requirements is presented in the Flight Manual in such a way that the distances required in each case can be directly compared. The most limiting of them is used to calculate the field-length maximum TOW (FLL TOW). Depending on the aircraft type, this comparison may be done automatically by presenting the all-power-units operating and the one-engine-inoperative net distances together as a single distance based on the most severe case, or by separate presentation accompanied by a statement that the limiting distance required is the greater of the two distances extracted.

In some circumstances the power-unit-failure case may not limit the maximum TOW as severely as the all-engines-operating case, due to the factorization imposed. This normally occurs with older turbo-propeller aircraft and not with modern transport aircraft unless ASDA greatly exceeds TODA. With old piston-engined aircraft the engine-out TODR always exceeds the all-engines TODR, and a large margin is available for any likely variations in the all-engines take-off performance. With turbine-engined aeroplanes this is not necessarily true, because variations in performance can occur when the power/weight ratio is so high that it causes the factored all-engines TODR to be greater than the average engine-out TODR.

22.1 GENERAL

22.1.1 Continued take-off data

The net data presented in the Flight Manual are based on the gross data for all-power-units-operating at maximum take-off power up to V_{EF}, at which point the most critical engine is assumed to fail. An allowance of two seconds is included in the computations for recognition of the failure and for the crew to react by carrying out the necessary drills and procedures to maintain control of the aircraft.

From V$_{EF}$, the data are scheduled at the one-engined-inoperative maximum contingency power, except in the all-engines-operating case for which the whole take- off is scheduled at the maximum take-off power. The data presented make due allowance for the effect that the failure of a power unit has on power-operated services such as the undercarriage, and the adverse affect that the operation of other auxiliary services such as cabin pressurization, engine air cleaning and electrical loads have on the remaining power available.

Credit is taken by the manufacturers in the calculation of performance data for automatic feathering, reverse thrust, air brakes or spoilers, and a suitable allowance is made for the probability of them becoming inoperative. No allowance is made for aircraft variable cooling gills, other than the setting required for cooling dictated by the aerodrome altitude and temperature.

22.1.1 Abandoned take-off data

In the abandoned take-off case, all power units are assumed to be operating at maximum take-off power up to V$_{EF}$. From this point the power which would be automatically achieved by the live engines until the throttles are fully closed is used. If reverse thrust is a recognized technique this will also be credited, as will the use of emergency braking systems and anti-skid devices, when fitted, for use in the accelerate/stop manoeuvre.

22.1.3 Variable configuration data

For aircraft having more than one take-off flap setting and/or refrigerant power augmentation, separate performance data are scheduled in the Flight Manual for each condition. Credit for power augmentation when establishing TODR may only be taken if the aircraft carries 1.2 times the quantity of refrigerant required in the all-engines-operating case or 1.05 times the amount required in the one-engine-inoperative case, whichever is the greater. The relevant quantity can be calculated from the appropriate graph.

22.2 FIELD LENGTH REQUIREMENTS ANALYSIS

The speed of V$_1$ is dependent on many variables, including field lengths available, runway conditions, meteorological conditions and aircraft characteristics. In demonstrating the effect a change of TOW has on V$_1$, however, these factors are assumed to remain constant. For any given flap setting, both V$_R$ and V$_2$ vary directly with TOW – i.e. an increase in TOW directly increases both V$_R$ and V$_2$. In the event of an engine failure, acceleration from V$_1$ to V$_R$ is decreased. An increase in TOW would cause this acceleration to be further decreased, in addition to the decreased acceleration up to V$_1$. Thus the distance to V$_1$ and from V$_1$ to V$_R$ are both increased if the TOW is increased. V$_1$ therefore changes with TOW, but not in direct proportion to the change of weight because of the influence the relative values of the available field lengths have on V$_1$.

The ratio of V$_1$ to V$_R$ is a common factor in all field length calculations and is influenced by TOW. It is therefore a useful parameter to analyse, comparing the effect the relative field-lengths have on limiting the TOW. Some older aircraft use the V_1/V_2 ratio in their Flight Manuals, where using the same reasoning results in the same conclusions. BCARs and JARs impose limitations on the values of V_1, setting the minimum at V_{MCG} plus the speed increase in two seconds, the recognition and reaction time, and the maximum at V_R. Thus the V_1/V_R ratio is limited to a minimum of about 0.76 and a maximum value of 1.0.

22.2.1 Take-Off Run Required (TORR)

When analysing the TORR it is only necessary to consider the continued-take-off case because the abandoned-take-off case is covered by EMDR. Thus if a power unit fails, successive examples at the increased TOWs show both V_R and V_2 increase with weight. Because it is only the take-off-continued case under consideration, then it is desirable for V_1 to occur later at a faster speed. In which case the distance to V_1 will increase due to the higher TOW, and the decreased acceleration on reduced power will result in the distance from V_1 to V_R being increased. Thus when TORR is considered in isolation, an increase in TOW not only increases V_1, V_R and V_2 but also increases the V_1/V_R ratio. When the V_1/V_R ratio is plotted on a graph against TOW this increase appears as a curve. An upper limit on TOW is imposed by the all-engines-operating case, which appears as a vertical straight line on the analysis graph. Thus at any point to the left of

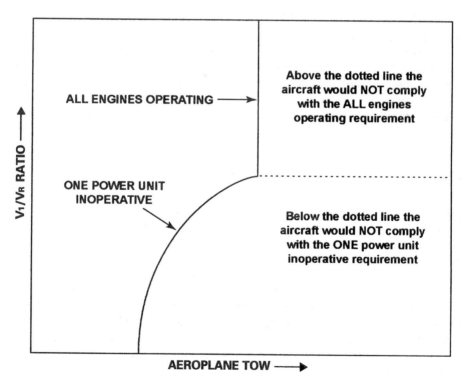

Fig. 22.1   TORR analysis.

the graph-line the requirements are attained and the continued take-off is safe. From Fig. 22.1 it can be seen that if the aircraft is light it is possible to experience a power-unit failure earlier in the take-off run and still comply with the requirements than it is for a heavy aircraft.

22.2.2 Accelerate/Stop Distance Required (ASDR)

In the case of an abandoned take-off, the decision at V_1, when a power unit failed, plainly has been to stop. It is therefore the distance required to stop that is the limiting factor. This distance is directly affected by the surface condition and aircraft weight. On a wet surface the stopping distance required is greater than it is on a dry surface for the same TOW. Stopping distance is also greater if the surface condition remains the same but the TOW is increased.

Thus, it is possible for a light aeroplane to have an engine failure later in the take-off run and still stop within ASDA than it is for a heavy aeroplane. If all other factors are ignored, V_1 decreases and V_R increases with an increase in TOW, which causes the V_1/V_R ratio to reduce. If these facts are plotted graphically, as in Fig. 22.2, they appear as a straight line sloping downward to the right as TOW increases. At any point below the graph-line the aircraft can comply with the requirements and is able stop within the available stopway but above the line it cannot.

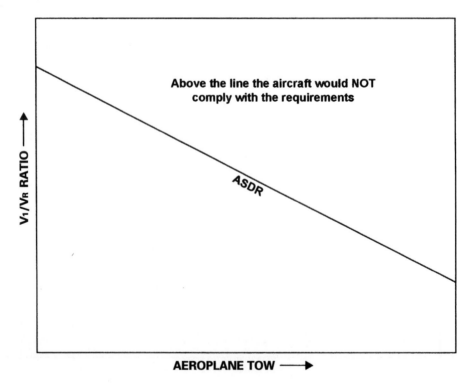

Fig. 22.2 ASDR analysis.

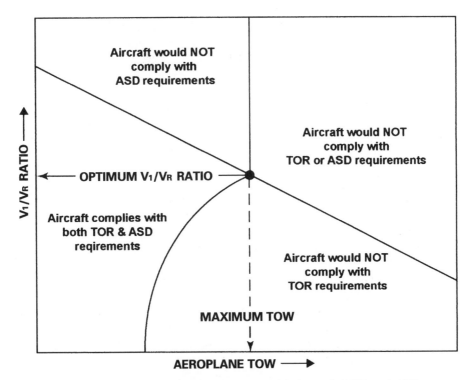

Fig. 22.3 The optimum V_1/V_R ratio and TOW, considering only TOR and ASD requirements.

22.2.3 TORR vs. ASDR

When both TORR and ASDR are taken together, achievement of the maximum TOW involves a conflict of requirements. If the decision at V_1 is to continue then a later and faster V_1 is desirable; but, if the decision at V_1 is to abandon take-off, it is better to have a lower V_1 which gives a greater braking distance from a decreased speed.

To satisfy both requirements, the graphical plot for each case is superimposed on the other, as illustrated in Fig. 22.3. The optimum V_1/V_R ratio is then at the intersection of the two graph lines. Note, however, that this produces the maximum TOW when only these two requirements are considered. Further limitations may be imposed by the TODR.

If Fig. 22.3 was to be plotted as a speed against distance graph at the maximum TOW using the full length of ASDA and TORA, it would appear as in Fig. 22.4. This clearly demonstrates the effect of an engine failure before, at and after V_1.

22.2.4 Take-Off Distance Required (TODR)

When only considering TODR if an engine fails, the decision at V_1 is to take-off. It is therefore desirable that V_1 and V_2 be close together to reduce the distance travelled when accelerating with one engine inoperative. If the TOW is increased, the distance to V_1 is increased and the distance onward to V_2 is also increased.

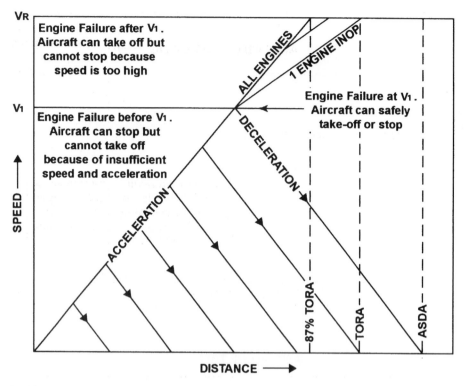

Fig. 22.4   Engine failure at maximum TOW.

Thus an increase in TOW in the TODR case increases V_1, V_R, V_2 and the V_1/V_R ratio. The increase, when shown graphically, is similar in appearance to the TORR graph, except that it is displaced to the left of the TORR graph-line if the clearway is much shorter than stopway and to the right of the TORR graph-line if the clearway is longer than stopway. The all-engines-operating requirement imposes an upper TOW limit at which the V_1/V_R ratio remains constant. This is shown by a vertical line on the analysis graph in Fig. 22.5.

It can be seen from the graph that at any position to the right of the graph line the aeroplane cannot comply with the requirements for this phase of flight, whereas to the left it can. This shows that a light aircraft can suffer a power unit failure earlier during the take-off run and still comply with this requirement than can a heavy one.

A full analysis of all the field-length requirements can be obtained by plotting all three graphs in Figs 22.1, 22.2 and 22.5 on to a single graph. The precise disposition of each graph line depends entirely on the relative field lengths. The limiting requirement is shown by the intersection furthest to the left. From this point a vertical line defines the maximum TOW permissible for the field-lengths available and is called the Field-Length-Limited TOW (FLL TOW). A horizontal line from the intersection indicates the maximum V_1/V_R ratio at this TOW. If the intersection is on the all-engines operating limiting graph-line, a range of V_1/V_R ratios is available to use. An example of each of the limiting factors is shown in Figs 22.6–22.9.

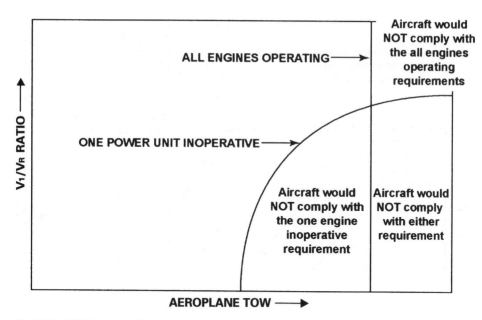

Fig. 22.5 TODR analysis.

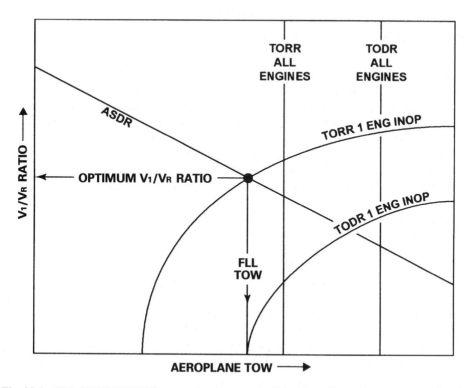

Fig. 22.6 FLL TOW TORR (one-engine-inoperative) limiting, all requirements considered.

22.2.5 FLL TOW TORR (one-engine-inoperative) limiting

The ASDR intersection with the one-engine-inoperative TORR line is the limiting intersection. See Fig. 22.6.

22.2.6 FLL TOW TORR (all-engines-operating) limiting

The limitation of ASDR intersects the TORR graph-line on the all-engines-operating portion of the line. The upper limit of the V_1/V_R ratio is defined by the horizontal at this intersection, and the lower limit is provided by the intersection of the TORR all-engines-operating graph line and the TORR one-engine-inoperative line. Maximum TOW, i.e. FLL TOW, is that limitation of the all-engines-operating vertical line. If all other conditions remain unaltered, the reason for the increased TOW and V_1/V_R ratio is that a larger stopway is available than in the previous example, such as would enable the aircraft to stop within ASDA at higher TOWs for the V_1/V_R ratio. The ASDR line therefore moves upward, providing a more relaxed limitation. See Fig. 22.7.

22.2.7 FLL TOW TODR (one-engine-inoperative) limiting

If no clearway, or only a very limited clearway, is available for use, it is possible that the requirements in the TODR case will be more limiting than the TORR

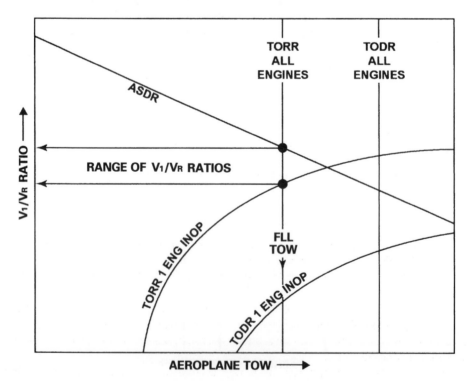

Fig. 22.7 TORR (all-engines-operating) limiting, all requirements considered.

requirements. When this happens, the TODR graph when plotted will fall to the left of the TORR graph line. The limiting intersection is in this case that of the ASDR and TODR one-engine-inoperative lines.

As the length of the clearway increases, so the TODR graph-line moves progressively to the right. By specifying a 'maximum usable clearway' it is sometimes possible to prevent it moving to the right of the TORR graph-line, thus ensuring that TORR is never the limiting factor. See Fig. 22.8.

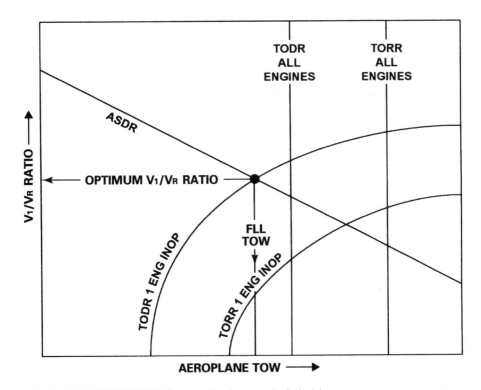

Fig. 22.8   FLL TOW TODR (one-engine-inoperative) limiting.

22.2.8 FLL TOW TODR (all-engines-operating)

If the stopway in the previous example were increased the limiting factor would become the TODR all-engines-operating graph line. As before, the intersection with ASDR provides the upper limit of the range of V_1/V_R ratios at the limiting TOW.

If some other limitation causes the TOW to be resticted to a weight lower than the maximum permissible, then a range of V_1/V_R ratios becomes available. It is usual to select the lowest ratio for turbo-jet aircraft and the highest ratio for propeller-driven aeroplanes. See Fig. 22.9.

The case of the engine failure at a TOW below the maximum field-length-limiting TOW is depicted on a graph of speed against distance in Fig. 22.10.

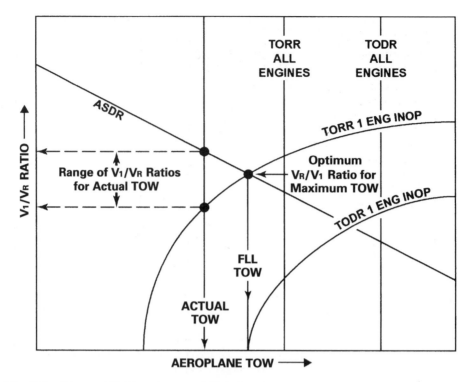

Fig. 22.9 Range of V_1/V_R ratios at TOWs below the maximum permissible.

22.3 WET RUNWAY ANALYSIS

The normal field-length requirements for a dry runway are satisfied by the limiting intersection at position A in Fig. 22.11. A wet take-off surface reduces the aeroplane's wheel braking capability. This is taken into account by reducing the decision speed for the field-lengths available, thus retaining the pilot's choice of action in the event of an engine failure. This is shown as point B on Fig. 22.11 and illustrates the severe reduction in the maximum TOW experienced if the usual requirements are applied.

Because of the acute effect of these demands, the CAA altered the requirements for aeroplanes operating from a wet runway of defined friction characteristics. The revised exigencies were devised to 'trade' a marked improvement in safety in the case of an abandoned take-off on a reference wet hard surface, against a relatively small degradation of safety in the event of a continued take-off from a wet runway V_1. These requirements permit screen height to be reduced to 15 ft and lift-off to be at the end of TORA.

The limiting intersection of the graph-lines for a reference wet hard surface is shown at position C. It gives only a relatively small increase of the maximum TOW above that for a dry surface. However, at this position the V_1 is shown to be much lower than decision speed for a dry runway. In the circumstances depicted in Fig. 22.11, the depreciated safety level can be slightly improved if the original dry run-

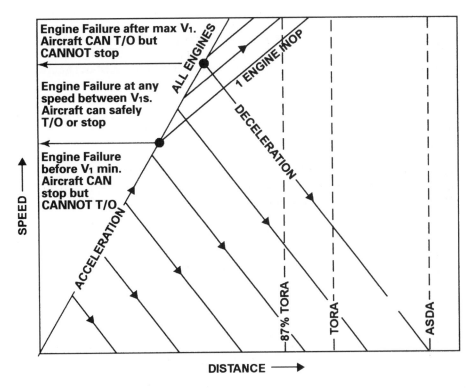

Fig. 22.10 Engine failure below maximum TOW.

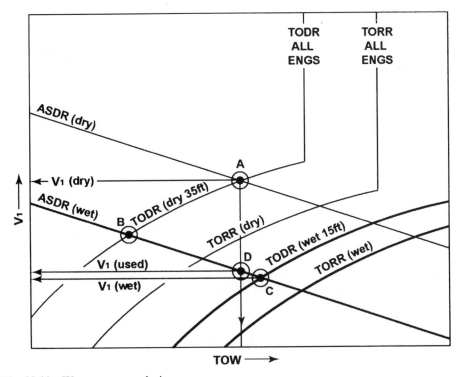

Fig. 22.11 Wet runway analysis.

way TOW is used in conjunction with the wet EMDR. This intersection is at point D on Fig. 22.11 and shows a small increase in V_1 above the wet runway value. The most important feature of this compromise arrangement is that screen height is increased to approximately 18 ft. On the graph it is the proportional distance of D between C (15 ft) and B (35 ft).

CHAPTER 23

Rapid Calculation Methods

In performance planning it is desirable to reduce the processes of calculation to a minimum. Four methods of computation are currently used by operators to calculate the field-length-limited TOW. They are the 'D' and 'X' graphical method, the 'D' and 'V_1/V_R' graph, the Balanced Field Graph and the Regulated Take-Off Graph (RTOG). The first method eliminates as many processes as possible within the regulations and can be used for any airfield or route. The second is a development of the first. The balanced field graph, although very easy to use, can be unnecessarily penalizing to the aircraft operator if a stopway or a clearway is available; whilst the fourth eliminates further processes but has the disadvantage that it can only be used for the departure aerodrome and the route for which it was designed.

No matter which method is used to complete the calculations the data will include, within the established operational limitations of the aeroplane, the following operational correction factors:

(1)   Not more than 50% of nominal wind components along the take-off path opposite to the direction of take-off, and not less than 150% of nominal wind components along the take-off path in the direction of take-off.

(2)   Effective runway gradients.

23.1 'D' AND 'X' GRAPHS

The 'D' and 'X' graph solution, usually only found in the Flight Manuals of older aeroplanes, eliminates the need to plot each limiting parameter on a consolidated graph. The figures extracted are simply compared and the lowest (the most limiting) of them accepted.

To understand the mechanics of the graphs, it is essential that the significance of each of the values be known. 'D' value represents the equivalent dry, level, hard surface distance in still air of the entry values being compared. The distances are then equated to a balanced field, but the power failure speed ratio (PFSR) associated with this distance requires correction to take account of any stopway or clearway used. The corrected balanced field PFSR is the 'X' value which is the ratio of V_1 to V_R.

When V_1 becomes equal to V_R, the ratio is 1.00 and is either for a balanced field or for an unbalanced field where available lengths are not limiting. 'D' and 'X' graphs are normally included in Flight Manuals to compare ASDA with TORA and TODA on separate pages. See Fig. 23.1. A further graph is used to comply with the all-engines-operating limitation imposed by TODA; this graph is substituted in the Flight Manuals on some aircraft by a check graph that ensures TODR all-engines-operating does not exceed TODA. Two conversion graphs are then provided to convert 'D' to a TOW and 'X' to a V_1/V_R ratio.

To ensure the Brake Energy limitation is not exceeded, a final graph is provided in the Flight Manual.

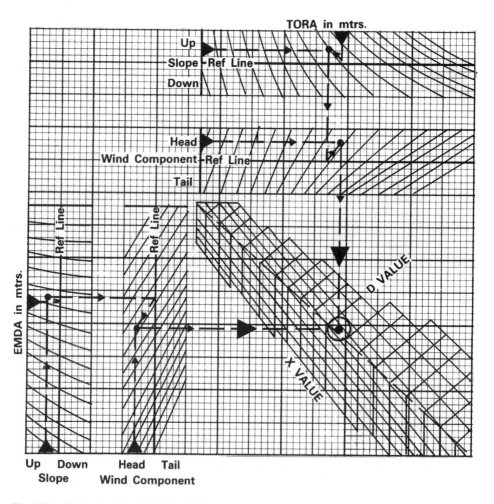

Fig. 23.1 Example 'D' and 'X' graph.

23.2 'D' AND V_1/V_R GRAPHS

The natural progression from the 'D' and 'X' graphs is the replacement of a further process without detracting from the accuracy of the results. Thus the 'X' value of the preceding method is replaced by V_1/V_R ratio. Exactly the same procedure is followed with these graphs except there is now no need to convert 'X' value to a V_1/V_R ratio. The lowest 'D' value and associated V_1/V_R ratio is selected and used for the calculation of the field-length limited TOW and V_1. An example is shown in Fig. 23.2.

23.3 BALANCED FIELD GRAPHS

When the field lengths under consideration are unbalanced, it is necessary to consider each length individually to find the limiting TOW and the associated V_1/V_R ratio. However, if the field lengths are balanced (i.e. if ASDA = TODA) then the requirements can be satisfied simultaneously in the case of a power unit failure at V_1. This problem can be solved by using a 'Balanced Field Graph' from which can be obtained the maximum TOW to comply with the ASDR with one-power-unit-inoperative, and the associated V_1/V_R ratio.

Should TORA, ASDA and TODA all be equal, then TORR will not be a limiting consideration (because of the factorization imposed by the requirements). If they are not all equal, then the calculated TOW *must* be checked against the TORR and the V_1/V_R ratio against the all-power-units-operating TODR to ensure that neither is limiting.

This simplified method of calculation unnecessarily penalizes the operator if the field lengths are unbalanced because credit is not taken for any excess stopway or clearway. If TOW is limited by any other factor such as Net Flight Path, En-Route or landing weight, to a weight below the balanced-field TOW, it is unnecessary to calculate the unbalanced field-length maximum TOW. In this case V_R is calculated for the actual TOW, and the original V_1/V_R ratio is used to calculate V_1. See Fig. 23.3.

There is no real advantage to using balanced-field distances for an unbalanced field apart from the reduced calculation effort. It is true that the safety margin, in the event of an engine failure at V_1, is increased but this is as a result of the reduced TOW rather than an increase in the safety factorization.

23.4 REGULATED TAKE-OFF GRAPHS

Although 'D' and 'V_1/V_R' graphs are a vast improvement on the original method of calculating TOW, in the opinion of many airlines the time taken to complete the performance plan is still unacceptably high. Scheduled carriers often have to make the same calculations for the same departure airport and even the same runway, the only changes being the ambient temperature and the wind component. Thus a system was devised that reduced the variable inputs to these two factors. For each departure airport, a chart is produced for each individual runway, on which all elements such as field-lengths, slope and obstacle heights are fixed. (With other rapid methods these are variable inputs.) Even the remaining variables can be limited to the annual range usually experienced at that airport. The operations staff, normally with the aid of a computer, calculate the maximum TOW for all combinations of tempera-

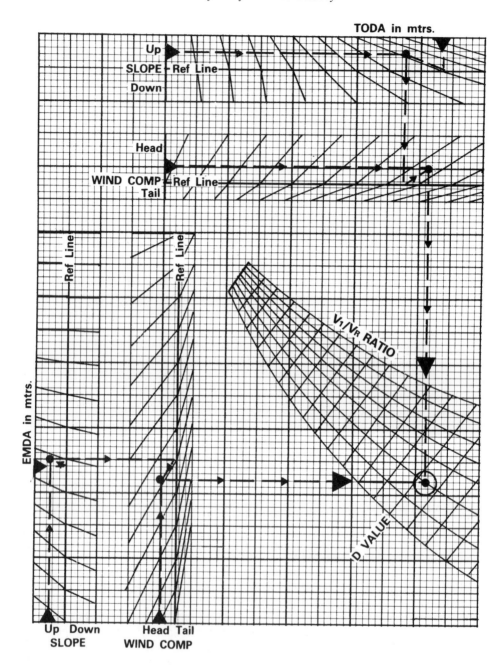

Fig. 23.2 Example D and V₁/Vᴿ graph (copyright British Aerospace).

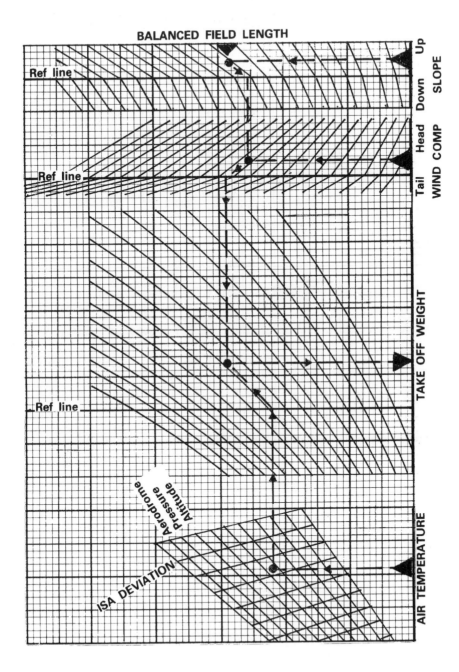

Fig. 23.3 Example balanced field graph (copyright British Aerospace).

Aircraft Type B74		Airfield HARTFORD		Runway 18L		
FLAP 10		A/D Elev. 230ft.		Slope 1%UP		
TOR		ED		TOD		
8450ft		8500ft		8550ft		
2567m		2591m		2606m		

WC	10Kt	5Kt	STILL	10Kt	20Kt	30Kt
Temp °C	Tail	Tail	AIR	Head	Head	Head
33	304·7	308·8	313·5	315·8	317·6	317·6
31	307·6	313·6	317·2	319·4	321·6	322·3
29	310·8	317·1	320·8	323·1	325·4	327·0
27	314·1	320·4	325·6	328·1	330·4	331·8
25	317·4	325·2	329·4	331·9	334·2	336·8
23	320·7	329·6	334·2	336·6	338·9	341·0
21	324·0	332·8	337·6	340·0	342·3	344·6
19	327·3	336·1	342·1	344·5	346·9	349·2
17	329·2	338·0	343·8	347·2	350·1	352·6
15	330·1	338·8	345·1	↓	↓	↓
13	330·9	339·7				
11	331·7	340·5	↓			
9	332·6	341·5	346·3			
7	333·5	342·4		↓		
5	334·3	↓			352·6	
3	335·2					
1	336·1	343·8	↓	↓	↓	↓

V₁ = CORRECTED Vᵣ −19 DRY or −29 WET

TEMP °C	VR/V2	VR/V2	VR/V2	VR/V2	VR/V2	VR/V2
1 to 12	2/0	2/0	6/4	8/5	11/7	13/9
13 to 20			4/2	6/4	8/5	11/7
21 to 25	↓	↓	5/3	7/5	10/7	12/9
26 to 32		3/1	7/5	9/7	11/8	12/10
33 to 35	↓	5/3	8/6	10/8	12/9	12/9

Fig. 23.4   Example RTOW.

ture and wind component for each runway, and produce a graph or table on which is listed the factors that were used in its production.

Thus the user is able to extract the TOW, V₁ and Vᵣ against the entering arguments of wind component and ambient temperature. These graphs are known as **Regulated Take-Off Graphs (RTOGs)** and are produced in manuals for particular aircraft types which include all of the airline's scheduled departure aerodromes. They can be regarded as pre-calculated TOW solutions that transfer the major work-load away from the crucial pre-take-off briefing period.

To ensure comprehensive coverage, a set of general graphs is included in the manual. These do not relate to any specific aerodrome but are suitably modified Flight Manual graphs. They include field-length charts, an obstacle clearance chart, a take-off WAT limit chart, a brake-energy limitation chart and a tyre-speed limitation chart. Usually the last two charts are only limiting at high airfields, high temperatures and heavy weights, or in tailwind conditions. The lowest TOW obtained from any of these charts is the maximum TOW limitation. See Figs 23.4 and 23.5.

SOUTHSTOP	Issue Date		Aircraft Type		FLAP	
Runway 08 (M)	Slope ·5% UP	Elev 130ft.				
TORA 5500ft.	ASDA 5500ft.	TODA 5500ft.				

OBSTACLES				TOW CORRECTION		
				FOR PRESSURE HEIGHT		
No	Height AMSL	Dist. from BRP	Offset	AMB. TEMP.	FOR -100ft.	FOR + 100ft.
1	13ft.	5650ft.	30ft. Left	-10 C	· 40Kgs.	-40Kgs.
2	45ft.	5700ft.	70ft. Right	0 ·C	· 75Kgs.	-80Kgs.
3	60ft.	10100ft.	100ft. Right	+ 15 ·C	· 110Kgs.	-125Kgs.
4	345ft.	19250ft.	100ft. Left	+ 30 ·C	· 120Kgs.	-130Kgs.
5	450ft.	22980ft.	160ft. Right			
6	510ft.	25500ft.	210ft. Right			

TOW	V1 10T	V1 0	V1 10H	V1 20H	VR	V2	VFTO
38000	117	117	118	120	124	137	175
37000	116	116	117	118	122	135	174
36000	114	114	116	116	120	133	172
35000	112	113	114	115	118	132	170
34000	110	111	112	113	116	130	168
33000	110	109	111	112	114	128	166
32000	108	108	109	111	112	126	162
31000	107	107	108	110	110	125	156
30000	107	107	107	107	107	123	154
29000	103	103	104	105	105	121	150
28000	101	102	102	103	103	119	148
27000	100	100	101	101	101	118	146
26000	98	98	98	98	98	116	144

AMBIENT TEMPERTURE C: ·10, 0, + 10, · 20, · 30

RTOW MAXIMUM · 40H · 30H · 20H · 10H · 0

WIND COMPONENT · 5T · 10T

FTOT APPROVED

NO TYRE SPEED LIMITATION CONSIDERED

87·9 88·8 89·6 90·3 91·1 91·6 91·3 90·5 89·5

N1% ANTI-ICING OFF

				FIELD LENGTH
	2	2	2	2	OBSTACLE No.

LANDING WEIGHT	LDA	10 Tail	10 Head	2	2	2	2	SEGMENT
AIRBRAKES OPEN	5500ft	33000Kgs.	34000Kgs.	LIMITING CONSIDERATION				

Fig. 23.5 Suggested RTOG for a four jet-engined aircraft.

CHAPTER 24

Take-off Abnormalities

The normal procedure used for a TOW analysis must be amended for any take-off abnormalities which can be accounted and scheduled. This will occur in the following circumstances:

(1) If, for any reason, the actual TOW is less than the field-length limited TOW and the operator wishes to take advantage of the unused clearway. Then it depends on the requirements of the operator how this distance may be utilized. Either of two procedures may be adopted:
    (a) If it is not desired to increase the TOW then a reduced power setting may be used to conserve engine life and reduce engine noise (see Section 24.1).
    (b) Should the operator wish to increase the TOW, beyond the limitation imposed by the climb limit or obstacle limit, then the aeroplane may be held on the ground during the take-off run until a higher speed is attained and so achieve the goal (see Section 24.2).
(2) If the aeroplane has an unserviceability which is deemed acceptable by its inclusion in the 'Configuration Deviation List', but adversely affects the calculated take-off performance, then due allowance must be made for the effect. These are known as conditional abnormalities of which there are two of significance. They are:
    (a) Reverse thrust inoperative (see Section 24.3.1).
    (b) Anti-skid inoperative (see Section 24.3.2).

24.1 VARIABLE THRUST TAKE-OFF

In recent years it has become apparent that engine reliability is a large factor to be considered in the assessment of aircraft safety and accident probability. If engine life can be conserved and the reliability increased, aircraft safety can be improved. A further benefit from conserving engine life is that it increases the flying time between engine changes, which from the operator's view-point improves economy.

A large proportion of take-offs are made below any of the limiting TOWs imposed by the requirements of the take-off or climb. Actual TOW is generally lower than the performance-limited TOW for the ambient temperature. Thus a proportion of the power obtained for take-off is not necessary to achieve the safety standards required. It is, therefore, possible to reduce the take-off thrust/power without affecting the safety standards achieved.

Any aircraft capable of taking advantage of this factor has an approved procedure detailed in the Flight Manual. It is known by a variety of names such as *Variable Thrust Take-Off, Graduated Power Take-Off, Factored Thrust Take-Off* and others. The procedure is optional and only used at the Captain's discretion, though the pilot obviously is encouraged to make use of it as much as possible, by the operator. As a safeguard the operators have to establish a periodic engine-condition monitoring system to ensure that the engines are capable of producing full take-off power/thrust if so required.

Take-off weight is in practice normally limited by either the field-length considerations, the take-off climb (see Chapter 25) or the Net Flight Path obstacle clearance (see Chapter 27) requirements. If none of these factors is limiting, take-off thrust may be reduced, within reason, until one of them becomes limiting. Thus the aircraft will be operating at or near a performance-limited condition.

This procedure is accepted by the CAA and JAA provided there is an approved procedure laid down in the Flight Manual, and that the minimum thrust stipulated for safe operations can be easily identified by the pilot. Generally the thrust reduction should *not* exceed 10% of the maximum take-off thrust. The CAA prohibits the use of this procedure in conjunction with:

(1) Icy or very slippery runway surfaces.
(2) Runways contaminated or covered in precipitation.
(3) Any non-standard take-off, e.g. one with reverse thrust inoperative.
(4) Increased V_2 procedure for improved obstacle clearance.
(5) Power Management Computer Unserviceable.

The method is to use the take-off performance and EPR for an assumed temperature at which the performance-limited TOW equals or exceeds the actual TOW. This temperature is higher than the ambient temperature and is used with the actual values of all other factors involved. It ensures that if an engine failure occurs at V_1, the reduced thrust is sufficient to take-off and climb without infringing any performance requirement or lowering of safety standards. In fact the performance will be slightly enhanced, because the density of the air is greater than that which was assumed. Although this produces better aircraft performance, it is usually recommended that if an engine failure occurs during operations with reduced take-off power, the remaining live engines be restored to full take-off power.

The actual take-off distance, take-off run and accelerate/stop distances at reduced thrust are less than those required at full take-off thrust and weight by about 1% for every 3°C that the actual temperature is below the assumed temperature. The effect of full reverse thrust is greater at the lower temperature, so the actual distance required in the abandoned take-off case is less than that calculated using the assumed temperature.

Variations in the technique used may be recommended for some aircraft that have contingency power settings. These aircraft have a greater amount of reserve power available in the event of an emergency and a special procedure is therefore detailed for them in their Flight Manual.

24.2 INCREASED V₂ TAKE-OFF

24.2.1 No NFP obstacles

If there are no obstacles in the take-off flight path that have to be considered, the climb maximum TOW will only be restricted by the minimum gradient requirements (see Chapter 25) of the climb. This limitation is imposed by the WAT limit graph (see Chapter 26). In the take-off phase, only the declared aerodrome distances available will cause the TOW to be restricted.

Thus if the declared aerodrome distances are in excess of the distances required and the only limiting factor is that of the WAT limit, this excess may be utilized to the advantage of the operator. It can be used to enable the aircraft to accelerate to a higher V_2 than normal. This will improve its take-off climb performance – which in turn enables the aircraft to take-off at a higher weight and still obtain the minimum take-off climb gradient requirements. This increased weight is subject to the limitations imposed by maximum tyre speed and brake energy capability.

In normal circumstances it is not permissible to take-off at a weight in excess of the WAT limited TOW because the gradient would not comply with the minimum acceptable gradient requirement, stipulated in JAR 25, and would be dangerously low. This is illustrated in Fig. 24.1. However, if the aeroplane at the heavier weight is held on the ground to an increased set of speeds the climb gradient is improved because the increased V_2 will approximate V_x, which is the speed used to attain the maximum climb gradient. Of course there are limitations imposed on how much the weight and speed may be increased, to ensure the procedure is safe. This limitation is effected by a balance of the limiting parameters on TOW, i.e. field-length, WAT and tyre-speed.

Excess available distance can thus be used to increase the maximum permissible TOW. The size of the increase is determined by the most inhibiting of the considerations remaining.

24.2.2 With NFP obstacles

If there are obstacles in the direction of take-off which limit the maximum TOW, it is possible that any excess distance available beyond the obstacle limited TODR may be used to improve obstacle clearance and provide a modest increase in TOW by utilizing the increased V_2 technique, subject to any restrictions imposed by V_{MBE} or the tyre speed limitation.

The increase in TOW achieved using this technique is limited by the balance of the field-length limited TOW, the obstacle limited TOW and the tyre speed limited TOW. This is because the distance to the limiting obstacle is reduced, from that which existed at the end of the TODR for the field-length limited TOW, and the net flight path must still clear the obstacle by the statutory minimum of 35 ft. The increase of weight is restricted in practice by using a different graphical procedure in the calculation. Figure 24.2 illustrates the effect of utilizing the increased V_2 procedure to improve obstacle clearance.

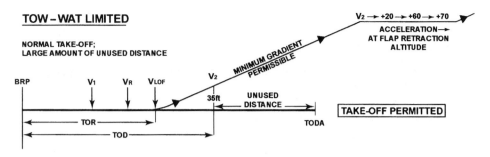

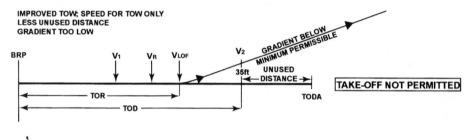

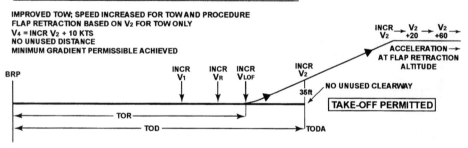

Fig. 24.1 Increased V_2 to improve TOW.

24.3 CONDITIONAL ABNORMALITIES

So far it has been assumed that all the ancillary equipment of the aeroplane is serviceable for take-off and that the runway surface is dry or just wet. Particular aeroplane types are permitted to take-off with certain ancillary equipment unserviceable. If any deviation to the usual take-off configuration is allowed, it may invoke extra operating limitations which will be clearly stated in the Flight Manual.

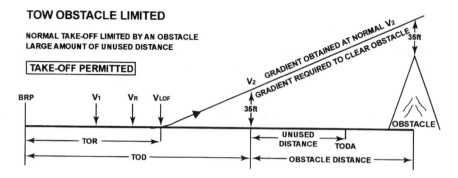

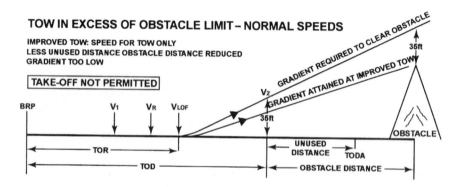

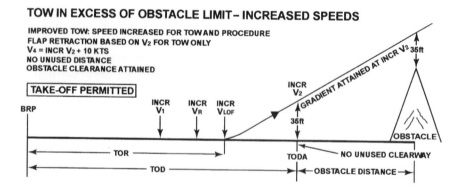

Fig. 24.2   Increased V2 to improve obstacle clearance.

24.3.1 Reverse thrust inoperative

Reverse thrust is one of the means of retardation used in the event of a take-off being abandoned. The actual emergency distance required from V1 is increased if this facility is not available on one or more engines. Although due allowance can be made for the unserviceability, performance cannot be scheduled for runway surfaces that are slush covered or very slippery, i.e. when the surface friction is significantly reduced for any reason. Thus take-offs may *not* be planned when reverse thrust is inoperative *and* the runway is icy or contaminated.

The method used to factorize the scheduled take-off performance for such an unserviceability is to correct the ASDA for runway slope, wind component and the effects of 'ACS packs ON'. This reduces the effective length of ASDA to become an equivalent distance of a fully serviceable aeroplane on a dry, level, hard surface in still air; it is this distance which is used in the take-off calculations. The corrections for this condition are made before completing the normal calculation procedure.

24.3.2 Anti-skid inoperative

The function of the anti-skid unit is to prevent the wheel-brakes locking, which would initially cause a skid to develop. On a dry surface such a skid would allow friction and heat to build up at the contact area of the tyre. Although this could seriously damage the tyre, it would not cause handling difficulties unless the heat plugs blew out and the tyre deflated. If the wheels become locked with the surface conditions other than dry, the resulting skids could cause control problems which could ultimately result in structural damage to the aeroplane.

The most dangerous position during take-off with this unserviceability is the point at which action is taken to abandon a take-off. Thus the distance that needs factorization to allow for this aspect is the ASDR. In practice, it is easier to factorize the ASDA to become an equivalent hard, dry, level distance in still air. Calculations to discover the field-length-limited TOW are completed in the normal manner, except that the corrected ASDA for 'anti-skid inoperative' is used in place of the normal corrected ASDA.

Although take-off in this condition is not permitted on a wet surface, the V_1 WET is calculated and used as V_1 DRY. The latest decision speed is between 8 and 10 kts lower than the correct speed for a dry surface condition. This reduces the emergency distance required. Remember that take-off is prohibited with anti-skid unserviceable if the runway is wet.

Test Paper 6

Q1. What percentage of the available distance is used to calculate the gross distance with all engines operating?:
    (a) 77%.
    (b) 87%.
    (c) 97%.
    (d) 107%.

Q2. The speed that an aeroplane must attain at screen height with one engine inoperative is:
    (a) V_1.
    (b) V_2.
    (c) V_3.
    (d) V_4.

Q3. The screen height when using a wet runway surface is assumed to be:
    (a) 15 ft.
    (b) 35 ft.
    (c) 50 ft.
    (d) 75 ft.

Q4. A range of V_1/V_R ratios is available:
    (a) Only when the all-engines-operating condition is limiting.
    (b) Only when the TOW is less than the FLL TOW.
    (c) When either the all-engines-operating condition is limiting or the TOW is less than the FLL TOW.
    (d) Only when the all-engines-operating condition is limiting and the TOW is less than the FLL TOW.

Q5. The 'D' value is:
    (a) The balanced field equivalent of an unbalanced field distance.
    (b) The equivalent dry, hard, level distance in still air, accounting the requirements.
    (c) EMDA factorized for wind and slope.
    (d) TODA factorized for wind and slope.

Q6. A 'variable thrust' take-off is permitted with:
  (a) Very slippery surfaces.
  (b) 'Increased V_2' technique to improve obstacle clearance.
  (c) Reverse thrust inoperative.
  (d) None of the above.

Q7. Using a 'balanced field' graph for take-off calculations when the field distances are 'unbalanced' will:
  (a) Improve the maximum permissible TOW.
  (b) Have no effect on TOW.
  (c) Decrease the maximum permissible TOW.
  (d) Increase the minimum permissible TOW.

Q8. The speed V_1 may never exceed:
  (a) Only V_R.
  (b) Only V_{MBE}.
  (c) V_{MCG}.
  (d) Either V_R or V_{MBE}.

Q9. During take-off, in the event of a power unit failure before V_1 then take-off:
  (a) May be abandoned.
  (b) May be continued.
  (c) Should be abandoned.
  (d) Should normally be continued.

Q10. Which of the following is the correct definition for take-off run?:
  (a) The distance from V_{LOF} to 35 ft above Reference Zero.
  (b) The distance from the start of the take-off run to the first upstanding obstacle in the take-off flight path, not exceeding a distance of 1.5 × TORA.
  (c) The distance from the start of the take-off run the point at which the wheels leave the ground.
  (d) The distance from the start of the take-off run to 35 ft above Reference Zero.

Q11. During take-off, in the event of a power unit failure after V_1 then take-off:
  (a) May be abandoned.
  (b) May be continued.
  (c) Should be abandoned.
  (d) Should normally be continued.

Q12. When a range of V_1/V_R ratios is available for take-off:
  (a) Turbo-propeller and turbo-jet aeroplanes use the lower value.
  (b) Turbo-propeller and turbo-jet aeroplanes use the upper value.
  (c) Turbo-propeller aeroplanes use the higher value and turbo-jet aeroplanes use the lower value.
  (d) Turbo-propeller aeroplanes use the lower value and turbo-jet aeroplanes use the higher value.

Q13. The value of V_1 WET relative to V_1 DRY is:
    (a) 8 to 10 kts lower.
    (b) 8 to 10 kts higher.
    (c) Both are the same.
    (d) 3 to 5 kts lower.

Q14. The minimum time interval in seconds between V_{LOF} and the initiation of undercarriage retraction is:
    (a) 2 s.
    (b) 3 s.
    (c) 4 s.
    (d) 5 s.

Q15. The maximum time difference in seconds between V_1 WET and V_1 DRY is:
    (a) 2 s.
    (b) 3 s.
    (c) 4 s.
    (d) 5 s.

CHAPTER 25

The Take-off Climb Requirements

For the purposes of producing climb path performance data for Class 'A' aeroplanes, it is assumed that the most critical engine fails at V$_{EF}$. In the continued take-off case, it is further assumed that the take-off phase of flight is successfully completed by the end of TODR. Thus at this point the aircraft is 35 ft above the datum surface level, Reference Zero (RZ), in the take-off configuration and must climb to a safe height of 1500 ft above the same datum. This phase of flight is the take-off climb during which all obstacles must be cleared by the stipulated safe margin, the aircraft configuration must be changed in a pre-ordained manner to its en-route configuration and the prescribed minimum performance level *must* be achieved if the aircraft is to be acknowledged as operating to Class 'A' standards. The requirements and regulations that must be observed are:

(1) The aircraft configuration change requirements.
(2) The gradient diminishment requirements.
(3) The minimum gradient requirements.
(4) The obstacle clearance regulations. These are specified in *JAR-OPS 1.495* and *AN(G)R 7(3)(b)* and are dealt with in depth in Chapter 27.

> *Reference Zero (RZ) is defined as an horizontal plane 35 ft vertically beneath the aeroplane at the end of TODR. The climb path data assumes one engine becomes inoperative at V$_{EF}$.*

25.1 AIRCRAFT CONFIGURATION CHANGE REQUIREMENTS

To ensure that the change of configuration *and* minimum performance level are achieved in a safe manner, the take-off climb to 1500 ft above RZ, referred to as the **Take-off Flight Path**, may be either a continuous take-off path or divided into segments. The end of each segment is defined by the completion of a change in configuration, power, thrust or speed or by the attainment of a performance requirement. Thus the specific number of segments depends on the aircraft type and its configuration at take-off. The minimum number of segments permissible is three and the maximum is six. *JAR 25.111(d)(1).*

To ensure adequate coverage of this phase of flight, two examples of the Take-off

Flight Path are described in this chapter. The first is for a turbo-prop aircraft and has a six-segmented, and the second is that of a jet aircraft having a four-segmented climb. Because these descriptions may differ considerably from the prescribed procedure for a specific aircraft type, it is essential that the aircraft Flight Manual be consulted for the detailed procedure to be used and the recommended flight technique to be adopted for that aeroplane.

25.1.1 Example 1: Turbo-propeller driven aircraft (Fig. 25.1)

1st segment The first segment commences at the end of TODR at 35 ft above RZ. At this point the undercarriage is selected UP and the propeller of the inoperative power unit is in the process of feathering. The time between lift-off and the initiation of undercarriage retraction is never less than three seconds. *ACJ 25.111(b)2.* Maximum take-off power is set on the operative engines and a speed of V2 maintained throughout the segment. When the undercarriage is fully retracted *and* the propeller is fully feathered, the segment is complete. *JAR 25.111(c)(4).* This point is the commencement of the second segment.

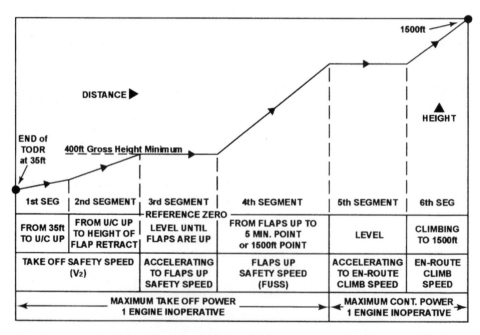

Fig. 25.1 Typical six-segment take-off flight path.

2nd segment The pilot has completed two actions of the 'cleaning-up' process and has now to climb the aircraft to a safe height at which the flaps, which are still in the take-off position, can be retracted. The CAA and the JAA dictate that the minimum *gross* height of flap retraction, and if water methanol is used to increase the power developed during take-off the minimum gross height at which it may be switched off, is 400 ft above RZ. *JAR 25.111(c)(4)*. Power and speed remain unchanged for the whole segment, which is complete when the aircraft achieves the selected flap retraction height. The aircraft Flight Manual specifies the maximum gross height of flap retraction. Therefore, the pilot has a band of heights from which to select the height at which to initiate flap retraction. The choice made depends on the relative position and height of obstacles in the take-off flight path obstacle domain but the choice must be made at the performance planning stage. The corrected *gross* height of flap retraction is that which is used to calculate the pressure altitude increment which, when added to the airfield pressure altitude and corrected for instrument error, is the altitude indicated on the altimeter at which to level the aircraft prior to flap retraction (see Chapter 4).

The climb gradient attained in the second segment decreases as the segment progresses. If flap retraction is delayed then the segment extends over a greater distance and the change of gradient becomes significant.

3rd segment On reaching the selected gross height of flap retraction, which is the commencement of the third segment, the aircraft is levelled and accelerated to the Flaps-Up Safety Speed (FUSS) with the power setting unchanged. On attaining the appropriate retraction speed for each setting the flaps are selected UP to the next setting. This segment is not complete until the flaps have reached the en-route setting, the water-methanol, if used, is switched off and the speed increased to FUSS. *It is not permissible to switch off the water-methanol before the flaps reach the en-route position.*

4th segment The fourth segment begins when the flap is completely retracted and FUSS is obtained. The climb is now recommenced and sustained until the aircraft reaches a height of 1500 ft above RZ, or until the time limit of five minutes from the start of the take-off run is reached.

5th segment At 1500 ft above RZ or the height attained after five minutes the aircraft is once again levelled and accelerated to the en-route climb speed. This is the fifth segment and is flown with the power set at the maximum contingency setting with one-engine-inoperative.

6th segment If the aircraft does not achieve 1500 ft above RZ because of the time limit imposed then the climb is resumed. This then is the sixth segment, which begins on attaining the en-route climb speed, and ends on reaching 1500 ft above RZ.

25.1.2 Example 2: Turbo-jet aircraft (Fig. 25.2)

1st segment The first segment of this NFP commences at the end of TODR at 35 ft above RZ. At this point the undercarriage is selected UP. It is never less than three seconds after lift-off. *ACJ 25.111(b)2*. Take-off thrust is established and used to achieve a speed of V_2 which is retained throughout the segment. The point at which the landing gear is fully retracted denotes the end of the first segment and the beginning of the second.

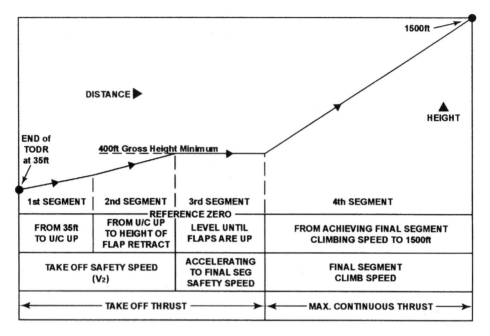

Fig. 25.2 Typical four-segment take-off flight path.

2nd segment Except for undercarriage retraction in the first segment the aeroplane configuration may not be changed nor may the power or thrust be altered until a height of at least 400 ft gross height above RZ has been attained. Therefore, the thrust and speed remain the same as the first segment. However, the gradient of climb obtained will be greater than that of the first segment because of the reduced drag resulting from undercarriage retraction. The climb is continued until the elected height of flap retraction is reached. This height must be between 400 ft *gross* and 1500 ft above RZ, although it may be restricted by any time limit imposed on the use of take-off thrust. Any restriction on the height of flap retraction is clearly stated in the Flight Manual for the aeroplane type. The second segment ends on reaching the elected flap retraction height. *JAR 25.111(c)(4).*

3rd segment The third segment is usually a level, acceleration segment for most aircraft but some aeroplanes have a sufficient excess of power available over power required that they are able to continue to climb *and* to accelerate, although the climb gradient may be less than that of the second segment. The speed is increased during this segment to the retraction speed for each flap setting, on attaining the appropriate retraction speed the flaps are selected UP to the next setting until they are fully retracted. When 0°-flap is obtained the acceleration is continued until the flaps up safety speed is achieved. This is the target speed for this segment and is often referred to as the final segment climb speed.

   If the take-off thrust time limit is reached before this speed is achieved then maximum continuous thrust *must* be set and the acceleration continued with this reduced power. The point at which the speed is obtained is the end of the segment.

4th segment   The final segment climb speed is maintained throughout the segment until 1500 ft above RZ is achieved. If the take-off thrust time limit is reached during this segment then the speed must be sustained at the reduced power setting. This will reduce the climb gradient attained.

25.3 THE RELATIONSHIP OF NFP TO GFP

The next aspect that requires consideration is that of the minimum climb performance levels which are specified in JARs. Minimum gross gradients of climb are detailed for each segment of the flight path. In addition to these details the percentage reduction that must be applied to the gross gradients attained to obtain the net gradients is specified for each group of aircraft, which are sub-divided according to the number of engines.

To achieve the gross performance used in the original computations, the aircraft must be flown at V2 up to flap retraction height, and from this point to 1500 ft above datum surface level at the speed stated in the Flight Manual as that used by the manufacturers for these purposes. The power used to establish the Gross Flight Path (GFP) is Maximum Take-off Power, Maximum Contingency Power and Intermediate Contingency Power, in sequence, up to the maximum permissible individual or total time, whichever is the least.

25.4 GRADIENT DIMINISHMENT REQUIREMENTS

The complete take-off climb phase and the profile most aeroplanes of the type could be reasonably expected to achieve is referred to as the **Gross Flight Path (GFP)**. The height accomplished at the end of each segment is the height at which the next segment commences and thus forms a continuous flight path. The flight path ends once the aircraft has reached a net height of 1500ft above Reference Zero *and* has accelerated to the en-route climb speed. Those aircraft certificated to JAR 25 safety levels have to comply with a set of *gross* gradient requirements for the one-engine-inoperative case which are detailed in *JAR 25.111(c)(3) and 121(b) & (c)*. See Table 25.1.

To ensure the safety probability level of 10^{-6} is preserved the gross gradients achieved by any Class 'A' aeroplane are diminished by 0.8% for twin-engined aircraft, 0.9% for three-engined aeroplanes and 1.0% for four-engined aircraft. *JAR 25.115*. Application of the specified diminishment to the gross gradients of the GFP produce the net gradients of the Net Flight Path (NFP); i.e. the net climb gradients are always less than the gross climb gradients. *It is the NFP that is used to calculate obstacle clearance.*

The length of any *climb* segment of the NFP is exactly equal to the length of the same segment in the GFP, but the gradient is diminished by the amount specified. If any particular GFP segment is horizontal, the same segment of the NFP is horizontal, and the gross acceleration in level flight is diminished by an acceleration equivalent to the specified gradient margin thus increasing the length of the the NFP level segments. See Fig. 25.3.

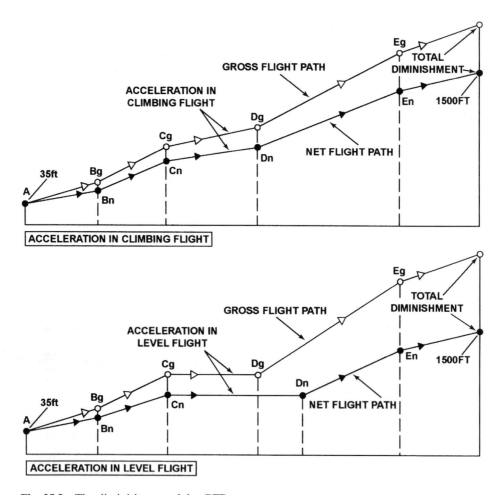

Fig. 25.3 The diminishment of the GFP.

25.5 MINIMUM GRADIENT REQUIREMENTS

The flight path graphs produced by the manufacturers are made up of the loci of the most limiting gradients of the one-engine-inoperative net flight paths. Although the first segment embraces a portion that benefits from 'ground effect' and a portion which does not gain from this phenomenon, the gradient quoted for this segment is based on the aeroplane's performance without 'ground effect'. Gradients quoted for the third segment are equivalent accelerations.

The minimum acceptable gradients for each segment of the flight path, irrespective of the wind component, are specified in JAR 25 and are reproduced in Table 25.1. Originally there was an all-engines-operating gross gradient requirement of 5.2% in the second segment and 4.0% in the final climb segment imposed by JAR (BB) 25.119 for all Class 'A' aircraft. This requirement has been withdrawn and all that remains is an all-engines-operating landing-climb requirement of 3.2%. *JAR 25.111(d)(3) & 119.*

Table 25.1 Minimum climb gradient requirements. *JAR 25.111, 115, 119, 121.*

	One-engine-inoperative gradient %					
Number of power units	2		3		4	
GFP diminishment	0.8%		0.9%		1.0%	
Segment	G	N	G	N	G	N
1st with auto-feather and turbo-jet aircraft	0	−0.8*	0.3	−0.6*	0.5	−0.5*
2nd segment	2.4	1.6	2.7	1.8	3.0	2.0
3rd segment	1.2	0.4	1.5	0.6	1.7	0.7
Final climb	1.2	0.4	1.5	0.6	1.7	0.7

* Subject to JAR 25.111(c)(1) that the GFP slopes must be positive at all points.

To comply with all of the requirements of JARs and AN(G)Rs, the climb achieved must be compared with that which is needed to give adequate clearance of obstacles. Therefore, the NFP must be plotted on a terrain profile. However, if the climb path is free of obstacles, this is an unnecessary chore which may be omitted. Nevertheless, it is still essential to ensure that the minimum performance climb gradients required are achieved. This is done by the use of a relatively simple graph, the WAT-limit graph which is covered in detail in Chapter 26. Obstacle clearance is dealt with in Chapters 27 and 28.

CHAPTER 26

Weight–Altitude–Temperature Limitation

The limitations on TOW so far discussed have been those imposed by the field lengths and aircraft controllability. If these restrictions are observed then the maximum TOW calculated will ensure that the aircraft can safely take-off and climb to screen height. But that is all that is guaranteed by observing the field-length-limited TOW. It is clearly desirable that the climb performance should also be covered by a guarantee to ensure that the required minimum gradients of the Take-off Flight Path are accomplished.

For a normal take-off the thrust levers are set to obtain maximum take-off power during the ground run. This setting is maintained until the maximum power time limit is reached. The amount of thrust and lift produced, and hence the weight supported by any aircraft at a set power output is dependent on the density of the air. The denser the air, the greater the weight it can support. Density varies with altitude and temperature; the denser atmosphere at low temperature and/or low altitude is the most suitable for these purposes. Thus if the power is set at take-off thrust there is, for any combination of pressure altitude and temperature, a maximum weight that can be lifted. However this weight may be restricted by the requirement to attain the specified minimum climb gradients of the NFP.

In Chapter 25 it was shown what minimum climb gradients or equivalent gradients are considered by the JAA to be safe for each segment of the NFP. *These are still-air gradients* because the wind component is accounted in any obstacle clearance calculations that may be necessary. It is the most severe gradient of these segment requirements that limits the maximum weight at which an aircraft, using take-off power, will be able to comply with all the requirements of the NFP. Usually the most severe requirement is that of the second segment, but for some aircraft configurations the most limiting gradient may be that of the third, fourth or fifth segments.

The maximum TOW which ensures that the aircraft will comply with all the gradient requirements of the NFP is termed the Weight–Altitude–Temperature (WAT) limited TOW.

In some countries this is referred to as the 'climb-limited take-off mass'.

The WAT limit thus provides the required performance guarantee for the take-off climb and must not be exceeded. *AN(G)R 7(1) and JAR-OPS 1.490(a).*

If the actual TOW exceeds the WAT-limited TOW, the guarantee is invalidated and a lower standard of performance will be obtained in which the rate of climb

208

achieved could be dangerously low. In fact this situation is prevented from arising because AN(G)R 7(1) and JAR-OPS 1.490(a) state unequivocally that under no circumstances may the TOW exceed the maximum TOW for the pressure altitude and air temperature obtaining at the aerodrome at which the take-off is made, if the aircraft is to be considered as operating to Class 'A' performance standards.

There is one exception to this rule which is the 'Increased V_2' procedure discussed in Chapter 24.

> The WAT-limit is therefore the maximum TOW at which an aircraft can comply with the most severe requirements of the NFP, both with all-engines-operating and with the critical power unit inoperative, at the pressure altitude and the air temperature under consideration.

It decreases with increase of pressure altitude and/or ambient temperature and also whenever the air conditioning or anti-icing systems are used. It does NOT take into account obstacle clearance or any requirement or limitation other than the gradient requirements of the NFP.

26.1 GRAPHICAL PRESENTATION

The WAT limitation on TOW for each configuration is presented as a set of curves. Separate curves may be provided for each take-off flap setting permitted for the aircraft type and, if the use of coolant is permitted, both with and without the use of the coolant. Aircraft having a capacity for power augmentation using a coolant, e.g. water-methanol, may use and take credit for its use in the Net Flight Path if the quantity of refrigerant available is $1.1 \times$ the actual amount that would be consumed by the aircraft in climbing from the end of TODR to the point at which the coolant is assumed to cease being used. The manufacturers include separate performance schedules in the Flight Manual for aircraft using water-methanol. An additional graph is provided in these aircraft Flight Manuals to enable the pilot to calculate the total amount of water-methanol required for the take-off and climb. Some manufacturers seek to reduce the number of graphs in the Flight Manual by introducing correction grids and/or correction tables to the main WAT limit graph so that it covers all configurations for that aeroplane.

Apart from the WAT limitations imposed on TOW, additional restrictions are imposed on different aircraft types by different configurations or ancillary equipment which, when employed, reduce the aircraft's ability to obtain the required minimum climb gradient.

A graph is provided in the Flight Manuals of all Class 'A' aircraft to enable the WAT-limited TOW to be calculated. This graph, for aircraft having no additional performance limitations, is a straight-line type with entering arguments of pressure altitude and ISA deviation. (See Fig. 26.1.)

Generally, propeller-driven aircraft have a wider variety of configurations that can be used for take-off than do turbo-jet aircraft. If an aircraft has more than one take-off flap setting, the larger-angled setting would produce a shorter ground run but a reduced gradient of climb and would require a greater flap retraction distance in the third segment, not only because of the larger angle of

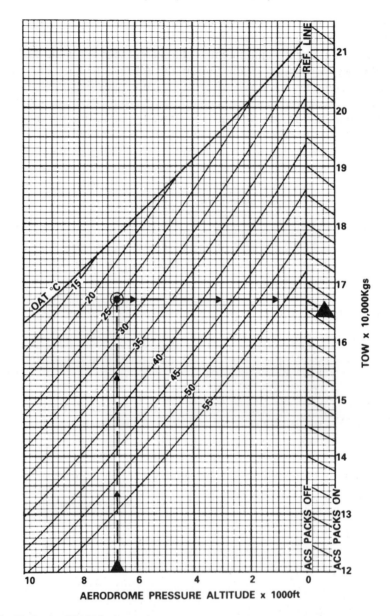

Fig. 26.1 Turbo-jet WAT limit graph.

flap to be retracted but also the reduced rate of acceleration to the flaps-up safety speed (FUSS) caused by the low lift/drag ratio. This results in a shallower initial climb, and thus a decrease in the WAT-limited TOW. A lower flap setting increases the lift/drag ratio and improves the acceleration rate, which results in the aircraft being able to accomplish the NFP gradient requirements more easily and consequently at an improved WAT-limited TOW. A flapless take-off reduces the performance below that of the high angled flap setting for take-off because there is no additional lift derived which can be traded-off against drag but it produces the best climb gradient possible.

Although the gradient requirement of the second segment is the steepest of the whole NFP, and for a large number of aircraft types is the most limiting, aircraft using water-methanol for take-off may be more restricted by the gradient requirement of a subsequent segment. After the third segment is complete the assistance obtained from the coolant to improve the performance ceases, and even the lower gradient requirements of the remaining segments may be difficult to attain. If this is so, it is necessary to limit TOW to ensure that the minimum gradients

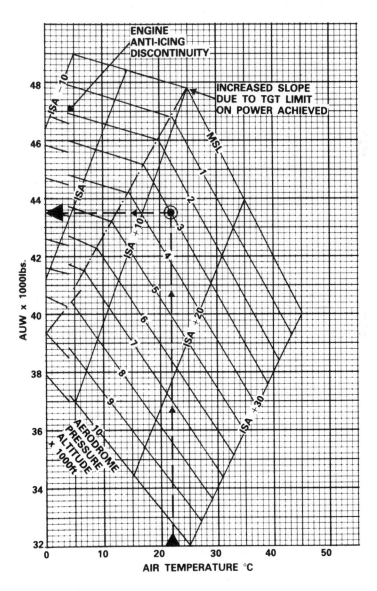

Fig. 26.2 WAT limit graph abnormalities (copyright British Aerospace).

of all segments of the NFP are accomplished. Thus the WAT-limited TOW ensures that the most severe requirement of the NFP is achieved for the conditions and configurations under consideration.

Because all permissible configurations must be scheduled in the Flight Manual the graphs tend to be more complicated and of a different shape to those of other aircraft. The more ancillary equipment used for take-off, the greater is the risk of causing a further limitation on the take-off performance. If TOW has to be restricted, because of the use of this equipment, to ensure compliance with the regulations, it is usually apparent from the format and layout of the WAT limit graph used in the Flight Manual when it is seen to be of a more complex nature. A typical example of this type of graph is that of a turbo-prop aircraft having water-methanol injection, engine anti-icing and limited power output, shown in Fig. 26.2.

For this aircraft, using engine anti-icing decreases the power available at temperatures below +9°C ambient temperature, which appears on the WAT curve as a discontinuity throughout the pressure altitude range. The maximum power that can be achieved is limited by the upper limit of the Turbine Gas Temperature (TGT) or by the gearbox torque limit.

Water-methanol injection effectively increases the mass flow and causes an increase in the power available up to the TGT limit. At the end of the third segment the water-methanol is switched off. This reduces the power available.

To ensure that the minimum gradients are attained in the remaining segments, the graph restricts the maximum TOW. This is shown by the increased slope of the matrix beyond the chain-dotted line.

When the WAT-limited TOWs for different configurations are equal, it indicates that the limiting gradient occurs after the aircraft has been 'cleaned up' at the end of the third segment and the configuration for all take-off conditions has been made the same, i.e. the limitation occurs in the fourth, fifth or sixth segments.

The factors which produce the best initial climb performance are *low* aerodrome *pressure altitude, low* ambient *temperature, low flap setting* and *use of coolant for power augmentation.* Its performance would be further enhanced if the engine anti-icing system, the air-conditioning system or any combination of these are switched off and the power management computer switched on.

CHAPTER 27

Obstacle Clearance

Although use of the WAT-limit graph will ensure that the most severe gradient requirements of the NFP are achieved, it will not guarantee that the aircraft will clear any obstacles that may be encountered in the take-off climb path. The JAA specify in JAR-OPS 1.495 the dimensions of the area, referred to as the **obstacle accountability area** or **domain**, sometimes called the 'funnel', in which it is considered necessary to avoid all obstacles, and the minimum vertical separation by which they must be cleared. The dimensions of the obstacle domain area are different for each performance Class of aeroplanes.

The maximum take-off weight that clears all of the accountable obstacles by the statutory minimum is referred to as the Obstacle Limited TOW.

27.1 THE OBSTACLE ACCOUNTABILITY AREA

For Class 'A' aeroplanes the obstacle domain commences at the end of TODA, or the end of TOD if a turn is scheduled before the end of TODA, and ends when the aircraft reaches a net height of 1500 ft above Reference Zero (RZ). The area has a starting semi-width of 90 m, or if the wing span is less than 60 m a semi-width of (60 m + $\frac{1}{2}$ wing span), either side of the intended line of flight, and expands at the rate of one eighth of the distance travelled along the line of flight from the end of TODA (i.e. Distance × 0.125) until the maximum width either side of the planned track is achieved (see Table 27.1). From this position a rectangle is drawn with sides parallel to the intended track to the point at which the aeroplane attains a net height of 1500 ft above RZ. *JAR-OPS 1.495(d) and (e)*. Its shape, therefore, is a funnel followed by a rectangle. Figure 27.1 illustrates the shape of the obstacle domain.

Table 27.1 Class 'A' obstacle accountability area maximum semi-width.

Change of track direction	0°–15°		Over 15°	
Required navigational accuracy	Distance*	Width	Distance	Width
Able to maintain accuracy	1680 m	300 m	4080 m	600 m
Unable to maintain accuracy	4080 m	600 m	6480 m	900 m

*Distance from TODA to maximum semi-width quoted.

213

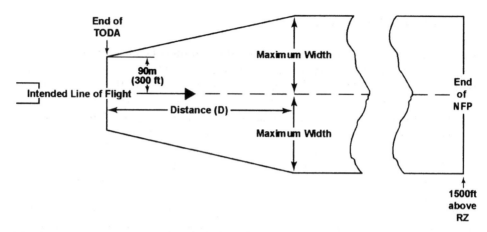

Fig. 27.1 Take-off obstacle accountability area.

The distance along track, from the end of TODA, at which the domain maximum width is initially reached, D, can be calculated by using the formula:

$$D = 8 \times [\text{Maximum semi-width} - 90\,\text{m}] \text{ if wing span is } 90\,\text{m or more or}$$
$$D = 8 \times [\text{Maximum semi-width} - (60\,\text{m} + \tfrac{1}{2}\text{ wing span})] \text{ if less than } 90\,\text{m}.$$

For all Class 'A' aeroplanes the obstacle domain is a fixed shape, with only the length of the final rectangle being a variable. The total length of the domain is determined by the distance taken for the aeroplane to reach 1500 ft above RZ, which in NFP calculations, is measured from the end of TODR. Before this distance can be used to determine the end of the obstacle domain, it must be reduced by the difference between TODR and TODA. Remember that the end of TODA is a fixed position on the ground, but that the end of TODR is a variable depending on many factors for its position. This means that the end of the obstacle domain cannot be determined until the actual TOW is known.

27.2 OBSTACLE CHART COVERAGE

The information required regarding the obstacles within the domain is obtained from an airfield type 'A' chart. These were described in Chapter 6 and depicted in Fig. 6.2. Remember the obstacle distance is measured from the BRP and the elevation is quoted above mean sea level. The take-off climb area of the chart for the runway commences at a width of 180 m at the end of TODA, which is the same width as the obstacle domain at this point. The chart area expands at the rate of one eighth of the distance travelled from the end of TODA, the same as the obstacle domain but extends to a distance of 15 000 m from the end of TODA, whereas the obstacle domain ends when the aeroplane attains 1500 ft above RZ. If the obstacle domain extends beyond the end of the type 'A' chart, an Ordnance Survey Chart of scale 1:10 000 should be used to obtain obstacle distances and elevations. The method used to determine obstacle clearance is described in Chapters 28 and 29.

27.3 VERTICAL SEPARATION

Obstacles encountered within the defined domain must be cleared by a minimum vertical interval of 35 ft in unbanked flight, or by 50 ft during a turn if it is intended that the aeroplane shall change its direction of flight by more than 15°, at a height above 400 ft gross, using a bank angle greater than 15° and not more than 25°, assuming the take-off was made on a dry runway. *JAR-OPS 1.495(c)(2). If the take-off was from a wet or contaminated runway screen height is then only 15 ft and close-in obstacles may only be cleared by this amount. IEM OPS 1.495(a).* The net aeroplane height at an obstacle is used to calculate the gross aeroplane height from which can be determined the aeroplane pressure altitude and altimeter indication at that point.

If it is planned to avoid an obstacle by turning, then this will impose further performance restrictions on the aeroplane, because turns can only be planned to occur when the power, speed and configuration of the aeroplane are constant. This is because it is impossible for the manufacturers to schedule the turn performance of an aircraft for segments during which these changes occur.

27.4 VERTICAL CLEARANCE CALCULATION

With the obstacles which require further consideration now being known, it is next necessary to determine the amount of clearance obtained by the NFP and, if this is legally insufficient, by how much the TOW must be reduced to achieve the minimum legal vertical separation. Two methods are currently in use to solve this problem, they are the **Profile-Plot** and the **Obstacle-Clearance Chart** methods.

The first method is used in Flight Manuals of older certificated aircraft and requires a scale plot of the NFP profile to be drawn from a fixed datum point. The obstacles within the domain are then plotted relative to the same fixed datum on the graph profile to enable the vertical separation of the aircraft from the obstacle to be assessed.

If the minimum vertical separation is not achieved, TOW is then reduced by an arbitrary amount and a new NFP calculated and plotted. The resulting clearance of each profile is then plotted on a separate graph and, assuming a linear change of obstacle clearance with change of weight, the exact weight at which the minimum permissible clearance is obtained can be assessed. This method is a lengthy procedure which can be improved by various short cuts described in Chapter 28. Alternatively the obstacle may be avoided by a planned turn as described in Chapter 29.

The second method utilizes obstacle clearance charts to determine the vertical separation from any obstacle. These do not require a special plot to be made because the graph consists of a series of NFP profiles plotted from the end of TODR. Obstacles are plotted directly on to the Flight Manual graph, and the vertical separation is assessed from the graph. If the necessary clearance minimum is not obtained, TOW may have to be reduced or one of a variety of methods may be employed to improve the climb performance.

27.5 RELATING THE PUBLISHED OBSTACLE DETAILS TO THE NFP

The first major difficulty with obstacle clearance calculations is that all the information must be related to a common reference point. All obstacles in the obstacle domain must have their details corrected, *before* commencement of the calculations, to relate them to the datum of the graph to be used for this purpose. There are commonly two datum points that may be utilized in the graphs, either of which may be used by the manufacturers. Both use the horizontal plane at the end of the TODR, which is Reference Zero, for the measurement of height but the distance reference point may be either the brakes release point or the end of TODR. Thus each requires a different method of correction to be employed.

27.5.1 Level runways

The only point common to both the NFP and the type 'A' chart (see Chapter 6) is the position at the commencement of the take-off run, referred to as the Brake Release Point (BRP). To determine the height of an obstacle above Reference Zero it is necessary to subtract the elevation of the BRP above mean sea level from the elevation of the obstacle. If the graph distance datum is the BRP no distance correction is necessary. However, if the graph datum is the end of the TODR then the length of the TODR must be subtracted from the published obstacle distance. See Fig. 27.2.

27.4.2 Sloping runways

The end of TODR on a sloping runway will be at a different elevation to that of the BRP. This causes an apparent change to the obstacle height above Reference Zero. If the reference datum is the BRP then no distance correction is necessary but if it is the end of the TODR then once again the published distance must be reduced by the length of the TODR.

To correct the published obstacle elevation to become a height above Reference Zero the elevation of the end of the TODR must be subtracted from the obstacle elevation. The elevation at the end of the TODR can be calculated by adding for an upsloping runway, or subtracting for a downsloping runway, the elevation correction, which is equal to the TODR in feet multiplied by the runway slope, and applying it to the elevation of the BRP. See Figs 27.3 and 27.4.

This calculation may be summarized by the following formulae:

End of TODR elevation = BRP elevation $\pm$ (TODR in feet $\times$ Runway Slope).
Obstacle height above RZ = Obstacle elevation $-$ End of TODR elevation.
Obstacle distance from the end of TODR = Obstacle distance from BRP $-$ TODR.

Example: BRP elevation 2300 ft AMSL; TODR 3000 m; Obstacle elevation 3900 ft AMSL; Obstacle distance from BRP 10 000 m; Runway slope 2% upslope.

Solution
1. Corrected obstacle distance = 10 000 m $-$ 3000 m = 7000 m
2. End of TODR elevation = 2300 + [(3000 × 3.28) × 2%] = 2300 + 196.8 ft
                                      = 2496.8 ft.
Obstacle height above RZ = 3900 $-$ 2496.8 = 1403.2 ft.

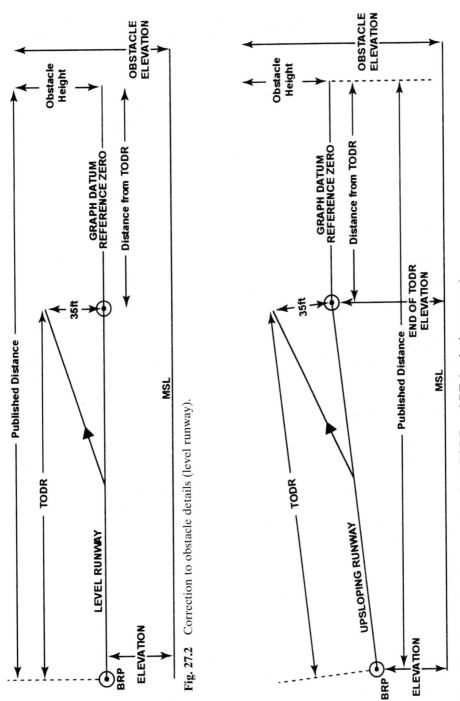

Fig. 27.2 Correction to obstacle details (level runway).

Fig. 27.3 The relationship of an obstacle to TODR and RZ (upsloping runway).

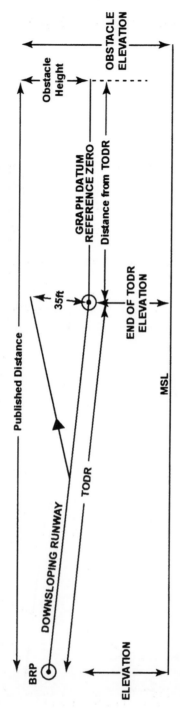

Fig. 27.4   The relationship of an obstacle to TODR and RZ (downsloping runway).

CHAPTER 28

The Profile Plot

This Chapter is included for operators of aircraft whose Flight Manuals do not include Obstacle Clearance Charts.

The profile plot is a side view of the NFP plotted segment by segment from the datum used. Two main datum points can be used – either the end of the take-off distance required (TODR) or the Brakes Release Point (BRP). TODR is a variable position, changing with TOW, flap setting, wind component, air density and runway slope, and to which obstacles can be related only with difficulty. BRP, however, is a fixed point at the beginning of TORA to which obstacles can be related easily. This chapter is a general guide to the method employed using BRP as the datum.

28.1 PLOTTING THE PROFILE

Because the obstacle and runway details are fixed, a skeleton profile graph can be drawn using BRP as the datum for each runway likely to be used, at any particular aerodrome. The greatest advantage of this method is that because so much of the data is fixed the operator can pre-print standard graphs in bulk.

All parts of the NFP, except the third and fifth segments which are level, can be solved by simple geometric right-angle triangles in which two factors are known enabling the third to be calculated. If a segment distance/height conversion chart is included in the Flight Manual, the calculation is unnecessary because the answer extracted from the segment graph can be easily converted to a plottable distance or height. The terms used and their relationship are illustrated in Fig. 28.1.

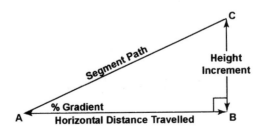

Fig. 28.1 The segment triangle.

From the segment triangle it can be seen that:

tan Gradient = Height Increment/Horizontal Distance

Gradient % = BC/AB

Horizontal Distance Travelled = BC/Gradient %

Height Increment = Gradient % × Horizontal Distance.

To account the effect of the along track wind component the horizontal distance should be divided by the TAS and multiplied by the groundspeed.

The NFP is worked out by solving the triangle or equivalent for each of the segments, then plotting the results as discussed above. It is best if a table similar to Table 28.1 is completed before attempting to draw a profile. In the example shown the BRP elevation is 2000 ft AMSL, the runway slope is 1.5% UP, the gross height of flap retraction is 600 ft in still air and there are four obstacles for which the corrected details related to BRP are as follows:

(1)   Distance 15 000 ft; Elevation 2430 ft AMSL; Height 430 ft above BRP.
(2)   Distance 30 000 ft; Elevation 2830 ft AMSL; Height 830 ft above BRP.
(3)   Distance 42 000 ft; Elevation 3430 ft AMSL; Height 1430 ft above BRP.
(4)   Distance 45 000 ft; Elevation 3430 ft AMSL; Height 1430 ft above BRP.

Table 28.1   Example of a completed NFP proforma.

CORRECTION TO RZ + 120 ft

Segment	Net gradient (%)	Height above BRP at		Segment increment		Distance from BRP
		Start of segment	End of segment	Height	Distance	
	(a)	(b)	(c)	(d)	(e)	(f)
1 TODR	1.5%	0	155	120	8000	8000
2 FIRST	3%	155	215	60	2000	10 000
3 SECOND	5%	215	655	440	8800	18 800
4 THIRD	0%	655	655	0	5000	23 800
5 FOURTH	4%	655	1620	965	24 125	47 925
6 FIFTH	0%	1620	1620	0	4000	51 925

Using the Flight Manual and the segment triangle formulae the details of the NFP were calculated and entered on the proforma as in Table 28.1. These details were then plotted on a profile graph as in Fig. 28.2. If the NFP does not clear the plotted obstacles by at least the minimum amount (the example did not clear Obstacle 3) then the TOW will have to be reduced until this minimum is achieved.

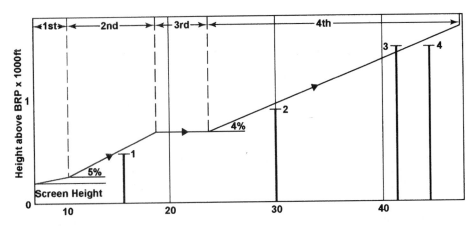

Fig. 28.2 Example of a plotted NFP profile.

It is extremely important to remember that when calculating the First Segment the net gradient of climb should be extracted as accurately as possible, because it is used as the entering argument in later graphs for other segments.

28.2 OBSTACLE CLEARANCE BY TOW REDUCTION

If, on the original NFP profile plot, the obstacles in the domain are not cleared by the statutory minimum vertical clearance of 35 ft, further calculations are necessary to find the exact TOW that will enable the aircraft to achieve this minimum separation. The TOW is first arbitrarily reduced by an amount that will assuredly achieve the desired result. For medium sized aircraft by about 3000 lb and for larger aircraft aircraft by about 5000 lb.

Initially reduce the original TOW by the selected amount to obtain the first revised TOW. The second revised TOW is obtained by reducing the first revised TOW by the same amount. Recalculate the whole NFP for each of these TOWs. The new profiles may be plotted on the same graph because the fixed reference datum remains unchanged – i.e. brakes release point (BRP) at the beginning of TODR. The obstacles do not require replotting because they were plotted from this datum in the first instance.

At the limiting obstacle, measure the vertical clearance of each NFP. It is best if the revised NFPs are plotted in different colours for clarity. Plot these vertical clearances on a separate interpolation graph as illustrated in Fig. 28.3.

In this assessment it is assumed that the resulting vertical clearances change linearly with change of weight. Generally this assumption is accurate if the sample TOWs are not widely separated. The TOW achieving the minimum legally permissible clearance is then found by dropping a vertical from the intersection of the graph line with the minimum vertical clearance line.

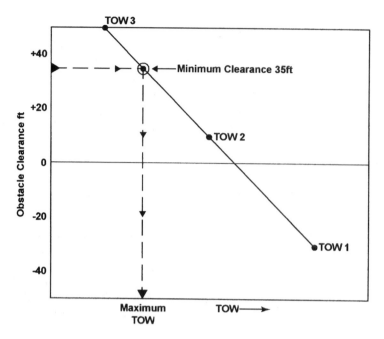

Fig. 28.3   TOW interpolation to obtain obstacle clearance.

28.3 RAPID CHECK OF OBSTACLE CLEARANCE

It will be realized that plotting the whole NFP and obstacles can be a lengthy procedure. It is therefore desirable to use short cuts, where possible, to eliminate any unnecessary work. From Table 28.1 it will be realized that the segment attaining the lowest gradient for any particular type of aircraft is the first.

If the procedure for drawing up the NFP graph is slightly changed, it could prove worth while. First draw the axes of the graph and only calculate the NFP to the end of the first segment. Now plot all the obstacles that have to be considered. (This may have already been done if it is a standard profile.) Plot the gradient of the first segment for the approximate length of the whole NFP. If all the obstacles are cleared by 35 ft, there is no need to continue with the NFP calculations and plot, because gradients attained in the other segments will be much steeper. See Fig. 28.4.

28.4 LEVEL-OFF HEIGHT

For most aircraft there is a maximum limit imposed on the length of time take-off thrust may be used. Usually it is five minutes, at which time the thrust must be reduced to the maximum continuous power setting. It is necessary to ensure that the flaps are retracted and the aeroplane accelerated to the final segment climb speed *before* the power is reduced. If, on a normal take-off, the time limit is likely to be reached during the second segment, then a limitation is imposed on the maximum level-off height, to ensure that the 'clean up' procedure is complete before the time limit is reached.

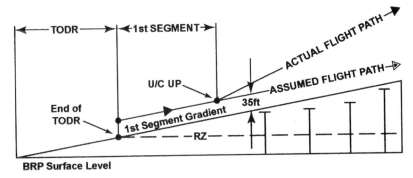

Fig. 28.4 Rapid check of NFP obstacles (copyright British Aerospace).

If, however, the time limit is attained during the fourth segment, then the aeroplane should be levelled just prior to the time limit. The power is then reduced to the maximum continuous setting and the aeroplane is then accelerated to the final segment climb speed. On achieving this speed the climb is resumed and continued at the reduced power until the aircraft reaches a height of 1500 ft above RZ. In such circumstances there will be two additional segments. The fifth segment is level and extends from the power reduction point to the position at which the final segment climb speed is regained. On attaining this speed the climb is resumed until 1500 ft above RZ is achieved; this is the sixth segment.

CHAPTER 29

Planned Turns

The only method so far considered to obtain the requisite clearance of obstacles in the take-off climb path domain has been to reduce the TOW, which improved the climb gradient enough to enable the aircraft to attain the minimum legal vertical separation. An alternative method which is legally permissible is to plan a change of direction in the climb path and its associated obstacle domain in such a manner that the limiting obstacle is no longer positioned inside the revised domain and therefore does not need consideration. Turns are authorized as a means of obstacle avoidance by *JAR-OPS 1.495*, which imposes limitations and restrictions on how it may be achieved.

29.1 VERTICAL CLEARANCE OF OBSTACLES

If the angle of bank used to execute a turn in the take-off climb path exceeds 15°, then the minimum permissible legal vertical interval above any obstacle encountered *during* the turn is automatically increased to 50 ft. *JAR-OPS 1.495(c)(2)*.

29.2 BANK ANGLE RESTRICTIONS

(1) Turns are *not* permitted in the take-off climb path below a height of 50 ft or a height equal to one half of the wing span, whichever is the greater, above the elevation of the horizontal plane at the end of the *take-off run available*.
(2) Above the height in (1) and up to a height of 400 ft above the elevation of the horizontal plane at the end of the *take-off distance required*, Reference Zero, the maximum bank angle is not permitted to exceed 15°, unless a special procedure, approved by the JAA, is being used.
(3) At heights in excess of 400 ft above Reference Zero the maximum angle of bank must not exceed 25°, unless a special procedure, approved by the JAA, is being used. *JAR-OPS 1.495(c)*.

29.3 AIRCRAFT PERFORMANCE IN A CLIMBING TURN

In level unbanked flight, weight acts vertically downward and is opposed by lift. The arrangement of these two forces acting on an aeroplane during a level turn is shown in Fig. 29.1. Weight still acts vertically downward and lift still acts upward along the aeroplane's normal axis. The force now opposing weight is the vertical component of lift which is equal to lift multiplied by the cosine of the angle of bank. This vertical component is insufficient to counteract the effect of weight. Additional lift is required to fully balance the weight; this can be produced only by increasing the angle of attack. If this is done it results in a decrease of the airspeed which reduces the amount of additional lift generated. This loss can be restored only by increasing the thrust.

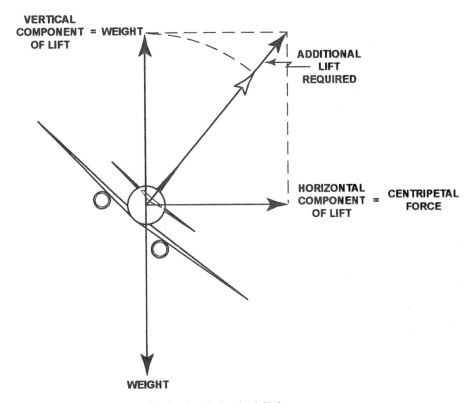

Fig. 29.1 Weight and lift distribution in banked flight.

The horizontal component of lift, which is equal to lift multiplied by the sine of the bank angle, is the centripetal force which causes the aeroplane to maintain a curved path. The load factor at a constant TAS is dependent on the bank angle, i.e. Load factor = (Total lift × cosine bank angle)/Total Weight.

However, during the climb after take-off with one engine inoperative, the power is set at the maximum permissible setting for that phase of flight and the speed is maintained at V_2. The thrust produced at this power setting must overcome the total of drag plus the rearward component of weight, which is equal to the weight multiplied by the cosine of the climb angle, as described in Chapter 14. Thus the thrust available is fully utilized and there is no extra thrust available to compensate for the reduced vertical component of lift. Consequently the performance in a climbing turn is diminished, the stalling speed increased, the airspeed, the climb gradient and the rate of climb are all decreased. Despite this if a turn using more than 20° of bank is made the speed must be increased to ensure there is an adequate margin above the stall. This further depletes the aeroplane's performance and results in a much decreased gradient and rate of climb.

Most manufacturers specify the climb gradient decrement for a 15° banked turn in the Flight Manual. For bank angles of less than 15° a proportionate amount should be applied. *AMC OPS 1.495(c)(4)*. To ensure an adequate stall margin and gradient correction for bank angles greater than 15°, in the absence of information from the manufacturers, the JAA provide the information shown in Table 29.1 in *AMC OPS 1.495(c)(4) Paragraph 2.*

Table 29.1   Climb gradient and speed correction for turns.

Bank	Speed	Gradient correction
15°	V_2	1 × Flight Manual 15° gradient loss
20°	$V_2 + 5\,\text{kts}$	2 × Flight Manual 15° gradient loss
25°	$V_2 + 10\,\text{kts}$	3 × Flight Manual 15° gradient loss

29.4 SCHEDULED TURNS WITH INCREASED BANK ANGLES

If a departure procedure with one-engine-inoperative requires a turn using a bank angle greater than the maximum permitted for normal turns then the procedure must be approved by the JAA. To obtain such approval the following criteria must be observed:

(1) Sufficient data must be included in the Flight Manual to enable the construction of the flight path accounting the increased bank angles and the associated speeds.
(2) Visual guidance must be available for navigation accuracy.
(3) The weather minima and wind limitations must be specified for each runway, and approved by the JAA.
(4) Adequate training in accordance with the requirements of JAR-OPS 1.975.
(5) The maximum bank angle must not exceed 20° between 200 ft and 400 ft above Reference Zero or 30° at heights above 400 ft above Reference Zero. *JAR-OPS 1.495(c)(3).*

29.5 LATERAL AVOIDANCE OF OBSTACLES

The maximum width of the obstacle accountability area varies with the navigational accuracy with which the climb can be executed and the change of direction required. These widths are specified in JAR-OPS 1.495(a) and (e) and are summarized in Table 27.1.

29.6 SAFE ROUTING

It is incumbent on the operator to establish a safe route to be followed after take-off in the event of an engine failure. It must avoid all obstacles to comply with either the en-route requirements of JAR-OPS 1.500 or the landing requirements at the departure aerodrome or the departure alternate aerodrome. *JAR-OPS 1.495(f)*.

A procedure requiring a turn in the take-off climb path must be planned in advance to be used in the event of a power unit failure, if this differs from the all-engines-operating route a 'deviation point' must be established. Should obstacle clearance beyond this point be marginal with all engines operating it should be checked that the minimum clearance will be achieved in the event of an engine failure. If the legal minimum clearance cannot be guaranteed beyond the 'deviation point' with one engine inoperative then the aircraft must be flown along the one-engine- inoperative route even if an engine failure has not occurred before this point is reached. *IEM OPS 1.495(f)*.

Some Standard Instrument Departures (SIDs) at particular aerodromes require that all turns be made below 1500 ft for all conditions and configurations. In such cases the procedure must be detailed in the Operations Manual, and obstacle clearance along the SID route must be checked. If detailed obstacle data for the SID are not available, the route must be plotted on a large-scale chart of the climb area and the appropriate obstacle domain examined for further obstacles. For such operations the point at which the turn must be commenced is usually readily identifiable by the pilot flying on instruments. Ideally the same method should be utilized in all circumstances when a turn is to be made as part of the climbing process.

Manufacturers are unable to produce data for any phase of flight unless the aeroplane is in a constant configuration and being flown at a constant speed. In the take-off climb path these conditions are met only in the second and fourth segments, therefore, turns are normally restricted to these segments. However, the Flight Manual for every aircraft type contains a statement giving the precise details of when turns are permitted in the NFP and to what angle of bank those turns are limited.

Obstacle details are given on the airfield type 'A' charts, which are related to the runway direction and are produced to the dimensions given in Chapter 6. Obstacle information outside of this area must be obtained from a large-scale chart. It is therefore essential to keep the change of direction to a minimum to ensure that the revised domain has adequate chart coverage. Small heading changes are also easily made and do not significantly affect the aircraft's climb performance. To minimize the angle of turn necessary to avoid any particular obstacle, it is essential to commence the turn as early as possible in the NFP. The most advantageous point to start turning is, therefore, at the beginning of the second segment, provided this does not bring more limiting obstacles into the NFP domain. For some aeroplanes this segment is relatively short and does not enable the aircraft to change direction by large angles before the segment ends. In such cases it is necessary to plan the turn in two phases with the first phase finishing at the beginning of the third segment, at which point the wings must be levelled before the flaps are retracted and the aircraft accelerated. The second phase of the turn commences at the start of the fourth segment. The necessity for this complicated procedure may be avoided if an extended second-segment technique, when permitted, is employed.

After the NFP obstacle domain has been plotted, it is necessary to ascertain which obstacle is the most limiting and the direction in which the aircraft must take avoidance action. Besides the obstacle itself, consideration must be given to the surrounding and subsequent topography before deciding on the direction in which the turn is to be made. It is pointless to plan a turn to avoid one obstacle only to discover that the domain of the new track encompasses obstacles more limiting, or just as limiting as the original. Contours as well as spot heights must be considered in this assessment because a turn towards ground having steep gradients may well clear a limiting area quicker than will a turn towards gradually sloping ground. See Fig. 29.2.

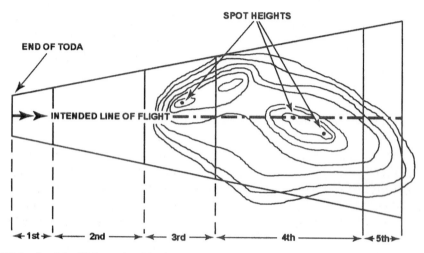

Fig. 29.2   Straight flight path with obstacles.

The direction of turn having been decided, the next step is to calculate the amount of change in direction that is necessary to position the obstacle outside the revised domain. The procedure employed to obtain such a separation is to measure the domain half-width at the position of the obstacle – i.e. from the centre-line to the outside of the original domain – then to plot a circle centred on the obstacle with a radius of half the NFP width, and draw an arc around the obstacle on the side on which the avoidance track will pass it. From the NFP centre-line at the start of the second segment, draw the tangent to this arc. With a protractor measure the angular difference between the original track and the new track. This is the change of direction required and is illustrated in Fig. 29.2.

If this plotting method is considered undesirable, it may be substituted by a calculation method if both the offset distance required to clear the obstacle and the distance to the obstacle from the start of the segment are known. The change of direction required can be calculated from the formula:

$$\text{Tan Angle of Change} = \frac{\text{Obstacle Avoidance Distance Required}}{\text{Obstacle Distance from Segment Start}}$$

This problem can also be solved by using the graph in Fig. 29.3.

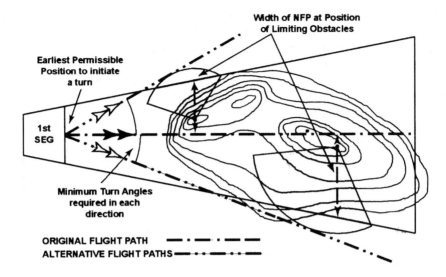

Fig. 29.3   Turn determination by plotting.

All Flight Manuals contain the basic information necessary to enable the details of a turn to be calculated and plotted. These are the radius of turn, distance travelled and time taken. They are derived from the inputs of CAS, pressure altitude, ambient temperature and the amount of change of direction required. The main reason these data are required is to enable allowance to be made for the effect that wind will have on the track.

The displacement of the track made good from the intended track is located by plotting downwind from the end-of-turn position a distance in metres of (windspeed in knots × time in seconds × 0.514) or in feet (windspeed in fps × time in seconds). This is shown in Fig. 29.4. When possible the wind should be used to assist the aircraft to obtain the required obstacle clearance. Thus turns should, by choice, always be made to the downwind side of the obstacle. If it is necessary to turn into wind, allowance must be made when planning the turn for the fact that the track actually made good will be *downwind* of the still-air track. Thus the amount of change in direction must be increased so that the clearance required is still achieved.

It will be seen from Fig. 29.5 that an obstacle is positioned 200 m left of the centre-line and 9000 m from the end of TODA. To place the obstacle outside of the domain the offset required is either 1100 m left or 700 m right, so the smaller change of direction is to the right. The change of heading required is calculated as:

$$\text{Tan angle of change} = \frac{\text{Domain semi-width} - \text{obstacle offset}}{\text{Distance from start of segment}}$$

From beginning of 2nd Segment at 1000 m from TODA: $\text{Tan} = \dfrac{(900 - 200)}{8000} = 5°$

From beginning of 4th Segment at 7000 m from TODA: $\text{Tan} = \dfrac{(900 - 200)}{2000} = 19°$

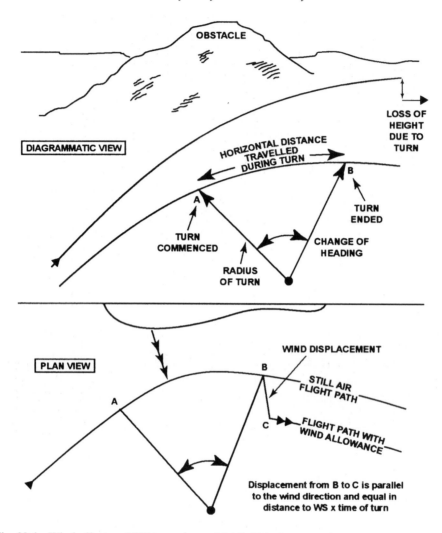

Fig. 29.4   Wind effect on NFP turns (copyright British Aerospace).

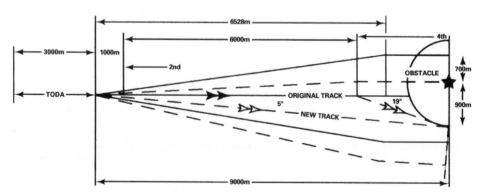

Fig. 29.5   Calculated heading change.

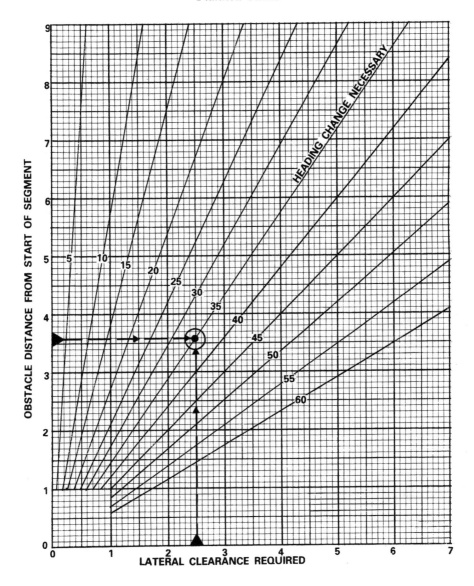

Fig. 29.6 Calculation of heading change.

Test Paper 7

Q1. Reference zero is defined as an imaginary horizontal plane passing through a point 35 ft vertically beneath the aeroplane at the end of:
  (a) TORR.
  (b) TORA.
  (c) TODA.
  (d) TODR.

Q2. The second segment of the Net Flight Path ends:
  (a) When the undercarriage is fully retracted.
  (b) At 400 ft gross height.
  (c) On reaching the selected flap retraction height.
  (d) When the flaps are fully retracted.

Q3. The speed to be maintained throughout the second segment is:
  (a) V_1.
  (b) V_2.
  (c) V_3.
  (d) V_4.

Q4. The diminishment to be applied to the gross gradient to obtain the net gradient for a twin-engined aeroplane is:
  (a) 0.7%.
  (b) 0.8%.
  (c) 0.9%.
  (d) 1.0%.

Q5. The Net Flight Path terminates when the aeroplane attains a height above reference zero of:
  (a) 1500 ft net.
  (b) 1500 ft gross.
  (c) 1200 ft net.
  (d) 1200 ft gross.

Q6. The WAT limited TOW ensures that the aircraft, with the critical power unit inoperative will:
  (a) Comply with all take-off requirements.
  (b) Comply with the most severe gradient requirement of the NFP.

(c) Ensure all that obstacles are cleared by the statutory minimum.

(d) Ensure that TODR does not exceed TODA.

Q7. Measured from the end of TODA, the distance at which the obstacle accountability area for an aircraft of 40 m wing span, which cannot maintain navigational accuracy and for which a change of direction greater than 15° is planned, will reach its maximum width is:

(a) 6600 m.

(b) 6560 m.

(c) 6528 m.

(d) 6400 m.

Q8. The minimum legal vertical interval by which an aeroplane may pass over an obstacle within the accountability area is:

(a) 35 m in unbanked flight and 50 m in banked flight.

(b) 50 ft in unbanked flight and 35 ft in banked flight.

(c) 35 ft in unbanked flight and 50 m in banked flight.

(d) 35 ft in unbanked flight and 50 ft in banked flight.

Q9. The fourth segment of the net flight path commences when the aeroplane attains:

(a) 400 ft gross height.

(b) The final segment climb speed.

(c) Flap retraction altitude.

(d) 1500 ft net height.

Q10. The minimum gross gradient in the second segment of the net flight path, for a twin-engined aeroplane, that is deemed acceptable by the JAA is:

(a) 1.8%.

(b) 2.4%.

(c) 2.7%.

(d) 3.0%.

Q11. A 'flat rating cut-off' is imposed on some Flight Manual graphs. Its purpose is to ensure that when the air density is:

(a) High the engines do not exceed their maximum operating temperature.

(b) Low the thrust developed does not fall below the minimum acceptable.

(c) High the thrust developed does not fall below the minimum acceptable.

(d) Low the engines reach their normal operating temperature.

Q12. For a change of direction of 10° in the climb path, if the required navigational accuracy cannot be maintained, the maximum semi-width of the obstacle accountability area is:

(a) 300 m.

(b) 500 m.

(c) 600 m.

(d) 900 m.

Q13. Given: TODR 2500 m; Runway slope 1.5% downhill; BRP elevation 2100 ft AMSL; Obstacle elevation 4000 ft AMSL; Obstacle distance 6000 m from BRP. The obstacle height above Reference Zero is:
  (a) 2023 ft.
  (b) 2072 ft.
  (c) 1777 ft.
  (d) 1728 ft.

Q14. Given: Climb gradient in still air 3.5%; Height gain 560 ft. The horizontal distance travelled in the climb in still air is:
  (a) 19.25 nm.
  (b) 2.63 nm.
  (c) 16.76 nm.
  (d) 6.31 nm.

Q15. Given: Obstacle distance 21 000 m from the BRP; Obstacle height 2000 ft. At the obstacle an aeroplane of weight 160 000 kg is at a height of 2300 ft above Reference Zero. The same aeroplane at a weight of 170 000 kg would be at a height of 1900 ft at the obstacle. The aircraft weight that will clear the obstacle by the statutory minimum is:
  (a) 163 375 kg.
  (b) 164 600 kg.
  (c) 165 400 kg.
  (d) 166 625 kg.

Q16. The speed required by JAR-OPS to be flown during a 25° banked climbing turn is:
  (a) V_2.
  (b) V_2 + 5 kts.
  (c) V_2 + 10 kts.
  (d) V_2 + 15 kts.

Q17. Given: Rate of climb 1210 fpm. The ground distance taken to climb from 10 000 ft to 33 000 ft at a TAS of 300 kts with a 50 kt headwind component is:
  (a) 79 nm.
  (b) 95 nm.
  (c) 111 nm.
  (d) 136 nm.

Q18. Given: Rate of climb 1500 fpm; TAS 300 kts; Wind component 50 kts headwind. The gradient of climb is:
  (a) 4.2%.
  (b) 4.9%.
  (c) 5.2%.
  (d) 5.9%.

Q19. Given: Windspeed 30 kts; Change of direction 60°. The downwind displacement of the end of a rate one turn is:
- (a) 600 ft.
- (b) 1013 ft.
- (c) 332 ft.
- (d) 332 m.

CHAPTER 30

The En-Route Regulations and Requirements

For the purpose of assessing an aircraft's performance capability, the JAA divides a flight into separate phases in each of which it is assumed that the critical power unit fails. A scheduled performance Class 'A' aeroplane must be capable of suffering an engine failure at any stage of flight from V_1 onward and then continuing safely to its planned destination, alternate or diversion aerodrome and of then landing. A single engine failure is 'reasonably probable', and the degree of risk of a second failure is dependent on the number of engines and the time elapsed since the first engine failed. The purpose of the en-route regulations and requirements for public transport aircraft is to ensure that any incident is survivable. To this end the probability of a double power unit failure on a twin-engined aircraft has been deemed 'extremely remote'.

The en-route phase of flight commences at the end of the NFP, at 1500 ft above RZ, and continues to the point at which the aircraft reaches 1500 ft above the surface level of the destination or alternate aerodrome as appropriate. This phase differs from all the other phases because in it a two-power-units-inoperative consideration is imposed on all aircraft.

30.1 EN-ROUTE REQUIRED NAVIGATION PERFORMANCE.

For each of the airspace areas of the world the controlling authorities specify the minimum acceptable navigational accuracy within their defined airspace, in the appropriate area document, e.g. ICAO DOC 7030, ICAO DOC 9613, RNP/RNAV. Referred to as the required navigation performance (RNP) it is expressed in nautical miles and is the maximum distance from the intended position, within which an aeroplane must remain for at least 95% of its flying time in that area, which is ascribed the term 'containment level'.

For example RNP 12.6 means all aircraft flying in that particular airspace must remain within 12.6 nm. of their intended position for at least 95% of their flying time in that airspace.

RNP accounts the navigation signal error, the airborne sensor error, the display error and any flight technical error in the horizontal plane. The operator must select from the approved navigation systems for that particular area those that will be used to attain the required accuracy. *IEM OPS 1.243.*

30.2 GRADIENT DIMINISHMENT REQUIREMENTS

For all en-route calculations only the *net* descent path and the *net* stabilizing altitude (see Chapter 31) may be used to determine obstacle clearance. The one-engine-inoperative and two-engines-inoperative *net* flight paths are derived from the *gross* climb performance diminished by the amounts specified by *JAR 25.123(b) & (c)*, when the remaining engines are set at Maximum Continuous thrust. The gross gradient diminishments demanded by the airworthiness requirements to obtain the net drift-down gradients are shown in Table 30.1.

Table 30.1   En-route gross gradient diminishments.

Maximum Continuous Power set on the live engines.		
Number of engines	1 Engine inoperative	2 Engines inoperative
Two	−1.1%	–
Three	−1.4%	−0.3%
Four	−1.6%	−0.5%

30.3 TERMINAL AERODROMES

The following definitions of terminal aerodromes are those to be used for the en-route scheduling of Class 'A' aeroplanes.

30.3.1 Adequate aerodrome

For an aerodrome to be considered 'adequate', it must be available at the anticipated time of use and equipped with the necessary ancillary services (such as ATC, lighting, communications, weather reporting, navaids and safety cover) with at least one let-down aid available for an instrument approach.

30.3.2 Suitable aerodrome

A 'suitable' aerodrome is an adequate aerodrome where, at the anticipated time of use, the actual or forecast weather, or any combination thereof, is at or above the normal operating minima. *IEM-OPS 1.220.*

30.4 ALL CLASS 'A' AIRCRAFT

30.4.1 One-engine inoperative en-route scheduling regulations

The following rules and requirements for the one-engine-inoperative case apply to any route or *planned* diversion therefrom for all Class 'A' aeroplanes.

(a) Route planning conditions For an aircraft to be considered to be operating to Class 'A' performance standards, following a single-engine failure, not only must it be capable of reaching a suitable aerodrome at a height from which it can land safely, with the operative engine(s) set at the maximum continuous rating, as demanded by ANOs but it must also, in so doing, comply with essential conditions specified in JAR-OPS 1.500 & 1.505 with regard to this aspect of flight. These conditions are that, *in the forecast meteorological conditions for the flight*, the aeroplane must clear all terrain and obstructions contained in an area extending 5nm. either side of the intended track, provided the aeroplane maintains a navigational accuracy within the 95% containment level, from the power-unit failure point to the aerodrome selected for landing, by a minimum vertical interval of 2000 ft during the drift-down descent from the cruise altitude, *JAR-OPS 1.500(c)*, or by 1000 ft with a positive rate of climb. *JAR-OPS 1.500(b) & AMC OPS 1.500.*

Additionally, on reaching a height of 1500 ft above the landing surface level the aircraft is required to be able to attain a *net* gradient greater than 0%. *JAR-OPS 1.500(a)*. The airfield selected for landing must enable the aircraft to comply satisfactorily with the landing requirements of JAR-OPS 1.515 or 1.520. See Chapter 33.

The JAA requires the aircraft operator to increase the obstacle domain from 5nm. to 10nm. either side of track, if the navigational accuracy does not meet the 95% containment level. *JAR-OPS 1.500(d).*

(b) Minimum cruise altitude When scheduling a flight, the minimum cruise altitude should be determined assuming an engine failure at the most critical point in accordance with *AMC OPS 1.500*, as described in Chapter 31.

(c) Aircraft configuration If the forecast meteorological conditions are such that it is possible that the aircraft's ice protection system *may* have to be used, the aircraft operator, when planning the flight, must assume that it *will* be in use at the time of engine failure, and any reduction in aircraft performance so caused must be taken into account. *JAR-OPS 1.500(a) & 1.520(b).*

(d) Use of fuel The graphs produced by the manufacturers for drift-down calculations assume that Maximum Continuous Power or Thrust is set on the 'live' engines following an engine failure, however, credit for the reduction in AUW due to the fuel consumed during the descent is restricted to 80% of that which would actually be used. This restriction is already built into the graphs. *ACJ 25.123.*

(e) Fuel jettisoning Fuel jettisoning is permitted to an extent consistent with reaching the aerodrome of intended landing with the required fuel reserves, if a safe procedure is used. *JAR-OPS 1.500(c)(3) & 1.505(e).*

If an aircraft has a fuel jettisoning capability, and if this equipment is operated in accordance with the relevant procedures contained in the Flight Manual, the reduction in AUW so achieved may be credited in any subsequent calculations. Fuel jettisoning should be commenced at the beginning of the drift-down. The manufacturers usually produce separate graphs with and without fuel jettisoning available. Any adverse effects of the jettisoning equipment to the aircraft's performance must also be accounted for by the manufacturers. These cause and are shown as reduced gradients of climb or increased gradients of descent in the Flight Manual.

(f) Landing aerodrome   After an engine failure en-route the aerodrome selected for landing must meet the following criteria:

(1)   The performance of the aeroplane must comply with the requirements of JAR-OPS 1.510, 1.515 and 1.520 at the expected landing weight.
(2)   The actual weather reports (METARS) or forecasts (TAFS) or any combination thereof, and field condition reports indicate a safe landing can be made at the estimated time of arrival.

30.5 THREE- AND FOUR-ENGINED AIRCRAFT

30.5.1 Two-engines-inoperative en-route scheduling

The regulations for the one-power-unit and two-power-units-inoperative condition are exactly the same, except that two engines are assumed to fail *simultaneously* at the most critical point of that portion of the route where the aeroplane is more than a distance equivalent to 90 minutes at the **all-engines-operating long range cruise speed** at ISA deviation 0°C, in still air, from a suitable landing aerodrome at which the landing requirements can be met. *JAR-OPS 1.505(c)*. Also, on arrival at 1500 ft over the selected destination aerodrome the aeroplane must be capable of flying level for a further 15 minutes. *JAR-OPS 1.505(f)*. Inability to comply with the requirements for two-power-units-inoperative exacts the penalty of restricting the routes on which it is permissible to operate that aeroplane type. This is commonly referred to as the '**90-Minute Rule**'. *JAR-OPS 1.505(c)*.

This route restriction, therefore, is appropriate to three- or four-engined aircraft for which the manufacturers have not scheduled two-engines-inoperative data *and* to those aircraft for which the necessary data are scheduled but which are unable to comply with the regulations. If such is the case, then aircraft must be routed to remain within the requisite distance of a suitable alternate airfield and must comply with the one-power-unit-inoperative requirements, if it is to be considered as operating to Class 'A' standards.

It should be remembered that all these requirements and considerations are imposed for the purposes of performance flight planning. The two-power-unit-inoperative requirement therefore only applies to those aircraft which have the data scheduled *and* have a route that at some point exceeds the stipulated distance from a *suitable* landing airfield. If these requirements are not complied with, the double-engine-failure potentiality would become greater than a 'remote probability' and an acceptable safety standard would not be attained.

30.5.2 Over water speed

To maintain the incident probability rate at 10^{-6} it is necessary for an aircraft not having an acceptable two-engines-inoperative performance standard to remain

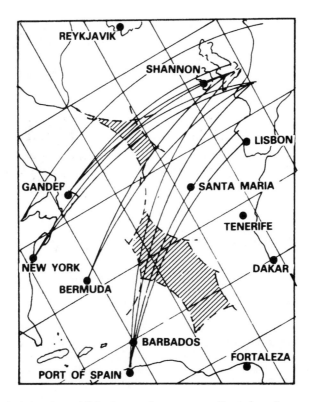

Fig. 30.1 North Atlantic prohibited areas for non-compliant aircraft.

within a distance from an aerodrome, at which it can land *and* comply with the landing requirements, that could be covered in two hours at the reduced TAS which would be attainable after it had suffered a single engine failure. This distance is approximately equal to 90 minutes' flying time at the all-power-units-operating economical cruising speed, which is the configuration and speed that would have existed before the incident occurred.

This speed varies with AUW and temperature, but for simplicity a representative TAS is selected for each aeroplane type, which is promulgated in the Flight Manual, and is to be used for calculating any route limitation. It is commonly referred to as the '**Over Water Speed**'. *V.A. Note No. 9 Issue 1. dated 9 August, 1984.*

If an aircraft with an all-engines-operating economical cruising speed of 500 kts is unable to comply with the two-engines-inoperative requirements, this cruising speed limits the routes the aircraft may fly to within 750 nm. of the nearest *suitable* aerodrome at which it can comply with the appropriate landing requirements. This restriction for the North Atlantic is illustrated in Fig. 30.1.

30.6 TWIN-ENGINED AIRCRAFT

Route restriction   The regulation restricting route structures, the '90-Minute Rule', was originally introduced during the piston-engine era to maintain the safety level required, despite the poor relative standard of engine reliability. Engine reliability is measured by the number of unscheduled engine changes that have to be carried out, per thousand flying hours, because of failure or the possibility of failure. Modern twin-engined aircraft, with their technically superior, more reliable and safer propulsion units, auxiliary units and navigation systems were unnecessarily restricted by this regulation. To alleviate the situation in June 1989 the CAA introduced new regulations which divided twin-engined aircraft in two groups to account for this fact. These have been adopted by the JAA and are promulgated in JAA Information Leaflet 20. These became known as the 'Extended Twin-Engine Operation Regulations' (ETOPS or EROPS) and are published in CAP 513. The two groups of aircraft are categorized as ETOPS and Non-ETOPS.

30.6.1 Non-ETOPS aeroplanes

(a) Aircraft over 45 360 kg MTWA or having 20 or more passenger seats Any aircraft certificated, for the purposes of public transport, to carry *more* than 19 passengers *or* having a maximum authorized take-off weight *exceeding* 45 360 kg is prohibited from operating over any route that contains a point further than one hour's flying time (in still air) at the normal **one-engined-inoperative cruise speed** (known as the threshold distance) from an *adequate* aerodrome unless it complies with the requirements for Extended Range Twin Operations (ETOPS) or is given specific clearance by the CAA/JAA so to do. *JAR-OPS 1.245(a)(1).*

(b) Aircraft having less than 20 passenger seats and aircraft having an MTWA of less than 45 360 kg Any aircraft certificated, for the purposes of public transport, to carry less than 20 passengers and aircraft having a maximum authorized take-off weight of less than 45 360 kg is prohibited from operating on any route having a point more than 90 minutes' still-air flying time at the normal all-engines-operating speed from a *suitable* landing aerodrome at which compliance with the landing requirements can be made.

Maximum distance from an adequate aerodrome The following factors should be accounted by the manufacturer to determine the speed to be used, not exceeding V_{MO}, to calculate the maximum distance from an *adequate* aerodrome:

(1) *Temperature.* ISA deviation 0°C.
(2) *Cruise Level.*
    (a) Jet propelled aeroplanes: FL170 or the gross stabilizing altitude whichever is the lower. (See Chapter 31.)
    (b) Propeller driven aeroplanes: FL80 or the gross stabilizing altitude whichever is the lower.
(3) *Thrust or Power.* Maximum continuous thrust or power with one-engine-inoperative.
(4) *Weight.* The weight of the aeroplane after take-off from an aerodrome at mean sea level at maximum TOW, an all-engines-operating climb to the optimum

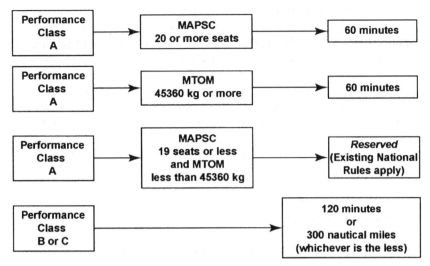

Notes:
1. MAPSC – Maximum Approved Passenger Seating Configuration
2. MTOM – Maximum Take-Off Mass

Fig. 30.2   Maximum distance from an adequate aerodrome. *IEM OPS 1.245(a)*.

long-range cruise altitude and a cruise at the long-range cruise speed with all-engines-operating until 60 minutes after take-off. *JAR-OPS 1.245(b)*.

30.6.2 Extended Range Twin Operations (ETOPS)

The complete rules and regulations regarding Extended Range Twin Operations (ETOPs) are contained in CAP 513. An airline that fulfils the criteria expounded in CAP 513 with regard to its aircraft's systems reliability may be granted permission for 'extended range twin operations'. This enables the airline to operate within an area where the standard maximum diversion time, from any point along the proposed route to a *suitable* aerodrome, known as the 'Rule Time', is 120 minutes or less (as specified by the CAA) at the **normal one-engine-inoperative cruise speed** (in still air). This area will be stated in the Air Operator's Certificate issued by the CAA.

After six months' satisfactory operations the CAA may permit the distance from a *suitable* aerodrome to be increased by 15%, that is to increase the 'Rule Time' to 138 minutes. After 12 months at this 'Rule Time' if the airline has satisfactorily carried out extensive ETOPs flights, the CAA may, on application, increase the 'Rule Time' up to a maximum of 180 minutes. Such permission will only be granted if the operator can prove an ability to meet the additional special requirements specified in CAP 513 Chapter 4.6.2.(b) with regard to Maintenance and Practices and Procedures, Crew Training and Equipment.

An example of the North Atlantic ETOPS areas for an aeroplane having a TAS of 420 kts is shown in Fig. 30.3.

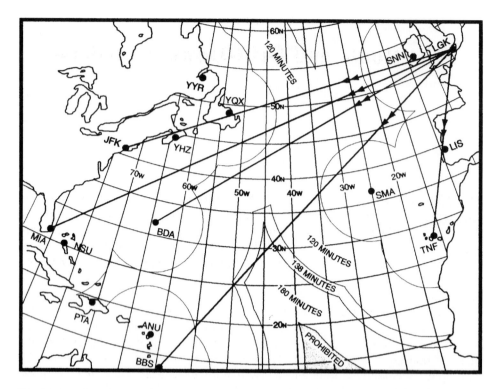

Fig. 30.3   Example of North Atlantic ETOPS areas at 420 kts.

CHAPTER 31

The Route and Drift-Down Technique

The ability of an aeroplane to comply with the appropriate en-route regulations and requirements depends on three factors – the aircraft's performance characteristics, the type of terrain over which it is flying and the type of climate experienced in that area. The performance capabilities of all aeroplanes are reduced by high ambient temperatures, and this can cause terrain clearance to become a problem in mountainous areas. For aircraft that already have low performance characteristics it can become an acute problem.

It is therefore necessary to ascertain whether or not the aircraft has a terrain clearance problem. If it has, a course of action should be pre-determined for specific sectors of the en-route phase. The alternatives available are either to divert from the planned track to a suitable en-route diversion airfield which fulfils the aircraft's landing requirements, or to reduce TOW to enable the aircraft to comply with the en-route regulations and requirements and maintain the planned route, or to re-route the aircraft away from the obstacles so that it no longer has a problem. Since the operator will always want the payload to be as large as possible to maximize profits, the alternatives must be compared to discover which requires the least reduction in payload.

31.1 CEILINGS

31.1.1 All-engines-operating ceilings

The ceiling of an aeroplane is that altitude at which attains a 0% gradient of climb. There are three types of ceiling:

(1) *The absolute ceiling*. The pressure altitude at which the aeroplane has a gross rate of climb of 0 fpm is referred to as the absolute ceiling. It has no practical value because it would take too long to achieve.
(2) *The gross ceiling*. The gross ceiling is assumed to exist at the pressure altitude at which the gross rate of climb for a propeller-driven aeroplane has fallen to 100 fpm or for a jet-engined aircraft to 500 fpm. This is often referred to as the 'service ceiling' because it is the maximum pressure altitude that can be used for practical purposes.
(3) *The net ceiling*. The net ceiling is assumed to be at the pressure altitude at which the gross rate of climb for a propeller-driven aeroplane has fallen to

150 fpm or for a jet-engined aeroplane to 750 fpm. This is normally the maximum pressure altitude which should be used to schedule the cruise.

31.2 DRIFT-DOWN TECHNIQUE

In the event of a power unit failure, the pilot's immediate action is to execute the appropriate emergency drills and to maintain altitude until any excess speed has decayed to drift-down speed. After that measures must be taken to accomplish the planned intentions.

If the aircraft is cruising above the maximum relight altitude when the power unit became inoperative, the initial descent technique is determined by the cause of the failure and the possibility of relighting the engine. If relight is a distinct possibility, a normal one-engine-inoperative descent should be initiated to enable the aircraft to reach the maximum relight altitude as soon as possible. However, if the cause of the engine failure is not obvious and relighting is only a remote possibility, from a performance viewpoint it is better to reduce the rate of descent to the lowest compatible with ATC requirements. This second method is the normal technique used if the engine failure occurs below the maximum relight altitude and terrain clearance is the only consideration.

The aircraft is descended at drift-down speed until it automatically levels off at that airspeed. The steepness of the descent path is dependent on the difference in altitude between the aircraft cruising level and the stabilizing altitude. If there is a considerable difference, the initial descent path will be relatively steep, but as the altitude difference diminishes the gradient becomes shallower until the path eventually becomes level. Use of this technique enables the distance travelled and descent time taken to be extended to the maximum.

In practice, an aeroplane suffering an engine failure will perform much better than the performance plan would indicate. This is because the *net* descent path is used for all planning calculations which is steeper and terminates at a lower stabilizing pressure altitude than actually would be experienced.

31.3 DRIFT-DOWN SPEED

The drift-down speed is the minimum IAS at which it is considered to be safe to climb, at the current weight and pressure altitude. The aeroplane will *not* climb unless the ambient temperature is such to enable it so to do. It will continue its slow descent, hence its name 'drift-down', until this condition obtains. The pressure altitude at which this occurs is called the 'stabilizing altitude'.

Because fuel is being used by the live engine(s) during the descent the aeroplane weight is decreasing as well as its pressure altitude. Therefore, the drift-down IAS must be revised continuously throughout the descent. The profile of such a descent is referred to as the 'drift-down path'.

Thus, the drift-down speed will produce a 0% gradient of climb at stabilizing altitude.

31.4 STABILIZING ALTITUDES

31.4.1 One-engine-inoperative stabilizing altitudes

The ceiling with one-engine-inoperative is referred to as the one-engine-inoperative stabilizing altitude. The stabilizing altitude is dependent on the AUW and the ambient temperature for its value. It is lower at heavy weight and/or high temperatures. Therefore, if the temperature remains constant along the route as the fuel is burnt and the weight reduces the stabilizing altitude increases. There are three types of stabilizing altitude:

(a) The absolute stabilizing altitude   The pressure altitude at which the aeroplane has a gross rate of climb of 0 fpm, with one-engine-inoperative, is referred to as the absolute stabilizing altitude. This is the maximum pressure altitude at which the aeroplane, having suffered an engine failure, is likely to cease drifting-down in the prevailing conditions.

(b) The gross stabilizing altitude   The gross stablizing altitude with one-engine-inoperative is assumed to exist at the pressure altitude at which the gross rate of climb for a propeller-driven aeroplane has fallen to 100 fpm or for a jet-engined aircraft to 500 fpm. It is that altitude at which the average pilot flying the average aeroplane is most likely to cease drifting down after an engine failure.

(c) The net stabilizing altitude   The net stabilizing altitude is assumed to be the pressure altitude at which the gross rate of climb with one-engine-inoperative for a propeller-driven aeroplane has fallen to 150 fpm or for a jet-engined aeroplane to 750 fpm. The net stabilizing altitude is that which must be used for comparison with the terrain and obstructions in the en-route obstacle domain. It is considerably lower than the gross stabilizing altitude and will ensure that the aeroplane will clear all terrain and obstructions by a more than adequate margin.

31.4.2 Two-engines-inoperative stabilizing altitudes

The definitions and descriptions of these stabilizing altitudes are the same as the preceding paragraph except two-engines-inoperative should be substituted for one-engine-inoperative.

31.5 ROUTE PROFILE COMPARISON

To determine whether or not an aircraft has a terrain clearance problem along the planned route it is necessary to obtain a terrain profile of the route on which all obstacles within the specified obstacle domain are shown. A profile of the aeroplane's stabilizing altitudes must then be plotted on the terrain profile chart starting with that at the TOW at the departure aerodrome and finishing with with that at the landing weight at the destination or alternate airfield, if one has been nominated. If the temperature remains constant along the route then a straight line is drawn

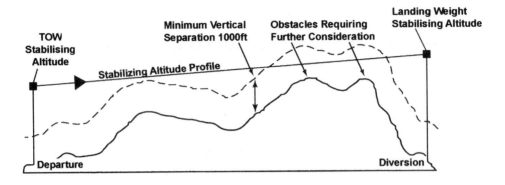

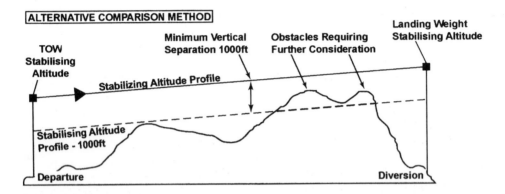

Fig. 31.1　Comparison of stabilizing altitude with terrain profile.

between the two altitudes. However, if the route temperature is not constant, it is necessary to calculate and plot the stabilizing altitude at selected AUW intervals along the route. These are then joined up to form a profile. The flight stabilizing altitude profile so obtained is pessimistic because no allowance has been made for the distance travelled during the climb (or descent) or for the AUW reduction resulting from the fuel burn-off during these phases.

By comparing the aircraft's stabilizing profile and the terrain profile, it is possible to rapidly assess whether or not the aircraft will comply with the terrain clearance regulations. Remember, all obstacles must be cleared by 1000 ft so it is necessary to either draw a (terrain + 1000 ft) profile or to reduce the aircraft stabilizing altitude profile by 1000 ft before comparison is made between the two profiles. If there is no conflict between the two profiles no further calculation is necessary. In fact the vertical separation achieved will actually be greater than that measured from the profile. See Fig. 31.1. *JAR-OPS 1.500(b)*.

31.5.1 The Effect of Wind Velocity

During the drift-down, wind velocity affects the path travelled and can be crucial in obtaining or not obtaining the requisite clearance. The distance travelled during the descent will be shortened into wind and lengthened downwind, and the drift-down path must be adjusted at each stage of the calculations to compensate for the effect experienced. The object of plotting drift-down profiles is to discover whether or not the terrain is limiting on TOW, and if so by what amount. *JAR-OPS 1.500(c)(2).*

31.5.2 Single obstacle

Should the profile comparison reveal that the aircraft does not adequately clear all en-route obstacles, it is necessary to proceed with the elimination of alternatives one step further. The planned route may still be suitable without reducing TOW, but to determine this it is essential to examine the profiles in more detail. If the aircraft's compliance is only prevented by one obstacle along the route, there is no problem if the obstacle is situated before the point of no return (PNR) is reached. This is because the aircraft may descend away from the obstacle in either direction. But if the obstacle is beyond the PNR, it may prove to be a limiting obstacle if the descent path from the PNR does not give the requisite vertical clearance of the obstacle. TOW will then have to be reduced if no suitable alternate aerodrome is available from this point, but the exact descent profile would have to be plotted to determine the precise weight reduction. See Fig. 31.3.

31.6 DETERMINING THE MOST CRITICAL POINT

From the route stabilizing altitude profile and the route terrain profile comparison ascertain the two most significant obstacles. They are those which are highest above the stabilizing altitude profile. Measure the distance between them. The procedure is now exactly the same as that for calculating the navigational critical point or equal time point. Use the formula $X = DH/(O + H)$ where X is the distance from the first obstacle to the critical point, D is the distance between the obstacles, H is the

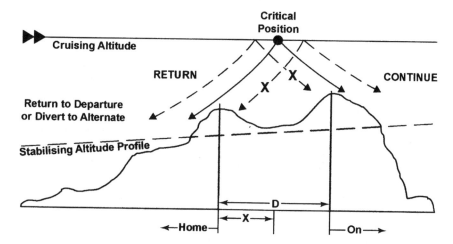

Fig. 31.2 Determining the most critical point.

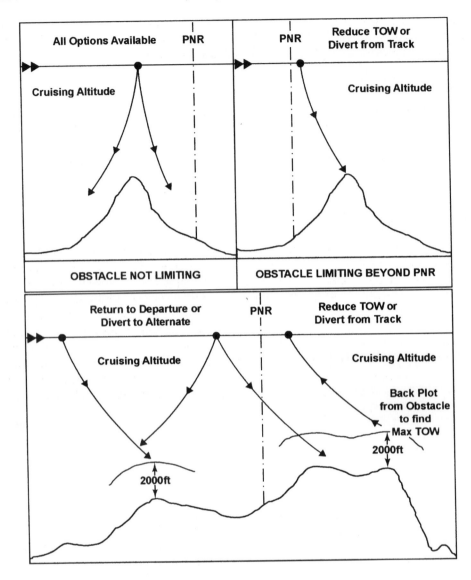

Fig. 31.3   Alternative procedures when obstacle limited en-route.

groundspeed back to the first obstacle and O is the groundspeed on to the second obstacle. Plot the distance X from the first obstacle to locate the most critical point, this is the assumed point of engine failure. See Fig. 31.2.

31.7 EN-ROUTE TERRAIN CLEARANCE CALCULATION

If the stabilizing altitude along the intended route does not clear all terrain and obstructions within the appropriate domain by 1000 ft and there is more than one significant obstacle then it is essential to make the necessary calculations to ensure compliance with *JAR-OPS 1.500*. Either of two methods commended by *AMC OPS 1.500* may be used, but each has disadvantages. They are:

31.7.1 Published minimum flight levels

By inspecting the appropriate charts the minimum en-route altitude (MEA) or minimum off route altitude (MORA) may be determined and used as the one-engine-inoperative stabilizing altitude. This has the disadvantage that unless a detailed drift-down path is to be constructed, it may impose a severe weight penalty. However, it has the advantage that a detailed terrain profile chart is not required and the normal topographical maps or route charts can be used.

31.7.2 Drift-down analysis

If the weight penalty associated with the MEA/MORA method is unacceptable, detailed drift-down paths must be calculated and plotted on a terrain profile chart to ensure all obstacles are avoided by a minimum vertical interval of 2000 ft during the drift-down. This method assumes an engine failure to have occurred at the *most* critical point, the critical position, between the two most significant obstacles along the route. The location of this point is dependent on the distance separating the obstacles and the mean wind velocity during the drift-down. The advantage of this method is that it produces the highest permissible en-route weight limitation, but the disadvantages are that the calculations are complex and the drift-down path must be plotted on a detailed route terrain profile chart, which will have to be specially obtained.

31.8 PLOTTING THE DRIFT-DOWN PROFILE

The procedure to be followed to plot the drift-down path is:

(1) Determine the AUW at the most critical point, i.e. TOW minus the fuel used from take-off to reach this point.
(2) Divide the descent path into segments and calculate the distance travelled in each segment until the obstacle is reached. A full description of this procedure is given in Chapter 32.
(3) Determine the aeroplane pressure altitude at the obstacle. If it does not equal or exceed a 2000 ft vertical interval then an arbitrary lower weight must be selected and the whole procedure repeated. This will facilitate the calculation of the exact weight that will clear the obstacle by the statutory minimum.
(4) Repeat (2) and (3) for the second obstacle.
(5) Plot both profiles. Where they intersect is the minimum cruise altitude for the flight. However, due allowance must be made for decision making.
(6) If a route terrain profile is not available the minimum flight altitude may be used to calculate the minimum cruise altitude as shown in Fig. 31.4, which will result in an excessive clearance of the obstacle and may cause a large weight penalty. *AMC OPS 1.500*.

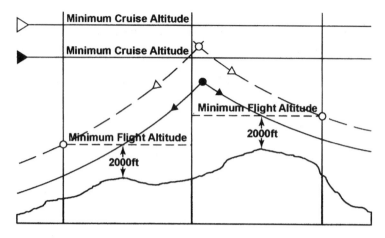

Fig. 31.4   The minimum cruise altitude.

Note: If MEA or MORA is at or below 6000 ft only 1000 ft clearance of obstacles is guaranteed. If such is the case 1000 ft should be added to the quoted value to enable it to be used in the drift-down calculations.

31.8.1 En-route alternate aerodromes

If a suitable alternate aerodrome is available which has no en-route limiting terrain and above which the aircraft can maintain 0% net gradient at 1500 ft, there is no need to plot any descent paths because an alternative course of action exists which does not restrict TOW. It is therefore only necessary to consider the drift-down in both directions from the assumed engine failure position to determine the most limiting path when no alternative course of action is available. However, when a limiting obstacle is beyond PNR and there is no en-route alternate aerodrome, the maximum TOW must be limited to that which will ensure that the drift-down path forward along track will adequately clear the obstacle.

In some circumstances, when a choice of drift-down path directions exists, the action to be taken in the event of an engine failure must be predetermined because of the terrain profile. This requires that the route be divided into sectors each having its own direction of drift-down. There are, of course, occasions when the pre-determined action is precluded by weather conditions or by some other factor that cannot be forecast. In that case it is necessary to restrict TOW, so ensuring that the original alternative is excluded from consideration.

31.9 FUEL JETTISONING

If an aircraft has a fuel-jettisoning capability, the aircraft operator is allowed by the regulations to assume that this facility will be available in the event of a power unit failure. Thus if the TOW is restricted by terrain clearance requirements, the operator may take into account the effects of fuel jettisoning to reduce or eliminate this limitation. At the planning stage the maximum AUW that will ensure adequate terrain clearance does not need to be converted to become a TOW limitation. The time taken to complete the fuel jettison procedure is calculated by the formula:

$$\text{(Actual AUW – Terrain-Clearance AUW)/Rate of Fuel Jettison.}$$

Fuel jettisoning must be complete before the Estimated Time of Arrival (ETA) overhead the limiting terrain. The latest time by which fuel jettisoning should begin is that ETA minus the time taken to complete the jettison procedure.

In the event of an engine failure, fuel jettisoning would be of greatest benefit if it is begun as soon as possible after the engine failure. At the latest it must have begun by the calculated position of fuel jettison. If the power unit failure occurs when the aircraft has passed this point, it will not be necessary to jettison so much fuel to achieve the required terrain clearance. It may even be unnecessary to jettison any – the exact amount will depend on the relative positions of the obstacle and the failure point. To determine the exact amount to jettison, a drift-down profile has to be plotted in flight. However, at the planning stage it is only permissible to assume that the most adverse set of conditions will prevail and to ensure that the maximum AUW at the commencement of the planned drift-down is not exceeded in the performance plan unless the jettison flow rate can reduce the actual AUW to this figure by the required position.

A further factor that cannot be ignored when considering fuel-jettisoning as a means of overcoming a terrain clearance problem is that of the amount of fuel required to reach the destination or selected diversion aerodrome at reduced speed. If the fuel required to the landing aerodrome exceeds the amount that would be available after stabilization, fuel jettisoning cannot be considered as an alternative procedure. *JAR-OPS 1.500(c)(3).*

An aeroplane experiencing a power unit failure will in fact drift-down on the *gross* descent path from the cruising pressure altitude. The profile will be shallower than that of the net descent path and is shorter because the *gross* stabilizing pressure altitude is much higher than the planned net stabilizing pressure altitude. If the technique of a normal one-engine-inoperative descent followed by a drift-down is employed, it may prove to be unacceptable to ATC in areas of dense traffic. Thus even though an emergency has been declared, it may only be permissible to descend from cruising altitude to the stabilizing altitude at the normal rate of descent. This will drastically reduce the time taken and the distance covered, and this restriction alone may prove to be a route limitation and require a different route to be selected.

In summary then, a full drift-down path profile need only be calculated if the stabilizing altitude profile does not clear more than one obstacle anywhere along track, or if it does not clear one obstacle beyond PNR *and* there is no alternative escape route to a suitable diversion aerodrome in either case.

CHAPTER 32

Drift-Down Calculations and Presentation

Terrain clearance is primarily a planning restriction which, if observed, guarantees that the aircraft will comply with the regulations and requirements. For this reason predetermined procedures must be stipulated for each route to ensure compliance with the regulations.

The performance flight planner's task is to determine how the terrain clearance regulations and requirements are best satisfied with the minimum reduction in TOW. The selection of a suitable route from departure to destination aerodrome depends on the aircraft's ability to comply with the regulations and requirements described in Chapter 30. Aircraft unable to comply with two-engines-inoperative have their basic route structure automatically restricted by the '60-Minute Rule' or the '90-Minute Rule' unless permitted to operate under ETOPs regulations. Thus the planner must use all of the data available to arrive at an acceptable solution which complies with the regulations and requirements.

In flight, the problem is to discover whether it is necessary to utilize the pre-determined alternative procedure or whether the flight has already progressed sufficiently along track, at the time of engine failure, for it to continue on its planned route and still obtain the requisite obstacle clearance.

A second in-flight consideration is that of the double incident for which there can be no prearranged procedure. This situation will arise if an aircraft having suffered an engine failure is prevented from following the planned alternative course of action by unforecast conditions such as weather below limits or the alternate aerodrome runways being unusable. Because of the nature of all these circum-stances they are not planning considerations. But they do require a drift-down path to be calculated and plotted in flight.

32.1 THE DRIFT-DOWN PROFILE

Because the drift-down path is not a constant angle of descent, but a path which is initially steep becoming shallower as the descent progresses, it is necessary to cal-culate the descent gradient at selected intervals to ensure accurate representation of the profile. The interval normally selected is either 2000 ft or 4000 ft, and *the gra-dient is calculated for the mid-height of each altitude band, using the mean AUW and mean temperature.* The drift-down is divided into altitude blocks starting at the cruising altitude and continuing down to the obstacle pressure altitude plus 1000 ft or stabilizing pressure altitude.

When back plotting for performance planning purposes, to find the limiting AUW, the drift-down path is commenced at the lowest altitude band, the base of which is the height of the obstacle plus 1000 ft. This lowest band will probably not be a whole two or four thousand feet block because its depth is dependent on the exact height of the obstacle, but nevertheless it is calculated in exactly the same manner as a block of normal depth. The gradient for each block is calculated up to and including the block that has as its upper limit the cruising altitude.

For an accurate drift-down path to be plotted, the AUW must be revised throughout the descent to allow for the fuel used. The mean TAS must also be revised to enable the distance travelled to be adjusted for wind and changing drift-down speed.

32.2 THE DRIFT-DOWN PROFILE CALCULATION – PLANNING

The descent profile is constructed by using the hypotenuses of altitude block triangles. The calculation is commenced at the lowest block for which it is necessary to ascertain the AUW at stabilizing altitude. Enter the appropriate graph with the obstacle pressure altitude plus 1000 ft and ISA deviation and extract the AUW which gives a net gradient of 0% at this altitude.

Re-enter the graph with the AUW, adjusted for fuel burn-off, and the mid-height of the lowest altitude band – extract the net gradient. Using the altitude interval and the net gradient, the horizontal distance travelled can be calculated and then corrected for wind component. The corrected horizontal distance is then plotted against the altitude band on the profile chart. This procedure is repeated for each altitude band until the cruising level is reached. Each hypotenuse is joined to form a continuous drift-down profile which must be plotted on the terrain profile. The relationship of gradient, altitude descended and distance travelled is depicted in Fig. 32.1, which also shows how each altitude block triangle is joined to the next to form a profile.

Note the terrain profile vertical axis must be re-labelled to become pressure altitude before the drift-down profile can be plotted.

The formula for calculating the horizontal distance travelled is as follows:

$$\text{Air Distance Travelled in nm.} = \frac{\text{Change in Height}}{\text{Gradient}} \times \frac{100\,\text{nm.}}{6080}$$

$$\text{Gradient} = \frac{\text{Change in Height}}{\text{Air Distance in nm.}} \times \frac{100\,\text{nm.}}{6080}$$

Which for a 2000 ft interval, can be transposed as

$$\text{Distance in nm.} = \frac{2000}{\text{Gradient}} \times \frac{100\,\text{nm.}}{6080} = \frac{32.89\,\text{nm.}}{\text{Gradient}}$$

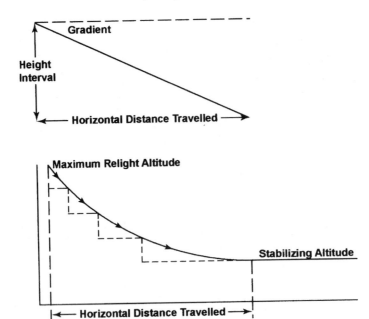

Fig. 32.1   The drift-down profile.

or for a 4000 ft interval as:

$$\text{Distance in nm.} = \frac{4000}{\text{Gradient}} \times \frac{100\,\text{nm.}}{6080} = \frac{65.79\,\text{nm.}}{\text{Gradient}}$$

Either of these equations can be solved using Fig. 32.2, which may be used even for the final altitude block of the descent despite the fact that it is likely to be a block of non-standard depth. By calculating the drift-down in this manner, the terrain-limited AUW can be determined relative to the obstacle along track. This terrain-limited AUW can be converted to a TOW limitation by using the all-engines fuel consumption for the time taken from take-off to get to the assumed position of engine failure. This then is a further TOW limitation that requires consideration when determining the eventual maximum TOW.

32.3 WIND EFFECT

The adjustment to the drift-down path for the effect of wind is made by altering the negative gradient extracted from the graphs in the proportion of TAS to G/S in such a way that:

Wind Effective Gradient = Still Air Gradient × (TAS / Groundspeed)

or

Ground Distance Travelled = Still Air Distance Travelled × (Groundspeed / TAS).

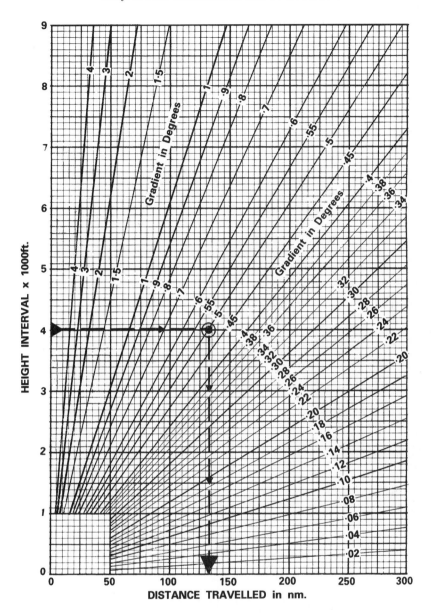

Fig. 32.2 Conversion of drift-down gradient (for use en-route).

The TAS is calculated from the Flight Manual using the aircraft AUW and pressure altitude at the mid-position of each altitude band to determine the IAS. By using the ISA deviation and Dalton Computer or Airtour CRP 5, this figure is then converted to TAS. Apply the given wind component to the TAS, to determine the ground-speed and the ground distance travelled accordingly. Alternatively use the graph at Fig. 32.3.

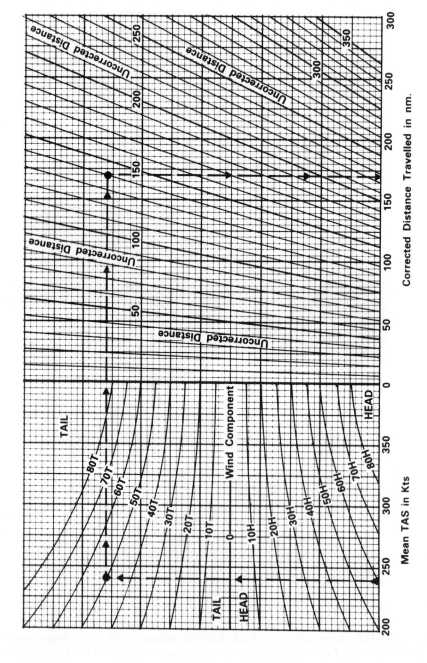

Fig. 32.3   Wind corrected horizontal distance.

If the rate of descent instead of the gradient of descent is known then the ground distance travelled in the descent can be found by using the formula:

Ground Distance in nm. = (Change of height / Rate of descent) × (Groundspeed/60)

It follows then that if the two formulae produce the same ground distance then they are equal and it is possible to calculate the gradient of descent from the rate of descent and the TAS or vice versa.

$$\frac{\text{Change of height}}{\text{Gradient}} \times \frac{100}{6080} \times \frac{\text{Groundspeed}}{\text{TAS}} = \frac{\text{Change of height}}{\text{Rate of descent}} \times \frac{\text{Groundspeed}}{60}$$

Then, by transposition and cancellation:

$$\text{Gradient of descent} = \frac{\text{Rate of descent}}{\text{TAS}} \times \frac{6000}{6080}.$$

For example: Given: Rate of descent 1500 fpm; TAS 500 kts.

$$\text{Gradient of descent} = \frac{1500}{500} \times \frac{6000}{6080} = 2.96\%$$

For all practical purposes *the still-air gradient of descent may be found by simply dividing the rate of descent in fpm by the TAS in kts.* Or the wind effective gradient may be found by dividing the rate of descent in fpm by the groundspeed in kts.

32.4 ANTI-ICING SYSTEM EFFECT

Anti-icing systems, when used, adversely affect aircraft performance, particularly after an engine failure. The gradient of a drift-down descent is increased by the operation of such systems, and the resultant effect may be presented to aircraft operators in the Flight Manual in one of three ways. A correction grid may be included in the en-route climb gradient graphs, but in some Flight Manuals the data may be presented by using separate graphs to depict the en-route climb gradients both with and without the anti-icing systems operating.

The third method sometimes used by the manufacturers is a statement in words of the correction to be applied to the gradient, printed in bold lettering on the same page as the en-route climb gradient graph.

32.5 ALTITUDE DATUM

To ensure that the plotted position of the assumed engine failure point is accurate, it is necessary to relate the drift-down profile correctly to the limiting obstacle under consideration. Therefore, the profile and the obstacle must be compared using the same datum. The aircraft in the cruise configuration is normally flown at pressure altitudes, i.e. with the altimeter sub-scale set to 1013.2 hPa. Obstacle heights, however, are related to MSL which, if a true comparison is to be made between aircraft and obstacle heights, requires MSL pressure (QNH) to be set on the altimeter sub-scale. Unless the MSL pressure happens to equal 1013.2 hPa, it is necessary to correct one set of information to the datum of the other. Because all performance graphs use pressure altitude as a datum, it is easiest to convert obstacle heights to become obstacle pressure altitudes. The correction necessary for this conversion is calculated by subtracting QNH from 1013.2 hPa and multiplying the result by 30. This correction is then added to obstacle height if QNH is lower than 1013.2 hPa and subtracted if it is higher.

$$\text{Obstacle Pressure Altitude} = \text{Obstacle Height} + [30 \times (1013.2 - \text{QNH})]$$

Alternatively the conversion of Obstacle Height to Pressure Altitude can be made using a graph such as that in Fig. 32.4. (See Chapter 4 for a full explanation of this correction.)

32.6 GRAPHICAL PRESENTATIONS

Three types of graph are used for the presentation of drift-down information – a stabilizing height graph, a descent net gradient chart and a composite chart. The stablizing height chart has entering arguments of the AUW and ISA deviation at the engine failure point, and enables the user to extract the stabilizing altitude. The fuel used during the descent, and the consequent progressive AUW decrease, is accounted for in the graph by portraying the stabilizing altitude for the AUW at the bottom of the descent against the AUW at the time of engine failure. These graphs are of little use for plotting a drift-down path profile but are of great value as a rapid method of plotting the stabilizing altitude profile.

The second type of graph presents the net gradient of climb with one-engine-inoperative (or two-engines-inoperative) against the entering arguments of pressure altitude, AUW and ISA deviation. These graphs have a correcting grid for use when the anti-icing systems are operated and enable the complete drift-down profile to be plotted.

The composite type of graph is rather complex but is extremely useful for making all the computations for the drift-down. From the graph can be obtained the drift-down IAS, the stabilizing altitude, the fuel used, the time taken and the distance travelled corrected for wind. An example is shown in Fig. 32.5.

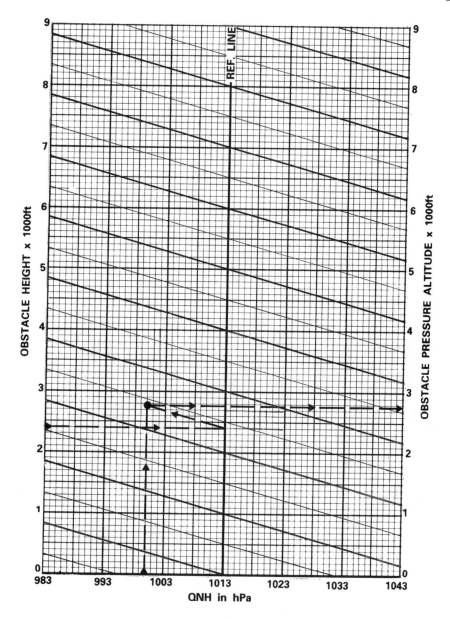

Fig. 32.4 Conversion of obstacle height to pressure altitude (for use en-route).

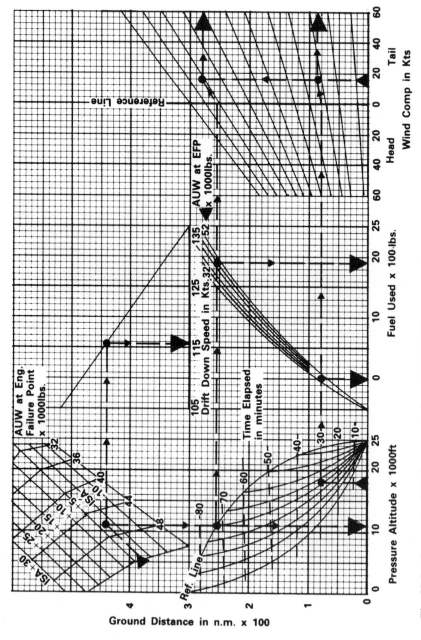

Fig. 32.5 Composite drift-down graph (copyright British Aerospace).

Test Paper 8

Q1. The minimum semi-width of the en-route obstacle domain permitted by the JAA is:
    (a) 5 nm.
    (b) 10 nm.
    (c) 15 nm.
    (d) 20 nm.

Q2. The minimum height above the landing aerodrome surface level at which a Class 'A' aeroplane with one-engine-inoperative must be able to attain a net gradient of greater than 0% is:
    (a) 1000 ft.
    (b) 1500 ft.
    (c) 2000 ft.
    (d) 2500 ft.

Q3. Stabilizing altitude is defined as that pressure altitude:
    (a) Which is 2000 ft above all obstacles in the en-route domain.
    (b) At which a 0% gradient is obtained in the configuration being considered.
    (c) At which a 0% gradient is obtained with all engines operating.
    (d) At 1500 ft above the landing aerodrome surface level.

Q4. Given: Still air descent gradient 4%; TAS 400 kts; Wind component 50 kts tail. The ground distance travelled in a descent from 32 000 ft to 8000 ft is:
    (a) 99 nm.
    (b) 88 nm.
    (c) 111 nm.
    (d) 123 nm.

Q5. Given: Rate of descent 1450 fpm; TAS 400 kts. The gradient of descent with a 50 kts headwind is:
    (a) 1.1%.
    (b) 3.58%.
    (c) 4.14%.
    (d) 3.63%.

Q6. For scheduling purposes, credit for fuel jettisoning during drift-down after

suffering an engine failure:
- (a) Is not permitted.
- (b) May be taken if the system is proven to be serviceable before take-off.
- (c) May only be taken above the maximum relight altitude.
- (d) May only be taken if sufficient fuel remains to reach the alternate aerodrome with the appropriate reserves.

Q7. The wind effect on the distance travelled during a drift-down:
- (a) May be ignored.
- (b) Shortens the distance downwind.
- (c) Equals the still-air distance × TAS / Groundspeed.
- (d) Equals the still-air distance × Groundspeed / TAS.

Q8. If a three-engined aeroplane suffers a double engine failure and is unable to comply with the en-route requirements, it may not be scheduled on a route which is further from a suitable landing aerodrome than the distance covered at the over water speed in still-air for a period of:
- (a) 60 minutes.
- (b) 90 minutes.
- (c) 120 minutes.
- (d) 138 minutes.

Q9. The minimum legal vertical interval by which an aeroplane may pass over an obstacle in the obstacle domain, during a drift-down descent is:
- (a) 1000 ft.
- (b) 1500 ft.
- (c) 2000 ft.
- (d) 2500 ft.

CHAPTER 33

The Landing Regulations

The landing phase commences at 1500 ft above the surface of the landing aerodrome and continues to the end of the landing ground roll. As with all other phases of flight, Class 'A' aeroplanes must comply with the regulations of JAR-OPS and the minimum performance requirements of JAR 25. There are many types of landing, it may be scheduled or unscheduled, normal or short, onto a dry, wet or contaminated surface, after a normal or steep approach path. No matter which of these combinations the specified regulations and requirements must be obeyed. The maximum landing weight is the *lowest* of the field-length limited landing weight, the structural limited landing weight and the weight-altitude-temperature limited landing weight.

33.1 ALL LANDING FIELD-LENGTH CALCULATIONS

33.1.1 Wind component

Operational regulations and requirements specify that the wind component to be used for all performance calculations is 50% of a forecast headwind or 150% of a forecast tailwind. This factorization is usually already accounted for in the Flight Manual on the wind component grid by the slope of the graph lines or adjustment of the scale. *AN(G)R 7(7)(b)(v)(bb), JAR 25.125(e) and ACJ 25.1587(b)(7)1.*

33.1.2 Surface condition

All UK Flight Manuals contain data for landing on a wet runway. There is, therefore, no mention of the surface condition in AN(G)Rs because an acceptable level of safety will be achieved for both wet and dry runways. However, if such is not the case then *JAR-OPS 1.515* specifies the factorization that must be used in the landing weight calculations and is detailed in Chapter 34.

33.2 SCHEDULED LANDING FIELD-LENGTH CALCULATIONS

The time span between planning a flight and landing may be considerable. In view of this the forecast temperature, wind velocity and runway in use may be incorrect. The

JAA, through the medium of JAR-OPS, therefore, impose additional regulations to restrict the use of such data without penalizing the operator unnecessarily. These are *the despatch rules and apply to all planned or scheduled* landing field-length calculations, for both the destination and alternate aerodromes.

The despatch rules formulated by the CAA, were adopted and modified by the JAA. They were not designed to cater for all contingencies and only apply to calculations made before the flight commences, but they are designed such that if correctly applied the crew should not have to make critical performance decisions in flight. The manner in which the field-length-limited landing weight is calculated is determined by whether or not the computation is made at the pre-flight planning stage. If it is, then it is referred to as a 'scheduled' landing field-length weight calculation for which the despatch rules apply. *AIC 11/1998 (Pink 164) Paragraph 3.2.*

When approaching or arriving overhead the scheduled landing aerodrome the pilot will be informed of the surface temperature, wind velocity, runway in use and surface condition. At this time, the actual landing weight may be either more or less than the maximum calculated in the performance Flight Plan. Unless there is a significant difference between the actual and planned details, no account need be taken for this, because the safety factors used in the scheduled landing distances allow for any reasonable variation from the planned landing weight. However, the actual landing weight should never exceed the structural landing weight limit, except in an emergency. Should the conditions be considerably different to those for which the landing was scheduled then the calculated field-length limited landing weight should be revised.

33.2.1 The Despatch Rules

The rules applied to the pre-flight field-length landing weight calculations are:

(1) Operators *must* take account of runway slope, in the scheduled landing weight calculations, if it exceeds 2%. Slopes of a lower magnitude need not be accounted in the field-length limited landing weight calculations.

   This rule is made, according to AIC 11/1998 (Pink 164) Paragraph 3.4.1, on the following assumptions:
   (a) The landing would normally be into wind.
   (b) The effect of wind on LDR is usually greater than that of slope when landing into wind.
   (c) That in still air conditions the landing would be made uphill.
   (d) On any runway the LDA is the same in both directions.
(2) For aerodromes at which a choice of runways is available, the limiting runway is taken to be that which produces the lowest landing weight. It is assumed that the aeroplane will land on the most favourable runway in still air. This is normally the longest runway on which the aeroplane can be landed within 60% of the LDA for jet aircraft, or 70% of the LDA for turbo-propeller driven aeroplanes, as appropriate. More specific details of these factors are in Chapter 34.
(3) It is assumed that the aeroplane will land on the most likely runway to be assigned considering the probable wind velocity, the ground handling char-

acteristics of the aeroplane, the landing aids available, the terrain, noise abatement procedures and Air Traffic Control requirements.

(4) If the destination has a single runway which is so short that a specific headwind is required for compliance, then, an aeroplane may be despatched if *two* alternate aerodromes are designated on the flight plan, at which full compliance of *all* the landing requirements can be attained.

(5) If an operator is unable to comply with (3) above for the destination aerodrome, the aeroplane may be despatched if *one* alternate aerodrome is nominated on the flight plan at which full compliance with *all* the landing requirements can be achieved. *JAR-OPS 1.515(b), (c), (d) & (e).*

33.3 IN-FLIGHT LANDING FIELD-LENGTH CALCULATIONS

The despatch rules are designed to ensure that on arrival at the destination at least one runway will be available for landing either at the destination or at a designated alternate aerodrome. Thus critical performance decisions should not have to be made in flight if the pre-flight computations have been completed correctly. However, it is not possible to foresee all in-flight occurrences and to make due allowance for them. It may be necessary to divert en-route to an aerodrome which was not included in the performance flight plan, in which case it would be necessary to complete the landing calculations for the selected aerodrome in flight. If such is the case, all of the aerodrome detailed information should be used in the calculations; *the despatch rules do not apply in flight.*

CHAPTER 34

The Landing Requirements

The legislation devised by the JAA for the landing phase is unlike that which concerns other performance phases because it allows for the possibility of a double incident such as engine failure followed by a diversion to a designated aerodrome, or vice-versa. Thus it is designed for the highest level of safety possible, with a view to ensuring that if the regulations are followed, a safe landing at either the destination or the alternate airfield will, from the performance viewpoint, be guaranteed.

Originally there were two sets of minimum landing performance requirements standards from which manufacturers could choose to certificate new aircraft types, which were based on different safety factors and associated conditions. They are termed the 'Arbitrary' and 'Reference' systems and were initially published in BCAR's Section D. When JAR 25 was introduced, in 1974, both systems were transferred to this document and were referred to as the 'First' and 'Second' methods of landing certification. The Flight Manual will clearly state which system was used for certification purposes. However, in response to pressure from other European countries the UK eventually withdrew both from JAR 25. They were then summarized and published in AIC 11/1998 (Pink 164).

Although the details of both systems are contained in this AIC *only the 'Arbitrary' system is now available for aircraft certification.* Irrespective of the system used, the landing distance is made up of two parts, an airborne distance from screen height, at the runway threshold, to touchdown and a ground roll from touchdown to a full stop. *AIC 11/1998 (Pink 164) Paragraph 2.2.*

The gross landing distance is established using the specified parameters of the method used and is regarded as the theoretical minimum distance that an average pilot would take to land from screen height using *maximum* braking to stop. To determine the net landing distance the gross landing distance is multiplied by a specified field-length safety factor, which accounts for normal operational variabilities. This is the level of performance an average pilot could realistically expect to attain using *normal* braking. The distance obtained from the Flight Manual landing distance graphs is the net distance. *AIC 11/1998 (Pink 164) Paragraph 2.4.* The net landing distance required must never exceed the landing distance available. *AN(G)R 7(7)(a)(i) & (ii). JAR-OPS 1.515(a).*

In-flight landing performance calculations   If the flight has proceeded as scheduled with only minor variations to the planned temperature, FL or route then re-calculation of the landing performance is unnecessary. The safety factorization accounts for any reasonable variation to these conditions. However, if there is a major deviation from the planned conditions, or if doubt exists about the landing calculations, then they should be re-computed using the actual wind component, slope and temperature to determine an accurate landing weight or distance.

34.1 LANDING FIELD-LENGTH REQUIREMENTS

The landing distance is measured from screen height at the beginning of the landing distance available to the point at which the aeroplane comes to a complete stop at the end of the landing ground roll. The screen height is 50 ft for a normal approach path but can be as low as 35 ft after a steep approach. The landing distance required is that which is calculated accounting the requirements of both JAR-OPS and JAR 25.

The landing graphs   The data produced by the manufacturers for the landing field-length calculations account the following assumptions:

(1) The aeroplane is in the landing configuration and has made a stabilized approach with a CAS of not less than V_{MCL} or $1.3V_S$, whichever is the greater, to screen height. The speed used to determine the landing distance for a manual landing is V_{REF} which should be increased in turbulent conditions.
(2) Normal changes to the configuration, power or thrust, and speed are made in accordance with the established procedure and that no changes to configuration, addition to power or thrust, or nose depression are made after reaching screen height. *ACJ 25.125(a)(3)*.
(3) The landing is made by an average pilot without excessive vertical acceleration or wheel braking and is on a hard, dry, level runway.
(4) Any means of retardation available that is safe, reliable and does not require exceptional skill to control the aeroplane may be used.
(5) Any device dependent on the operation of any engine which significantly reduces the landing distance is not accounted, unless an alternative means of operation is available should the engine be inoperative. *JAR 25.125(a) and (f)*.

34.1.1 General requirements

Configuration   The aircraft must be in the landing configuration for the approach. No changes of configuration, addition of thrust or nose depression are permitted after reaching screen height. *JAR 25.125(a)(1) & (3); ACJ 25.125(a)(3)*.

Retardation   The pilot is permitted to use all means of retardation on the landing ground run for which there is a recognized procedure laid down in the Flight Manual. The brakes are to be used judiciously to prevent excessive wear of brakes and tyres. They should not be applied until the main wheels are firmly on the ground. However, if permitted, automatic braking systems may be selected 'on' before touchdown. Other means of retardation may be used if it is safe and reliable and does not adversely affect the controllability of the aeroplane. *JAR 25.125(b); ACJ 25.125(b)*.

Abnormal configurations   If it is permitted to operate the aeroplane with any of the retardation devices unserviceable, or if the use of reverse thrust is prohibited for noise abatement reasons, then the corrections or allowances that must be made to account for the effects on the landing distance and/or weight are stated in the Flight Manual. *AIC 11/1998 (Pink 164) Paragraph 6.*

If any device is used that depends on the operation of a specific engine, *and* if the LDR is significantly increased with that engine inoperative, then the landing distance must be determined with that engine inoperative. *JAR 25.125(c).*

Abnormal approach speeds   If V_{AT} has to be increased because of wind shear, gusty or turbulent conditions and the adjusted speed exceeds $V_{REF} + 7$ kts then the calculated landing distance must be corrected by the formula:

$$\text{Corrected LDR} = \text{LDR} \times V_{AT}^2/(V_{REF} + 7)^2.$$

Notice to AOC holders 5/94

34.1.2 Dry runway requirements

The JAA has determined that for safety reasons the landing distance on a dry runway must not exceed 60% of the landing distance available for jet-engined aeroplanes or 70% of the LDA for turbo-propeller aircraft. This means that all data for landing field-length calculations must include a factor of 1.67 for jet aircraft and 1.43 for turbo-prop aeroplanes. The safety factorization for short-field landing data will be specified by the JAA on approval of such operations. *JAR-OPS 1.515(a).*

If V_{MCL} exceeds 1.3Vs, at any practicable landing weight, then the landing distance determined by the manufacturers must be specified for an approach speed of V_{MCL} or 1.3Vs, whichever is the greater. Practicable landing weight is defined as empty weight plus the weight of fuel required for a 100 nm. diversion and 30 minutes hold, plus the weight of the minimum flight and cabin crew and 10% of the maximum payload. *ACJ 25.125(a)(2).* See Fig. 34.1.

34.1.3 Wet runway requirements

If the weather report (METAR) or forecast (TAF), or any combination thereof, indicate that at the estimated time of arrival the runway is likely to be wet then the landing distance required is to be the calculated landing distance for a dry runway increased by 15%. In other words, the dry runway LDR multiplied by a factor of 1.15. A wet runway is defined in Chapter 10. *JAR-OPS 1.520(a).*

If the Aeroplane Flight Manual (AFM) contains specific additional information regarding landing on a wet runway, then the landing distance available must not be less than the LDR on a dry runway. *JAR-OPS 1.520(c).* See Fig. 34.2.

34.1.4 Contaminated runway requirements

A runway is considered to be contaminated if there is 3 mm or more of water, wet snow or slush on the surface *or* a covering of 10 mm of dry snow *or* ice. Any landing

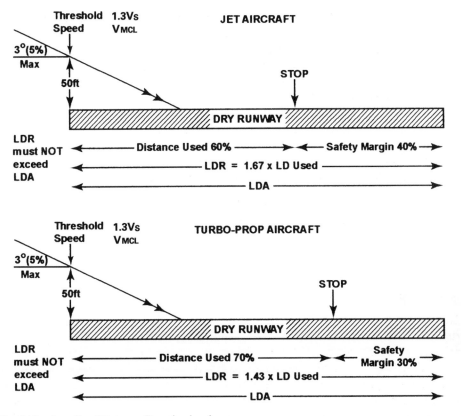

Fig. 34.1 Landing Distance Required – dry runway.

restriction or factorization that must be made to account for the surface condition is stated in the Flight Manual. Nevertheless, because of the risks involved, a landing on a contaminated surface should be avoided if possible. *AIC 11/1998 (Pink 164) Paragraph 5.2.*

If the METAR, TAF or any combination thereof, for the estimated time of arrival, indicate that the runway is likely to be contaminated then the LDA must be at least the length of the greater of:

(1) The dry landing distance required, and
(2) The landing distance required, calculated using JAA approved contaminated landing distance data or equivalent, multiplied by 1.15.

If the AFM contains specific additional information regarding landing on contaminated surfaces, then the landing distance available on a specially prepared contaminated surface must not be less than the LDR for a runway using the normal safety factorization. *JAR-OPS 1.520(b), (d) & (e).*

This means that the safety margin provided on a contaminated runway is no less than 48% for jet aircraft and 39% for turbo-prop aeroplanes. (See Fig. 34.2). But if the landing is to be made on a specially prepared contaminated surface a greater

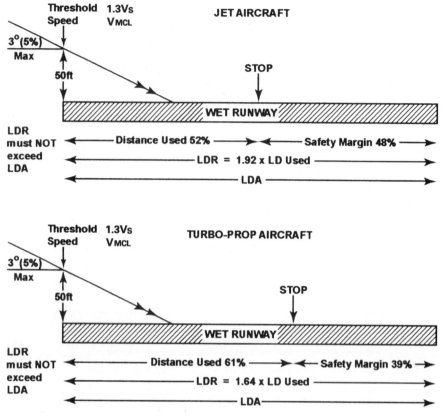

Fig. 34.2 Landing Distance Required – wet runway.

distance may be accounted and the safety margins accordingly reduced to 40% for jet aircraft and 30% for turbo-prop aeroplanes (see Fig. 34.1). However, any landing on a contaminated surface will normally utilize some of the safety margin no matter how well it is executed. *JAR-OPS 1.520(e)*.

34.1.5 Normal approaches

The approach to the screen height must be made at a descent gradient of 5% or less (3° glide path) flown at a constant speed, not less than the greatest of 1.3 Vs and Vmcl, with the aircraft in the landing configuration. In still air the maximum rate of descent allowed is 500 fpm. *JAR 25.125(a), ACJ 25.125(a)(2), V.A. Note No. 9 Issue 1 dated 9 August, 1984.*

34.1.6 Steep approaches

A steep approach is one that has a glideslope angle of 4.5° or more and a screen height of less than 50 ft but not less than 35 ft. Such approaches will be approved by the JAA provided the following criteria are met:

(1) **Aeroplane Flight Manual**. The AFM contains:
 (a) Field-length data determined using normal safety factorization.
 (b) Maximum glideslope angle and any other limitations.
 (c) The normal steep approach procedure and any abnormal or emergency procedures.
(2) **Aerodrome**. At least a visual glidepath indicating system is available at any aerodrome at which approval is sought for a steep approach.
(3) **Weather Minima**. The weather minima specified for each runway is approved and accounts:
 (a) Significant obstacles.
 (b) Glideslope and runway aids available.
 (c) Minimum visual reference at DH and MDA.
 (d) Aircraft aids available.
 (e) Missed approach criteria.
 (f) AFM limitations and procedures.
 (g) Pilot qualification and special aerodrome familiarization.
Appendix 1 to JAR-OPS 1.515(a)(3).

34.1.7 Short-field landings

Approval   The JAA will only approve the use of the short-field landing technique if there is clearly a public need and an operational necessity to employ such a landing technique, which may be due to the isolation of the aerodrome or to the physical inability to extend the runway. If such is the case, then approval will be given if a screen height of 50 ft can be cleared at the beginning of the declared safe area and the following criteria met:

(1) The vertical distance from the pilot's eyes and the lowest part of the wheels is 3 m or less.
(2) The Operations Manual must specify:
 (a) The minimum visibility/RVR for operations, which must be 1.5 km or greater.
 (b) The minimum wind limitations.
 (c) The minimum pilot experience and training requirements.
 (d) Any special familiarization requirement.
 (e) Any additional conditions the JAA may impose.

Landing distance calculations   The landing data provided for short-field landings must comply with the requirements for a dry dunway with the normal factorization. The landing distance used may consist of the LDA plus the length of any declared safe area. Only in exceptional circumstances will approval be given for a steep approach followed by a short-field landing. *JAR-OPS 1.515(a)(4).*
 The declared safe area must:

(1) Not exceed 90 m in length.
(2) Have a semi-width equal to the width of the runway or the aeroplane wing-span, whichever is the greater.

(3) Be free of obstructions or depressions liable to hazard an undershooting aeroplane.
(4) Be free of mobile objects at the time of use.
(5) Have a slope not exceeding 5% upward or 2% downward in the direction of landing.
(6) Have a uniform load-bearing strength but not necessarily the same as the LDA.

The landing field-length data based on measurements of actual landings and factorized in accordance with AIC 11/1998 (Pink 164) allows for such deviations as the aircraft travelling at a speed greater than the recommended approach speed, landing on a wet runway, the actual height being greater than screen height at the beginning of the LDA, and the retardation devices scheduled to be used not functioning. *AIC 11/1998 (Pink 164) Paragraph 2.5.*

CHAPTER 35

Landing Weight–Altitude–Temperature Limitation

It has been shown how the various requirements ensure that the LDR never exceeds the LDA, no matter what the surface condition. It is also essential to maintain the same level of safety if the aircraft is unable to land at the first attempt and has to go around as a result of a baulked landing or discontinued approach. To achieve this, the JAA specify the minimum gradient of climb that an aircraft must be able to achieve after an approach is terminated or a landing run abandoned.

35.1 THE APPROACH CLIMB

A missed approach is one that is discontinued at or above decision height from which the subsequent climb is referred to as the 'approach climb'. It is assumed that the aeroplane has approach flap set and that the *critical engine is inoperative* when the decision to go-around is made. At this point the undercarriage (landing gear) is retracted and the remaining live engine(s) are set to take-off power or thrust. The aeroplane is then climbed at a speed not exceeding 1.5 Vs to establish a minimum gross gradient of climb of 2.1% for twin-engined aircraft, 2.4% for three-engined aeroplanes or 2.7% for four-engined aeroplanes. The minimum permissible gradient must be achieved at the maximum landing weight permitted for the prevailing conditions, so that an aircraft lighter than this will always perform better than the minimum stipulated. The climb speed used to produce the WAT limitation graph is a maximum of 1.5Vs, if acceleration to this speed can be achieved within 10 000 ft from initiation of the discontinued approach procedure. If it cannot, the speed used is the maximum that can be achieved in this distance as stated in the Flight Manual. *JAR 25.121(d).* In an emergency, fuel dumping may be used to reduce the weight so as to attain the required speed and climb gradient. See Fig. 35.1.

If, however, the approach is made on instruments, with a decision height below 200 ft, the aeroplane, in the go-around configuration, must attain a minimum gross gradient of 2.5% or the published aerodrome minimum climb gradient, whichever is the higher. This gradient is based on the airfield obstacle clearance surface slope. *JAR-OPS 1.510(b) & (c) and IEM OPS 1.510(b) & (c).*

An approach may be discontinued at any point between commencing descent at 1500 ft AGL and decision height. *ANO Article 96* defines decision height as that which is specified by the operator as being the minimum height to which an approach to landing can safely be made without visual reference to the ground. *Once the aircraft has passed decision height, however, it is committed to land, unless it has all power units operating normally*, in which case in the event of the runway becoming blocked during the landing run, it may carry out a baulked landing procedure.

35.2 THE LANDING CLIMB

The climb made after a baulked landing is called the 'landing climb' for which the aeroplane is assumed to be in the landing configuration. After touchdown the throttles/thrust levers are advanced to the maximum take-off power position for the ambient conditions. Data provided for this maneouvre are based on the assumption that *all engines are operating* and the power is that which is available eight seconds after the power setting is made. If the aircraft has an automatic configuration-change facility, the configuration used in producing the landing WAT limitation graphs is the configuration that would exist five seconds after the initiation of the baulked landing procedure. The aeroplane is then climbed at a speed of 1.15Vs for four-engined aeroplanes, and 1.2Vs for all other types of aircraft. However, the speed must never be less than the greater of 1.3Vs and V_{MCL}, to ensure a gross gradient of climb of 3.2% is attained. *JAR 25.119*.

35.3 WEIGHT–ALTITUDE–TEMPERATURE (WAT) LIMITATION

The weight of the aeroplane at the estimated time of landing must not exceed that as limited by the altitude and temperature to guarantee that the minimum gradient requirements of both the all-engines-operating and the one-engine-inoperative configurations will be attained.

The gradient attained by an aeroplane is determined by the power/weight ratio. With the throttles/thrust levers at the maximum setting, the power and lift obtained are dependent on air density. The greater the air density, the higher the power output and lift generated and, consequently, the heavier the AUW that can be sustained at a particular gradient. Therefore, the maximum AUW at the minimum climb gradient required for any specific configuration is limited by air density which is determined by a combination of altitude and temperature.

This restriction on the landing weight is adversely affected by high aerodrome pressure altitude, high ambient temperature, high angled flap setting and the use of ancillary equipment such as air conditioning or anti-icing. Any one or any combination of these conditions will diminish the ability of the aeroplane to climb, resulting in a reduced climb gradient and, if the aeroplane is to comply with the minimum gradient requirement, a reduced WAT-limited landing weight.

The limitation is usually imposed by means of a Weight-Altitude-Temperature (WAT) limit graph for landing. If observed, *the WAT-limitation will ensure the stipulated minimum climb gradient with one-power-unit-inoperative from decision height, and the steeper gradient of climb on full take-off power from the landing surface level will be attained.* The landing weight of the aeroplane may never exceed

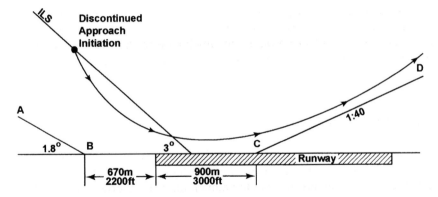

Fig. 35.1 The Optimum Discontinued Approach Path.

the WAT-limited landing weight for the estimated time of landing. *AN(G)Rs 7(6). JAR-OPS 1.510(a).*

35.4 LANDING WAT-LIMIT GRAPHS

The basic layout of the Landing WAT-limit graphs is similar to that of Take-Off WAT-limit graphs. Pressure altitude and air temperature are combined in such a manner that the limiting landing weight is easily extracted. For some aeroplane types the graphs for with and without reverse thrust are combined.

Turbo-prop aeroplanes have a wider variety of configurations available and have separate graphs for each flap setting, with and without water-methanol and have similar features to those described in Chapter 26.

Test Paper 9

Q1. For scheduled landing weight calculations, runway slope must be used:
  (a) When landing into wind.
  (b) When the crosswind is out of limits.
  (c) When it exceeds 2%.
  (d) For a one-way runway only when there is a tail-wind component.

Q2. The screen height for a normal approach and landing for a Class 'A' aeroplane is:
  (a) 30 ft.
  (b) 35 ft.
  (c) 50 ft.
  (d) 60 ft.

Q3. The minimum depth of wet snow for a runway to be considered to be contaminated is:
  (a) 3 mm.
  (b) 10 mm.
  (c) 12 mm.
  (d) 15 mm.

Q4. In the scheduled landing weight calulations the approximate safety margin allowed for a jet-engined aeroplane on a wet runway is:
  (a) 30%.
  (a) 40%.
  (c) 48%.
  (d) 52%.

Q5. The minimum gross gradient of climb permitted with one-engine-inoperative for a three-engined aeroplane approach climb is:
  (a) 2.0%.
  (b) 2.1%.
  (c) 2.3%.
  (d) 2.4%.

Q6. If reverse thrust is not used the safety level is acceptable:
  (a) When there is a tailwind.
  (b) When the runway is damp.

   (c) When there are strong crosswinds.
   (d) When LDA < 140% LDR for a wet runway.

Q7. The maximum glide-path angle permitted in the normal landing calculations is:
   (a) 3.0°.
   (b) 3.5°.
   (c) 4.0°.
   (d) 4.5°.

Q8. The minimum gross gradient of climb after a baulked landing is:
   (a) 2.3%.
   (b) 2.4%.
   (c) 2.7%.
   (d) 3.2%.

Q9. The safety margin included in the landing distance graphs for a turbo-propeller aeroplane on a dry runway is:
   (a) 30%.
   (b) 40%.
   (c) 48%.
   (d) 52%.

Q10. The maximum ground slope permissible in the direction of landing in any declared safe area is:
   (a) 2% upward and 2% downward.
   (b) 5% upward and 5% downward.
   (c) 5% upward and 2% downward.
   (d) 2% upward and 5% downward.

CHAPTER 36

Maximum Landing Weight

The requirements described in Chapters 34 and 35 are quite specific, and when applying for certification manufacturers must demonstrate that their aircraft is capable of achieving the stipulated minima. It is the application of these requirements to a given situation that is open to errors of interpretation. JAR-OPS details the method to be used in every set of circumstances, and this chapter is devoted to explaining the exact meaning and practical application of these rules.

The maximum planned landing weight is the lowest of the following individual limiting weights:

(1)   The maximum structural-limited landing weight,
(2)   The landing WAT limitation, and
(3)   The field-length-limited landing weight.

This maximum must be calculated for both the destination and the planned alternate aerodromes. The fuel used between the destination and the alternate aerodromes must be added to the maximum landing weight for the alternate aerodrome so that it can be compared with that of the destination airfield to determine which is the lowest and thus the most limiting. If fuel is not to be wasted, this then is the maximum AUW at which it may be planned to arrive overhead the destination aerodrome. If this is lower than the maximum destination landing weight, it becomes the limiting landing weight.

Factors affecting the landing weight which require consideration can be divided into the structural limitation, the minimum climb requirements and the field-length requirements. To complete the necessary calculations in the most efficient manner they should be made in the sequence shown in Fig. 36.1.

36.1 STRUCTURAL LIMITATION

The structural limitation is absolute and may not be exceeded without authority, except in an emergency. Most landing weight graphs have this limitation marked on both the WAT-limit and landing field-length distance graphs.

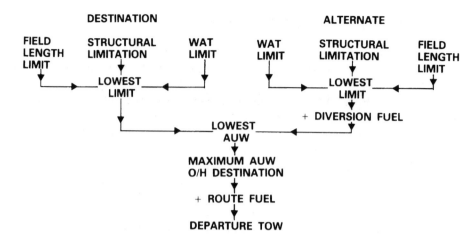

Fig. 36.1 Determination of limiting landing weight.

36.2 WAT LIMITATION

The minimum climb requirements will be achieved if the WAT-limited landing weight is observed. JAR-OPS categorically states that the landing weight of the aeroplane *shall not* exceed the maximum landing weight specified for the altitude and the expected air temperature for the estimated time of landing at the aerodrome at which it is intended to land, or at any alternate aerodrome. *JAR-OPS 1.510(a)*.

36.3 FIELD-LENGTH LIMITATION

The landing distance required *must not* exceed the landing distance available at either the destination or the alternate aerodromes. This requirement can be transposed so as to mean that the aircraft landing weight *must not* exceed the field-length-limited landing weight at the aerodrome of intended landing or at the alternate aerodrome. *JAR-OPS 1.510(b)*.

The method of comparison and elimination is shown in Fig. 36.1, from which it can be seen that, in addition to a safe landing being ensured by calculation of the maximum landing weight, a further limiting TOW can be calculated which requires comparison with all the other limitations on TOW.

36.4 FORECAST ZERO WIND COMPONENT

When the wind component is being calculated from the forecast wind velocity, it sometimes happens that for a particular runway the calculated component is zero – i.e. the wind direction is 90° to the runway. If this runway has a length and slope advantage over the alternative runway which has a headwind component, it may be prudent to select it for landing so as to maximize landing weight – always provided that the calculated crosswind is within the aircraft's limits.

36.5 PROCEDURE FOR EXCESSIVE ACTUAL LANDING WEIGHT

JAR-OPS require only that the landing weight should be checked for compliance with the regulations in the forecast wind and temperatures for the estimated time of arrival. This procedure is carried out at the flight planning stage. If the actual meteorological conditions during flight are more favourable than forecast, the actual landing weight may exceed the calculated maximum landing weight. It is merely laid down that such excess weight be 'reasonable', and that actual landing weight does not exceed the maximum structural weight. The difficulty lies in defining what is considered to be a 'reasonable' weight variation.

The various safety margins already included in the landing weight calculations take account of the fact that the aircraft may arrive at a higher weight than that calculated; but there is a limit to the variation of weight offset. It is therefore recommended that on arrival at the landing aerodrome the landing distance required be calculated using the actual figures for landing weight, runway in use, wind component and gradient to ensure that the LDR does not exceed the LDA. If it does, fuel should be burned off or jettisoned until the permissible weight is achieved.

36.6 NOISE ABATEMENT ON LANDING

Operating crews may be asked to avoid using reverse thrust on landing for noise abatement reasons. The captain's prime concern is the safety of the aeroplane and passengers not the comfort of those on the ground. Good airmanship demands that if the reverse thrust is serviceable then 'reverse idle' must be selected for landing. If this is not done the safety 'probability' factor is adversely affected. *AIC 103/1997 (Pink 56).*

Scheduled performance data with reverse thrust unserviceable is included in the Flight Manuals of particular aeroplane types but the probability factor used in the calculations assumes this event to be a relatively infrequent occurrence. If reverse thrust is not used because of noise abatement it would become a frequent occurrence and render the calculations and assumptions void.

The safety level is degraded to an *unacceptable* extent if reverse thrust is not used on landing when:

(1)   The whole runway surface is contaminated.
(2)   There is a tailwind component.
(3)   Strong cross-winds cause V_{AT} to be increased.
(4)   There is a known unserviceability of any retardation device.
(5)   LDA $< 140\%$ LDR for a wet runway.
(6)   The landing is made in an abnormal configuration.

CHAPTER 37
Maximum Take-off Weight

It has been shown in this part of the book that, for performance planning purposes, any flight can be divided into four separate and distinct phases.

The first phase begins at the start of the take-off roll and ends at the point at which the aircraft attains screen height at the end of TODR. This position is also the beginning of the second stage, which continues until the aeroplane obtains a height of 1500 ft above Reference Zero. The second part of the climb from 1500 ft to the route cruising altitude is considered to be part of the en-route phase, and is the third phase, which also includes the initial descent from cruising altitude down to 1500 ft above the landing surface level. The fourth and final phase commences at this point and finishes at the end of the landing run.

If an alternate to the destination aerodrome has been designated on the Flight Plan, the original simple case becomes more complicated because it is mandatory that a performance plan be also completed to the diversion airfield. Thus it becomes necessary to plan as additional stages to the basic performance plan both the en-route phase to, and the landing phase at, the alternate aerodrome from the position of the missed approach at the destination airfield.

For each phase of the performance plan a different maximum limiting weight can be calculated. These maxima are dependent on the topography, the meteorological conditions, the aircraft configuration and the regulations which must be obeyed.

Although safety is the prime concern throughout, the factor which predominantly influences the calculations can vary from one phase to the next. The aeroplane must be able to perform above a given minimum level within the constraints of the meteorological conditions and the airfield dimensions or the obstacle clearance required. To a certain extent it is the primary and secondary considerations which influence the sequence of calculations at the performance planning stage.

No legislation prohibits an aeroplane from arriving overhead either a destination or an alternate aerodrome at a weight in excess of the maximum permitted landing weight, but there are a number of legally enforceable regulations which prevent it from actually landing overweight. For this reason it is sometimes necessary for the pilot to decrease aircraft weight by either jettisoning fuel or by holding overhead to burn off fuel. Both these actions are wasteful and uneconomic. Planning to arrive at the landing aerodrome at anything much above the maximum landing weight wastes fuel, payload capacity, hours of airframe and engine life – and any prudent operator plans to utilize an aircraft to the maximum economic advantage.

It is obviously essential that the performance plan should take account of the possibility of a diversion from over the destination aerodrome, and sufficient fuel must be available for this. The minimum amount of fuel considered essential for safe operation on arrival over the alternate aerodrome is specified in the Operations Manual for each aircraft type, and allowance must be made in the performance plan for this weight, even if it is not likely to be used.

The whole essence of performance planning is to ensure that the flight can be conducted in the safest possible manner, with every foreseeable contingency taken into consideration.

Although every phase of any planned flight can be sub-divided, and even though for every sub-division there is an individual limiting weight, there will be for every phase only one over-riding maximum weight. Any limiting weight which is not a TOW can be converted, for comparison purposes, to become a limiting TOW for any stage.

The maximum TOW for the whole flight will be the lowest limiting TOW from the list which follows.

With these points firmly in mind, the recommended order in which the facts should be taken into account in planning calculations is as follows:

(1) **Alternate aerodrome: maximum landing weight**
   (a) Certificate of Airworthiness structural limitation.
   (b) Runway bearing strength limitation.
   (c) Field-length requirements, i.e. LDR.
   (d) Minimum landing-climb gradient, i.e. WAT-limited landing weight.
   (e) Runway contamination limited landing weight.

(2) **Destination aerodrome: maximum landing weight**
   (a) Certificate of Airworthiness structural limitation.
   (b) Runway bearing strength limitation.
   (c) Field-length requirements, i.e. LDR.
   (d) Minimum landing-climb gradient, i.e. WAT-limited landing weight.
   (e) Runway contamination limited landing weight.

(3) **En-route obstacle clearance: maximum take-off weight**
   (a) En-route terrain clearance to destination aerodrome.
   (b) En-route terrain clearance to the planned alternate aerodrome.

(4) **Departure aerodrome: maximum take-off weight**
   (a) Certificate of Airworthiness structural limitation.
   (b) Runway bearing strength limitation, i.e. LCN or SIWL.
   (c) Field length requirements, i.e. TORR, ASDR, TODR.
   (d) The maximum V_1/V_R ratio as a single limiting value.
   (e) The maximum brake energy absorption capacity, i.e. V_{MBE}.
   (f) The maximum tyre speed limitation.
   (g) The contaminated runway limited weight.

(5) **NFP obstacle clearance: maximum take-off weight**
   (a) Maximum climb gradient requirements, i.e. WAT-limited TOW.
   (b) Noise abatement regulations and restrictions.
   (c) Obstacle clearance after take-off, i.e. NFP.
   (d) Maximum time limitation on power setting.

The advantages of completing the performance planning calculations in the fore-going sequence are that it avoids the possibility of arriving over the landing aero-drome above the maximum permissible landing weight, and eliminates any unnecessary obstacle clearance calculations. The process of calculation and elim-ination is depicted in Fig. 37.1.

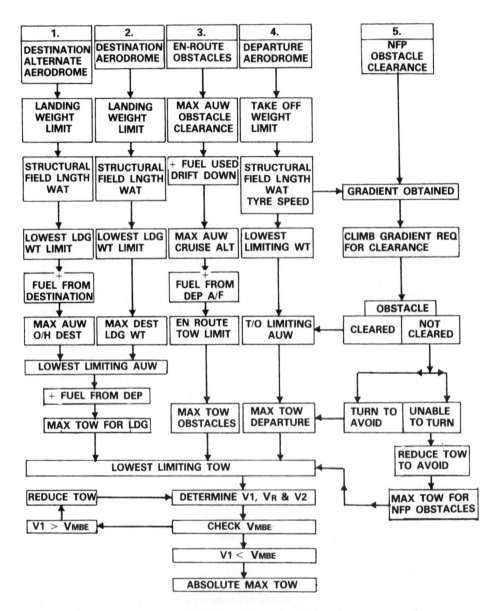

Fig. 37.1 The sequence of calculations for maximum TOW.

CHAPTER 38

Requirement Anomalies

Up to this point, each phase of flight has been considered in isolation. Short-comings in the current legislation *when the flight is considered as a whole* have therefore not become apparent. JARs and AN(G)Rs are regulations which are legally enforceable for each phase of any flight, and which indeed provide comprehensive legal coverage for that phase. When the legal package for a complete flight is considered, however, obvious defects emerge that could, in some circumstances, unnecessarily penalize the aeroplane operator. For instance, the rules and regulations governing take-off and NFP phases conveniently dove-tail together; but, if a plan view of the flight from the end of the NFP to the end of the landing run is drawn, it reveals shortcomings in the existing legislation. The maximum half-width of the obstacle domain at the end of the NFP is 900 m. Any obstacle within the domain width appropriate to the conditions must be cleared by a vertical interval of at least 35 ft. At this point the obstacle domain suddenly increases to a half-width of 5 or 10 nm., as appropriate, but because the distance of TODR is variable, so also is the distance of the end of the NFP. Not only does the width of the domain dramatically increase but so also does the minimum vertical interval from 35 ft to 1000 ft. See Fig. 38.1.

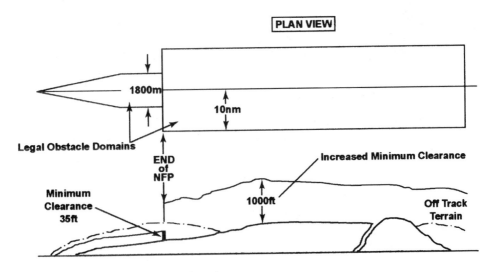

Fig. 38.1 Comparative obstacle domains.

Or again, the NFP assumes a power unit failure at V_1 on take-off, but terrain clearance regulations set out in JAR-OPS 1.505(b) require that an aircraft with two power units become(s) inoperative be capable of clearing all obstacles by 2000 ft between the failure point and the aerodrome of intended landing. This means that the aircraft must be capable of continuing its climb to stabilizing altitude and so achieving at least the minimum obstacle clearance.

For jet aircraft having an excess of power available over power required that may seem a problem which is no problem at all, but for a turbo-prop aeroplane which lacks such an excess of power, the requirement as it stands can pose real difficulties. If, for instance, an obstacle that could just be cleared by the minimum height clearance is positioned in the domain but near the end of the NFP, any TOW reduction which may be imposed by some other requirement will reduce TODR. This effectively 'repositions' the obstacle into the en-route domain where a larger vertical separation is required. So if no alternative routing is available, TOW will have to be yet further reduced.

One of the major British airlines overcomes this anomaly in the Regulations by imposing a graduated obstacle-clearance requirement for all obstacles within the domain. The minimum vertical separation from obstacles is progressively increased at the rate of 100 ft per 1 nm. travelled along track, from the end of the NFP until the minimum legal en-route vertical separation of 1000 ft is achieved. See Fig. 38.2.

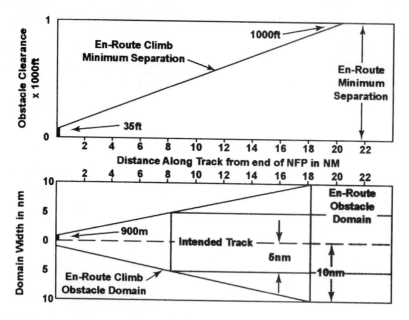

Fig. 38.2 Suggested transition from NFP to en-route obstacle clearance domains.

A similar improvement could be suggested for the descent phase of flight. JAR-OPS provides good coverage for the en-route phase, but no separate regulation exists for the descent of the aeroplane. The implications of JAR-OPS 1.500 for Class 'A' aeroplanes are that, if a power unit failure is experienced, the aircraft must clear all obstacles within the en-route domain up to and including the aerodrome of intended landing by at least 2000 ft during the descent or by 1000 ft in level flight. The same Regulation also specifies the minimum gradient climb at 1500 ft over the selected aerodrome must be positive. There is no regulation detailing a descent obstacle domain, or a minimum vertical separation for the descent, from cruising altitude to 1500 ft. It follows then that the en-route regulations are also mandatory for this phase and that if a diversion is initiated from overhead the destination, the same rules apply until overhead the alternate aerodrome. Here again no specified domain nor any vertical clearance for obstacles are laid down for the final descent and approach to land. It can only be assumed that the area to be considered in this instance is a funnel converging at the rate of 1:8 until it becomes a half-width of ($\frac{1}{2}$ wingspan + 60 m) or 90 m as appropriate at the runway threshold, and that the vertical separation from obstacles within this domain is reduced to screen height. These would seem to be logical parameters for the descent, but because there is no legislation specifically covering this phase, the en-route requirements are those that *must* be followed in practice.

As the law currently stands therefore, it can unnecessarily penalize the aeroplane operator by compelling the consideration of certain obstacles, and their minimum clearance limits, which could reasonably be regarded as being outside the domain in question. Good airmanship demands an accurate top-of-descent fix before a descent is begun and then an intermediate descent fix during the descent, so the aircraft's position in relation to obstacles in practice can be accurately determined.

A similar situation exists with respect to the missed-approach climb. Although no regulation exists that requires the operator to take obstacles positioned in the overshoot area into consideration, they cannot be ignored.

In this instance it is suggested that it would be prudent to assume that the aircraft, having attempted but failed to land, achieves no climb at all before it reaches the end of the TORA. The NFP in the case of the approach-climb commences at 200 ft above the landing surface level and continues until the aircraft achieves 1500 ft above that datum. The obstacles which should be considered are those lying in the missed-approach obstacle domain. In this instance, it is suggested that the domain should commence with a half-width of (60 m + $\frac{1}{2}$ wingspan) or 90 m as appropriate at the end of TORA and then expand at the normal rate, 1:8, to a maximum half-width of 900 m.

Obstacles in this area would have to be cleared by a minimum vertical separation of 35 ft in straight flight, or of 50 ft in turning flight. At this stage of flight the aircraft is usually at a comparatively low AUW, so it should have no difficulty in obtaining the necessary vertical separation under normal operating conditions. The minimum obstacle-clearance altitude will of course be more difficult to achieve under severe operating conditions such as high temperatures and high aerodrome elevations. Indeed, at certain aerodromes in some mountainous areas of South America, for some small Class 'A' public transport aircraft, the missed-approach case becomes, when diversion to an alternate aerodrome is being initiated, a limiting factor for the initial TOW from the departure airfield.

The landing performance requirements and method of application are fully covered by JAR's landing field-length requirements.

Irrespective of the quantity or quality of legislation, performance planning does not replace good airmanship. It is complementary to it, and its prime purpose is to relieve the pilot of having to make critical decisions about performance at a time when there is already considerable pressure.

Test Paper 10

Q1. Given: R/W 27 touchdown elevation 277 ft, TORA 2000 m, EMDA 2100 m, TODA 2300 m. R/W 09 touchdown elevation 167 ft, TORA 2200 m, EMDA 2300 m, TODA 2400 m. The runway slope for R/W 09 is:
- (a) 1.52% up.
- (b) 1.52% down.
- (c) 1.68% up.
- (d) 1.68% down.

Q2. The altimeter sub-scale of an aircraft is set to 1013.2 hPa and is not reset during flight. If the aircraft flies from an area of high pressure to an area of low pressure the altimeter reading will:
- (a) Over-read.
- (b) Under-read.
- (c) Remain the same.
- (d) Decrease.

Q3. At FL320 the ambient temperature is –34°C. The temperature deviation is:
- (a) +15°C.
- (b) –15°C.
- (c) +30°C.
- (d) –30°C.

Q4. During take-off, in the event of a power unit failure after V_1 then take-off:
- (a) May be abandoned.
- (b) May be continued.
- (c) Should be abandoned.
- (d) Should normally be continued.

Q5. The maximum angle of bank permitted for scheduled turns below 400 ft is:
- (a) 5°.
- (b) 10°.
- (c) 15°.
- (d) 20°.

Q6. If the graph datum for the net flight path is the brakes release point and the obstacle details are quoted from the end of TODA the corrections made for a downsloping runway produce an apparent:
  (a) Increase to the height and decrease to the distance.
  (b) Decrease to the height and increase to the distance.
  (c) Increase to the height and increase to the distance.
  (d) Increase to the height and leave to the distance unchanged.

Q7. The maximum level-off height limit is imposed on second segment climbs to ensure:
  (a) The 'clean up' procedure is complete before the maximum take-off power time limit is reached.
  (b) The minimum gradient requirements of the fourth segment are attained.
  (c) All the minimum gradient requirements of the net flight path are attained.
  (d) The legal minimum vertical separation of all the obstacles in the obstacle domain is achieved.

Q8. An obstacle is 1000 m from the end of TODA and 210 m left of the centre-line. For an aeroplane having a 36 m wing span it is:
  (a) 7 m inside of the domain.
  (b) 7 m outside of the domain.
  (c) 1 m inside of the domain.
  (d) 1 m outside of the domain.

Q9. The downwind displacement of a turn measured in metres equals:
  (a) WS in knots × turn time in seconds × 0.514.
  (b) WS in fps × turn time in seconds.
  (c) WS in knots × turn time in seconds.
  (d) $\frac{1}{2}$ × WS in fps × turn time in seconds.

Q10. 'Over Water Speed' may be defined as:
  (a) A representative TAS used for calculating any route restriction.
  (b) The speed attained with one-engine-inoperative over water.
  (c) The speed attained with all engines operating at the service ceiling.
  (d) The speed attained at stabilizing altitude with one-engine-inoperative.

Q11. Given: Rate of descent 1000 fpm; TAS 200 kts; G/S 250 kts; The wind effective gradient is:
  (a) 3%.
  (b) 4%.
  (c) 5%.
  (d) 6%.

Q12. A drift-down descent is made from 32 000 ft pressure altitude to 8000 ft pressure altitude. The gradient of descent is 5%; TAS 200 kts; G/S 250 kts. The distance travelled in the descent is:

(a) 99 nm.
(b) 79 nm.
(c) 63 nm.
(d) 47 nm.

Q13. The effect that a change of flap setting from 10° to 30° for take-off has is to:
  (a) Increase the ground run distance and decrease the WAT TOW.
  (b) Decrease the ground run distance and decrease the WAT TOW.
  (c) Decrease the ground run distance and increase the WAT TOW.
  (d) Increase the ground run distance and decrease the climb gradient.

Q14. The maximum width of the obstacle accountability area for a Class 'A' aeroplane having a wing span of 40 m and requiring a track change of 20° with no means of accurate track keeping will be reached at a distance of how many metres from the end of TODA?:
  (a) 4160 m.
  (b) 6480 m.
  (c) 6560 m.
  (d) 2760 m.

Q15. In the absence of specific instructions in the AFM the maximum crosswind permitted for a take-off on a contaminated runway is:
  (a) 5 kts.
  (b) 10 kts.
  (c) 15 kts.
  (d) 20 kts.

PART 3

CLASS 'B' AEROPLANES: THEORY

Class 'B' aeroplanes include all propeller driven aeroplanes with a maximum approved passenger seating configuration of nine or less *and* a maximum take-off weight of 5700 kg or less.

Any twin-engined aeroplane included in this Class which cannot attain the minimum climb standards specified in Appendix 1 to JAR-OPS 1.525(b) shall be treated as a single-engined aeroplane. Performance accountability for engine failure on a multi-engined aeroplane need not be considered below a height of 300 ft.

IEM OPS 1.535 Paragraph 1.

Single-engined aeroplanes are prohibited from operating at night or in IMC (except under special VFR), and are restricted to routes or areas in which surfaces are available to permit a safe forced landing to be executed.

JAR-OPS 1.470(b).

Class 'B' aeroplanes as defined above are referred to as 'normal utility and aerobatic aeroplanes' in JAR 23. The Class 'B' Specimen aeroplanes used by JAA FCL as representative are the Seneca 220T (multi-engined type) and the Bonanza (single-engined).

CHAPTER 39

The Field-Length Requirements

Manufacturers of multi-engined Class 'B' aeroplanes are not required to provide data to account an engine failure below 300 ft above the take-off surface level. *IEM OPS 1.535.*

39.1 TAKE-OFF PERFORMANCE

The speeds used during take-off differ from those of a Class 'A' aeroplane because engine failure is not accounted. Whilst V_{MCG} and V_{MC} are defined in precisely the same manner V_{EF}, V_1 and V_2 do not apply to this Class of aeroplanes. The speeds used for take-off are:

39.1.1 Rotation speed

This is defined in JAR 23 as the speed at which the pilot makes a control input with the intention of lifting the aeroplane out of contact with the runway or the water surface. V_R must *not* be less than:

(1)   The greater of 1.05 V_{MC} or 1.1V_{S_1} for twin-engined land planes.
(2) V_{S_1} for single-engined aeroplanes.
(3)   For seaplanes and amphibians, taking off from water, a safe speed accounting turbulence and engine failure.

39.1.2 Screen height speed

At a screen height of 50 ft the free-air safety speed. ie. the lowest speed at which it is considered safe must not be less than:

(1)   For twin-engined aeroplanes the highest of:
      (a) 1.1 V_{MC}.
      (b) 1.2 V_{S_1}.
      (c) The safe speed for continued flight or land back allowing for the effect of turbulence and critical engine failure.

(2) For single-engined aeroplanes the higher of:
   (a) $1.2Vs_1$.
   (b) A safe re-land speed allowing for turbulence and engine failure.

If an engine does fail during take-off, then to ensure the accident probability rate is no worse than 10^{-6} additional requirements are imposed by the JAA on the take-off. These are restrictions imposed in such a manner that if an engine fails during the ground run or the take-off distance up to screen height it is possible to safely continue the take-off or to re-land the aeroplane and brake to a halt

Should an engine failure occur after reaching screen height, 50 ft, and before reaching 300 ft, if the aeroplane cannot continue the climb, it is assumed that the pilot will make a forced landing straight ahead. However, if an engine failure occurs above 300 ft it is assumed that the pilot will complete a circuit and re-land. The visibility quoted in Table 39.1 is considered to be the minimum necessary to complete the appropriate procedure safely.

Table 39.1 Take-off RVR/visibility.

Assumed height of engine failure (ft)	RVR/visibility[a] (m)
< 50	200
51–100	300
101–150	400
151–200	500
201–300	1000
> 300	1500[b]

[a] For the initial part of the TOR pilot assessment may be used in place of the RVR/visibility.
[b] Also applicable if no positive flight path can be constructed.

This imposes a restriction on the minimum acceptable RVR/visibility for the take-off, because it is dependent on the minimum height of the one-engine-inoperative data provided by the manufacturers in the AFM. The details of this restriction given in *JAR-OPS 1.430(3)(ii)* are shown in Table 39.1.

Therefore, if the manufacturer has not provided any data to account an engine failure below 300 ft above the aerodrome surface level then the minimum visibility acceptable for take-off is 1500 m.

39.1.3 Take-off distance

The take-off distance from brakes release point to 50 ft is determined from the appropriate graph and is an unfactored distance. The graph accounts the following:

(1) The take-off weight.
(2) The aerodrome pressure altitude and the ambient temperature, i.e. the air density.
(3) Take-off power selected.
(4) Flaps set at the take-off position.
(5) Undercarriage (landing gear) extended.

As with Class 'A' aeroplanes the maximum take-off weight calculations are in two parts, the field-length limitation and the weight–altitude–temperature (WAT) limitation, the lower of which is the maximum take-off weight.

39.2 FIELD-LENGTH REQUIREMENTS

To comply with the field-length requirements the operator must account:

(1) The aeroplane weight at the commencement of the TOR.
(2) The air density.
(3) The runway surface type and condition.
(4) The runway slope in the direction of take-off.
(5) 50% of any reported headwind or 150% of any reported tailwind.
     JAR-OPS 1.530(c).

Most manufacturers include these data in the field-length graphs by a series of grids in the graph using a hard, dry, level concrete runway in still-air at MSL as the datum for the graph. If the surface type, condition and slope are not accounted in the graph they must be allowed for by using the information in *AMC OPS 1.530* which is detailed in the next two paragraphs.

39.2.1 Surface correction factor

For take-off on a grass surface, up to 20 cm long, which has firm sub-soil the take-off distance determined from the graph must be increased by mutiplying by a factor of 1.2 if it is dry, or 1.3 if it is wet. However, if the grass is very short and wet the distance may increase significantly, possibly up to 1.6 times the unfactored distance. *AMC OPS 1.530(c)(4).*

39.2.2 Runway slope correction factor

The take-off distance must be increased by 5% for each 1% of upslope. Runway slope is confined to 2% for normal operations, however, the JAA may approve slopes in excess of this if the correction factor is acceptable. *A downsloping runway may not be accounted.* A factor is calculated by adding the percentage increase recommended by the requirement at 5% for every 1% upslope then dividing the increased amount by 100, eg. For a 1% upslope the factor is 105/100 = 1.05. *AMC OPS 1.530(c)(5).*

39.3 TAKE-OFF DISTANCE REQUIREMENTS

39.3.1 Aerodrome with no clearway or stopway

The 1.25 × take-off distance must not exceed the TORA, i.e. TOD may not exceed 80% of TORA. See Fig. 39.1.

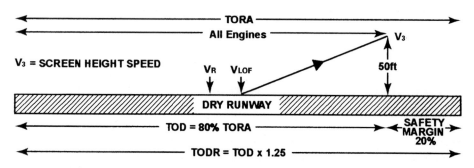

Fig. 39.1 TODR for an airfield with no stopway or clearway.

39.3.2 With stopway and/or clearway available

The unfactored TOD must not exceed any of the following (see Fig. 39.2):

(1) TORA.
(2) When multiplied by 1.15, TODA, i.e. TOD may not exceed 87% of TODA.
(3) When multiplied by 1.3, ASDA, i.e. TOD may not exceed 77% of ASDA. *JAR-OPS 1.530(b).*

Should the field-length graphs not contain the appropriate correction grids for runway slope and surface condition then these corrections will have to be applied by the pilot. If the calculation is to determine the maximum scheduled field-length limited TOW, then the pilot will also have to apply the safety factor appropriate to the aerodrome distances as specified above.

39.3.3 Take-off calculations

The procedure for determining the actual take-off distance to the point at which screen height is attained is as follows, but if the take-off distance *required* is to be determined then the appropriate safety factor must also be applied.

(1) Determine the graphical distance.
(2) Determine the slope correction factor for an upsloping runway.
(3) Ascertain the surface correction factor.
(4) Apply the factors to the graphical distance, i.e. Graphical distance × slope factor × surface factor = Take-off Distance.
(5) Take-off Distance Required = Take-off Distance × safety factor.

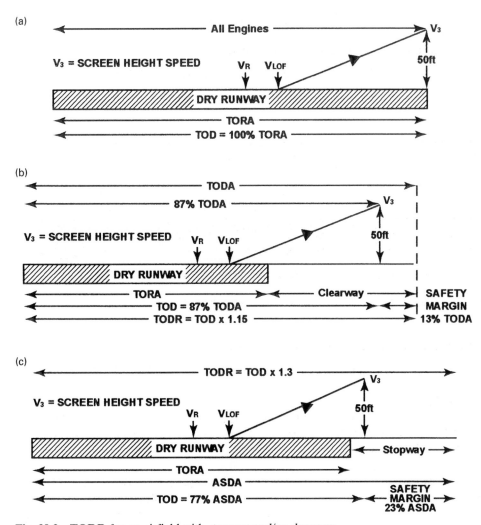

Fig. 39.2 TODR for an airfield with stopway and/or clearway.

39.3.4 Field-length limited TOW calculation

The distances available for take-off at an aerodrome are published in the AIP. To calculate the field-length limited TOW the following procedure appropriate to the aerodrome should be utilized.

Aerodrome with no stopway or clearway

(1) Determine the TORA from the AIP.
(2) Calculate the slope correction factor.
(3) Ascertain the surface correction factor.
(4) The regulatory safety factor imposed by JAR-OPS is always 1.25 for this type of aerodrome.

(5) Divide the TORA by the slope correction factor, the surface correction factor and the regulatory safety factor to obtain the factored distance available.
(6) Enter the graph at the distance axis and enter with the factored distance to obtain the field-length limited TOW.

Aerodrome with a stopway and/or clearway

(1) Ascertain the values of the TORA, ASDA and TODA from the AIP.
(2) Calculate the runway slope correction factor.
(3) Decide the runway surface correction factor.
(4) The regulatory safety factors from JAR-OPS are 1.0 for TORA, 1.3 for ASDA and 1.15 for TODA.
(5) Divide each of the available distances by the runway slope correction factor, the surface correction factor and by the appropriate regulatory safety factor to obtain three factored distances.
(6) Select the shortest of these factored distances and enter the distance axis of the field-length graph to determine the field-length limited TOW.

CHAPTER 40

The Take-off Climb Requirements

All Class 'B' aeroplanes must comply with the minimum acceptable climb gradient requirements of *Appendix to JAR-OPS 1.525(b)* which are based on *JAR 23.63(c)(1) and (2)* but only aeroplanes having two or more engines have to obey the obstacle clearance requirements.

40.1 MINIMUM CLIMB GRADIENT REQUIREMENTS

40.1.1 All engines operating

The gradient of climb from 50 ft to the assumed height of engine failure, for compliance with the obstacle clearance requirements, is equal to the average gradient of climb during the climb and transition to the en-route configuration multiplied by 0.77. This equates to the distance travelled multiplied by 1.3. For compliance with the minimum acceptable gradient requirement *the gradient must not be less than 4%* with:

(1) All engines operating at take-off power.
(2) The undercarriage (landing gear) extended, unless it can be retracted in seven seconds or less.
(3) Flaps in the take-off position.
(4) A climbing speed equal to the higher of $1.1V_{MC}$ and $1.2V_{S_1}$.
    JAR-OPS 1.535(a)(4) and Appendix to JAR-OPS 1.525(b)(a)(1).

40.1.2 One-engine-inoperative

The gradient of climb from the assumed height of engine failure to 1500 ft above reference zero is equal to the one-engine-inoperative en-route climb gradient shown in the AFM.

(1) At 400 ft above the take-off surface level this must be *measurably positive* with:
    (a) The critical engine inoperative and its propeller feathered.
    (b) Maximum take-off power set on the live engine.
    (c) Undercarriage (landing gear) retracted.
    (d) Flaps set in the take-off position.
    (e) Climb speed equal to that attained at 50 ft. *JAR-OPS 1.535(5) and Appendix to JAR-OPS 1.525(b)(a)(2)(i).*

303

(2) At 1500 ft above the take-off surface level the steady gradient of climb *must not be less than 0.75%* with:
     (a) The critical engine inoperative and its propeller feathered.
     (b) Maximum continuous power set on the live engine.
     (c) Undercarriage (landing gear) retracted.
     (d) Flaps retracted.
     (e) Speed not less than 1.2Vs$_1$. *JAR-OPS 1.535(5) and Appendix to JAR-OPS 1.525(b)(a)(2)(ii).*

40.2 WEIGHT–ALTITUDE–TEMPERATURE LIMITATION ON TOW

JAR-OPS 1.530(a) states that the take-off weight must not exceed that specified in the AFM for the pressure altitude and ambient temperature at the aerodrome at which the take-off is to be made. This requirement means that the gradients attained in the take-off climb may not be less than those specified in *JAR 23.63(c)(1) and (2)* which are detailed in Sections 40.1.1 and 40.1.2 above.

Some AFMs do not contain graphs which enable either the climb gradient or the weight–altitude–temperature (WAT) limited take-off weight to be immediately determined. This does not mean that the requirements can be ignored. It means that either the aeroplane TOW is not WAT limited within the specified environmental envelope or that rate of climb graphs are provided. Often the maximum aerodrome pressure altitude from which it is permitted to operate the aeroplane prevents the imposition of a WAT limitation on TOW.

The still-air gradient is that which is used to determine the WAT limitation on TOW. If the AFM contains climb gradient graphs these can be utilized to determine any limitation on TOW caused by compliance with the minimum acceptable gradient requirements. However, should the AFM contain only graphs from which the rate of climb can be determined then it is necessary to use the following formula to calculate any limitation:

$$\text{Still-air Gradient} = \frac{\text{ROC}}{\text{TAS}} \times \frac{6000}{6080}\,\%.$$

By transposition this becomes:

ROC required = Still-air gradient required × TAS × 6080/6000,

which can be shortened to be:

ROC required = Still-air gradient required × TAS × 1.013.

For all practical purposes the 1.013 can be ignored; thus, the formula becomes:

ROC required = Still-air gradient required × TAS.

Using this formula with the requirements then the ROC required are:

(1) All engines operating at screen height = 4 × TAS/100 in kts.
(2) One-engine-inoperative at 400 ft = 0.1 × TAS/100 in kts.
(3) One-engine-inoperative at 1500 ft = 0.75 × TAS/100 in kts.

40.3 SPECIMEN TWIN-ENGINED AEROPLANE – CAP 698

This aeroplane is prohibited from using aerodromes above 8000 ft pressure altitude. Using the most adverse conditions of the maximum certificated TOW and ISA +25°C this aeroplane does not have a limitation imposed on TOW by any of the gradient requirements. *In other words TOW is never WAT limited.*

40.4 SPECIMEN SINGLE-ENGINED AEROPLANE – CAP 698

For this aeroplane only the all-engines-operating gradient requirement needs consideration. To determine the WAT limited TOW the following procedure must be adopted:

(1) Draw an horizontal line from 4% gradient, on the right vertical axis of the graph, left through the weight grid.
(2) Enter the left carpet at the ambient temperature, proceed vertically to the aerodrome pressure altitude. From this intersection travel horizontally right to the weight grid reference-line.
(3) At this point parallel the grid lines to intersect the horizontal input from the 4% gradient. At the intersection drop a vertical to the carpet to read the WAT limited TOW.

40.5 OBSTACLE CLEARANCE REQUIREMENTS

The 'see and avoid' principle is employed for obstacle clearance in the climb. That is, all the time the pilot can see an obstacle it can be avoided. However, on entering cloud or becoming IMC the obstacle can no longer be avoided visually and the worst circumstance must be assumed, i.e. that the aeroplane has suffered an engine failure.

40.5.1 The obstacle accountability area

For Class 'B' aeroplanes the obstacle domain commences at the end of TODA, or the end of TOD if a turn is scheduled before the end of TODA, and ends when the aircraft reaches a height of 1500 ft above Reference Zero. The area has a starting semi-width of 90 m, or if the wing span is less than 60 m, a semi-width of (60 m + $\frac{1}{2}$ wing span), either side of the intended line of flight, and expands at the rate of one eighth of the distance travelled along the line of flight from the end of TODA until the maximum width either side of the planned track is achieved. (See Table 40.1.) From this position a rectangle is drawn with sides parallel to the intended track to

Table 40.1 Class 'B' obstacle accountability area maximum semi-width.

| Change of track direction | 0°–15° | | Over 15° | |
Required navigational accuracy	Distance	Width	Distance	Width
VMC*	1680 m	300 m	4080 m	600 m
IMC	4080 m	600 m	6480 m	900 m

Distance from TODA to maximum semi-width quoted.

* Visual guidance is considered to be the most accurate means of track keeping to avoid obstacles after take-off. However, if there are navigational aids available to the pilot which enable the same track keeping accuracy and are used for such a purpose, then if the change of track required is 15° or less, the maximum width of the visual accountability area may be used in IMC. This allowance may not be employed if the required change of track is greater than 15°. *JAR-OPS 1.535(b)(1).*

the point at which the aeroplane attains a height of 1500 ft above RZ. *JAR-OPS 1.535(a)*. Its shape is, therefore, a funnel followed by a rectangle. The distance along track, from the end of TODA, at which the domain initially reaches its maximum width can be calculated by using the formula:

$D = 8 \times$ [Maximum semi-width – 90 m] if wing span is 90 m or more *or*
$D = 8 \times$ [Maximum semi-width – (60 m + $\frac{1}{2}$ wing span)] if less than 90 m.

For all Class 'B' aeroplanes the obstacle domain is a fixed shape, with the length of the final rectangle being a variable. The total length of the domain is determined by the distance taken for the aeroplane to reach 1500 ft above RZ, which in NFP calculations, is measured from the end of TODR. Remember that the end of TODA is a fixed position on the ground, but that the end of TODR is a variable depending on many factors for its position. This means that the end of the obstacle domain cannot be determined until the actual TOW is known. Therefore the length of the obstacle domain is equal to the distance from the end of TODR to 1500 ft minus the distance (TODA − TODR).

40.5.2 Visual guidance

For each aerodrome in the Operations Manual the minimum cloud ceiling and visibility essential to enable safe visual guidance to avoid obstacles after take-off must be specified. The safe visual climb-out path must:

(1) Have sufficient ground reference points to facilitate obstacle clearance analysis.
(2) Be within the capabilities of the aeroplane regarding speed, bank and wind effect.
(3) Be fully described in writing or diagrams in the manual.
(4) Have the limiting environmental conditions specified, i.e. wind, cloud, visibility, lighting etc. *Appendix 1 to JAR-OPS 1.535(b)(1) & (c)(1).*

40.5.3 Minimum vertical separation

All aeroplanes with two or more power units must clear all obstacles in the domain by a minimum vertical separation of 50 ft. *JAR-OPS 1.535(a).*

40.5.4 The climb in IMC

For the purposes of obstacle clearance it must be assumed that the critical engine becomes inoperative at the point where visual reference is lost, i.e. on entering cloud. *JAR-OPS 1.535(a)(3)*.

40.5.5 Scheduled turns

The aeroplane must not be banked below 50 ft and thereafter the maximum angle of bank is 15°. *JAR-OPS 1.535(a)(2)*.

40.6 OBSTACLE CLEARANCE CALCULATIONS

40.6.1 Adjustment of obstacle details

Any obstacle within the obstacle accountability area must have its details adjusted to relate its position to the end of TODR and Reference Zero, in accordance with Chapter 27 of this book, before commencing calculation.

40.6.2 The calculation of distance travelled

The distance travelled along track in nm. from the end of TODR is calculated using the height gain and the gradient or rate of climb. Dependent on the graphs available in the AFM, one of the following two formulae may be utilized for the calculations:

Rate of climb graphs available

$$\text{Distance in nm.} = \frac{\text{Height gain}}{\text{ROC}} \times \frac{\text{Groundspeed}}{60}.$$

Climb gradient graphs available

$$\text{Distance in nm.} = \frac{\text{Height gain}}{\text{Gradient}} \times \frac{100}{6080} \times \frac{\text{Groundspeed}}{\text{TAS}}.$$

If the calculation is for obstacle clearance purposes then the all-engines-operating gradient is multiplied by 0.77 or the distance travelled multiplied by 1.3. Remember that at the commencement of the climb path the aeroplane will be at 50 ft above Reference Zero.

40.6.3 The calculation of height gain

To determine the height of the aeroplane at a specific distance in nm. from the end of TODR then the above formulae may be transposed:

(1) $\text{Height gain} = \dfrac{\text{Distance} \times \text{ROC} \times 60 \text{ ft}}{\text{Groundspeed}}.$

(2) $\text{Height gain} = \dfrac{\text{Distance} \times \text{Gradient} \times 6080 \times \text{TAS}}{100 \times \text{Groundspeed}}.$

CHAPTER 41

The En-Route Requirements

The en-route phase extends from 1500 ft above the take-off surface level at the end of the net flight path to 1000 ft above the landing aerodrome surface level. When scheduling or planning this part of the flight the worst circumstance must be assumed, that is that an engine fails.

For twin-engined aeroplanes this will entail a drift-down descent until it reaches the maximum altitude at which it can maintain level flight with one engine inoperative. On reaching this altitude it must be able to continue the flight to an aerodrome at which it can comply with all the landing requirements without flying below the minimum safe altitude for the route.

A single-engined aeroplane suffering an engine failure would have to make a glide descent to a suitable area at which a forced landing can be made safely. All high ground and obstacles must be visually avoided during the descent. Therefore, a single-engined public transport aeroplane may not be flown at night or in IMC because the pilot would be unable to see any obstacle or high ground to take avoiding action. *JAR-OPS 1.525(a)*. If the route is above a layer of cloud that extends below the route minimum safe altitude then the 'see and avoid' principle imposes a further limitation on single-engined aircraft, and prohibits such a flight despite the fact that the flight conditions may be VMC above the cloud. *IEM OPS 1.542.1*.

41.1 IN-FLIGHT PROCEDURE FOR TWIN-ENGINED AEROPLANES

On experiencing an engine failure en-route the pilot of a twin-engined public transport aeroplane should take the following actions:

(1) Execute the emergency feathering or shut-down drills and select maximum continuous power on the live engine.
(2) Maintain level flight and allow the airspeed to decay to the speed recommended by the manufacturers for the descent, the 'drift-down' speed.
(3) Maintain the aeroplane in a level attitude at this speed. Initially the descent path is relatively steep becoming shallower as the descent progresses until the aeroplane eventually maintains altitude at the drift-down speed. This is referred to as the 'stabilizing altitude'.

41.2 IN-FLIGHT PROCEDURE SINGLE-ENGINED AEROPLANES

In the event of an engine failure the pilot of a single-engined aeroplane should take the following actions:

(1) Carry out the emergency feathering drills.
(2) Maintain level flight and allow the speed to decay to the 'drift-down' speed.
(3) Select a suitable area in which to make a forced landing, taking into account:
    (a) Clearance of the intervening terrain.
    (b) The wind direction and speed selecting an approach into wind, if possible, so as to reduce the groundspeed on landing to a minimum.
    (c) The nature and condition of the landing surface.
    (d) The position of any built-up areas relative to the approach and landing.
    (e) The position and altitude of the sun. If it is at low altitude try to avoid approaching into sun.
(4) Execute the forced landing drills for the aeroplane type.

The rules and regulations applicable to the en-route phase of flight are designed to attain the maximum safety possible. It is, therefore, essential that only net values of gradient, rate of descent and distance are used in the planning calculations to ascertain the exact drift-down path relative to any obstacles or high ground until the stabilizing altitude is attained.

41.3 THE ASSUMED MAXIMUM CEILING

To comply with the en-route requirements the aeroplane may not be assumed to be flying, *with all engines operating*, at an altitude exceeding that at which the rate of climb equals 300 fpm with maximum continuous power set. *JAR-OPS 1.540(b)(1) & 542(b)(1).*

41.4 MULTI-ENGINED AEROPLANE EN-ROUTE REQUIREMENTS

(1) In the event of an engine failure, in the meteorological conditions expected for the flight and with maximum continuous power set on the live engine(s), an aeroplane must be capable of continuing the flight at or above the minimum safe altitude (MSA) to 1000 ft above the aerodrome of intended landing. *JAR-OPS 1.540(a).*
(2) The net gradient of climb is to be the gross gradient of climb decreased by 0.5% and the net gradient of descent is the gross gradient of descent increased by 0.5%. *JAR-OPS 1.540(b)(2).*

41.5 SINGLE-ENGINED AEROPLANE EN-ROUTE REQUIREMENTS

(1) In the event of engine failure en-route the aeroplane in the meteorological conditions expected for the flight, must be capable of gliding to a place on land at which a safe forced landing can be made. *JAR-OPS 1.542(a).*

(2)   The net gradient of descent is to be the gross gradient of descent increased by 0.5%. *JAR-OPS 1.542(b)(2)*.

41.6 MAXIMUM AUW EN-ROUTE

41.6.1 Multi-engined aeroplanes

The maximum AUW that a multi-engined aeroplane may be along the route is that which will allow a 300 fpm rate of climb at MSA, in the prevailing conditions, with all engines operating within the maximum continuous power rating. In other words the maximum assumed altitude and MSA are coincident.

41.6.2 Single-engined aeroplanes

The maximum AUW that a single-engined aeroplane may be en-route is that weight which will attain a 300 fpm rate of climb at the altitude from which the aeroplane, in the prevailing conditions, can glide to a suitable place for a safe landing to be made.

41.7 DRIFT-DOWN PATH CALCULATIONS

The calculations necessary to determine the distance travelled or height loss during a drift-down are precisely the same as those for Class 'A' aeroplanes. The formulae to be used are those stated in Chapter 32. It must be remembered that the gradient or rate of descent used must be that which obtains at the mean height of the drift-down being considered. If the descent gradient derived from the graph available for this purpose is a gross gradient then it must be increased by 0.5% to become a net gradient.

CHAPTER 42

The Landing Requirements

The landing phase commences when the aeroplane has reached 1000 ft above the aerodrome surface level and ends at the point at which the aeroplane comes to a full stop after landing. As with every other phase the target probability is 10^{-6} and there is a set of minimum performance requirements and operating regulations that must be observed to attain the desired safety level.

There are two sets of minimum acceptable performance requirements for the landing phase. The first is to ensure that in the event of a missed approach or a baulked landing the aeroplane can safely climb away. This is the weight–altitude–temperature (WAT) limitation on landing weight, sometimes referred to as the 'climb limit' on landing weight. The second is to ensure that the landing distance required does not exceed the landing distance available to enable the required safety level to be obtained. This is the field-length limitation on landing weight.

42.1 THE WEIGHT–ALTITUDE–TEMPERATURE LIMITATION

The limitation imposed on the landing weight by virtue of the climb gradient requirements may not be exceeded in any circumstances. It comprises two elements which both apply to multi-engined aeroplanes but only the all-engines-operating requirement applies to single-engined aeroplanes. *JAR-OPS 1.535(b).*

42.1.1 All-engines-operating

In the event of a baulked landing the aeroplane in the landing configuration must attain a landing climb gradient of at least 2.5% in the ambient density conditions. The power assumed for this limitation is that which would obtain eight seconds after the throttles are opened to maximum take-off power. Furthermore, the aeroplane is assumed to be climbing at VREF with the undercarriage (landing gear) extended and flaps at the landing setting. *Appendix to JAR-OPS 1.525(b)(b)(1).*

42.1.2 One-engine-inoperative

This requirement only applies to multi-engined aeroplanes and demands a minimum gradient, in the approach climb from decision height, to be at least 0.75% at 1500 ft above the aerodrome surface level. The assumptions included in this requirement are that the aeroplane has maximum continuous power set on the remaining live engines and is climbing at $1.2V_{S_1}$ with the flaps and undecarriage retracted. *Appendix to JAR-OPS 1.525(b)(b)(2).*

42.2 THE FIELD-LENGTH-LIMITED LANDING WEIGHT

The requirements for the Field-Length-Limited (FLL) landing weight can be divided into those for a dry runway and those for a wet or contaminated runway. For compliance with either of the requirements the following must be accounted:

(1)   Aerodrome pressure altitude and ambient temperature.
(2)   50% of any headwind and 150% of any tailwind.
(3)   The runway surface nature and condition.
(4)   The runway slope in the direction of landing. *JAR-OPS 1.550(b).*

42.3 THE DESPATCH RULES

The 'despatch rules' are a set of operating regulations which are used when scheduling or planning a landing. They are designed to ensure that at least one runway at the destination aerodrome will be available for landing on arrival, so that performance decisions do not have to be made during this critical phase of flight. As such they do not penalize the operator unnecessarily, but do attain the target probability. These rules do *not* apply to any landing calculations made during flight. They are:

(1)   The aeroplane will land on the most favourable runway in still-air.
(2)   The aeroplane will land on the runway most likely to be assigned considering the forecast wind, the aeroplane ground handling characteristics, the landing aids available, the surrounding terrain and any noise abatement regulations in force. *IEM OPS 1.550(c).*
(3)   If the operator is unable to comply with (2) above for the destination aerodrome, the aeroplane may still be despatched if an alternate aerodrome is designated on the flight plan which permits full compliance with all the requirements. *JAR-OPS 1.550(c) & (d).*

42.2 DRY RUNWAY REQUIREMENTS

The landing distance required (LDR) is that distance measured from the threshold to the point at which the aeroplane comes to a full stop after landing. The normal approach path is $3°$ (5.2%) descent, at a speed of V_{REF}, the greater of V_{MC} and $1.3V_{MSO}$, to arrive at a screen height of 50 ft. However, steep approaches are permitted, with the specific approval of the JAA, of $4.5°$ or more to a screen height of between 50 ft and 35 ft.

42.2.1 Dry, hard runway surface

The LDR may not exceed 70% of the LDA. Thus 30% of the LDA is the safety margin. Net LDR = LD $\times$ 1.43. See Fig. 42.1. *JAR-OPS 1.550(a).*

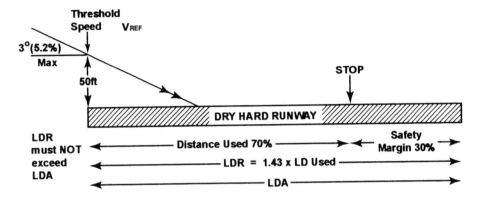

Fig. 42.1   LDR for a dry, hard runway surface.

42.2.2 Dry, grass runway surface

Landings are permitted on grass runways provided the grass length does not exceed 20 cm and only wheel impressions, not rutting, will occur. In these circumstances the Net LDR on a grass runway = LD × 1.43 × 1.15 = LD × 1.64. This means that 39% is the safety margin for a grass runway. See Fig. 42.2. *AMC OPS 1.550(b)(3).*

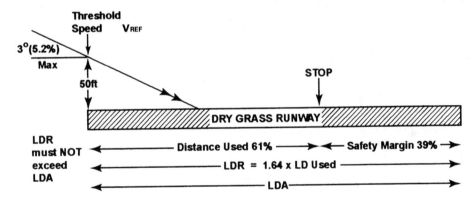

Fig. 42.2   LDR for a dry, grass runway surface.

42.2.3 Runway slope

Unless otherwise stated in the AFM the LDR must be increased by 5% for each 1% of runway downslope. Slopes in excess of 2% require the acceptance of the JAA. *No credit may be taken for any runway upslope.* Therefore, the factor to be applied is a variable dependent on the actual runway slope. *AMC OPS 1.550(b)(4).*

42.2.4 Steep approaches

Approval may be given by the JAA to use an approach path of 4.5° or more if the following criteria are met:

(1) The AFM must state the maximum approved glideslope and any other limitations or procedures imposed on steep approaches.
(2) Any correction factor to be applied to the AFM data when using a steep approach technique must be stated in the AFM.
(3) The aerodrome must have a suitable glide path reference system comprising a visual approach indicating system (VASI).
(4) The weather minima must be specified for each runway that may be used with steep approach.

42.3 WET RUNWAY REQUIREMENTS

If the meteorological actual report (METAR) or the forecast (TAF) for the estimated time of arrival indicates that the landing runway will be covered with water less than 3 mm deep then it is considered to be wet but if the depth exceeds 3 mm and more than 25% of the runway surface is covered then it is contaminated.

The LDR for a wet runway is to be 115% of the LDR for a dry runway. If the LDA is less than this amount but greater than the dry runway LDR then it may be used if the AFM contains specific additional information regarding the LDR on wet runways. *JAR-OPS 1.555(a) & (c).*

42.3.1 Wet, hard runway surface

The factorization used to calculate the LDR must still account the safety factorization for a dry runway. Thus the Net LDR for a wet, hard runway surface is the gross landing distance × 1.43 × 1.15. Therefore, the Net LDR for a wet, hard runway = the gross LD × 1.645. This ensures a safety margin of 39% of the LDA. See Fig. 42.3. *JAR-OPS 1.555(a).*

43.2.2 Wet, grass runway surface

The safety factorization for a dry grass runway surface must be accounted in the factorization for a wet grass runway. Therefore, the Net LDR = Dry, hard

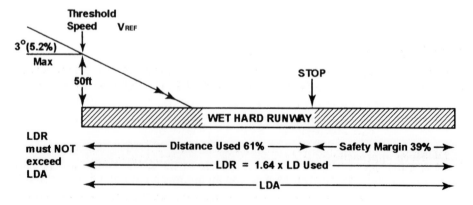

Fig. 42.3 LDR for a wet, hard runway surface.

LD × 1.2 × 1.43 × 1.15. = Dry, hard LD × 1.9734. This provides a safety margin of 49.3% of the LDA. See Fig. 42.4. *JAR-OPS 1.555(c)*.

Note: If the grass is very short and wet, the factor of 1.15 should be replaced by a factor of 1.6 which allows a 63.5% safety margin. *IEM OPS 1.555(a)*.

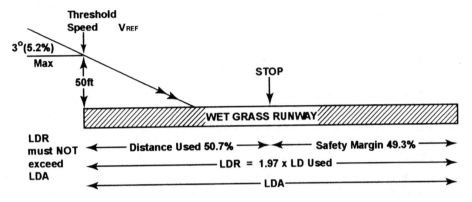

Fig. 42.4   LDR for a wet, grass runway surface.

42.3.3 Contaminated runway surface

If the meteorological reports or forecast conditions for the estimated time of arrival indicate the runway surface is likely to be contaminated then the LDR must be calculated from the data approved by the JAA in the AFM and must not exceed the LDA. *JAR-OPS 1.555(b)*.

42.4 SHORT LANDING OPERATIONS

Any short landing operations must have the approval of the JAA before being planned or executed. The distance used for the calculation of the field-length-limited landing weight is the sum of the declared landing distance available and the length of the declared safe area. The screen height at the beginning of the declared safe area is a minimum of 50 ft. See Fig. 42.5.

42.4.1 Declared safe area

This is an area, approved by the aerodrome authority, situated on the approach path to the runway and adjoining the beginning of the LDA. It has a maximum length of

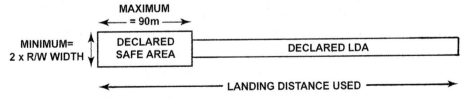

Fig. 42.5   Landing distance used.

90 metres and a minimum semi-width equal to the runway width either side of the extended runway centre-line. It must be free of obstructions, ditches and depressions which could be hazardous to an aeroplane undershooting the runway. The surface slope of the area must not exceed 5% upward or 2% downward in the direction of landing. It does not require the same load-bearing strength as the LDA.

42.4.2 Short landing requirements

In addition to the normal landing requirements operators must comply with the following:

(1) *Weather*. The weather minima must be specified and approved for each runway and shall not be less than VFR or the non-precision minima.
(2) *Pilot*. The requirements that must be complied with regarding briefing and experience must be detailed in the Operations Manual.
(3) *Safety*. The JAA may impose such additional conditions that it considers necessary for safety reasons, accounting the aircraft type, the approach aids and the missed approach/baulked landing considerations. *Appendix 2 to JAR-OPS 1.550(a)*.

Test Paper 11

Q1. The safety margin allowed in the take-off calculations for a Class 'B' aeroplane operating on a hard, dry, level runway with no stopway or clearway is:
  (a) 80% of TORA.
  (b) 60% of TORA.
  (c) 40% of TORA.
  (d) 20% of TORA.

Q2. If a Class 'B' aeroplane is to take-off on a dry, grass runway the additional factorization to be made to TODR for the nature of the surface is:
  (a) × 1.15.
  (b) × 1.2.
  (c) × 1.3.
  (d) × 1.6.

Q3. In the take-off calculations for a Class 'B' aeroplane the factorization to be applied to the TODR for an upslope of 0.8% is:
  (a) × 1.03.
  (b) × 1.04.
  (c) × 1.05.
  (d) × 1.06.

Q4. The maximum angle of bank permitted, after take-off, below 50 ft for a Class 'B' aeroplane is:
  (a) 0°.
  (b) 5°.
  (c) 10°.
  (d) 15°.

Q5. In the net flight path obstacle clearance calculations for a Class 'B' aeroplane the gradient to be used to the assumed engine failure height is the average all-engines-operating gradient multiplied by:
  (a) 1.15.
  (b) 1.05.
  (c) 0.95.
  (d) 0.77.

Q6. For a Class 'B' aeroplane the maximum semi-width of the obstacle account-ability area for a track change of 15° for an aeroplane with a 60 m wing span with accurate track keeping aids, is reached at a distance from the end of the TODA of:
(a) 1680 m.
(b) 2400 m.
(c) 4080 m.
(d) 648 m.

Q7. The maximum altitude that may be assumed in en-route calculations for a Class 'B' aeroplane is the altitude at which, with all engines operating, the aeroplane attains a rate of climb of:
(a) 100 fpm.
(b) 200 fpm.
(c) 300 fpm.
(d) 500 fpm.

Q8. To obtain the net gradient of descent, in the drift-down, for a Class 'B' aero-plane the gross gradient must be increased by:
(a) 1.0%.
(b) 0.75%.
(c) 0.5%.
(d) 0.25%.

Q9. For a Class 'B' aeroplane the factorization to be applied to the AFM landing distance to determine the landing distance required on a short, wet, grass runway with a 2% downslope is:
(a) 2.9.
(b) 2.5.
(c) 2.0.
(d) 1.9.

PART 4

CLASS 'C' AEROPLANES: THEORY

Class 'C' aeroplanes include all those aircraft powered by reciprocating engines with a maximum approved passenger seating configuration of more than nine *or* a maximum weight exceeding 5700 kg.

Class 'C' aeroplanes are *not* included in either the ATPL or CPL performance examinations for the JAA licence.

CHAPTER 43

The Field-Length Requirements

Manufacturers of Class 'C' aeroplanes are not legally required to provide data to account an engine failure during take-off in the AFM. Therefore, some provide the information and some do not. Irrespective of which the case may be, all Class 'C' aeroplane flight manuals must account the following in the data presented.

(a) Air Density   The aerodrome pressure altitude and ambient temperature. *JAR-OPS 1.565(d)(1) & (2).*

(b) Along track wind component   50% of any headwind and 150% of any tailwind. *JAR-OPS 1.565(d)(5).*

(c) Runway alignment   The reduction that must be made to the available distances to account for runway alignment. See Chapter 5. *IEM OPS 1.565(d)(6).*

(d) Runway slope   An allowance of an increase to the take-off distance of 5% for each 1% of runway upslope in the direction of take-off. Slopes exceeding 2% must be approved for use by the JAA. *Credit may not be taken for any downslope. AMC OPS 1.565(d)(4).*

(e) Runway surface   The nature and condition of the runway surface must be accounted. If the manufacturer does not recommend a factor to be used then that which is in the current AIC must be used. *IEM OPS 1.565(d)(3).*

43.1 ENGINE FAILURE ACCOUNTED IN THE AFM

If data are provided which account an engine failure during take-off then the actual distances travelled during the take-off must not exceed the available distances. That is:

(1)   TOR must not exceed TORA.
(2)   ASD must not exceed ASDA.
(3)   TOD must not exceed TODA. *JAR-OPS 1.565(c).*

Only one V_1 may be used for rejecting or continuing the take-off. Although a range of V_1s may be available, because the actual TOW is less than the field-length-limited take-off weight, only one may be selected as the decision speed. *JAR-OPS 1.565(c)(4)*.

The maximum calculated TOW for a wet or contaminated runway may not exceed the field-length-limited TOW for a dry runway for the same conditions. *JAR-OPS 1.565(c)(5)*.

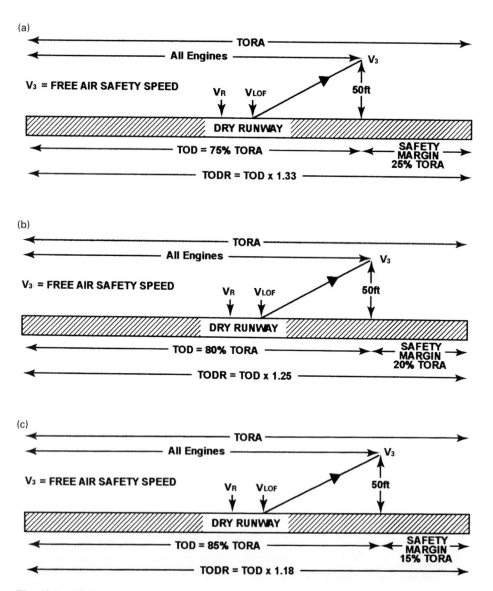

Fig. 43.1 TOD factorization: engine failure *not* accounted in the AFM. (a) Twin-engined aeroplanes. (b) Three-engined aeroplanes. (c) Four-engined aeroplanes.

43.2 ENGINE FAILURE *NOT* ACCOUNTED IN THE AFM

If the data in the AFM do not account an engine failure during take-off then the factorized *distance* must not exceed the take-off *run* available. The take-off *distance* must be factorized by multiplying by:

(1) 1.33 for twin-engined aeroplanes, thus providing a 25% safety margin.
(2) 1.25 for three-engined aeroplanes, which provides a 20% safety margin.
(3) 1.18 for four-engined aeroplanes, providing a 15% safety margin. See Fig. 43.1. *JAR-OPS 1.565(b)*.

CHAPTER 44

The Take-off Climb Requirements

44.1 THE WEIGHT–ALTITUDE–TEMPERATURE LIMITATION

The operator must ensure that the TOW does not exceed the maximum specified in the AFM appropriate to the pressure altitude and ambient temperature. This is based on the minimum acceptable rate of climb of 300 fpm, with all engines operating, and 150 fpm, with one-engine-inoperative, at a height of 1000 ft above the aerodrome surface level, whichever is the most limiting. See Chapter 26. *JAR-OPS 1.565(a)*.

44.2 OBSTACLE CLEARANCE

44.2.1 The obstacle accountability area

For Class 'C' aeroplanes the obstacle domain commences at the end of TODA, and ends when the aircraft reaches a height of 1500 ft above Reference Zero (RZ). The area has a starting semi-width of 90 m, or if the wing span is less than 60 m a semi-width of $(60\,m + \frac{1}{2}$ wing span), either side of the intended line of flight, and expands at the rate of one eighth of the distance travelled along the line of flight from the end of TODA until the maximum width either side of the planned track is achieved (see Table 44.1). From this position a rectangle is drawn with sides parallel to the

Table 44.1 Class 'C' obstacle accountability area maximum semi-width.

Change of track direction	0°–15°		Over 15°	
Required nav. accuracy	150 m		300 m	
Attainable/not attainable	Distance	Width	Distance	Width
Attainable*	1680 m	300 m	4080 m	600 m
Not attainable	4080 m	600 m	6480 m	900 m

Distance from TODA to maximum semi-width quoted.
* Visual guidance is considered to be the most accurate means of track keeping to avoid obstacles after take-off. Provided the external references used are visible from the flight deck more than 45° from the intended track with a depression of less than 20° and the cloud ceiling and visibility are such that the obstacles and/or ground reference points are easily identified. *AMC OPS 1.570(e)(1) & (f)(1)*.

intended track to the point at which the aeroplane attains a height of 1500 ft above RZ. *JAR-OPS 1.570(a)*. Its shape is, therefore, a funnel followed by a rectangle. For all Class 'C' aeroplanes the obstacle domain is a fixed shape, with the length of the final rectangle being a variable. The total length of the domain is determined by the distance taken for the aeroplane to reach 1500 ft above RZ, which in NFP calculations, is measured from the end of TODR. Remember that the end of TODA is a fixed position on the ground, but that the end of TODR is a variable depending on many factors for its position. This means that the end of the obstacle domain cannot be determined until the actual TOW is known. Therefore, the length of the obstacle domain is equal to the distance from the end of TODR to 1500 ft minus the distance (TODA – TODR). See Fig. 44.1.

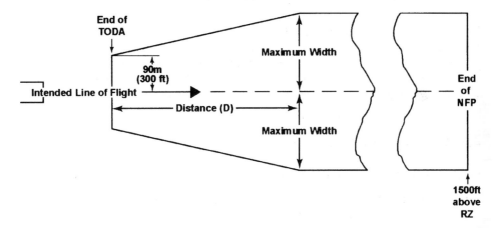

Fig. 44.1 Take-off obstacle accountability area.

The distance along track, from the end of TODA, at which the domain initially reaches its maximum width can be calculated by using the formula:

$D = 8 \times$ [Maximum semi-width − 90 m] if wing span is 90 m or more *or*
$D = 8 \times$ [Maximum semi-width − (60 m + $\frac{1}{2}$ wing span)] if less than 90 m.

44.2.2 Visual guidance

For each aerodrome in the Operations Manual the minimum cloud ceiling and visibility essential to enable safe visual guidance to avoid obstacles after take-off must be specified. The safe visual climb-out path must:

(1) Have sufficient ground reference points to facilitate obstacle clearance analysis.
(2) Be within the capabilities of the aeroplane regarding speed, bank and wind effect.
(3) Be fully described in writing or diagrams in the manual.
(4) Have the limiting environmental conditions specified, i.e. wind, cloud, visibility, lighting etc. *AMC OPS 1.570(e)(1) & (f)(1)*.

44.2.3 Minimum vertical separation

All aeroplanes must clear all obstacles in the domain by a minimum vertical separation of 50 ft + (0.01 × D) where 'D' is the distance from the end of TODA. *JAR-OPS 1.570(a)*.

44.2.4 Safe routing

An operator must establish a procedure, to be used for contingency purposes, which provides a safe route avoiding all obstacles to the take-off alternate aerodrome or return to the departure aerodrome to enable compliance with the obstacle clearance requirements. *JAR-OPS 1.570(g)*.

44.3 BANK ANGLE RESTRICTIONS

(1) Turns are *not* permitted in the take-off climb path below a height of 50 ft, above the elevation of the horizontal plane at the end of the *take-off distance required, i.e. Reference Zero. JAR-OPS 1.570(d)*.

(2) From a height of 50 ft up to a height of 400 ft above the elevation of the horizontal plane at the end of the *take-off distance required*, Reference Zero, the maximum bank angle is not permitted to exceed 15°, unless a special procedure, approved by the JAA, is being used. *JAR-OPS 1.570(d)*.

(3) At heights in excess of 400 ft above Reference Zero the maximum angle of bank must not exceed 25°. *JAR-OPS 1.570(d)*.

Table 44.2 Class 'C' climb gradient and speed correction for turns. *AMC OPS 1.570(d)*.

Bank	Speed	Gradient correction
15°	V_2	1 × Flight Manual 15° gradient loss
20°	V_2 + 5 kts	2 × Flight Manual 15° gradient loss
25°	V_2 + 10 kts	3 × Flight Manual 15° gradient loss

44.4 OBSTACLE CLEARANCE CALCULATIONS

44.4.1 Adjustment of obstacle details

Any obstacle within the obstacle accountability area must have its details adjusted to relate its position to the end of TODR and Reference Zero, in accordance with Chapter 27 of this book, before commencing calculation.

44.4.2 The calculation of distance travelled

The distance travelled along track in nm. from the end of TODR is calculated using the height gain and the gradient or rate of climb. Dependent on the graphs available in the AFM, one of the following two formulae may be utilized for the calculations:

(1)   Rate of climb graphs available

$$\text{Distance in nm.} = \frac{\text{Height gain}}{\text{ROC}} \times \frac{\text{Groundspeed}}{60}$$

(2)   Climb gradient graphs available

$$\text{Distance in nm.} = \frac{\text{Height gain}}{\text{Gradient}} \times \frac{100}{6080} \times \frac{\text{Groundspeed}}{\text{TAS}}$$

Remember that at the commencement of the climb path the aeroplane will be at 50 ft above Reference Zero.

44.4.3 The calculation of height gain

To determine the height of the aeroplane at a specific distance in nm. from the end of TODR then the above formulae may be transposed:

(1) $\text{Height gain} = \dfrac{\text{Distance} \times \text{ROC} \times 60 \text{ ft}}{\text{Groundspeed}}$

(2) $\text{Height gain} = \dfrac{\text{Distance} \times \text{Gradient} \times 6080 \times \text{TAS}}{100 \times \text{Groundspeed}}.$

CHAPTER 45

The En-Route Requirements

The en-route phase of flight commences at the end of the NFP, at 1500 ft above RZ, and continues to the point at which the aircraft reaches 1500 ft above the surface level of the destination or alternate aerodrome as appropriate. This phase differs from all the other phases because in it a two-power-units-inoperative consideration is imposed on all aircraft.

A single engine failure is 'reasonably probable', and the degree of risk of a second failure is dependent on the number of engines and the time elapsed since the first engine failed. The purpose of the en-route regulations and requirements for public transport aircraft is to ensure that any incident is survivable. To this end the probability of a double power unit failure on a twin-engined aircraft has been deemed 'extremely remote'.

45.1 EN-ROUTE REQUIRED NAVIGATION PERFORMANCE

For each of the airspace areas of the world the controlling authorities specify the minimum acceptable navigational accuracy within their defined airspace, in the appropriate area document, e.g. ICAO DOC 7030, ICAO DOC 9613, RNP/RNAV. Referred to as the Required Navigation Performance (RNP) it is expressed in nautical miles and is the maximum distance from the intended position, within which an aeroplane must remain for at least 95% of its flying time in that area, which is ascribed the term 'containment level'.

For example RNP 12.6 means all aircraft flying in that particular airspace must remain within 12.6 nm. of their intended position for at least 95% of their flying time in that airspace.

RNP accounts the navigation signal error, the airborne sensor error, the display error and any flight technical error in the horizontal plane. The operator must select from the approved navigation systems for that particular area those that will be used to attain the required accuracy. *IEM OPS 1.243*.

45.1.1 Fuel jettisoning

In the event of one or two engines becoming inoperative fuel jettisoning is permitted to an extent consistent with reaching the aerodrome of intended landing with the required fuel reserves, if a safe procedure is used. *JAR-OPS 1.580(e) & 585(g)*.

45.2 RATE OF DESCENT DIMINISHMENT REQUIREMENT

For all en-route calculations only the *net* descent path and the *net* stabilizing altitude may be used to determine obstacle clearance. The one-engine-inoperative and two-engines-inoperative net flight paths are derived from the gross rate of descent increased by 150 fpm when the remaining engines are set at Maximum Continuous thrust. *JAR-OPS 1.580(c) & 585(e).*

45.3 EN-ROUTE SCHEDULING

There are three sets of requirements that must be obeyed, in the meteorological conditions forecast for the flight, when scheduling a flight:

45.3.1 All-engines-operating requirements

At any point on the route, or planned diversion, the aeroplane must be able to climb at 300 fpm with maximum continuous power set on all engines at MSA and at the minimum altitude necessary for compliance with the one- and two-engine inoperative requirements. *JAR-OPS 1.575.*

45.3.2 One-engine-inoperative requirements

The following rules and requirements for the one-engine-inoperative case apply to any route or *planned* diversion therefrom for all Class 'C' aeroplanes.

Route planning conditions   For an aircraft to be considered to be operating to Class 'C' performance standards, following a single-engine failure, not only must it be capable of reaching a suitable aerodrome at a height from which it can land safely, with the operative engine(s) set at the maximum continuous rating, as demanded by JAR-OPS but it must also, in so doing, comply with essential conditions specified in JAR-OPS 1.580 with regard to this aspect of flight. These conditions are that, *in the forecast meteorological conditions for the flight,* the aeroplane must clear all terrain and obstructions contained in an area extending 5 nm. either side of the intended track, provided the aeroplane maintains a navigational accuracy within the 95% containment level, from the power-unit failure point to the aerodrome selected for landing, by a minimum vertical interval of 2000 ft during the drift-down descent from the cruise altitude, or by 1000 ft in level flight with a positive rate of climb. *JAR-OPS 1.580(a)(1) & 1.580(a)(2) and AMC OPS 1.580.*

Additionally, on reaching a height of 1500 ft above the landing surface level the aircraft is required to be able to attain a *positive* slope, i.e. a gross rate of climb of 151 fpm. *JAR-OPS 1.580(b)*. The airfield selected for landing must enable the aircraft to comply satisfactorily with the landing requirements of JAR-OPS 1.595 or 1.600.

The JAA requires the aircraft operator to increase the obstacle domain from 5 nm. to 10 nm. either side of track, if the navigational accuracy does not meet the 95% containment level. *JAR-OPS 1.580(d).*

45.3.3 Two-engines-inoperative (three- and four-engined aircraft)

The regulations for the one-power-unit- and two-power-units-inoperative conditions are exactly the same, except that two engines are assumed to fail *simultaneously* at the most critical point of that portion of the route where the aeroplane is more than a distance equivalent to 90 minutes at the *all-engines-operating long range cruise speed* at ISA deviation 0°C, in still air, from a suitable landing aerodrome at which the landing requirements can be met. *JAR-OPS 1.585(c)*. Also on arrival at 1500 ft over the selected destination aerodrome the aeroplane must be capable of flying level for a further 15 minutes. *JAR-OPS 1.585(d)*.

Inability to comply with this requirement exacts the penalty of restricting the routes on which it is permissible to operate an aeroplane. This is commonly referred to as the '**90-Minute Rule**'. This route restriction applies to twin-engined aeroplanes and, therefore, is appropriate to three- or four-engined aircraft for which the manufacturers have not scheduled two-engines-inoperative data *and* to those aircraft for which the necessary data are scheduled but which are unable to comply with the regulations. If such is the case, then aircraft must be routed to remain within the requisite distance of a suitable alternate airfield and must comply with the one-power-unit-inoperative requirements, if it is to be considered as operating to Class 'C' standards. *JAR-OPS 1.585(c)*.

Route planning conditions   For an aircraft to be considered to be operating to Class 'C' performance standards, following a double engine failure, not only must it be capable of reaching a suitable aerodrome at a height from which it can land safely, with the operative engine(s) set at the maximum continuous rating, as demanded by ANOs but it must also, in so doing, comply with essential conditions specified in JAR-OPS 1.585 with regard to this aspect of flight. These conditions are that, *in the forecast meteorological conditions for the flight,* the aeroplane must clear all terrain and obstructions contained in an area extending 5 nm. either side of the intended track, provided the aeroplane maintains a navigational accuracy within the 95% containment level, from the power-unit failure point to the aerodrome selected for landing, by a minimum vertical interval of 2000 ft. *JAR-OPS 1.585(b)*.

Additionally, on reaching a height of 1500 ft above the landing surface level the aircraft is required to be able to maintain level flight for a period of 15 minutes. *JAR-OPS 1.585(d)*. The airfield selected for landing must enable the aircraft to comply satisfactorily with the landing requirements of JAR-OPS 1.595 or 1.560 (see Chapter 46). *JAR-OPS 1.580(a)*.

The JAA requires the aircraft operator to increase the obstacle domain from 5 nm. to 10 nm. either side of track, if the navigational accuracy does not meet the 95% containment level. *JAR-OPS 1.585(f)*.

CHAPTER 46

The Landing Requirements

The landing phase commences when the aeroplane has reached 1500 ft above the aerodrome surface level and ends at the point at which the aeroplane comes to a full stop after landing. As with every other phase the target probability is 10^{-6} and there is a set of minimum performance requirements and operating regulations that must be observed to attain the desired safety level.

There are two sets of minimum acceptable performance requirements for the landing phase. The first is to ensure that in the event of a missed approach or a baulked landing the aeroplane can safely climb away. This is the weight–altitude–temperature (WAT) limitation on landing weight, sometimes referred to as the 'climb limit' on landing weight. The second is to ensure that the landing distance required does not exceed the landing distance available to enable the required safety level to be obtained. This is the field-length limitation on landing weight.

46.1 THE WEIGHT–ALTITUDE–TEMPERATURE LIMITATION

The limitation imposed on the landing weight by virtue of the climb gradient requirements may not be exceeded in any circumstances. It comprises two elements the details of which are not specified in JAR-OPS. *JAR-OPS 1.590.*

The following are the assumptions made by the author.

46.1.1 All-engines-operating

In the event of a baulked landing the aeroplane in the landing configuration must attain a gradient of climb of 3.2% at the aerodrome surface level in the ambient density conditions. The power assumed for this limitation is that which would obtain eight seconds after the throttles are opened to maximum take-off power. Furthermore, the aeroplane is assumed to be climbing at V_{MCL} with the undercarriage (landing gear) extended and flaps at the landing setting.

46.1.2 One-engine-inoperative

This requirement demands a minimum gradient of climb of 2.1% for twin-engined aeroplanes, 2.4% for three-engined aircraft and 2.7% for four-engined aeroplanes in the approach climb from decision height, with maximum continuous power set on the remaining live engines and a climbing speed of $1.2V_{S_1}$ with the flaps and undercarriage retracted.

46.2 THE FIELD-LENGTH-LIMITED LANDING WEIGHT

The requirements for the Field-Length-Limited (FLL) landing weight can be divided into those for a dry runway and those for a wet or contaminated runway. For compliance with either of the requirements the following must be accounted:

(1) Aerodrome pressure altitude and ambient temperature.
(2) 50% of any headwind and 150% of any tailwind.
(3) The runway surface nature and condition.
(4) The runway slope in the direction of landing. *JAR-OPS 1.595(b).*

46.3 THE DESPATCH RULES

The 'despatch rules' are a set of operating regulations which are used when scheduling or planning a landing. They are designed to ensure that at least one runway at the destination aerodrome will be available for landing on arrival, so that performance decisions do not have to be made during this critical phase of flight. As such they do not penalize the operator unnecessarily, but do attain the target probability. These rules do *not* apply to any landing calculations made during flight. They are:

(1) The aeroplane will land on the most favourable runway in still-air.
(2) The aeroplane will land on the runway most likely to be assigned considering the forecast wind, the aeroplane ground handling characteristics, the landing aids available and the surrounding terrain. *JAR-OPS 1.595(c) and IEM OPS 1.595(c).*
(3) If the operator is unable to comply with (2) above for the destination aerodrome, the aeroplane may still be despatched if an alternate aerodrome is designated on the flight plan which permits full compliance with all the requirements. *JAR-OPS 1.595(d).*

46.4 DRY RUNWAY REQUIREMENTS

The landing distance required (LDR) is that distance measured from the threshold to the point at which the aeroplane comes to a full stop after landing. The normal approach path is $3°$ (5%) descent, at a speed of 1.3Vs, to arrive at a screen height of 50 ft.

46.4.1 Dry, hard runway surface

The LDR may not exceed 70% of the LDA. Thus 30% of the LDA is the safety margin. Net LDR = LD × 1.43. See Fig. 46.1. *JAR-OPS 1.595(a).*

46.4.2 Dry, grass runway surface

Landings are permitted on grass runways provided the grass length does not exceed 20 cm and only wheel impressions, not rutting, will occur. In these circumstances the

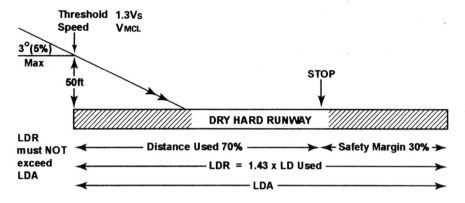

Fig. 46.1 LDR for a dry, hard runway surface.

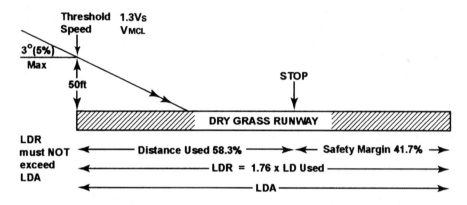

Fig. 46.2 LDR for a dry, grass runway surface.

Net LDR on a grass runway = LD × 1.43 × 1.2 = LD × 1.716. This means that 41.7% is the safety margin for a grass runway. See Fig. 46.2. *AMC OPS 1.595(b)(3).*

46.4.3 Runway slope

Unless otherwise stated in the AFM the LDR must be increased by 5% for each 1% of runway downslope. Slopes in excess of 2% require the acceptance of the JAA. *No credit may be taken for any runway upslope.* Therefore, the factor to be applied is a variable dependent on the actual runway slope. *AMC OPS 1.595(b)(4).*

46.5 WET AND CONTAMINATED RUNWAY REQUIREMENTS

If the meteorological actual report (METAR) or the forecast (TAF) for the estimated time of arrival indicates that the landing runway will be covered with water less than 3 mm deep then it is considered to be wet but if the depth exceeds 3 mm and more than 25% of the runway surface is covered then it is contaminated. The LDR for a wet runway is to be 115% of the LDR for a dry runway. *JAR-OPS 1.600(a) & (c).*

46.5.1 Wet, hard runway surface

The factorization used to calculate the LDR must still account the safety factorization for a dry runway. Thus the Net LDR for a wet, hard runway surface is the gross landing distance × 1.43 × 1.15. Therefore, the Net LDR for a wet, hard runway = the gross LD × 1.645. This ensures a safety margin of 39% of the LDA. See Fig. 46.3. *JAR-OPS 1.600(a)*.

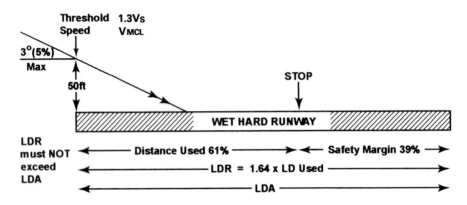

Fig. 46.3 LDR for a wet, hard runway surface.

46.5.2 Wet, grass runway surface

The safety factorization for a dry grass runway surface must be accounted in the factorization for a wet grass runway. Therefore, the Net LDR = Dry, hard LD × 1.2 × 1.43 × 1.15 = Dry, hard LD × 1.9734. This provides a safety margin of 49.3% of the LDA. See Fig. 46.4. *JAR-OPS 1.595(b)(3) & 600(a)*.

Note: If the grass is very short and wet the factor of 1.15 should be replaced by a factor of 1.6 which allows a 63.5% safety margin. IEM OPS 1.555(a).

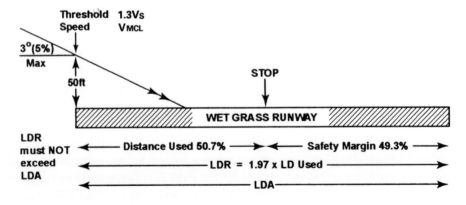

Fig. 46.4 LDR for a wet, grass runway surface.

46.5.3 Contaminated runway surface

If the meteorological reports or forecast conditions for the estimated time of arrival indicate the runway surface is likely to be contaminated then the LDR must be calculated from the data approved by the JAA in the AFM and must not exceed the LDA. *JAR-OPS 1.600(b).*

CHAPTER 47

Speed

Approach-Climb Speed   This is the recommended speed for initial climb-out after a missed approach is initiated at or above decision height. It ensures that the aircraft, with the critical power-unit inoperative, at the maximum landing weight and in the configuration achieved 15 seconds after initiation (i.e. undercarriage retracted), will be able to maintain the minimum climb gradient required. For Class 'A' aeroplanes the gradient is 2.1% for twin-engined aeroplanes, 2.4% for three-engined aircraft and 2.7% for four-engined aeroplanes. The speed must not exceed 1.5Vs. *JAR 25.121(d)(3).*

Buffet Speed   This is the speed at which the aerodynamic airflow becomes turbulent and causes uncontrollable vibration of the airframe. *JAR 25.251.*

Calibrated Airspeed (CAS) is the indicated airspeed, corrected for position and instrument error. It is equal to True Airspeed at MSL in a Standard Atmosphere. *JAR 1 page 1-3 and ICAO Annex 6 page 44.*

Cruising Speed   The representative TAS, quoted to the nearest 10 kts, used for aeroplanes of the type to calculate their compliance with AN(G)Rs regarding over-water flight and two-engines-inoperative data.

Equivalent Airspeed (EAS)   The Calibrated Airspeed corrected for compressibility at the particular pressure altitude under consideration. It is equal to Calibrated Airspeed in a Standard Atmosphere. *JAR 1 page 1-6.*

Flaps-Up Safety Speed (FUSS)   (V2 0° Flap) This speed is the safety speed used during the fourth segment of a six-segment net flight path for older turbo-propeller aeroplanes. It is equal to 1.2Vs. Sometimes it is called the **Initial En-Route Climb Speed**.

Indicated Airspeed (IAS) is the speed as shown by the pitot/static airspeed indicator calibrated to reflect Standard Atmosphere adiabatic compressible flow at MSL and uncorrected for airspeed system errors. *JAR 1 page 1-8.*

Landing Approach Speed   The calibrated airspeed in the landing configuration that must be maintained down to screen height 50 ft during a stabilized approach. It must not be less than 1.3Vs at any practicable landing weight. *JAR 25.125(a)*.

Landing-Climb Speed   This is the recommended speed for the initial climb-out after a baulked landing. It ensures that the aircraft, with *all-power-units-operating* and in the landing configuration, at the power obtained eight seconds after initiation, achieves a minimum gross gradient of climb of 3.2%. The speed, which is never less than VMCL and must not exceed the greater of 1.3Vs and VMCL, is exactly determined by AUW and the flap-setting on landing. It is 1.15Vs for four-engined aeroplanes and 1.2Vs for all other Class 'A' aeroplanes. *JAR 25.119(b)*.

Maximum Abandonment Speed   The highest speed from which a take-off with all engines operating on a very slippery or contaminated surface can be abandoned with a reasonable degree of safety. It does not guarantee the aeroplane will stop within the Accelerate/Stop Distance Available. It is *not* a V1 speed, and does not imply an ability to continue take-off after suffering an engine failure. It may well be lower than VMCG.

Normal One-Engine-Inoperative Cruise Speed   The TAS calculated, for ISA conditions from the one-engine-inoperative cruise control data for the aeroplane, at the AUW obtained two hours after take-off at the maximum authorized TOW and climbing to and maintaining the all-engines-operating optimum initial cruise level for long range cruise.

True Airspeed (TAS)   True Airspeed is the Equivalent Airspeed corrected for density error and is the true speed of the aircraft relative to the undisturbed air. *JAR 1 page 1-12*.

V1   Commonly referred to as decision speed, V1 is determined by the relative field-lengths, aircraft configuration and AUW and is the speed at which the pilot, in the event of a power unit failure, must decide whether to abandon or to continue the take-off. It is at this speed that the aircraft can be safely brought to rest on the ground or safely become airborne. Engine failure before this speed demands the abandonment of take-off. Above this speed the aircraft is committed to becoming airborne even if an engine fails.

If TOW is less than the maximum TOW determined by the field-lengths, a range of V1s is available. Turbo-jet aircraft generally use the lower value, dictated by the actual TOW. Piston or turbo-prop aircraft should use the higher value, determined by the field lengths. The manufacturer may alternatively recommend a value to use. V1 is never less than VEF plus the speed increase after engine failure to the point at which the pilot applies the first means of retardation, nor greater than VR or VMBE. There is a two-second delay built into V1 to allow for the recognition of and the reaction to the failure by the pilot. *JAR 25.107(a)(2)*.

V1/VR ratio   The power-failure speed ratio is one of the parameters used in the Flight Manual as a convenient method of presenting take-off data. The V1/V2 ratio was once used for this purpose, but has been superseded in modern Flight Manuals by the V_1/V_R ratio. Both V_R and V_2 are dependent on the aircraft AUW and flap setting. V_1 is a variable determined by field-length and aerodrome take-off conditions. If the AUW and V_1/V_R ratio are known, the calculation of V_1 is a relatively simple procedure.

V_2 The take-off safety speed, sometimes called the **Free Air Safety Speed**, is the speed which the aircraft is legally required to attain on reaching screen height with one-power-unit-inoperative. It varies with air density, TOW and flap setting, but must not be less than V_{2min} or V_R + the increment attained [according to JAR 25.111(c)(2)] before reaching screen height with the operative power units set at Maximum Take-off Power. *JAR 25.107(c); JAR 1 page 1-11.*

V_{2min} The minimum take-off safety speed, is the minimum speed that V_2 may be in terms of calibrated airspeed. It is never less than:

(1) $1.2V_S$ for
    (a)   Two-engined and three-engined turbo-prop aeroplanes; and
    (b)   Turbo-jet aeroplanes without provisions for obtaining a significant reduction in the one-engine-inoperative power-on stalling speed;
(2) $1.15V_S$ for
    (a)   Turbo-prop aeroplanes with more than three engines; and
    (b)   Turbo-jet aircraft with provisions for obtaining a significant reduction in the one-engine-inoperative power-on stalling speed; and
(3) $1.1V_{MC}$. *JAR 25.107(b); JAR 1 page 1-16.*

V_3 The steady initial climb speed, with all-engines-operating, which must be achieved by screen height, and which is never less than V_2 + 10 kts. *JAR 1 page 1-16.*

V_4 The steady take-off climb speed, with all-engines-operating, using the scheduled techniques and achieved by 400 ft gross height. It is never less than $1.2 V_{MCA}$ or $1.3V_{MS_1}$, and is such that the gross flight path attained does not fall below the gross flight path from which the net flight path is derived.

V_5 There is no official recognition or definition of this term which is often incorrectly used to refer to the One-Engine-Inoperative En-route Climb Speed.

V_A The design maneouvring speed. *JAR 25.335(c).*

V_{AT} – Target Threshold Speed – is the speed at which the pilot aims to cross the threshold when landing. It is an average speed calculated for *the conditions of light winds and slight turbulence*, and is determined by the AUW and flap setting. It may be related either to the all-power-units-operating condition (V_{AT_0}), to the one-power-unit-inoperative (V_{AT_1}) condition, or to the two-power-units-inoperative (V_{AT_2}) condition. These terms were deleted from JAR 1 but are still used in JAR-OPS 1.430(c) to categorize aeroplanes.

V_{AT_0} That target threshold speed for an all-power-units-operating approach which is not less than any of the following:

(1) V_{MS_1} + 22 kts, or 1.3V_{MS_0}.
(2) V_{MCL}.
(3)   The minimum demonstrated threshold speed + 5 kts.
(4)   The final steady approach speed − 10 kts.
(5)   1.08 × the pre-stall buffet speed in steady flight.

V_{AT_1} The target threshold speed for a one-power-unit-inoperative approach which is not less than any of the following:

(1) V_{AT_0}.
(2) V_{MCL} (with the critical power unit inoperative) + 5 kts.
(3) V_{MCL} (with two power units inoperative) for three- and four-engined aircraft.
(4)   The final steady approach speed with the critical power unit inoperative − 10 kts.

V_B The design speed for maximum gust intensity. *JAR 25.335(d)*.

V_C The design cruising speed. *JAR 25.335(a)*.

V_D The design diving speed. *JAR 25.335(b)*.

V_{DD} The design drag devices speed. *JAR 25.335(f)*.

V_{EF} The calibrated speed at which, for the purposes of performance calculations, it is assumed that the most critical power unit fails. It is never less than V_{MCG}. *JAR 25.107(a)(1)*.

V_F The design flap speed. It may not be less than:

(1)   1.6V_{S_1} with take-off flap at the maximum TOW.
(2)   1.8V_{S_1} with approach flap at the maximum landing weight.
(3)   1.8V_{S_0} with land flap at the maximum landing weight. *JAR 25.335(e)(3)*.

V_{FE} The maximum speed at which it is safe to fly with the flaps in a prescribed extended position. *JAR 25.1511; JAR 1 pages 1-7 & 1-15*.

V_{FTO} Final Take-Off Speed – the speed of the aeroplane at the end of the take-off path in the fourth segment, of a four segment net flight path, with *one power unit inoperative*, and the remaining engines set at the maximum continuous power setting, in the en-route configuration. The speed may not be less than 1.25V_S and the climb gradient may not be less than 1.2% for twin-engined aeroplanes, 1.5% for three-engined aircraft and 1.7% for four-engined aeroplanes. This speed is sometimes called the **Final Segment Speed** or the **Final En-Route Climb Speed**. *JAR 25.121(c) & JAR 1 pages 1-6 & 1-15*.

V_{GO} This is the lowest decision speed from which a continued take-off is possible within the Take-Off Distance Available (TODA). *AMJ 25X1591 Paragraph 3.2.1.c Note.*

V_{IMD} The velocity of minimum drag is the speed achieved at the lowest point of the total drag curve.

V_{IMP} The velocity of minimum power is the speed attained at the lowest point on the power curve.

V_{LE} The maximum speed at which the aeroplane may be safely flown with the undercarriage extended. *JAR 1 pages 1-8 & 1-15 & JAR 25.1515(b).*

V_{LO} The maximum speed at which the undercarriage (landing gear) may be safely extended or retracted. *JAR 1 pages 1-8 & 1-15, & JAR 25.1515(a).*

V_{LOF} Lift-Off Speed – the speed at which the main wheels will leave the ground if the aircraft is rotated about its lateral axis at V_R. It is a direct function of aircraft weight and flap setting, and is sometimes called **Unstick Speed**. *JAR 25.107(f) & JAR 1 page 1-15.*

V_{MBE} Maximum Brake-Energy Speed – the maximum speed on the ground from which the aircraft can be safely brought to a halt within the energy-absorbing capabilities of the brakes. It may limit V_1 in combinations of high TOW, temperature, altitude, downhill slope and tailwind.

V_{MC} The Minimum Control Speed – the lowest calibrated airspeed at maximum take-off power at which, if the critical power unit suddenly becomes inoperative, it is possible to recover control to maintain a heading within 20° of the original heading, without using more than 5° of bank. V_{MC} is always greater than V_{MCG} but may not exceed $1.2V_S$. *JAR 25.149(b), (c) & (d) and ICAO Annex 6 page 49.*

V_{MCA} The minimum control speed in the take-off climb. *JAR 1 page 1-15.*

V_{MCG} The minimum control speed on the ground at maximum take-off power is such that, if the critical power unit becomes inoperative, it is possible *by aerodynamic means alone*, without the use of nosewheel steering, using normal piloting skill to maintain a parallel path not more than 30 ft laterally from the original path. V_{MCG} is never greater than V_{MC}. *JAR 25.149(e).*

V_{MCL} The minimum control speed on approach to land with *all engines operating* is the lowest speed that may be used for this phase of flight. It is obtainable at all power settings up to the maximum for level flight. It is such that, if a wing-mounted power unit becomes inoperative, it is possible to recover control using no more than 5° of bank so as to maintain straight flight without encountering flight characteristics which would prejudice maintenance of an accurate approach. *JAR 25.149(f) & JAR 1 page 1-15.*

V_{MCL_1} The minimum control speed on approach to land with *one-engine-inoperative*. It is such that it is possible to maintain straight flight using no more than 5° of bank without encountering flight characteristics which would prejudice maintenance of an accurate approach. *JAR 25.149(g)*.

V_{MCL_2} The minimum control speed on approach to land for three-engined and four-engined aeroplanes with *two-engines-inoperative*. It is such that it is possible to maintain straight flight using no more than 5° of bank without encountering flight characteristics which would prejudice maintenance of an accurate approach. *JAR 25.149(h)*.

V_{MO}/M_{MO} The Maximum Operating Speed (or Mach number, whichever is critical at a particular altitude) which must not be deliberately exceeded in any flight condition. This speed is that which, allowing for moderate upsets, ensures the aircraft will remain free from buffet or other undesirable flying qualities associated with compressibility. It must not exceed V_C. *JAR 25.1505*.

V_{MS} The lowest possible stalling speed, V_S, for any combination of AUW and atmospheric conditions with power off, at which a large, not immediately controllable, pitching or rolling motion is encountered.

V_{MS_0} The lowest possible stalling speed, V_{S_0} (or if no stall is obtainable, the minimum steady-flight speed) with the wing-flaps in the landing setting, for any combination of AUW and atmospheric conditions.

V_{MS_1} The lowest possible stalling speed, V_{S_1} (or if no stall is obtainable, the minimum steady-flight speed) with the aeroplane in the configuration appropriate to the case under consideration, for any combination of AUW and atmospheric conditions.

V_{MU} The lowest possible unstick speed, V_{US}, for any combination of AUW and atmospheric conditions, at and above which it is possible to leave the ground and climb, without undue hazard, to screen height, with all-power-units-operating. A margin of 5 kts between the lowest nose-wheel raising speed and V_R would normally be considered adequate. *JAR 25.107(d), ACJ 25.107(d)*.

V_{NE} The speed which must *never* be exceeded. *JAR 1 page 1-15*.

V_P The Hydroplaning (Aquaplaning) Speed is the speed at which loss of directional control on the ground becomes total, by reason of the decrease in surface friction caused by contaminant on the runway surface.

V_R Rotation Speed. This is the speed at which, in both the all-engines-operating and the one-engine-inoperative cases the makers recommend that on the take-off ground-run the pilot initiates a change in the aircraft attitude, by raising the nose-wheel and rotating the aircraft about its lateral axis, so that it lifts off the ground at a speed of not less than $1.1V_{MU}$ with all engines operating, or $1.05V_{MU}$ with one-engine-inoperative, and attains V_2 on reaching screen height. V_R is never less than V_1 or $1.05V_{MC}$. Its exact value depends on TOW and flap setting, and varies with pressure altitude and temperature. *JAR 25.107(e), ACJ 25.107(e) & JAR 1 page 1-15.*

V_{RA} The speed recommended for the aeroplane to be flown in turbulence. It is not less than the maximum gust intensity speed, nor greater than ($V_{MO} - 35$ kts). *JAR 25X1517; ACJ 25X1517 & JAR 1 page 1-15.*

V_{REF} Reference Landing Speed – the speed of the aeroplane, in the specified landing configuration, at screen height, which is used to determine the landing distance for manual landings. *JAR 1 page 1-11.*

V_S The Calibrated Stalling Speed. It is not less than 94% of the minimum calibrated speed in flight at which the aeroplane can develop lift equal to its own weight for the configuration under consideration and is the minimum steady flight speed at which the aircraft remains controllable. *JAR 25.103(b) & JAR 1 page 1-15.*

V_{S_0} The stalling speed (or if no stalling speed is obtainable, the minimum steady-flight speed) with the wing-flaps in the landing setting. *JAR 1 page 1-15 & ICAO Annex 6 page 45.*

V_{S_1} The stalling speed (or if no stalling speed is obtainable, the minimum steady-flight speed) with the aeroplane in the configuration appropriate to the case under consideration. *JAR 1 page 1-15 & ICAO Annex 6 page 45.*

$V_{S_{1g}}$ The speed at which the aeroplane develops lift equal to its weight. It is V_S factorized to allow for the excess of weight over lift during the stall. *JAR 25.103(c) & JAR 1 page 1-15.*

V_{SR} – The reference stalling speed.

V_{SR_0} – The reference stalling speed in the landing configuration.

V_{SR_1} – The reference stalling speed in a specific configuration.

V_{SW} – The speed at which the onset of natural or artificial stall warning occurs.

V_{STOP} The highest decision speed from which the aeroplane can stop within ASDA in the event of an abandoned take-off. *AMJ 25X1591 Paragraph 3.2.1.c Note.*

$V_{T_{max}}$ The maximum safe threshold speed is the speed used to determine compliance with the landing field-length requirements. If exceeded, the required field-lengths may well exceed the landing distance available, and the approach should be immediately discontinued. The exact speed is V_{AT_0} plus a predetermined figure which is dependent on the aircraft type – usually about 15 kts. *JAR 1 page 1-15.*

$V_{T_{min}}$ The minimum safe threshold speed is the lowest approach speed which should be maintained at or before the threshold. It is the higher of V_{IMD} + 5 kts or $V_{S_{1g}}$ + 20%. Approaches made below this speed may result in loss of control.

V_{US} The speed at which the wheels of an aircraft will leave the ground if it is rotated at V_R. It is often referred to as **unstick speed** and is the same as V_{LOF}.

V_X The speed used to climb at the maximum gradient of climb. If the climb is to be with one-engine-inoperative for three- or four-engined aircraft then the speed is referred to as V_{X_1}.

V_Y The speed used to climb at the maximum rate of climb. If the climb is to be with one-engine-inoperative for three- or four-engined aircraft then the speed is referred to as V_{Y_1}.

$V_{Y_{se}}$ The speed used to climb at the maximum rate of climb in a twin-engined aeroplane with one-engine-inoperative.

V_{ZF} The minimum safe maneouvring speed with zero flap. This speed is used in noise abatement procedures. *ICAO DOC 8168 PANS-OPS Volume 1 page 5-5.*

CHAPTER 48

Distance, Height and Weight

48.1 DISTANCE

Aeroplane Reference Field Length The *minimum* field length required for take-off at *maximum* certificated take-off weight, calculated for MSL, in standard atmospheric conditions and still-air, and with zero runway slope. The precise distance required for a particular aircraft type is given in the Aeroplane Flight Manual or equivalent data-sheet from the manufacturer. *CAP 168 Chapter 3 Paragraph 2.2.*

Accelerate/Stop Distance (ASD) The distance taken by an aeroplane to accelerate from the brakes release point to V_1 and then brake safely to a halt in the prevailing conditions.

Accelerate/Stop Distance Available (ASDA) The total distance available for an aircraft to accelerate to V_1, to abandon take-off and then to brake safely to a halt. The distance available is therefore TORA plus stopway. It is sometimes referred to as the **Emergency Distance Available (EMDA)**. If no stopway exists, EMDA/ASDA = TORA. *AN(G)R Paragraph 5(3); CAP 168 Chapter 3 Paragraph 13.1(b); ICAO Annex 6 page 44 & JAR-OPS 1.480(a)(1).*

Accelerate/Stop Distance Required (ASDR) The calculated distance required for an aircraft to accelerate to V_1 and then brake to a halt. It is factorized for safety purposes, and is calculated from the Flight Manual for the environmental conditions and configuration there specified. *ICAO Annex 6 page 49.*

Balanced Field Lengths If the declared distances for a particular runway direction are such that ASDA = TODA then it is considered to have a **Balanced Field Length**. In other words, it has a clearway equal in length to the stopway *or* it has neither stopway nor clearway at all. *CAP 168 Chapter 3 Appendix 3c Paragraph 2.1.3.*

Clearway This is an area beyond the end of TORA, in the direction of the extended centre-line which is free of obstacles liable to cause damage to the aeroplane during the climb after take-off. Its length is limited by the first upstanding non-frangible obstacle liable to endanger the aeroplane in flight, however, the declared length must not exceed 50% of the length of the associated TORA. The clearway has a starting semi-width of half the runway strip for the visual runway with which it is associated, at the end of TORA, and expands for UK aerodromes, of

Codes 3 and 4, to a semi-width of 90 m, by the end of its length. The shape of the clearway for UK aerodromes is, therefore, a truncated triangle. For aerodromes using the ICAO standards the area is a rectangle having a semi-width of 75 m. *JAR 1 page 1-3; CAP 168 Chapter 3 Paragraph 9; ICAO Annex 14 pages 2 & 14.*

'D' Value   The equivalent dry, level, hard surface, still air value of the field lengths being compared, after accounting for the surface condition, use of ACS packs, slope, wind component and the necessary factorization demanded by the Airworthiness requirements is known as the **'D' value**.

Landing Distance Available (LDA)   The distance declared by an aerodrome operating authority as being available for landing. It must be free of all non-frangible obstacles and have uniform characteristics of slope, bearing strength and braking coefficient. The LDA commences at the runway threshold and extends for the length of the runway. This distance usually corresponds to the physical length of the runway pavement, but on some runways the threshold is displaced so that allowance may be made for obstacles in the approach path to the runway, in which case the LDA is foreshortened. *AN(G)R Paragraph 5(3); CAP 168 Chapter 3 Paragraph 13.1(d); ICAO Annex 6 page 44; JAR-OPS 1.480(a)(5).*

Nautical Mile   The International Nautical Mile which is a distance of 6080 ft and equal to 1852 m. *ANO 96 and ICAO Annex 5 page 7.*

Stopway   An obstacle-free rectangular area beyond the end of TORA, having the same width as the associated runway, over which an aircraft may safely roll in an emergency without hazard to its occupants or structural damage to itself. The braking coefficient, strength and slope of a stopway are similar to those of the runway itself. The slope may change at a rate not exceeding 0.3% per 30 m for Code 3 and 4 aerodromes. *JAR 1 page 1-9; CAP 168 Chapter 3 Paragraph 8; ICAO Annex 14 page 4.*

Take-Off Distance (TOD)   The distance taken by an aeroplane to accelerate from the brakes release point to V_R and then to climb to screen height in the prevailing conditions.

Take-Off Distance Available (TODA)   The distance declared by an aerodrome operating authority as being available for an aircraft to take-off and attain screen height. TODA may comprise TORA plus clearway, or (if no clearway is declared) just TORA alone. TODA is limited to a maximum length of 150% of TORA or the first non-frangible obstacle liable to damage the aeroplane during a continued take-off, whichever is the shorter. *AN(G)R Paragraph 5(3); CAP 168 Chapter 4 Paragraph 13.1(c); ICAO Annex 6 page 44.*

Take-Off Distance Required (TODR)   The calculated distance required for an aircraft to take-off and attain screen height. It is factorized for safety purposes, and is calculated from the Flight Manual for the environmental conditions and configuration there specified. *ICAO Annex 6 page 51.*

Take-Off Run (TOR)   The distance taken by an aeroplane to accelerate from the brakes release point to V$_{LOF}$ in the prevailing conditions.

Take-Off Run Available (TORA)   The distance declared by the airfield operating authority as being available in the direction of take-off, having uniform characteristics of braking coefficient, slope and load-bearing strength, and guaranteed free of all non-frangible obstacles. *AN(G)R Paragraph 5(3); CAP 168 Chapter 3 Paragraph 13.1(a); ICAO Annex 6 page 44; JAR-OPS 1.480(a)(9).*

Take-Off Run Required (TORR)   The calculated distance required to complete the take-off run, factorized by a specific percentage for safety purposes. The factor is determined by the specified environmental conditions and aircraft configuration given in the Flight Manual. *ICAO Annex 6 page 57.*

Unbalanced Field Length   If the declared distances for ASDA and TODA are of different lengths for a particular runway direction it is considered to be an **Unbalanced Field Length**.

48.2 HEIGHT

Absolute Ceiling   The altitude at which the rate of climb, with all engines operating, has reduced to 0 fpm. It has no practical value.

Aerodrome Elevation   The elevation of the highest usable point of the landing area of a given airfield, which is its vertical distance from mean sea level. *CAP 168 page xi. ICAO Annex 14 page 1 and DOC 8168 PANS-OPS Volume 1 page 1-1.*

Altitude   The vertical distance of a level, a point or an object considered as a point measured from MSL. *ICAO Annex 14 page 1 and DOC 8168 PANS-OPS Volume 1 page 1-1.*

Decision Altitude/Height   The point on the descent path at which a decision must be made during an ILS or PAR instrument approach, to either continue the approach or execute a missed approach procedure. A missed approach must be initiated if the visual reference to continue the approach has not been established by this height/altitude. Decision altitude is referenced to MSL and decision height is referenced to the threshold elevation. *JAR 1 page 1-4; ICAO Annex 6 page 1 and DOC 8168 PANS-OPS Volume 1 page 1-1.*

Elevation   The vertical distance of a fixed point measured above MSL. *ICAO DOC 8168 PANS-OPS Volume 1 page 1-1.*

Flight Level   A surface of constant pressure which is related to the standard atmosphere pressure level of 1013.2 hPa. It is referred to in terms of the pressure altitude divided by 100. Thus FL300 means pressure altitude 30 000 ft. *ICAO DOC 8168 PANS-OPS Volume 1 page 1-1.*

Gross Height   The average height reached by an average aeroplane flown by an average pilot. Gross height is that which is reduced for safety reasons to obtain net height. The amount of the reduction is dependent on the phase of flight and its value is specified by the JAA.

Height   The vertical distance of a point or object considered as a point measured from a specified datum. *BCAR K2-2 Paragraph 7.2.2; ICAO Annex 6 page 44 and DOC 8168 PANS-OPS Volume 1 page 1-2.*

Maximum Level-Off Height   The height at which the maximum time-limit imposed on the use of take-off thrust requires that an aircraft be levelled-off to enable it to accelerate and for its flaps to be retracted. The time limit is normally five minutes from the start of take-off – for which reason this limitation was once (and unofficially still is) referred to as the '5-Minute Point'. *JAR 1 page 1-13.*

Net Height   The gross height reached by an aeroplane reduced for safety reasons by a specified amount is referred to as net height. It is that which must be used to determine compliance with any obstacle clearance requirements.

Obstacle Elevation/Height   The vertical distance of the uppermost point of any non-frangible obstacle. If it is an elevation it is referenced to MSL and if it is a height it is referenced to Ordnance Datum.

Ordnance Datum   A horizontal plane passing through a point on the surface-level, of a particular runway, at the centre of the end of TODA. It was once used to calculate the height of all obstacles, for promulgation in the AIP by the airfield operator.

Pressure Altitude   The altitude of an aircraft above the pressure level of 1013.2 hPa. It can be ascertained by setting the altimeter sub-scale to 1013.2 hPa. and reading the indicated altitude. The word 'altitude' on performance charts refers strictly to pressure altitude.

Reference Zero (RZ)   An imaginary plane passing through a point 35 ft (or 50 ft) vertically beneath the aircraft at the end of TODR. It is used as the plane to which heights on the take-off flight path are related.

Screen Height   The height of an imaginary screen which an aircraft would *just* clear in an unbanked attitude, with the undercarriage extended. For take-off it is 'located' at the *end* of TODR and for landing at the *beginning* of LDR. *BCAR K2-2.7.2.4.*

Service Ceiling   The altitude at which a maximum rate of climb of 500 fpm (2.5 m/s) for jet aircraft is attained and 100 fpm (0.5 m/s) for propeller-driven aircraft is achieved, with all engines operating.

Standard Pressure Setting   An altimeter sub-scale setting of 1013.2 hPa.

QFE   The atmospheric pressure at the elevation of an aerodrome or runway threshold which, when set on the altimeter sub-scale, will cause it to read zero.

QNE   The indicated height on landing when the altimeter sub-scale is set to 1013.2 hPa, i.e. the pressure altitude of the runway.

QNH   The setting on the sub-scale of an altimeter which will cause the instrument to indicate the height of the ground above MSL when corrected for temperature. It is the normal altimeter setting used by civilian aeroplanes operating in the vicinity of an aerodrome.

48.3 WEIGHT

48.3.1 Weight and Mass

Most of us know what we mean when we use the term weight and become confused when the term mass is used in its place. In all of its documents the JAA insist on using the term mass whereas the majority of aviation documents produced by the manufacturers use the term weight. The following are the definitions of each of the terms and should help clarify the situation:

Mass   The quantity of matter in a body as measured by its inertia is referred to as its mass. It determines the force exerted on that body by gravity, which is inversely proportional to the mass. Gravity varies from place to place and also decreases with increased altitude above mean sea level.

Weight   The force exerted on a body by gravity is known as its weight and is dependent on the mass of the body and the strength of the gravitational force for its value. Weight = mass in kg × gravity in Newtons. Thus the weight of a body varies with its position and elevation above mean sea level but the mass does not change for the same body.

   The change of weight of an object due to its changed location is extremely small, even at 50 000 ft above mean sea level, however, it is technically incorrect and the term mass should be used. For the sake of simplicity I have retained the colloquial term weight throughout this book, which should be replaced when dealing with the JAA documents by the term mass. *IEM OPS 1.605.*

All-Up Weight (AUW)   The total weight of an aircraft, including fuel, crew and payload, at any specific time.

Basic Weight   The weight of an aircraft and all its basic equipment plus the declared quantity of unusable fuel and unusable oil. *BCAR A5-4 Paragraph 2.1.*

Design Minimum Weight   The lowest weight at which an aeroplane complies with the structural requirements necessary for its own safety. *BCAR K1-2.2.7.*

Design Maximum Weight The highest of the following weights at which an aeroplane complies with the structural requirements:

(1) **Design take-off weight** – For taxi-ing or landing at a reduced velocity of descent.
(2) **Design en-route weight** – For flight conditions other than those associated with take-off or landing.
(3) **Design landing weight** – For landing at the maximum velocity of descent. *JAR 25.25(a); JAR 23.25(a).*

Empty Weight The Flight Manual for each individual aircraft specifies the empty weight. It generally excludes fuel, crew and payload, but includes fixed ballast, unusable fuel, undrainable oil, total quantity of engine coolant, total quantity of hydraulic fluid, potable water and lavatory chemicals. Sometimes it is called the **Aircraft Prepared for Servicing (APS) Weight** or the **Dry Operating Weight**. *JAR 25.29(a); JAR 23.29(a); JAR-OPS 1.607(a).*

Gross Weight The weight of an aeroplane including everything and everybody carried in or on it at the commencement of the take-off run.

Landing Weight The gross weight of an aeroplane, including its contents, at the estimated time of landing, allowing for the weight of fuel and oil expected to be used during the flight to the destination or alternate aerodrome. *AN(G)R Paragraph 5(4)(a).*

Maximum Landing Weight The highest permissible weight of an aeroplane, including its contents, at touchdown. It is calculated after taking into account all relevant regulations and requirements, as well as structural limitations. *JAR-OPS 1.607(c).*

Maximum Take-Off Weight The highest permissible weight of an aeroplane, including its contents, at take-off. It is calculated in the same way as Maximum Landing Weight. *JAR-OPS 1.607(d).*

Maximum Total Weight Authorized (MTWA) The maximum total weight of an aircraft and its contents at which it may take-off in the most favourable circumstances anywhere in the world in accordance with its C of A.

Maximum WAT Limit Weight The highest weight at which all relevant climb minima can be achieved. *BCAR K1-2.2.5.*

Maximum Weight The lowest of the three following weights:

(1) The maximum weight at which take-off is permitted.
(2) The maximum weight at which flight other than take-off and landing is permitted.
(3) The maximum weight at which landing (other than in an emergency) is permitted.

Maximum Zero Fuel Weight (Max ZFW)   The maximum weight of an aircraft, excluding usable fuel, which its structural limitations allow. *JAR-OPS 1.607(b).*

Practicable Landing Weight   The empty weight plus fuel for a 100 nm. diversion and 30 minutes' hold, plus minimum flight and cabin crew and 10% of the maximum payload. *ACJ 25.125(a)(2).*

Traffic Load   The total weight of passengers, baggage and cargo, including any non-revenue load. *JAR-OPS 1.607(f).*

CHAPTER 49

Miscellaneous

49.1 AERODYNAMICS

Drag   That force acting on an aeroplane which directly opposes thrust.

Induced drag   That portion of the total drag caused by the movement of an aerofoil through the air.

Lift   That force acting on an aerofoil which is at right-angles to the direction of the airflow.

Profile drag   That portion of the total drag caused by the aerofoil shape, the boundary layer surface friction and poor streamlining.

Thrust   The force produced by the aircraft power units in a forward direction.

49.2 ATMOSPHERIC CONDITIONS

Humidity   The moisture content of the free air, excluding free water. It is usually expressed as a percentage of total saturation.

International Standard Atmosphere (ISA)   An atmosphere defined as a perfect dry gas at a temperature of + 15°C and a pressure of 1013.2 hPa (29.92 in.Hg) at MSL, and with a lapse rate of 1.98°C per 1000 ft (3.25°C per 500 m) from MSL to 36 090 ft where the temperature is assumed to be at −56.5°C.

49.3 EXTENDED RANGE TWIN OPERATIONS. *CAP 513*

Adequate Aerodrome   An aerodrome that is available at the anticipated time of use and equipped with the necessary ancillary services (such as ATC, lighting, communications, weather reporting, navaids and safety cover) and having at least one let-down aid available for an instrument approach.

ETOPS segment   This is the portion of an ETOPS flight that begins when the aeroplane is more than Threshold Distance from any *adequate* aerodrome and ends when the aeroplane is last more than the 'threshold distance' from any *adequate* aerodrome.

Rule distance   The distance travelled, in still air, in the Rule Time by an aeroplane, after shutting down one engine in normal cruise and flying at the speeds, power settings, and flight levels agreed with the CAA and specified in the Operations Manual, being the greatest distance that a twin-engined aeroplane may be from a *suitable* aerodrome for landing.

Rule time   The maximum diversion time that any point on the route may be from a *suitable* aerodrome for landing, as specified by the CAA and included in the Operations Manual.

Suitable aerodrome   A *suitable* aerodrome is an *adequate* aerodrome where, at the anticipated time of use, the weather report, or the weather forecasts, or any combination thereof, indicate that the weather conditions at the time of intended operation are likely to be at or above:

(1) **Single ILS/MLS or PAR**   The higher of 600 ft cloudbase AGL and 3 km (2 statute miles) visibility *or* 400 ft cloudbase above the lowest authorized minima and 1.5 km (1 statute mile) visibility.
(2) **Non-precision and circling approaches (inc SRA)**   The higher of 800 ft cloudbase AGL and 3 km (2 statute miles) visibility *or* 400 ft cloudbase above the lowest authorized minima and 1.5 km (1 statute mile) visibility.
(3) **Two or more ILS/MLS/PAR to separate runways**   Where the forecast wind and surface conditions will be available within the Rule Distance, whether at one or more airfields, the relevant Planning Minima cloudbase may be reduced by 200 ft and the visibility by 1 km (0.5 statute mile).

Threshold distance   The distance travelled in still air in 60 minutes by an aeroplane, after shutting down one engine in normal cruise and flying at the speeds, power settings, and flight levels agreed with the CAA and specified in the Operations Manual.

Threshold time   60 minutes.

49.4 OBSTACLES

Frangibility   The ability of an object to retain its structural integrity and stiffness up to a specified maximum load. *ICAO Annex 14 page 2.*

Frangible obstacle   An object which, when struck by a force imposing on it a load greater than a specified maximum, will distort, yield or break into pieces in such a way that it presents only minimum hazard to aircraft moving on the ground or in the air. *ICAO Annex 14 page 2.*

Obstacle   Any object which endangers the movement of aircraft on the ground or, if the object extends above a defined surface level, in the air. It can be a mobile or a fixed object, of either a permanent or temporary nature. *ICAO Annex 14 page 3.*

49.5 PERFORMANCE

Brakes Release Point (BRP)   The position at which the take-off roll begins, sometimes used as an alternative reference point for positions on the flight path.

Category II operation   A straight-in ILS approach to the runway of an airport under a Category II ILS instrument approach procedure issued by the CAA.

Climb gradient   The ratio of an aircraft's height to the horizontal distance travelled to gain that height, expressed as a percentage. TRUE gradients are used in performance graphs derived from TRUE rates of climb.

Decision point (V_1)   The latest point at which the pilot may decide to abandon a take-off by reason of an engine failure. It allows for the inherent delay in recognizing a failure, and is usually identified by means of an airspeed indicator. The airspeed indicating that decision point has been reached is never less than V_{MCG}, nor greater than V_R.

Gross Flight Path (GFP)   The profile path of an aeroplane after it has reached the end of TODR. The GFP is plotted using the gross performance data, and ends at the same horizontal distance from the point of take-off as does the NFP.

Gross performance   The measured performance of an aeroplane type adjusted in such a way that any particular aeroplane of that type has a 50% chance of exceeding the given level of performance at any time. *BCAR K2-2.7.5.3.*

Ground effect   When the aircraft is within the wing span height above the ground the proximity of the ground causes the downwash to be reduced. This effectively reduces the angle of attack of the wing which increases the lift produced. This phenomenon is referred to as 'ground effect'. An aeroplane is considered to be in 'ground effect' until it reaches a height equal to its wing span from the surface. *JAR 25.111(d).*

Measured performance   The average performance of an aeroplane or group of aeroplanes undergoing tests by an acceptable method under specified conditions. *BCAR K2-2.7.5.2.*

Net Flight Path (NFP)   The profile path of an aeroplane from the end of the TODR until it reaches 1500 ft net height above RZ. It is plotted using the net performance data.

Net performance   The gross performance of an aeroplane type diminished in a manner prescribed by the Airworthiness Requirements to allow for variations in performance not included in the Operational Regulations. Varying pilot techniques would be an example. *BCAR K2-2.7.5.4.*

Required navigation performance The navigational accuracy required for operation within a defined airspace. It is based on a combination of navigation signal error, airborne sensor error, display error and flight technical error in the horizontal plane. The aircraft must remain within the specified distance of its intended position for 95% of the time spent in that area. *IEM OPS 1.243 Paragraph 2.b.*

Runway Visual Range (RVR) The maximum distance that the runway markers can be clearly seen from a point 5 m above the centre-line. *ANO Article 96.*

Significant turn A steady banked turn which causes a change of direction in the horizontal plane of sufficient magnitude (15° or more) to require special account to be taken of it in flight path calculations.

49.6 POWER UNIT(S)

Bleed air Air taken from the main compressor of an engine to be used for cabin pressurization and/or other ancillary equipment.

Critical power unit The power unit or units which, if failed completely, would have the most adverse effect on the performance characteristics of an aeroplane. *JAR 1 page 1-4.*

Engine Pressure Ratio (EPR) The parameter used to determine thrust. It is the ratio of the maximum cycle pressure (compressor delivery pressure) to the intake air at ambient pressure.

Power augmentation Any recognized or accepted method of providing increased power output and improved performance over a short period of time. The term includes the injection of a refrigerant, the use of rockets and the reheat of exhaust gases.

Power unit A system of one or more engines, with ancillary parts, which can independently provide the required thrust. The inclusion in the term of short-period thrust-producing devices is specifically disallowed by JARs.

Power unit failure The complete and immediate loss of propulsive power from a faulty power-unit, save for the power momentarily provided by the inertia of the moving parts.

Reverse thrust A mechanical method of utilizing the thrust output of a power unit to help retard an aeroplane after a take-off has been abandoned, or during the landing run on the ground.

Target Engine Pressure Ratio (EPR)   The engine pressure ratio which is aimed to be achieved between 40 kts and 80 kts on the take-off ground run.

49.7 RANGE AND ENDURANCE

Maximum Endurance   The longest time that an aircraft can remain airborne using a given quantity of fuel.

Maximum Range   The greatest distance that an aeroplane can travel using a given quantity of fuel.

49.8 SURFACE AND AREAS

Baulked-Landing Surface   An inclined plane commencing at a specified distance after the threshold (at the elevation) of the runway, and extending between the inner transitional surfaces of the aerodrome area.

Braking Coefficient of Friction   The tangential force acting on an appropriately-loaded, smooth-tyred main wheel propelled across an aerodrome surface parallel to the plane of the wheel. The force is applied by the aerodrome surface, and is expressed as a proportion of the normal force acting on the tyre. The speed of slip is approximately equal to the speed of the aircraft.

Gradient (or Slope)   The ratio of a change of height to the horizontal distance travelled in gaining that height, expressed as a percentage. It is called the **slope** when the aerodrome surfaces are being described.

Landing Surface   For performance purposes, a plane of infinite extent and uniform slope extending in the direction of landing. *ICAO Annex 6 page 44.*

Reference Wet Hard Surface   A surface used for calculating the relationship between aeroplane groundspeed and the braking coefficient of friction.

Runway End Safety Area (RESA)   An area at the end of a runway strip primarily intended to reduce the risk of damage to an aeroplane under-shooting or over-running the runway. It is symmetrically disposed about the runway centre-line. *ICAO Annex 14 page 3.*

Runway Strip   An area of defined dimensions which includes the runway and the stopway, if present. Its purpose is to reduce the risk to aeroplanes taking off from, landing on or over-running the runway. *ICAO Annex 14 page 3.*

Take-Off Surface   For performance purposes, a plane of infinite extent and uniform slope extending in the direction of take-off. *ICAO Annex 6 page 44.*

Take-Off Climb Surface (TOCS)   A specified surface area or inclined plane extending beyond the end of the runway or clearway in the direction of take-off.

Water Equivalent Depth (WED)   The depth of any runway contaminant converted to an equivalent depth of water by multiplying the contaminant depth by its SG.

49.9 TEMPERATURE

Declared Temperature   The average temperature for the month being considered, plus half the standard deviation.

Indicated Temperature (IAT or TAT)   The static air temperature plus the heating rise caused by adiabatic compression, as indicated on the Total Air Temperature indicator.

Maximum Temperature   In relation to aeroplane performance, the highest temperature at any altitude at which all performance requirements can be fulfilled.

Minimum Temperature   In relation to aeroplane performance, the lowest temperature at any altitude at which all performance requirements can be fulfilled.

Outside Air Temperature (OAT or SAT)   The static or ambient temperature of free air at the relevant time.

Test Paper 12

Q1. The minimum legal vertical interval by which a Class 'A' aeroplane may pass over an obstacle within the domain is:
    (a) 35 m in unbanked flight and 50 m in banked flight.
    (b) 50 ft in unbanked flight and 35 ft in banked flight.
    (c) 35 ft in unbanked flight and 50 m in banked flight.
    (d) 35 ft in unbanked flight and 50 ft in banked flight.

Q2. After suffering an engine failure en-route, if a descent is necessary because of the inability of the aircraft to maintain altitude it should be made at a speed of:
    (a) V_2.
    (b) V_4.
    (c) Drift-down speed.
    (d) V_{AT}.

Q3. The maximum pressure altitude that may be assumed to schedule en-route performance calculation for Class 'B' aeroplanes is:
    (a) The cruise altitude at which 300 fpm ROC is achieved.
    (b) The service ceiling.
    (c) The performance ceiling.
    (d) The cruise altitude or maximum relight altitude whichever is the lower.

Q4. V_{GO} is:
    (a) The highest V_1 for a continued take-off is possible within TODA.
    (b) The lowest V_1 for a continued take-off is possible within TODA.
    (c) Equal to V_{LOF}.
    (d) Equal to V_R.

Q5. When a range of V_1 speeds is available, the maximum value is restricted by:
    (a) TORA.
    (b) ASDA.
    (c) TODA.
    (d) TORA or TODA.

Q6. The maximum permitted reduction to the normal thrust setting for take-off when making a variable thrust take-off is:
    (a) 6%.
    (b) 8%.

(c) 10%.

(d) 12%.

Q7. For a Class 'A aeroplane with all-engines-operating configuration the factorization imposed on the gross TODR to obtain the net TODR is:

(a) × 1.05.

(b) × 1.15.

(c) × 1.25.

(d) × 1.35.

Q8. Which of the following circumstances will cause the TODR to be more limiting to the field-length-limited TOW than the TORR?:

(a) TODA significantly longer than TORA.

(b) ASDA significantly longer than TORA.

(c) Stopway significantly longer than clearway.

(d) Clearway significantly longer than stopway.

Q9. A rigid pavement is described as one for which the bearing strength is derived from:

(a) A series of layers of compacted substance.

(d) A concrete slab.

(c) A strong sub-surface layer.

(d) A series of sub-surface layers.

Q10. The bearing strength beyond the end of the runway must not be less than ... of the associated runway strength:

(a) 70%.

(b) 50%.

(c) 30%.

(d) 25%.

Q11. The loss of braking efficiency caused by rubber deposits at the touchdown point on a wet runway is up to:

(a) 50%.

(b) 65%.

(c) 75%.

(d) 100%.

Q12. Aerodrome operators are permitted to accept aeroplanes with an LCN up to ... higher than the pavement PCN without restricting the number of movements:

(a) 5%.

(b) 10%.

(c) 15%.

(d) 20%.

Q13. The aquaplaning (hydroplaning) speed on a wet runway for a non-rotating tyre with a tyre pressure of 144 psi is:
   (a) 93 kts.
   (b) 108 kts.
   (c) 120 kts.
   (d) 144 kts.

Q14. Profile drag is not caused by:
   (a) Decreased forward speed of the aeroplane.
   (b) The aerofoil shape.
   (c) Boundary layer surface friction.
   (d) Inadequate streamlining.

Q15. The 'speed squared law' states:
   (a) Induced drag is inversely proportional to the speed squared.
   (b) Profile drag is proportional to the speed squared.
   (c) Total drag is squared in proportion to the speed.
   (d) Total drag increases in proportion to the square of the speed.

Q16. The gradient of climb:
   (a) Increases with increased altitude.
   (b) Decreases with increased altitude.
   (c) Is unaffected by altitude.
   (d) Increases with increased weight.

Q17. In a glide descent the forward speed is caused by:
   (a) Weight $\times$ sine glide angle.
   (b) Weight $\times$ cosine glide angle.
   (c) Weight $\times$ tangent glide angle.
   (d) Lift $\times$ tangent glide angle.

Q18. The maximum endurance for a piston/propeller-driven aeroplane is obtained at:
   (a) V_{IMD} at the most efficient altitude.
   (b) V_{IMP} at the lowest practible altitude.
   (c) $V_{l/D_{max}}$ at the highest praticable altitude.
   (d) V_{IMD} at the highest practible altitude.

Q19. The one-engine-inoperative net stabilizing altitude is that altitude at which for a piston/propeller aeroplane the rate of climb is:
   (a) 0 fpm.
   (b) 100 fpm.
   (c) 150 fpm.
   (d) 200 fpm.

Q20. An increased ambient temperature causes the aeroplane ceiling to:
   (a) Decrease.
   (b) Increase.

(c) Remain the same.
(d) Increase only if the temperature is greater than ISA.

Q21. The factorization to be applied to the landing distance for a jet aeroplane landing on a contaminated runway is:
(a) 1.92.
(b) 1.66.
(c) 1.43.
(d) 1.18.

Q22. During a climb at a constant IAS the climb gradient will:
(a) Increase with increase of altitude.
(b) Decrease with increase of altitude.
(c) Remain unchanged.
(d) Increase until the speed change point is reached.

Q23. If the ambient temperature increases, VMCG will:
(a) Increase.
(b) Decrease.
(c) Remain unchanged.
(d) Increase only if the altitude is also increased.

Q24. The maximum length that may be declared for the 'safe area' and used in short-field landing calculations is:
(a) 60 m.
(b) 75 m.
(c) 90 m.
(d) 50% of the LDA.

Q25. Given: Rate of descent 500 fpm; TAS 200 kts; wind component 50 kts tail. The gradient of descent is:
(a) 2.0%.
(b) 2.5%.
(c) 3.3%.
(d) 5.0%.

Q26. For take-off if the flap setting is changed from 0° to 10° it will:
(a) Increase the climb gradient and decrease the WAT limited TOW.
(b) Decrease the climb gradient and decrease the WAT limited TOW.
(c) Increase the climb gradient and increase the WAT limited TOW.
(d) Decrease the climb gradient and increase the WAT limited TOW.

Q27. During a descent at a constant Mach number and a constant rate of descent the gradient of descent and the pitch angle will:
(a) Increase and increase.
(b) Increase and decrease.
(c) Decrease and increase.
(d) Decrease and decrease.

Q28. The cause of the kink in the WAT limit graph for a turbo-propeller aeroplane
is caused by:
    (a) A decreased climb gradient.
    (b) Switching off the ACS packs.
    (c) Switching off the water-methanol injection.
    (d) The TGT limitation of the engines.

Q29. The effect a headwind has on the climb gradient and the rate of climb is:
    (a) Increase and decrease.
    (b) Increase and increase.
    (c) Increase and no effect.
    (d) Decrease and decrease.

Q30. The effect on the stalling IAS (accounting compressibility) of increasing
altitude, if all other conditions remain the same is that it:
    (a) Increases.
    (b) Decreases.
    (c) Remains the same.
    (d) Only increases above 20 000 ft.

Test Paper Answers

TEST PAPER 1

Q1. (b)	Q2. (c)	Q3. (a)	Q4. (c)	Q5. (d)
Q6. (b)	Q7. (d)	Q8. (a)	Q9. (a)	Q10. (c)
Q11. (c)	Q12. (b)	Q13. (a)	Q14. (d)	

TEST PAPER 2

Q1. (d)	Q2. (c)	Q3. (d)	Q4. (b)	Q5. (d)
Q6. (a)	Q7. (b)	Q8. (c)	Q9. (c)	Q10. (b).
Q11. (a)	Q12. (c)	Q13. (a)	Q14. (b)	

TEST PAPER 3

Q1. (c)	Q2. (b)	Q3. (a)	Q4. (b)	Q5. (c)
Q6. (a)	Q7. (d)	Q8. (d)	Q9. (b)	Q10. (a)

TEST PAPER 4

Q1. (a)	Q2. (c)	Q3. (b)	Q4. (b)	Q5. (c)
Q6. (c)	Q7. (a)	Q8. (d)	Q9. (c)	Q10. (d)
Q11. (c)	Q12. (b)	Q13. (c)	Q14. (a)	Q15. (b)

TEST PAPER 5

Q1. (c)	Q2. (a)	Q3. (c)	Q4. (b)	Q5. (b)
Q6. (c)	Q7. (c)	Q8. (b)	Q9. (c)	Q10. (b)
Q11. (b)	Q12. (a)	Q13. (d)	Q14. (a)	Q15. (c)
Q16. (c)	Q17. (d)	Q18. (b)	Q19. (d)	Q20. (d)

TEST PAPER 6

Q1. (b)	Q2. (b)	Q3. (a)	Q4. (c)	Q5. (b)
Q6. (d)	Q7. (c)	Q8. (d)	Q9. (c)	Q10. (c)
Q11. (d)	Q12. (c)	Q13. (a)	Q14. (b)	Q15. (c)

TEST PAPER 7

Q1. (d)	Q2. (c)	Q3. (b)	Q4. (b)	Q5. (a)
Q6. (b)	Q7. (b)	Q8. (d)	Q9. (b)	Q10. (b)
Q11. (a)	Q12. (c)	Q13. (a)	Q14. (b)	Q15. (d)
Q16. (c)	Q17. (a)	Q18. (d)	Q19. (b)	

TEST PAPER 8

Q1. (a)	Q2. (b)	Q3. (b)	Q4. (c)	Q5. (c)
Q6. (d)	Q7. (d)	Q8. (b)	Q9. (c)	

TEST PAPER 9

Q1. (c)	Q2. (c)	Q3. (a)	Q4. (c)	Q5. (d)
Q6. (b)	Q7. (a)	Q8. (d)	Q9. (a)	Q10. (c)

TEST PAPER 10

Q1. (c)	Q2. (a)	Q3. (a)	Q4. (d)	Q5. (c)
Q6. (b)	Q7. (a)	Q8. (b)	Q9. (a)	Q10. (a)
Q11. (b)	Q12. (a)	Q13. (b)	Q14. (c)	Q15. (b)

TEST PAPER 11

Q1. (d)	Q2. (b)	Q3. (b)	Q4. (a)	Q5. (d)
Q6. (a)	Q7. (c)	Q8. (c)	Q9. (a)	

TEST PAPER 12

Q1. (d)	Q2. (c)	Q3. (a)	Q4. (b)	Q5. (b)
Q6. (c)	Q7. (b)	Q8. (c)	Q9. (b)	Q10. (c)
Q11. (d)	Q12. (b)	Q13. (a)	Q14. (a)	Q15. (d)
Q16. (b)	Q17. (a)	Q18. (b)	Q19. (c)	Q20. (a)
Q21. (a)	Q22. (b)	Q23. (b)	Q24. (c)	Q25. (a)
Q26. (b)	Q27. (d)	Q28. (d)	Q29. (c)	Q30. (a)

Bibliography

The following are published by the Civil Aviation Authority (CAA), and available from Westward Digital, 37 Windsor Street, Cheltenham GL52 2OG, UK, telephone +44 (0)1242 283101.

Air Navigation Order.
Air Navigation (General) Regulations.
Extended Range Twin Operations (ETOPS). CAP 513.
Licensing of Aerodromes (1984). CAP 168.
Specimen Performance Charts. CAP 698.

The following are published by the Joint Aviation Authority (JAA), and also available from Westward Digital:

Joint Airworthiness Requirements (JAR).

The following are published by the International Civil Aviation Organization (ICAO), and available from ICAO Document Sales Unit, 1000 Sherbrooke Street West, Suite 400, Montreal, Quebec, Canada H3A 2R2:

ICAO Standards & Recommended Practices.

Index